MARITIME ORGANISATION, MANAGEMENT AND LIABILITY

This book identifies and examines the legal challenges facing the shipping industry and ship management today.

It first addresses flag state rules and private international law as organisational tools of the shipowner for establishing the applicable legal framework in an age of increasing regulatory activity and extraterritorial effect of legislation. It then focuses on sustainability requirements and the liability of shipping companies managing supply chains and ships as waste. The third section considers challenges stemming from times of financial crisis and deals with the cross-border impact of shipping insolvencies, the UNCITRAL Model Law, and the approaches of different jurisdictions. Finally, the fourth section concerns digitalisation and automation, including delivery on the basis of digital release codes, bills of lading based on blockchain technology, the use of web portals and data sharing, and particular aspects of the law relating to autonomous ships, notably in marine insurance and carriage of goods.

The book will be a useful resource for academics and practising lawyers working in shipping and maritime law.

Maritime Organisation, Management and Liability

A Legal Analysis of New Challenges in the Maritime Industry

Edited by
Stephen Girvin
and
Vibe Ulfbeck

•HART•
OXFORD • LONDON • NEW YORK • NEW DELHI • SYDNEY

HART PUBLISHING
Bloomsbury Publishing Plc
Kemp House, Chawley Park, Cumnor Hill, Oxford, OX2 9PH, UK
1385 Broadway, New York, NY 10018, USA
29 Earlsfort Terrace, Dublin 2, Ireland

HART PUBLISHING, the Hart/Stag logo, BLOOMSBURY and the Diana logo are trademarks of Bloomsbury Publishing Plc

First published in Great Britain 2021

A catalogue record for this book is available from the British Library.

Library of Congress Cataloging-in-Publication data

Names: Maritime organisation, management and liability (Conference) (2018 : Københavns universitet, Juridiske fakultet) | Girvin, Stephen, editor. | Ulfbeck, Vibe, editor. | Københavns universitet. Juridiske fakultet, host institution.

Title: Maritime organisation, management and liability : a legal analysis of new challenges in the maritime industry / edited by Stephen Girvin and Vibe Ulfbeck.

Description: Oxford, UK ; New York, NY : Hart Publishing, an imprint of Bloomsbury Publishing, 2021. | Includes bibliographical references and index.

Identifiers: LCCN 2021004276 (print) | LCCN 2021004277 (ebook) | ISBN 9781509942916 (hardback) | ISBN 9781509942954 (paperback) | ISBN 9781509942930 (pdf) | ISBN 9781509942923 (Epub)

Subjects: LCSH: Maritime law—Congresses. | LCGFT: Conference papers and proceedings.

Classification: LCC K4150.A6 M37 2018 (print) | LCC K4150.A6 (ebook) | DDC 343.09/6—dc23

LC record available at https://lccn.loc.gov/2021004276

LC ebook record available at https://lccn.loc.gov/2021004277

ISBN: HB: 978-1-50994-291-6
ePDF: 978-1-50994-293-0
ePub: 978-1-50994-292-3

Typeset by Compuscript Ltd, Shannon

PREFACE

In November 2018, five members of the Centre for Maritime Law (CML) at the National University of Singapore (NUS) boarded flights from a hot and humid Singapore bound for wintry Copenhagen to attend a conference hosted by the then Centre for Enterprise Liability (CEVIA) at the University of Copenhagen. Dr Anders Møllmann, an Associate Professor and member of CEVIA, and an Academic Fellow of CML provided the initial impetus. His departure for pastures new meant, however, that his involvement sadly ended prematurely. However, to the delight of all at CML, Vibe Ulfbeck generously picked up the ball and was a courteous and gracious host in Copenhagen. Members of CEVIA and colleagues from elsewhere were joined at the conference by an enthusiastic audience of maritime practitioners from the local bar and further afield. Our aim was to introduce new scholarship by experienced scholars and to highlight the work of up-and-coming scholars associated with our respective research centres.

Early in 2019 plans were put in place to generate written papers along the theme of the conference, with a view to possible publication. By this time, it no longer proved possible for all the original participants to contribute to the project. We are immensely grateful to Víctor Chacón, Carola Glinski, Michiel Spanjaart, Yoshifumi Tanaka and Mikis Tsimplis for their enthusiastic agreement to become involved in this book project. All but one of the authors of the book is associated with the maritime group in the Copenhagen research centre, now called the Centre for Private Governance (CEPRI), or the Centre for Maritime Law (CML) at NUS.

The editors would like to thank all the contributors for bearing with us during the long gestation period of this book. Little could any of us have imagined that the backdrop to writing and editing the book in 2020 would be the worldwide pandemic, COVID-19.

Stephen Girvin would like to acknowledge the assistance of Liwen Leung, his research assistant, for his care and attention in creating the tables, and eagle-eyed checking and rechecking of the individual chapters and proofs for accuracy. Stephen thanks CML's ever-willing manager, Rowena Goh, for her generous assistance throughout the planning and execution of the conference and this book.

CML acknowledges the generous funding provided by the Ministry of Law through its NUS Law Vision Project, which enabled us to participate in the conference on which this book is based. Vibe Ulfbeck would like to thank the Danish Orient Fund for providing the funding for CEPRI's larger project on management and organisation in the maritime sector of which this book project forms an important part.

Stephen Girvin and Vibe Ulfbeck would like to thank Roberta Bassi and Rosemarie Mearns of Hart Publishing for agreeing to publish this collection, and to Linda Staniford and Vicki Hillyard for their assistance in getting the book through the production stage. We are grateful to them all for bearing with us during the writing and production process, and making the project as enjoyable as book publishing can ever be.

Stephen Girvin
Centre for Maritime Law
Singapore
All Saints Day
1 November 2020

Vibe Ulfbeck
Centre for Private Governance
Copenhagen
1 November 2020

CONTENTS

MANAGEMENT AND ORGANISATION IN A DIGITALISED MARITIME SECTOR

MANAGEMENT AND ORGANISATION: AUTONOMOUS SHIPPING

LIST OF CONTRIBUTORS

Professor Ulrik Rammeskow BANG-PEDERSEN
Professor of Law, Faculty of Law, University of Copenhagen

Ms Luci CAREY
Research Associate, Centre for Maritime Law (CML), Faculty of Law, National University of Singapore
Admitted Lawyer, Western Australia

Dr Víctor CHACÓN
Senior Research Fellow, Centre for Maritime Law (CML), Faculty of Law, National University of Singapore
Lawyer, Republic of Panama

Professor Stephen GIRVIN
MPA Professor of Maritime Law
Director, Centre for Maritime Law (CML), Faculty of Law, National University of Singapore
An Advocate of the High Court of South Africa

Associate Professor Carola GLINSKI
Centre for Private Governance (CEPRI), Faculty of Law, University of Copenhagen
Lawyer, Germany

Associate Professor Paul MYBURGH
Deputy Director, Centre for Maritime Law (CML), Faculty of Law, National University of Singapore
An Advocate of the High Court of South Africa

Mr Elson ONG
Research Associate, Centre for Maritime Law (CML), Faculty of Law, National University of Singapore
An Advocate and Solicitor of the Supreme Court of Singapore

Dr Michiel SPANJAART
Academic Fellow, Centre for Maritime Law (CML), Faculty of Law, National University of Singapore
An Advocate and Principal, Trains & Co, Rotterdam

Professor Yoshifumi TANAKA
Professor of Law, Centre for Private Governance (CEPRI), Faculty of Law, University of Copenhagen

Professor Mikis TSIMPLIS
School of Law, City University of Hong Kong

Professor Vibe ULFBECK
Professor of Law; Director, Centre for Private Governance (CEPRI), Faculty of Law, University of Copenhagen; Board Member, Scandinavian Institute of Maritime Law

Dr Jingchen XU
Associate, Helmsman LLC, formerly Postdoctoral Fellow, Centre for Maritime Law (CML), Faculty of Law, National University of Singapore
Attorney-at-Law, New York State
Lawyer, People's Republic of China

TABLE OF CASES

Australia

Belgium

Canada

Denmark

European Union

Finland

Germany

Hong Kong SAR

The International Court of Justice

The International Tribunal for the Law of the Sea

Netherlands

New Zealand

Norway

Permanent Court of Arbitration

Singapore

United Kingdom

United States of America

TABLE OF LEGISLATION

Australia

Canada

Denmark

European Union

Finland

France

Germany

Hong Kong SAR

Liberia

Malaysia

Marshall Islands

Netherlands

New Zealand

Norway

Panama

Philippines

Russia

Saint Vincent and the Grenadines

Singapore

South Africa

South Korea

Sweden

United Kingdom

United States of America

TABLE OF INTERNATIONAL INSTRUMENTS

Management and Organisation of Shipping Enterprises: Public and Private Law Framework

1

Nationality Requirements: Flag State Rules from an International Law Perspective

YOSHIFUMI TANAKA*

I. Introduction

The aim of this chapter is to examine the issue of the nationality of a ship from the viewpoint of public international law. In international law, the nationality of a ship performs a dual function. The first is to establish the juridical link between a state and a ship flying its flag, and the second is to provide a basis for claims of a flag state before an adjudicatory body. The dual function of the nationality of a ship can be amplified as follows.

First, as there is no centralised authority governing the high seas in the international community, the legal order on the high seas is secured primarily by the flag state, that is, the state which has granted a ship the right to sail under its flag. The principle of the exclusive jurisdiction of the flag state is the key to the maintenance of legal order on the high seas.[1] That principle is provided in article 92(1) of the UN Convention on the Law of the Sea (hereinafter the LOSC):[2] 'Ships shall sail under the flag of one State only and, save in exceptional cases expressly provided for in international treaties or in this Convention, shall be subject to its exclusive jurisdiction on the high seas'. It could well be said that the principle of the exclusive jurisdiction of the flag state is part of customary international law. In international law, the role of that principle is twofold. First, by preventing any interference by other states with vessels flying its flag on the high seas, that principle ensures the freedom of activity of vessels on the high seas. Second, the flag states undertake responsibility for securing compliance with national and international laws

* Professor of Law, Centre for Private Governance, Faculty of Law, University of Copenhagen.

[1] According to Gidel, the principle of the exclusive jurisdiction of the flag states should be considered as a corollary of the *juridicité* (or 'juridicity') of the high seas. G Gidel, *Le droit international public de la mer: le temps de paix, vol I: Introduction, La haute mer* (reprint, Paris, Duchemin, 1981) 225.

[2] 1833 *UNTS* 3. In force on 16 November 1994.

regulating activities of ships flying its flag on the high seas.[3] While the obligations of the flag state are diverse,[4] article 94(1) obliges every state to 'effectively exercise its jurisdiction and control in administrative, technical and social matters over ships flying its flag'. In exercising the exclusive jurisdiction over vessels flying its flag, the nationality of a ship is of critical importance since it provides a basis for establishing the juridical link between a flag state and a ship flying its flag.[5]

Second, the exclusive jurisdiction of the flag state comprises both legislative and enforcement jurisdiction over vessels flying its flag. Accordingly, the flag state exercises enforcement jurisdiction over all peoples within its ships flying its flag regardless of their nationalities. In the words of the International Tribunal for the Law of the Sea (ITLOS): 'the ship, everything on it, and every person involved or interested in its operations are treated as an entity linked to the flag State. The nationalities of these persons are not relevant'.[6] In light of this, the flag state is entitled to make claims against other states in case of damage to its ship or injury to the seamen manning it, regardless of their nationality.[7] Thus the nationality of a ship provides the basis for making claims by the flag state before an international court or tribunal.

An issue that needs further consideration concerns the requirements to grant the nationality to a ship. Under article 91 of the LOSC:

> 1. Every State shall fix the conditions for the grant of its nationality to ships, for the registration of ships in its territory, and for the right to fly its flag. Ships have the nationality of the State whose flag they are entitled to fly. There must exist a genuine link between the State and the ship.
> 2. Every State shall issue to ships to which it has granted the right to fly its flag documents to that effect.[8]

Article 91 leaves to each state considerable discretion to decide requirements for granting its nationality to vessels. In the words of ITLOS: 'Determination of

[3] Y Tanaka, *The International Law of the Sea*, 3rd edn (Cambridge, Cambridge University Press, 2019) 190.

[4] ibid 191–92.

[5] See also Gidel, *Le droit international public de la mer* (1981) 74.

[6] The *M/V Saiga (No 2) (Saint Vincent and the Grenadines v Guinea)*, ITLOS Case No 2, Judgment, [1999] ITLOS Rep 10, 48, [106].

[7] The American Law Institute, *Restatement of the Law Third: The Foreign Relations Law of the United States*, vol 2 (American Law Institute Publishers, 1990) §502, Comment (h), 21. An issue that may arise in this regard is whether a tender flying the flag of another state would fall within the scope of 'its ship'. This issue arose in the 2013 case *M/V Louisa* between Saint Vincent and the Grenadines and Spain. This case was concerned with the legality of the arrest and detention of the *M/V Louisa*, a research vessel of Saint Vincent and the Grenadines, and its tender, the *Gemini III*, by Spain. In its submission before ITLOS, the applicant state, Saint Vincent and the Grenadines, contended that while the *Gemini III* was not flying its flag, it served as a tender for the *M/V Louisa* and was 'inextricably linked' to it. However, ITLOS considered that the *Gemini III* enjoyed an identity of its own. The Tribunal thus concluded that it lacked jurisdiction in respect to the *Gemini III*: *The M/V Louisa (Saint Vincent and the Grenadines v Kingdom of Spain)*, Judgment, [2013] ITLOS Rep 4, 31–32, [86]–[87].

[8] In the *M/V Saiga (No 2)*, ITLOS considered that art 91 'codifies a well-established rule of general international law': [1999] ITLOS Rep 36 [63].

the criteria and establishment of the procedures for granting and withdrawing nationality to ships are matters within the exclusive jurisdiction of the flag State'.[9] However, it is not suggested that the right of states to grant their nationality to ships is without limitation.[10] First, ships must sail under the flag of one state only in accordance with article 92(1) of the LOSC as well as customary international law.[11] It would seem to follow that a state may not grant its nationality to a ship which has already been granted the nationality of another state. Second, the right of the state to grant its nationality to vessels may also be qualified by specific treaties, such as the United Nations Convention on Conditions for Registration of Ships.[12] Third, and importantly, there must exist a genuine link between the state and the ship.

In reality, it is not uncommon for the nationality of a ship to be disputed by one of the disputing parties in international adjudication. In such cases, the question associated with the nationality of a ship may be subject to the dispute settlement procedures under Part XI of the LOSC.[13] When considering the requirements for the flag state to grant its nationality to a ship, four issues arise:

(1) How is it possible to verify the validity of the nationality of a ship?
(2) What are the elements necessary to establish a genuine link between a flag state and a ship?
(3) Is it possible for non-flag states to refuse to accept the nationality of a ship because of the absence of a genuine link?
(4) What are the implications of change of ownership of a ship for the nationality of the ship?

The jurisprudence of ITLOS sheds some light on those issues. Thus this chapter examines the four issues by analysing the jurisprudence of ITLOS. Following the Introduction, section II addresses the issue of verification of the nationality

[9] ibid 37 [65]. See also the Separate Opinion of Judge Wolfrum, ibid 97, [18]. The Supreme Court of the United States in *Lauritzen v Larsen* 345 US 571 (1953), 584 has also held that: 'Each state under international law may determine for itself the conditions on which it will grant its nationality to a merchant ship, thereby accepting responsibility for it and acquiring authority over it' (Jackson J). An early example of a statement on this matter can be found in the 1905 *Muscat Dhows* arbitration: *Affaire des Boutres de Mascate (France v Great Britain)* (1961) 11 *Reports of International Arbitral Awards* 83. See also DP O'Connell (IA Shearer ed), *The International Law of the Sea*, vol II (Oxford, Clarendon Press, 1984) 752–53.

[10] D König, 'Flags of Ships' in R Wolfrum (ed), *Max Planck Encyclopedia of Public International Law* (online edn) [21]; RA Barnes, 'Flag States' in D Rothwell, A Oude Elferink, KN Scott and T Stephens (eds), *Oxford Handbook on the Law of the Sea* (Oxford, Oxford University Press, 2015) 304, 306.

[11] Under art 92(2) of the LOSC, 'A ship which sails under the flags of two or more States, using them according to convenience, may not claim any of the nationalities in question with respect to any other State, and may be assimilated to a ship without nationality'.

[12] Not in force. For the text of the Convention, see (1986) 7 *Law of the Sea Bulletin* 87–106. See also art III(2) and (3) of the Agreement to Promote Compliance with International Conservation and Management Measures by Fishing Vessels on the High Seas. Entered into force 24 April 2003. The text is available at: www.fao.org/iuu-fishing/international-framework/fao-compliance-agreement/en. See also König, 'Flags of Ships' (n 10) [21].

[13] The *M/V Saiga (No 2)* [1999] ITLOS Rep 37 [65].

of a ship in international adjudication. Section III then considers the elements necessary to establish a genuine link between a flag state and a ship and the non-recognition of the nationality of a ship because of the absence of a genuine link between an alleged flag state and a ship. Section IV moves on to address the legal effect of change of ownership of a ship on the nationality of the ship. Finally, conclusions are presented in section V.

II. Verification of the Nationality of a Ship

As noted, the flag state is entitled to make claims with regard to a vessel flying its flag before an international court or tribunal. However, not infrequently, a defendant state disputes the validity of the nationality of a flag state granted to a ship concerned in international adjudication with a view to challenging the *locus standi* of the applicant state, the flag state. In that case, an international court or tribunal has to decide whether the ship concerned has the nationality of the flag state at the time of application. In this connection, two cases merit discussion: the *M/V Saiga (No 2)* and the *Grand Prince*.

A. The *M/V Saiga (No 2)* (1999)

A central issue of the *M/V Saiga (No 2)* related to the legality of supplying gas oil to fishing vessels in the exclusive economic zone (EEZ) of a third state. An oil tanker, the *Saiga*, was provisionally registered in Saint Vincent and the Grenadines on 12 March 1997.[14] On 24 October 1997, the *Saiga* supplied gas oil to three fishing vessels at the point of approximately 22 nautical miles from Guinea's island of Alcatraz. Subsequently the ship sailed towards another location. On 28 October 1997, the *Saiga* was awaiting the arrival of fishing vessels to which it was to supply gas oil in the south of the southern limit of the EEZ of Guinea. Yet the *Saiga* was arrested by a Guinean patrol boat and the ship and its crew were brought to Conakry, Guinea. The Master and six crew members – all of Ukrainian nationality – remained in Conakry until the vessel was released on 28 February 1998.[15]

In response, on 13 November 1997, Saint Vincent and the Grenadines submitted a request for the prompt release of the *Saiga* and its crew to ITLOS in accordance with article 292 of the LOSC.[16] The Tribunal, in its judgment of 4 December 1997, ordered that Guinea promptly release the *Saiga* and its crew upon the position

[14] ibid 27, [31].
[15] ibid 28, [32]–[33].
[16] *Application submitted by Saint Vincent and the Grenadines*, available at www.itlos.org/fileadmin/itlos/documents/cases/case_no_1/application_without_annexes__svg_131197_eng.pdf.

of bond or security, which consisted of the gas oil discharged from the *Saiga* by the authorities of Guinea plus an amount of US$400,000.[17] On 13 January 1998, Saint Vincent and the Grenadines further submitted the Request of provisional measures to ITLOS[18] and, on 11 March 1998, the Tribunal delivered the Order prescribing provisional measures.[19] The Tribunal then moved on to address the merits of the case.[20]

In the *M/V Saiga (No 2)* (merits), a contentious issue arose as to whether the *Saiga* had the nationality of Saint Vincent and the Grenadines at the time of its arrest.[21] According to ITLOS, 'In the case of merchant ships, the normal procedure used by states to grant nationality is registration in accordance with domestic legislation adopted for that purpose'.[22] The issue was then whether or not the *Saiga* was duly registered in accordance with the Merchant Shipping Act of Saint Vincent and the Grenadines at the time of the arrest.

As noted, the *Saiga* was registered in Saint Vincent and the Grenadines only provisionally. A crucial issue that arose in this regard was the legal effect of the Provisional Certificate of Registration. This document made it clear that: 'This Certificate expires on 12 September 1997'. Subsequently a Permanent Certificate of Registration was issued on 28 November 1997.[23] Guinea accordingly claimed that on the day of its arrest (that is, 28 October 1997), the *Saiga* was 'not validly registered under the flag of Saint Vincent and the Grenadines'.[24] Consequently, Guinea contended that the *Saiga* may be qualified to be a ship without nationality when it was arrested by the Guinean authority.[25] However, Saint Vincent and the Grenadines countered that when a vessel was registered under its flag, 'it remains so registered until deleted from the registry'.[26] According to Saint Vincent and the Grenadines, a provisional certificate of registration remained in force until the expiry of one year from the date of its issue pursuant to section 36(2) of the Merchant Shipping Act. Saint Vincent and the Grenadines thus argued that 'the Provisional Certificate in this case remained in force after 12 September 1997 and at all times material to the present dispute'.[27]

[17] The *M/V Saiga (Saint Vincent and the Grenadines v Guinea)*, ITLOS Case No 1, Prompt Release, Judgment [1997] ITLOS Rep 16, 37, [86].

[18] Request for the prescription of provisional measures submitted by Saint Vincent and the Grenadines, see: www.itlos.org/fileadmin/itlos/documents/cases/case_no_2/provisional_measures/request_without_annexes_svg_050198_eng.pdf.

[19] The *M/V Saiga (No 2) (Saint Vincent and the Grenadines v Guinea)*, Provisional Measures, Order of 11 March 1998, [1998] ITLOS Rep 24, 39–40, [50].

[20] Notification of Special Agreement, available at: www.itlos.org/cases/list-of-cases/case-no-2/#c3283.

[21] [1998] ITLOS Rep 36, [62].

[22] ibid 37, [64].

[23] ibid 34, [57].

[24] Judgment, [1999] ITLOS Rep 33 [55].

[25] ibid. See also Counter-Memorial Submitted by Guinea, 132–33, [10]; Rejoinder Submitted by Guinea, 433–34, [14]–[18].

[26] Reply Submitted by Saint Vincent and Grenadines, 253, [24]; Judgment, [1999] ITLOS Rep 34 [59].

[27] ibid 35, [60].

After examination of the arguments of the parties, ITLOS held that 'Saint Vincent and the Grenadines has produced evidence before the Tribunal to support its assertion that the *Saiga* was a ship entitled to fly its flag at the time of the incident giving rise to the dispute'.[28] To support this view, the Tribunal focused on the conduct of the Applicant. In the words of the Tribunal:

> Saint Vincent and the Grenadines has at all times material to the dispute operated on the basis that the *Saiga* was a ship of its nationality. It has acted as the flag State of the ship during all phases of the proceedings.[29]

In contrast, according to the Tribunal, Guinea failed to prove its contention that the *Saiga* did not have the nationality of Saint Vincent and the Grenadines at the time of arrest.[30] In this regard, the Tribunal stressed the fact that Guinea did not challenge the nationality of the ship at any time until the submission of its Counter-Memorial in October 1998.[31] In conclusion, the Tribunal rejected the objection to the admissibility of the claims of Saint Vincent and the Grenadines based on Guinea's contention that the *Saiga* was not registered in Saint Vincent and the Grenadines at the time of its arrest.[32] However, the Tribunal's view leaves some room for discussion. In this regard, three points can be made.

The first concerned the interpretation of section 36(2) of the Merchant Shipping Act of Saint Vincent and the Grenadines, which stipulates: 'The provisional certificate of registration issued under subsection (1) shall have the same effect as the ordinary certificate of registration until the expiry of one year from the date of issue'. Judge Wolfrum noted that section 36(2) does not say that 'a provisional certificate of registry has to be valid for 12 months; it further does not say that a provisional certificate whose validity has expired has the same effect as a permanent certificate'.[33] The learned judge thus concluded:

> Since the permanent registration of the *Saiga* was entered in the Register of ships of Saint Vincent and the Grenadines only on 28 November 1997 the Judgment should have come to the conclusion that the *Saiga* was, … not registered at the time of its arrest. The further and only possible conclusion to be drawn is that, …, the *Saiga* at the time of its arrest did not have the nationality of Saint Vincent and the Grenadines.[34]

Likewise, Judge Ndiaye considered:

> In the case of the *Saiga*, the validity of the registration was limited to 12 September 1997. And, since there was no extension of the provisional registration, the *Saiga* was a ship without nationality at the time of its arrest.[35]

[28] ibid 37, [67]. See also 38, [70].
[29] ibid 37, [68].
[30] ibid 38, [72].
[31] ibid 37–38, [68]–[69].
[32] ibid 69, [183(3)].
[33] Separate Opinion of Judge Wolfrum, ibid 100, [28].
[34] ibid 100, [26]. See also 96, [16].
[35] Dissenting Opinion of Judge Ndiaye, ibid 257, [91]. See also Separate Opinion of President Mensah, ibid 80–81, [5].

Furthermore, referring to the Brochure of Saint Vincent and the Grenadines under the heading of Provisional Registration Certificate,[36] Judge Chandrasekhara Rao argued:

> [A] provisional registration certificate is issued for six months and not for one year, that it requires extension if it were to be valid for more than the initial period of six months, and that such extension can be given 'under certain circumstances'. If this be so, it is illogical to hold that, by virtue of section 36(2), a provisional certificate issued for a period of six months would continue to be valid for a one-year period even when it fails to receive extension and without regard to the 'circumstances' of the case.[37]

In light of the above views, it was debatable whether, as Saint Vincent and the Grenadines argued, a provisional certificate of registration remained in force until the expiry of one year from the date of its issue.[38]

Second, if the interpretation of Saint Vincent and the Grenadines were correct, another problem arose concerning the deletion of previous nationality. Under section 37 of the Merchant Shipping Act of Saint Vincent and the Grenadines:

> The provisional certificate of registration shall cease to have effect if, before the expiry of sixty days from its date of issue, the owner of the ship in respect of which it was issued has failed to produce to the issuing authority —
>
> (a) a certificate issued by the government of the country of last registration of the ship (or other acceptable evidence) to show that the ship's registration in that country has been closed.

The *Saiga* was previously registered to Malta. However, Saint Vincent and the Grenadines failed to submit the certificate of deletion from the Registry of Malta, when the Tribunal required the parties to submit certain documentation on the registration of the *Saiga*.[39] Hence it was questionable whether the condition set out in section 37 could be met.

Third, as noted, the conduct of the applicant during the proceedings was key when verifying the nationality of the *Saiga*. If, as the Tribunal stated, 'the normal procedure used by states to grant nationality is registration in accordance with domestic legislation', a question arises why the conduct of the alleged flag state

[36] The brochure stated that: 'The Provisional Registration Certificate is issued for 6 months and can be extended under certain circumstances for a further period of 6 months'. Cited in Separate opinion of Judge Chandrasekhara Rao, [1999] ITLOS Rep 128 [7]. The statement was also referred to in the oral presentation by von Brevern, 11 March 1999, Verbatim Record, ITLOS/PV.99/8, 11.

[37] Separate opinion of Judge Chandrasekhara Rao, [1999] ITLOS Rep 128, [8]. See also the Separate Opinion of Judge Nelson, ibid 119–20.

[38] Scovazzi also questioned the nationality of the *Saiga*, stating that 'if registration is the normal procedure to grant nationality to ships, why the expiration of a certificate of registration should not also automatically entail that the nationality has expired?': T Scovazzi, 'ITLOS and Jurisdiction over Ships' in H Ringbom (ed), *Jurisdiction Over Ships: Post-UNCLOS Developments in the Law of the Sea* (Leiden, Nijhoff, 2015) 382, 391.

[39] Dissenting Opinion of Judge Warioba, [1999] ITLOS Rep 205 [22]–[24]; Dissenting Opinion of Judge Ndiaye, ibid 253–54, [78]–[82]. See also presentation of von Brevern, 20 March 1999, Verbatim Record, ITLOS/PV.99/18, 13.

should be needed as an additional condition for validating the nationality of a ship. As Judge Warioba pointedly observed:

> Either a ship is registered under those conditions or it is not registered. The behaviour of Saint Vincent and the Grenadines will not change what is in its law, it will not change the words on the Certificate of Registration, and it will not change what is inscribed in the Book of Registry.[40]

All in all, the validity of the Vincentian nationality of the *Saiga* at the time of arrest appears highly debatable. Nonetheless, ITLOS accepted the *locus standi* of Saint Vincent and the Grenadines in this case. In this connection, the Tribunal particularly stressed 'Guinea's failure to question the assertion of Saint Vincent and the Grenadines that it is the flag state of the *Saiga* when it had every reasonable opportunity to do so and its other conduct in the case'.[41] In the view of the Tribunal, 'in the particular circumstances of this case, it would not be consistent with justice if the Tribunal were to decline to deal with the merits of the dispute'.[42] Yet the meaning of 'justice' remains obscure. It appears that the Tribunal overlooked a technical irregularity with the registration of the *Saiga* in order to secure the consistency in its own jurisprudence.

B. The *Grand Prince* (2001)

The next case that needs consideration is the *Grand Prince* between Belize and France.[43] On 26 December 2000, the *Grand Prince*, a fishing vessel, was boarded by the French surveillance frigate *Nivose* in the EEZ of the Kerguelen Islands in the French Southern and Antarctic Territories[44] and was escorted under supervision to Port-des-Galets, Réunion.[45] Subsequently the court of first instance at Saint-Paul confirmed the arrest of the Grand Prince and declared that its release would be subject to the payment of a bond of 11,400,00 FF to be paid into the Deposits and Consignments Office.[46] On 23 January 2001, the criminal court ordered the confiscation of the vessel, its equipment and gear as well as the fishing products seized.[47] On 19 February 2001, the shipowner in vain submitted an application

[40] Dissenting Opinion of Judge Warioba, [1999] ITLOS Rep 212 [46]. See also T Scovazzi, 'The Contribution of the Tribunal to the Progressive Development of International Law' in ITLOS, *The Contribution of the International Tribunal for the Law of the Sea to the Rule of Law: 1996–2016* (Leiden, Nijhoff, 2018) 118, 156–57.

[41] [1999] ITLOS Rep 38–39 [73].

[42] ibid. See also Separate Opinion of President Mensah, ibid 86, [16]. Eventually Judges Mensah, Wolfrum, Nelson and Rao voted for para 3 of the operative part of the judgment.

[43] The *Grand Prince (Belize v France)*, ITLOS Case No 8, Prompt Release, Judgment [2001] ITLOS Rep 17.

[44] ibid 30, [35].

[45] ibid 30, [38]. According to the applicant, at the time of its detention the *Grand Prince* was going to be reflagged and registered in Brazil where the vessel had been allocated a fishing licence. ibid 29, [33].

[46] ibid 32, [46].

[47] ibid 33, [50].

to the Court of First Instance at Saint-Paul for the release of the *Grand Prince* upon presentation of a bank guarantee of 11,400,000FF.[48] Thus, on 21 March 2001, Belize instituted proceedings against France concerning the release of the *Grand Prince* under article 292 of the Convention before ITLOS. The *Grand Prince* can be contrasted with the *M/V Saiga (No 2)* in two respects.

First, in the *Grand Prince*, the defendant state (France) did not dispute the nationality of the vessel. Nonetheless, ITLOS examined the question regarding whether Belize was the flag state of the *Grand Prince* at the time of the application.[49] In this connection, the Tribunal made it clear that 'the Tribunal must satisfy itself that it has jurisdiction to deal with the case as submitted', even where there is no disagreement between the parties regarding the jurisdiction of the Tribunal.[50]

Second, by contrast with the *M/V Saiga (No 2)*, ITLOS denied the nationality of Belize of the *Grand Prince*. According to the Tribunal, 'The initial burden of establishing that Belize was the flag state when the Application was made is on the Applicant'.[51] A provisional patent of navigation of the *Grand Prince* was issued by the International Merchant Marine Registry of Belize (IMMARBE) on 16 October 2000 and the date of its expiration was 29 December 2000.[52] Accordingly, the provisional patent was already expired when Belize filed its application concerning the release of the *Grand Prince* on 21 March 2001. Furthermore, in the note verbal of 4 January 2001, the Ministry of Foreign Affairs of Belize stated that 'punitive measures being imposed by the Belizean authority is its de-registration effective today 4 January 2001'.[53] The question to be decided in this regard was 'whether the registration of the vessel in Belize continued following the expiry of the provisional patent of navigation or, as the case may be, was revived following the de-registration of the vessel with effect from 4 January 2001'.[54] In considering the question, the Tribunal took the view that 'When the note verbal spoke in terms of "de-registration effective today", the act of de-registration must be taken to have commenced with effect from 4 January 2001'.[55] According to the Tribunal,

> the Applicant did not act 'at all times material to the dispute' on the basis that the Grand Prince was a vessel of its nationality. To the contrary, on 4 January 2001, Belize communicated to France, by means of a note verbale from the Ministry of Foreign Affairs, its decision to de-register the *Grand Prince* with effect from 4 January 2001.[56]

[48] Ibid 34, [52]–[53].
[49] However, the tribunal's approach invited criticism from nine dissenting judges. Dissenting Opinion of Judges Caminos, Marotta Rangel, Yankov, Yamamoto, Akl, Vukas, Marsit, Eiriksson and Jesus, [2001] ITLOS Rep 66 [2].
[50] The *M/V Saiga (No 2)* [1999] ITLOS Rep 38 [40].
[51] The *Grand Prince* [2001] ITLOS Rep 38 [67].
[52] ibid 38, [69].
[53] ibid 39, [72].
[54] ibid 40, [76].
[55] ibid 43, [87].
[56] ibid 43, [89].

In light of this, the Tribunal concluded that 'the documentary evidence submitted by the Applicant fails to establish that Belize was the flag state of the vessel when the Application was made'.[57] It accordingly found, by 12 votes to nine, that it had no jurisdiction to hear the application.[58]

As shown in the voting record, however, the majority opinion was not free from controversy. Contrary to the majority opinion, the nine dissenters – Judges Caminos, Marotta Rangel, Yankov, Yamamoto, Akl, Vukas, Marsit, Eiriksson and Jesus – considered that it could not be concluded that the registration of the *Grand Prince* had been revoked by the Belize authorities. They further held that the statements of the competent Belize authorities that the *Grand Prince* was registered in Belize sufficed to discharge the initial burden of establishing that it had Belize nationality.[59] In this regard, two issues must be considered.

The first concerns the meaning of 'documents' under article 91(2) of the LOSC. A contentious issue in this regard was the value of communications from IMMARBE. As ITLOS itself noted, the IMMARBE communication dated 30 March 2001 stated that 'despite the expiration of the Patent of navigation and Ship station license, the vessel is still considered as registered in Belize'.[60] However, the Tribunal held:

> [T]he assertion that the vessel is 'still considered as registered in Belize' contains an element of fiction and does not provide sufficient basis for holding that Belize was the flag State of the vessel for the purposes of making an application under article 292 of the Convention. The IMMARBE communications cannot be treated as 'documents' within the meaning of article 91, paragraph 2, of the Convention.[61]

By contrast, the nine dissenters seemed to accept the value of the IMMARBE communications as evidence. In this connection, the dissenters indicated that according to later information provided by Belize to the French authorities and to the Tribunal, that is, the letter of 26 March 2001 from the Director and Senior Deputy Registrar of IMMARBE, the procedures of deregistration had been suspended.[62] In any event, the difference between the majority and dissenting opinions seems to suggest that there is no standard for deciding what documents will fall within the scope of article 91(2) of the LOSC.

The second issue concerns the consistency of the conduct of the alleged flag state. In accordance with the dictum of the *M/V Saiga (No 2)* judgment, the state must have 'at all times material to the dispute'.[63] As noted, the conduct of the applicant state also constituted a crucial element when examining the nationality of the

[57] ibid 44, [93].

[58] ibid 45, [95].

[59] Dissenting Opinion of Judges Caminos, Marotta Rangel, Yankov, Yamamoto, Akl, Vukas, Marsit, Eiriksson and Jesus, ibid 69, [14].

[60] The *Grand Prince* [2001] ITLOS Rep 42 [85].

[61] ibid.

[62] The Agent of France also acknowledged the suspension of the procedures of deregistration. Presentation of Alabrune, 6 April 2001, Verbatim Record, ITLOS/PV. 01/04, 5.

[63] The *M/V Saiga (No 2)* [1999] ITLOS Rep 37 [68].

Grand Prince. The *Grand Prince* judgment seems to suggest that the initiation of the deregistration of a ship constitutes an element that casts doubt whether a state acted at all times material to the dispute as the flag state. Apart from this, however, the Tribunal offered no further precision with regard to the standard for judging whether a state had at all times material to the dispute.

C. Summary

The following conclusions may be reached:

(1) The nationality of a ship is a question of fact that must be decided on the basis of evidence adduced by the parties. ITLOS can examine *proprio motu* the nationality of a ship, even though there is no disagreement between the parties on this matter.
(2) The initial burden of establishing that the ship concerned had its nationality when the application was made is on the applicant, the flag state. Where the flag state could discharge the initial burden of establishing that the ship concerned had its nationality, the other party (ie the respondent state) has to prove that the ship had not the nationality of the flag state at the time of the application. In this connection, the conduct of the parties constitutes a crucial element when determining the nationality or registration of a ship.
(3) Domestic laws and/or documents of a flag state can be the subject of an examination by the Tribunal. However, there is no established standard for deciding what documents will fall within the scope of article 91(2) of the LOSC. It appears that rules and standards concerning the evidence of the nationality of a ship remain less clear in the jurisprudence of ITLOS.

III. Implications of a Genuine Link for the Validity of the Nationality of a Ship

A. The Concept of Genuine Link

The next issue concerns the implications of a genuine link for the validity of the nationality of a ship. Article 94(1) requires that: 'Every State shall effectively exercise its jurisdiction and control in administrative, technical and social matters over ships flying its flag'. The juridical link between a state and a ship that is entitled to fly its flag is a prerequisite for securing effective exercise of the flag state jurisdiction. With a view to securing the juridical link, article 5(1) of the Geneva Convention on the High Seas[64] provides: 'There must exist a genuine link between

[64] 450 *UNTS* 11. In force 30 September 1962.

the State and the ship; in particular, the State must effectively exercise its jurisdiction and control in administrative, technical and social matters over ships flying its flag'.[65] Subsequently, the concept of genuine link was succeeded by article 91(1) of the LOSC. As ITLOS observed, 'the need for a genuine link between a ship and its flag State is to secure more effective implementation of the duties of the flag State'.[66] The requirement of a genuine link should mean to prevent non-compliance with relevant rules by states, in particular, flag of convenience states.[67]

Nonetheless, it is problematic that the contents of the requirement of a genuine link remains less clear. In fact, the Geneva Convention on the High Seas and the LOSC leave entirely unspecified the concept of a genuine link.[68] In this regard, the International Law Commission (ILC), which drafted the Geneva Convention, explained:

> The Commission does not consider it possible to state in any greater detail what form this link should take. This lack of precision made some members of the Commission question the advisability of inserting such a stipulation. But the majority of the Commission preferred a vague criterion to no criterion at all.[69]

However, the vagueness of the requirement of a genuine line entails a serious risk that its effectiveness will be undermined. With a view to tightening a genuine link between a flag state and the ships flying its flag, the UN Registration Convention was adopted in 1986.[70] This Convention elaborates several conditions with which the flag state shall comply, such as ownership of ships, manning of ships, and the management of ships and shipowning companies. To this day, however, this Convention has not entered into force. Indeed, it is doubtful whether any flag of convenience state will ratify this Convention. It therefore may have to be admitted that the attempt to tighten the requirement of a genuine link by a treaty has been unsuccessful in practice.

The requirement of a genuine link creates debatable issues in international adjudication. In particular, two issues merit highlighting. The first relates to the

[65] In this connection, it may be relevant to recall *Nottebohm (Liechtenstein v Guatemala)* [1955] ICJ Rep 4, 23. The International Court of Justice (ICJ) there ruled that a state cannot claim that the municipal rules governing the grant of its own nationality are entitled to recognition by another state 'unless it has acted in conformity with this general aim of making the legal bond of nationality accord with the individual's *genuine connection* with the State which assumes the defence of its citizens by means of protection as against other States' (emphasis added). Here one can find an analogy between the concept of 'genuine connection' and that of 'genuine link'.

[66] The *M/V Saiga (No 2)* [1999] ITLOS Rep 42 [83].

[67] Whilst there is no generally agreed definition, 'flag of convenience' or 'open registry' states refer, in essence, to states that permit foreign shipowners, having very little or virtually no real connection with those states, to register their ships under the flags of those states. R Churchill and V Lowe, *The Law of the Sea*, 3rd edn (Manchester, Manchester University Press, 1999) 258.

[68] Thus the concept of a genuine link has provoked strong criticism. See, eg, MS McDougal, WT Burke and IA Vlasio, 'The Maintenance of Public Order at Sea and the Nationality of Ships' (1960) 54 *American Journal of International Law* 25, 28.

[69] [1956] 2 *Yearbook of the International Law Commission* 279.

[70] Further, see HW Wefers Bettink, 'Open Registry, The Genuine Link and the 1986 Convention on Registration Conditions for Ships' (1987) 18 *Netherlands Yearbook of International Law* 69.

elements necessary to establish a 'genuine link' between a flag state and the ships flying its flag, and the second issue concerns the consequences to be attached to the absence of a genuine link. In considering the issues, the *M/V Saiga (No 2)* and *M/V Virginia G*[71] must be examined.

B. The *M/V Saiga (No 2)* (1999)

In the 1999 *M/V Saiga (No 2)*, two issues arose.[72] The first was whether there was a genuine link between the *Saiga* and Saint Vincent and the Grenadines at the time of the incident. On this issue, the opinions of the parties were sharply divided. Guinea contended that there was no genuine link between the *Saiga* and Saint Vincent and the Grenadines.[73] Guinea argued that 'a State cannot fulfil its obligations as a flag State under the Convention with regard to a ship unless it exercises prescriptive and enforcement jurisdiction over the owner or, as the case may be, the operator of the ship'.[74] In contrast, to establish the existence of the genuine link, Saint Vincent and the Grenadines highlighted, inter alia:

- the representation of the owner of the *Saiga* in Saint Vincent and the Grenadines by a company formed and established in that state;
- supervision of the *Saiga* by the Vincentian authorities to secure compliance with relevant conventions, such as the SOLAS and MARPOL;
- regular supervision of the *Saiga*'s seaworthiness through surveys.[75]

Arguably, the facts indicated by Saint Vincent and the Grenadines should have been objectively verified by ITLOS. Nonetheless, ITLOS did not examine these matters and simply stated that 'the evidence adduced by Guinea [was] not sufficient to justify its contention that there was no genuine link between the ship and Saint Vincent and the Grenadines at the material time'.[76] Thus the Tribunal missed an opportunity to clarify the requirements for establishing a genuine link between a flag state and a ship.

The second issue concerned the legal consequences of the absence of a genuine link set out in article 91(1) of the LOSC.[77] Guinea claimed that it was not obliged to recognise the claims of Saint Vincent and the Grenadines in relation to the *Saiga* because of the absence of genuine link between the vessel and Saint Vincent and the Grenadines.[78] Yet ITLOS did not support Guinea's view. In this regard, the

[71] The *M/V Virginia G (Panama/Guinea-Bissau)* ITLOS Case No 19, Judgment, [2014] ITLOS Rep 4.
[72] The *M/V Saiga (No 2)* [1999] ITLOS Rep 40 [79].
[73] ibid 39, [75]. See also Counter-Memorial Submitted by Guinea, 156–57, [72].
[74] The *M/V Saiga (No 2)* [1999] ITLOS Rep 39 [76].
[75] ibid 40, [78]. See also the Presentation by Plender, ITLOS/PV.99/1, 20.
[76] The *M/V Saiga (No 2)* [1999] ITLOS Rep 42 [87].
[77] ibid 40, [79].
[78] ibid 39, [75]–[76].

Tribunal noted that, in the legislative process leading to article 5(1) of the Geneva Convention on the High Seas, the proposal that the existence of a genuine link should be a basis for the recognition of nationality was not adopted.[79] Article 91 of the LOSC followed the approach of the Convention on the High Seas.

Furthermore, according to ITLOS, 'There is nothing in article 94 to permit a state which discovers evidence indicating the absence of proper jurisdiction and control by a flag state over a ship to refuse to recognise the right of the ship to fly the flag of the flag State'.[80] Hence ITLOS concluded:

> The purpose of the provisions of the convention on the need for a genuine link between a ship and its flag State is to secure more effective implementation of the duties of the flag State, and not to establish criteria by reference to which the validity of the registration of ships in a flag State may be challenged by other States.[81]

The dictum of the Tribunal can be interpreted to imply that the lack of a genuine link between a flag state and a ship, as such, does not affect the validity of the nationality of the ship.[82] As will be discussed next, the Tribunal addressed this issue again in the *M/V Virginia G* between Panama and Guinea-Bissau.

C. The *M/V Virginia G* (2014)

The *M/V Virginia G* was concerned with the legality of bunkering conducted by *M/V Virginia G*, an oil tanker flying the flag of Panama, in the EEZ of Guinea-Bissau. In this case, Guinea-Bissau raised objections to the admissibility of the claims of Panama and contended that there was no genuine link between the *M/V Virginia G* and Panama.[83] In this connection, two issues arose: the existence of a genuine link between the *M/V Virginia G* and Panama, and the legal consequences of the absence of the genuine link.

First, the existence of a genuine link between the flag state, that is, Panama and the *M/V Virginia G*, must be examined. Related to this, Guinea-Bissau claimed:

> From the conception of the 'genuine link' it follows that a flag State can only then effectively exercise its jurisdiction and control in administrative, technical and social matters over ships flying its flag, as required under article 94(1) of the Convention, when it can exercise appropriate jurisdiction and control also over the *owners* of the ships.[84]

In this connection, Guinea-Bissau further contended that 'a basic condition for the registration of a ship is that also the owner or operator of the ship is under

[79] ibid 40–41, [80].
[80] ibid 41, [82].
[81] ibid 42, [83].
[82] BH Oxman and V Bantz, 'THE M/V SAIGA (No 2) (*Saint Vincent and the Grenadines v Guinea*), Judgment (ITLOS Case No 2)' (2000) 94 *American Journal of International Law* 140, 148.
[83] The *M/V Virginia G* [2014] ITLOS Rep 41 [102].
[84] Emphasis original. Counter-Memorial of Guinea-Bissau, 13, [31].

the jurisdiction of the flag State'.[85] In response, Panama claimed that it '*does*, and did, effectively exercise its jurisdiction and control in administrative, technical and social matters over the *VIRGINIA G*'.[86] Related to this, Panama maintained that it imposed on the owner of the *M/V Virginia G*, Penn Lilac, an additional condition, a continuous synopsis record.[87] In considering the issue, ITLOS noted the following points:

- Panama's legislation sets out the conditions for granting Panamanian nationality to ships, for the registration of ships in its territory, and for the right to fly its flag;
- the requirement on shipowners to take specific actions, to carry out certain activities and to submit substantial information and documentation to fulfil all these requirements, in line with Panama's international obligations;
- the fact that the *M/V Virginia G* obtained the required documents and technical certificates;
- specific conditions on owners of vessels imposed by Panama, such as the requirement of a continuous synopsis record, in International Convention for the Safety of Life at Sea (SOLAS 1974);[88] and
- the fact that Panama delegated the conduct of annual safety inspection and the issuance of technical certificates to one of the recognised organisations (ie, Panama Shipping Registry Inc).[89]

The Tribunal considered that 'on the basis of information available to it, there [was] no reason to question that Panama exercised effective jurisdiction and control over the *M/V Virginia G* at the time of the incident'.[90] It thus concluded that 'a genuine link existed between Panama and the *M/V Virginia G* at the time of the incident'.[91] It is noteworthy that the Tribunal specified factors which need to be considered when examining the existence of a genuine link. In particular, the reference to the duties of shipowners merits attention. The analysis of the Tribunal is too succinct to draw any conclusions regarding the Tribunal's method of analysis of these factors. Furthermore, the Tribunal provided little explanation about the question whether the requirements mentioned by Panama were actually implemented.

The related issue that needs consideration concerns the meaning of genuine link. In this regard, the Tribunal stated:

> In the view of the Tribunal, once a ship is registered, the flag State is required, under article 94 of the Convention, to exercise effective jurisdiction and control over that ship

[85] ibid 14, [33]. See also presentation by Leitão, Verbatim Record, ITLOS/PV.13/C19/4/Rev.1, 3.
[86] Emphasis original. Reply of Panama, 22, [111].
[87] ibid 23, [114].
[88] The *M/V Virginia G* [2014] ITLOS Rep 45 [115].
[89] ibid 46, [116].
[90] ibid 45, [114].
[91] ibid 46, [117].

> in order to ensure that it operates in accordance with generally accepted international regulations, procedures and practices. This is the meaning of 'genuine link'.[92]

The phrase 'once a ship is registered' seems to imply that the requirement of a genuine link comes into play only after the registration of a ship or granting the nationality of a flag state to a ship. However, the ILC's commentary explicitly stated:

> *[B]efore* the grant of nationality is generally recognised, there must be a genuine link between the ship and the State granting permission to fly its flag … While leaving States a wide latitude in this respect, the Commission wished to make it clear that the grant of its flag to a ship cannot be a mere administrative formality, with no accompanying guarantee that the ship possess a real link with its new State.[93]

The commentary seems to suggest that a genuine link must exist when granting the nationality of a flag state to a ship.[94] In fact, it seems logical that the legal basis for securing a genuine link must already be provided in the municipal laws and regulations that set out the conditions for the nationality of a flag state to a ship. If not, a flag state cannot effectively control the activities of a vessel. It must also be noted that the requirement of a genuine link is provided in article 91 and headed 'Nationality of Ships'.[95] In light of the above reasons, it seems reasonable to consider that a genuine link must be incorporated into the conditions for granting the nationality of a flag state to a ship.

Second, as regards the legal consequences of the absence of a genuine link, ITLOS reaffirmed its dictum in the *M/V Saiga (No 2)* decision that

> article 91, paragraph 1, third sentence, of the Convention requiring a genuine link between the flag State and the ship should not be read as establishing prerequisites or conditions to be satisfied for the exercise of the right of the flag State to grant its nationality to ships.[96]

As the statement suggested, ITLOS consistently took the view that a state cannot refuse to recognise the right of the ship to fly the flag of the flag state because of the absence of a genuine link.[97] In light of the vagueness of the concept of genuine

[92] ibid 45, [113].

[93] Emphasis added: (1956) 2 *Yearbook of International Law Commission* 279.

[94] Scovazzi also considers that 'the conditions established under the national legislation of a state for granting its nationality to ships must be based on the existence of a genuine link between such state and the ship': Scovazzi, 'ITLOS and Jurisdiction over Ships' (2015) 385.

[95] See D Attard and P Mallia, 'The High Seas' in DJ Attard, M Fitzmaurice and NA Martínez Gutiérrez (eds), *The IMLI Manual on International Maritime Law*, vol 1 (Oxford, Oxford University Press, 2014) 239, 251.

[96] The *M/V Virginia G* [2014] ITLOS Rep 44 [110].

[97] In addition, one can find one precedent of a municipal court relating to this matter, that is, the *Magda Maria* of 1986. On 1 August 1981, the *Magda Maria*, flying the flag of Panama, was seized by the Dutch authorities on the high seas nine miles off the Dutch coast because of unauthorised broadcasting from the high seas. Before the Court of Appeal of the Hague, the Procurator-General claimed that the *Magda Maria* had become stateless owing to the absence of a genuine link as referred to in art 5 of the Geneva Convention on the High Seas. However, the Court of Appeal took the view that the concept of the genuine link 'does not imply that the Dutch Government has the right to recognise

link, it is arguable that unilateral discretion of state denying the nationality of vessels because of the absence of a genuine link may endanger the maintenance of a legal order on the high seas through the exclusive jurisdiction of the flag state.[98] In this sense, the Tribunal's interpretation seems to have some merits. However, it cannot pass unnoticed that this interpretation gives rise to a question regarding remedy for the violation of the obligation of a flag state to exercise effective jurisdiction and control over vessels flying its flag.

Under the LOSC, the only available remedy is that provided in article 94(6):

> A State which has clear grounds to believe that proper jurisdiction and control with respect to a ship have not been exercised may report the facts to the flag State. Upon receiving such a report, the flag State shall investigate the matter and, if appropriate, take any action necessary to remedy the situation.

In the situation where a genuine link between a flag state and a ship does not exist, however, it seems well probable that the flag state already knows the fact. This is particularly the case of flag of convenience states. If so, it seems unlikely that such a flag state would investigate the matter and take any action pursuant to article 94(6).[99] Therefore, serious doubts can be expressed regarding whether the right to report under article 94(6) alone would be adequate to secure effective implementation of the duties of the flag state.[100]

In this regard, it is notable that ITLOS, in its Advisory Opinion of 2015, added an obligation which is not explicitly provided in article 94(6), stating that 'the flag State is under the obligation to inform the reporting State about the action taken'.[101] If this does not occur, state responsibility for the breach of obligations of the flag state will arise.[102] In this case, there appears to be scope for arguing that the alleged flag state would lose the right to exercise its jurisdiction over the ship concerned and the right to claim before an international court or tribunal in respect of the ship.[103] Scovazzi has argued that 'the non-recognition of the right to grant the national flag could be a rightful countermeasure against a state

or otherwise the right to fly the Panamanian flag which was granted to the ship by Panama'. Further, 'it cannot be said on the basis of the examination at the sitting that the MS *Magda Maria* was stateless on account of the absence of a genuine link'. See *Compania Naviera Panlieve SA v Public Prosecutor (The MS Magda Maria)* (29 May 1986, Court of Appeal of The Hague, Netherlands), which was summarised in LANM Barnhoorn, 'Netherlands Judicial Decisions Involving Questions of Public International Law, 1987–1988' (1989) 20 *Netherlands Yearbook of International Law* 283, 349.

[98] See also McDougal, Burke and Vlasio, 'Maintenance' (1960) 35.

[99] Scovazzi, 'The Contribution of the Tribunal' (2018) 151.

[100] See also D Guilfoye, 'Article 94' in A Prölss (ed), *The United Nations Convention on the Law of the Sea: A Commentary* (München/Oxford, Beck/Hart, 2017) 707, 713.

[101] Request for Advisory Opinion submitted by the Sub-Regional Fisheries Commission, Advisory Opinion, 2 April 2015, [2015] ITLOS Rep 4, 36, [118].

[102] As Judge Anderson pointedly observed, the concept of a genuine link contains an element of good faith in the word 'genuine': Separate Opinion of Judge Anderson in the *M/V Saiga (No 2)* [1999] ITLOS Rep 132. Accordingly, the lack of a genuine link may also create state responsibility for a breach of the principle of good faith set out in art 300 of the LOSC.

[103] *cf* Attard and Mallia, 'The High Seas' (2014) 252.

that has persistently violated the obligation to ensure the existence of a genuine link'.[104] While this view is noteworthy, it has not yet been tested by state and judicial practice.[105] In any event, given that the prevention of illegal, unreported, and unregulated (IUU) fishing, vessel-source marine pollution, and the safety of navigation are becoming a matter for serious concern,[106] further consideration must be given to the remedy for the violation of the obligation of a flag state to exercise effective jurisdiction and control over vessels flying its flag.

D. Summary

The principal points discussed in this section can be summarised as follows:

(1) Where one of the disputing parties disputes the existence of a genuine link between a flag state and a ship before ITLOS, the existence of a genuine link is to be examined by the Tribunal. Thus a dispute regarding a genuine link may be subject to the dispute settlement procedures under the LOSC.
(2) When examining the existence of a genuine link between a flag state and a ship, there is a need to investigate various elements of municipal law and regulation. The scope of those elements is not well established in the jurisprudence of ITLOS and nor is there any standard for deciding whether a flag state effectively exercises its jurisdiction and control over ships.
(3) ITLOS has consistently taken the view that states cannot refuse to accept the nationality of a ship because of the absence of a genuine link between a flag state and the ship. Thus, the only remedy for the violation of the obligation to ensure a genuine link is the right to report under article 94(6) of the LOSC. This provision is of only modest utility to secure a genuine link.

IV. Implications of Change of Ownership for the Nationality of a Ship

The last issue that must be examined in this chapter concerns the implications of change of ownership for the nationality of a ship. In considering this issue, two cases

[104] Scovazzi (n 40) 152. See also Scovazzi (n 38) 386. Judge Jessup, in his Separate Opinion in *Barcelona Traction, Light and Power Company, Limited (Belgium v Spain) (New Application: 1962)*, also expressed the view that 'if a State purports to confer its nationality on ships by allowing them to fly its flag, without assuring that they meet such tests as management, ownership, jurisdiction and control, other States are not bound to recognise the asserted nationality of the ship': [1970] ICJ Rep 3, 161, 188.

[105] In this regard, an issue may arise whether the non-recognition of the right to grant the national flag can be regarded as a proportionate measure. See art 51 of the International Law Commission's Article on State Responsibility, reproduced in J Crawford, *The International Law Commission's Articles on State Responsibility: Introduction, Text and Commentaries* (Cambridge, Cambridge University Press, 2002) 61.

[106] See also Scovazzi (n 40) 153.

merit discussion: the *Juno Trader* between Saint Vincent and the Grenadines and Guinea-Bissau[107] and the *Tomimaru* between Japan and the Russian Federation.[108]

A. The *Juno Trader* (2004)

The essential issue of the *Juno Trader* was the prompt release of a refrigerated cargo vessel, the *Juno Trader*. The vessel was registered in Saint Vincent and the Grenadines on 14 February 1994. The Certificate of Registry was permanent.[109] On 26 September 2004, the *Juno Trader* crossed into the EEZ of Guinea-Bissau at a distance of about 40 nautical miles from the coast.[110] On that day, the *Juno Trader*, which was within the limits of the EEZ of Guinea-Bissau, was boarded by officers of the Fisheries Inspection Service of Guinea-Bissau.[111] The *Juno Trader* was escorted to the port of Bissau, Guinea-Bissau. On 27 September 2004, the master and the crew were detained on board under the surveillance of armed personnel.[112] In Minute No 14/CIMF/04 of 19 October 2004, the Interministerial Maritime Control Commission (IMCC) decided to impose fines on the *Juno Trader* and its master.[113] Against that background, on 18 November 2004, Saint Vincent and the Grenadines instituted proceedings before ITLOS against Guinea-Bissau concerning the release of the *Juno Trader* and its crew.[114]

In this case, Guinea-Bissau maintained that Saint Vincent and the Grenadines failed to discharge the initial burden of establishing that it was the flag state of the *Juno Trader* at the time of the filing of the application since the ownership of the *Juno Trader* had already reverted to the state of Guinea-Bissau.[115] In this connection, Guinea-Bissau argued that 'since 5 November 2004 the *Juno Trader* has been the property of the state of Guinea-Bissau'[116] and that 'it would seem a rather odd result that one sovereign state could be the flag state of a vessel that is the property of another sovereign state'.[117] However, Saint Vincent and the Grenadines

[107] The Juno Trader (Saint Vincent and the Grenadines v Guinea-Bissau), ITLOS Case No 13, Prompt Release, Judgment [2004] ITLOS Rep 17.
[108] *The Tomimaru (Japan v Russian Federation)*, Prompt Release, Judgment, [2005–2007] ITLOS Rep 74.
[109] The *Juno Trader* [2004] ITLOS Rep 28 [34].
[110] ibid 28, [36].
[111] ibid 29, [39].
[112] ibid 29, [40].
[113] ibid 31–32, [43].
[114] Application on behalf of Saint Vincent and the Grenadines, available at: www.itlos.org/fileadmin/itlos/documents/cases/case_no_13/Application.SVG.pdf. See also [2004] ITLOS Rep 21 [1].
[115] ibid 36, [58].
[116] Presentation by Staker, Verbatim Record, ITLOS/PV.04/03, 43 and 45. In this connection, the National Fisheries Inspection and Control Service (FISCAP) stated that the ownership of the *Juno Trader* had reverted to the state of Guinea-Bissau with effect from 5 November 2004 on failure to pay the fine imposed by the decision of the IMCC of 19 October 2004: The *Juno Trader* [2004] ITLOS Rep 34 [53].
[117] Presentation by Staker (ibid), 47.

countered that the execution of the decision of the IMCC was suspended by a decision of the Regional Court of Bissau.[118] On this issue, ITLOS held:

> [W]hatever may be the effect of a definitive change in the ownership of a vessel upon its nationality, the Tribunal considers that there is no legal basis in the particular circumstances of this case for holding that there has been a definitive change in the nationality of the *Juno Trader*.[119]

It thus found that 'there is no legal basis for the Respondent's claim that Saint Vincent and the Grenadines was not the flag state of the vessel on 18 November 2004, the date on which the Application for prompt release was submitted'.[120]

The Tribunal's view on this matter was succinct. However, the implications of change in the ownership of a ship on its nationality was further amplified by Judges Mensah and Wolfrum:

> In view of the important functions of the flag State as referred to in article 94 of the Convention and also the pivotal role of the flag State in the initiation of the procedure for the prompt release of a ship under article 292 of the Convention, …, it cannot easily be assumed that a change in ownership automatically leads to a change of the flag. … In the present case, there is no evidence that the alleged loss of the flag of the *Juno Trader* had any basis in the law of the flag State or the relevant provisions of the Convention.[121]

The learned judges also added:

> Equally, it is not tenable to argue that the *Juno Trader* has lost its flag in consequence of its alleged confiscation. Vessels without flags are the exception and, therefore, loss of flag of a ship cannot be assumed lightly.[122]

This view was echoed by Judge Ndiaye.[123] Overall ITLOS seems to have taken the view that change of ownership of a ship did not automatically lead to a change of the nationality of the ship. As will be discussed below, this point was further amplified by ITLOS in the *Tomimaru*.

B. The *Tomimaru* (2007)

The *Tomimaru* was a trawler flying the flag of Japan. The essential subject of the *Tomimaru* related to prompt release of the ship. On 31 October 2006, the *Tomimaru*, which was fishing in the western Bering Sea located in the EEZ of the Russian Federation, was boarded by officers of the Russian authority. According to the Russian Federation, an unaccounted amount of 5.5 tons of walleye pollack were discovered in the *Tomimaru*. Thus the vessel was escorted to Avachinskiy Bay for

[118] [2004] ITLOS Rep 36 [60].
[119] ibid 36, [63].
[120] ibid 37, [64].
[121] Joint Separate Opinion of Judges Mensah and Wolfrum, ibid 61, [10].
[122] ibid, [11].
[123] Separate Opinion of Judge Ndiaye, ibid 82, [28].

further investigation.[124] After the inspection of the *Tomimaru*, it was established that the trawler was engaged in illegal fishing.[125] Accordingly, a criminal case was instituted against the Master of the *Tomimaru* on 8 November 2006.[126] Despite the petition of the owner, on 28 December 2006 the Petropavlovsk-Kamchatskii City Court decided that the *Tomimaru* should be confiscated. When the owner of the vessel filed an appeal before the Kamchatka District Court, that court confirmed the decision of the Petropavlovsk-Kamchatskii City Court on 24 January 2007.[127] Thus Japan filed an application under article 292 of the LOSC for the release of the Tomimaru.[128] At the time of the application, the procedure was still pending before the Supreme Court of the Russian Federation.[129] After the closure of the hearing, however, the Tribunal was informed that the Supreme Court of the Russian Federation had dismissed the complaint concerning the confiscation of the Tomimaru.[130] In this connection, two issues arose: the impact of confiscation on the nationality of a vessel; and the the impact of confiscation on the application for the prompt release of the vessel.[131]

As regards the first issue, ITLOS stressed the distinction between the change of ownership of a vessel and the change of nationality of the vessel:

> In view of the important functions of the flag State as referred to in article 94 of the Convention and the pivotal role played by the flag State in the initiation of the procedure for the prompt release of a ship under article 292 of the Convention, it cannot be assumed that a change in ownership automatically leads to the change or loss of its flag.[132]

The Tribunal thus held that 'the confiscation of a vessel does not result *per se* in an automatic change of the flag or in its loss'.[133] The Tribunal's view is noteworthy.

As regards the second issue, the Tribunal distinguished two situations. In the situation where proceedings are still pending before the domestic courts of the detaining state, 'a decision to confiscate a vessel does not prevent the Tribunal from considering an application of prompt release of such vessel'.[134] In the situation where the procedures were finally ended before the domestic courts, however, the application for prompt releases was without object since 'a decision under article 292 of the Convention to release the vessel would contradict the decision which concluded the proceedings before the appropriate domestic fora and

[124] The *Tomimaru* [2007] ITLOS Rep 84 [24].
[125] ibid, [25].
[126] ibid, [26].
[127] ibid 89, [42]–[43].
[128] Application of Japan, available at www.itlos.org/fileadmin/itlos/documents/cases/case_no_15/application_japan_eng.1.pdf.
[129] [2007] ITLOS Rep 89 [43].
[130] ibid 90, [46].
[131] ibid 95, [69].
[132] ibid 95, [70].
[133] ibid.
[134] ibid 97, [78].

encroach upon national competences, thus contravening article 292, paragraph 3, of the Convention'.[135]

In conclusion, the Tribunal unanimously found that the application of Japan no longer had any object.[136] At the same time, the Tribunal notably added that 'confiscation of a fishing vessel must not be used in such a manner as to upset the balance of the interests of the flag State and of the coastal State established in the Convention'.[137] Specifically, it stressed that a decision to confiscate a vessel 'should not be taken in such a way as to prevent the shipowner from having recourse to available domestic judicial remedies, or as to prevent the flag state from resorting to the prompt release procedure set forth in the Convention'.[138] In so stating, the Tribunal seemed to strike a balance between the decision of domestic courts and the institution of prompt release under article 292 of the LOSC.

C. Summary

The above cursory consideration can be summarised in three points:

(1) ITLOS took the view that a change of ownership of a vessel and that of the nationality of a vessel are two distinct matters and that change of ownership of a vessel through confiscation does not per se result in an automatic change of the nationality of the vessel.
(2) Where proceedings are still pending before the domestic courts of the detaining state, a decision to confiscate a vessel does not prevent an application for the prompt release of such a vessel. Where confiscation of a vessel is finally confirmed by a domestic court, however, the application for prompt release is without object.
(3) A decision to confiscate a vessel should not be used as a means to prevent the flag state from resorting to the prompt release procedure under the LOSC.

V. Conclusions

The nationality of a ship is key to establishing the juridical link between a flag state and a ship flying its flag. In this sense, it is a prerequisite of the exclusive jurisdiction of the flag state. The above consideration seems to reveal the following conclusions.

First, while a state has a wide discretion to decide the conditions for granting its nationality to a ship, the nationality of a ship can be examined by ITLOS in its judicial proceedings. In that case, the relevant domestic laws are to be examined by

[135] ibid 97, [80].
[136] ibid 98, [82].
[137] ibid 96, [75].
[138] ibid 96, [76].

the Tribunal. However, the scope of the domestic documents that would fall within article 91(2) of the LOSC remains less clear. In addition, the rules and standards for evaluating evidence of the nationality of a ship need further clarification.

Second, the existence of a genuine link can be the subject of the dispute settlement procedures under the LOSC. In fact, ITLOS in the *M/V Saiga (No 2)* and *M/V Virginia G* examined the existence of a genuine link. Yet there is no established standard for deciding whether a flag state effectively exercises its jurisdiction and control over ships in the jurisprudence of ITLOS.

Third, according to ITLOS, states have no right to unilaterally refuse to accept the nationality of a ship because of the absence of a genuine link between a flag state and the ship. The only remedy available for the violation of the obligation to ensure a genuine link is the right to report provided in article 94(6) of the LOSC. ITLOS, in its Advisory Opinion of 2015, further added an obligation to inform the reporting state about the action taken to article 94(6). Even so, it may have to be admitted that the remedy under article 94(6) remains weak.

Fourth, the change of ownership of a vessel is distinct from the change of the nationality of a vessel. Accordingly, the change of ownership of a vessel through confiscation does not per se automatically change the nationality of the vessel.

Fifth, apart from an exceptional case, it seems difficult, if not impossible, for third states to challenge the validity of the nationality of a ship. Furthermore, the remedy for the violation of the obligation of a flag state to exercise effective jurisdiction and control over vessels flying its flag remains limited.

Overall it can be concluded that the existing rules favour flag states and that the remedy for the violation of flag state obligations remains weak. At present, however, to secure the exercise of effective jurisdiction and control over ships by the flag state is increasingly important particularly in the context of sustainable use of marine living resources, prevention of marine pollution and safety of navigation. In response, two options that are not mutually exclusive can be suggested.

The first is to strengthen the remedy in response to the alleged breach of the obligations of a flag state. In this regard, as noted, it may not be unreasonable to argue that a flag state would lose the right to claim before an international court or tribunal in respect of a ship concerned, if the flag state failed to comply with the obligation set out in article 94(6). If an adjudicatory body, such as ITLOS, declared that a flag state had no right to a claim concerning a ship in a particular case, it might be possible to argue that there would be no obligation for third states to accept the flag state's nationality of the ship in question.

The second option is to explore concerted mechanisms for preventing breaches of the relevant rules by vessels in specific fields. By way of illustration, many regional fisheries management organisations take non-flag measures. Port inspection could also be an alternative well worth considering in securing compliance with relevant rules concerning, inter alia, the conservation of marine living resources.[139]

[139] Tanaka *International Law of the Sea* (2019) 313–18.

2

Nationality Requirements: Implications for Shipping Enterprises

STEPHEN GIRVIN*

I. Introduction

It is the norm for a substantial majority of commercial ships to trade under flags differing from the flag of the state in which the owner is located.[1] The International Chamber of Shipping (ICS) confirms that 'there is nothing inherently unusual in an international ship registry system in which the owner of a ship may be located in a country other than the state whose flag the ship flies'.[2] Although there are notable variations, the tonnage of nationally flagged ships among the top 10 shipowning states[3] ranges from less than one per cent to 71.82 per cent while the proportion of foreign-flagged vessels of the same states ranges from 28.18 per cent to 99.46 per cent.[4] Some states have significantly higher numbers of national shipowners[5] and it is remarkable that the top shipowning states differ from the leading flags.[6]

Such raw statistics are, however, superficial. Shipowners and ship management companies are not much interested in statistics per se; standing in tonnage rankings is unlikely to be *the* compelling factor when making the decision on flag. More broadly, the choice of flag is not about nationality simpliciter but embraces

* MPA Professor of Maritime Law; Director, Centre for Maritime Law, Faculty of Law, National University of Singapore.

[1] More than 70% of the worldwide fleet in 2020: 'Review of Maritime Transport 2020' (UNCTAD, 2020) 41. For detailed coverage, see E Watt, *Ship Registration: Law and Practice*, 3rd edn (London, Informa, 2018).

[2] 'Shipping Industry Flag State Performance Table 2020/2021' (ICS, 2021) 3.

[3] Greece, Japan, China, Singapore, Hong Kong, Germany, Republic of Korea, Norway, Bermuda and the USA: UNCTAD, 'Review' (2020) 41. See also 'Top 10 Flag States 2019' *Lloyd's List* (3 December 2019).

[4] ibid.

[5] *cf*, eg, China, where 43.56% of the fleet is nationally owned (J Chen, KX Li, X Liu and H Li, 'The Development of Ship Registration Policy in China: Response to Flags of Convenience' (2017) 83 *Marine Policy* 22) and Hong Kong, where 71.82% is nationally owned: ibid.

[6] Currently Panama, Liberia, the Marshall Islands, Hong Kong and Singapore: UNCTAD (n 1) 44.

choices that are complex, involving commercial, legal, political and (occasionally) moral considerations.[7] Other factors come into play at the end of a vessel's trading life when the decision is made to scrap the vessel.[8] In recent years, there have been concerns about the proliferation of fraudulent registrations and registries of ships and the IMO is in the vanguard of efforts to stamp this out.[9]

This chapter examines the background to registration and the ascription of nationality to ships; the underlying legal principles are considered[10] together with the factors that may affect nationality choices for shipping enterprises.[11]

II. Registration

Nationality (or flag) typically requires registration, the entry of the particulars of the vessel into the public records of the state.[12] Although registration is traceable to Roman times,[13] the earliest statute mandating formal registration was the Navigation Act 1660,[14] requiring the owner of every foreign-built ship to make an oath before a customs officer at the home port of the ship that:

> [S]uch Ship or Vessel was *bona fide* and without fraud by him or them bought for a valuable consideration, expressing the sum, as also the time, place, and persons from whom it was bought … and that no foreigner directly or indirectly hath any part, interest, or share therein, and that upon such oath he or they shall receive a Certificate under the Hand or Seal of the said chief Officer or Officers of the Port where such person or persons so making Oath do reside, whereby such Ship or Vessel may for the future pass and be deemed as a Ship belonging to the said Port, and enjoy the privilege of such a Ship or Vessel.[15]

A formal system of registration requiring entry in the UK register was maintained,[16] culminating in the Merchant Shipping Act 1894. Section 2(1) of that Act explicitly stated that 'every British ship shall, unless exempted from Registry, be registered under this Act'.[17] As more and more colonies in the commonwealth became

[7] Watt, *Ship Registration* (2018) [6.17].

[8] See Glinski (ch 5). See also L McCarthy, 'A Final Flag of Convenience', *Lloyd's List* (28 February 2013); N Krigslund, 'Maersk Vessels Sailed Under Black-listed Flag for Final Journey' *TradeWinds* (17 October 2017).

[9] See below, IV(D).

[10] For the public international law background, see Tanaka (ch 1).

[11] The position within the EU is not covered. *cf Community Guidelines on State Aid to Maritime Transport* [2004] OJ C13/3; Watt (n 1) [6.10].

[12] *Liverpool Borough Bank v Turner* (1860) 1 J & H 159, 169, 70 ER 703, 707–09; *KeyBank National Association v The Ship 'Blaze'* [2007] 2 NZLR 271 [31].

[13] J Williams, 'The Function of Evidence in Roman Law' (1894) 20 *Law Magazine & Law Review* (5th ser) 73, 83.

[14] 12 Cha II, c 18.

[15] s 10.

[16] See JNK Mansell, *Flag State Responsibility* (Berlin, Springer, 2009) 26.

[17] Section 1 laid down the qualification for owning a British ship and included 'bodies corporate established under and subject to the laws of some part of Her Majesty's dominions, and having their principal place of business in those dominions' (s 1(d)).

independent, however, these requirements became increasingly dated, notably as those countries enacted their own domestic merchant shipping legislation. The UK system was revised in 1988,[18] replacing an *obligation* to register with an *entitlement* to register while a further revision in 1993, consolidated in 1995,[19] introduced a central register.[20]

Legislation setting up a system of registration is now *de rigeur* in the majority of flag states, including former British colonies, now commonwealth states, which started out following the British model.[21] The recognised functions of registration include:

(1) the allocation of a vessel to a specific state and its subjection to a single jurisdiction for the purposes, for example, of safety regulation, security aspects, crewing and discipline on board;
(2) the conferment of the right to fly the national flag;
(3) the right to diplomatic protection and consular assistance by the flag state;
(4) the right to naval protection by the flag state;
(5) the right to engage in certain activities within the territorial waters of the flag state – for example, coastal fishing, trading or in the case of a pleasure yacht, cruising between the ports of the flag state;
(6) in case of war, for determining the application of the rules of war and neutrality to a vessel; and
(7) publicity itself, the provisional of searchable, verifiable and authoritative information within the public domain.[22]

Although rare, a ship which possesses no nationality, a so-called 'stateless ship', has no right to enjoy the above protections.[23] In some cases, local legislation requires that the master of a ship declare to an officer of customs and excise 'the name of the nation to which he claims that the ship belongs'.[24] It is even more common for vessels arriving in port to provide pre-arrival notification which includes information about documentation held on board, including information concerning the ship's name and IMO number.[25]

[18] Merchant Shipping Act 1988.

[19] Merchant Shipping Act 1995, Part II. See below, VI(F).

[20] Merchant Shipping (Registration, etc) Act 1993.

[21] See, eg, Shipping Registration Act 1981 No 8 (Cth) (Australia); Merchant Shipping Act 1995 (rev edn, 1996), Part II (Singapore) and The Merchant Shipping (Registration of Ships) Regulations 1996, Reg 7 (rev edn, 1997) (Singapore); Ship Registration Act 1998 (South Africa); Ship Registration Act 1992 (New Zealand). See P Myburgh, 'The New Zealand Ship Registration Act 1992' [1993] *LMCLQ* 444.

[22] Watt (n 1) [1.29].

[23] See, eg, RR Churchill and RV Lowe, *The Law of the Sea*, 3rd edn (Manchester, Manchester University Press, 1999) 213.

[24] Shipping Registration Act 1981 No 8 (Cth) (Australia), s 31(1); Merchant Shipping Act 1995, s 6(1) (which reproduces s 68 of the 1894 Act); Ship Registration Act 1998 No 58 (South Africa), s 6(1); Ship Registration Act 1992 No 89 (New Zealand), s 59(1). There is no equivalent provision in the Singapore Merchant Shipping Act 1995, cap 179.

[25] See, eg, MPA Port Marine Circular No 20 of 2008 ('Revised Reporting Procedures for Notification and Confirmation of a Vessel's Arrival in Singapore') which specifies the information which must

III. Choices for Shipping Enterprises: Open Registries

A. Background

Before World War II, the UK, along with 11 other leading maritime nations,[26] owned 88 per cent of the world's fleet.[27] After World War II, however, there was a significant haemorrhage of tonnage from these countries in part because of the development of open registries, referred to pejoratively as 'flags of convenience',[28] which started with Panama in 1917[29] and Liberia in 1948,[30] but are associated with the prohibition era in the 1920s when cruise liners were reflagged in Panama to avoid US law banning the sale of alcohol aboard US ships.[31] Such 'flagging out' is also associated with an early twentieth-century example of British fishermen registering their vessels in Norway so as to avoid fishing restrictions[32] and others more than 200 years earlier.[33]

Open registries attracted increasingly adverse attention. The OECD in 1958 produced a study on 'flags of convenience'[34] in which it concluded that

> the laws of certain countries … allow, and indeed make it easy, for ships owned by foreign nationals or companies to fly their flags. This is in contrast to practice in maritime countries (and in many others) where the right to fly the national flag is subject to stringent conditions and involves far-reaching obligations.[35]

A few years later Boczek stated that:

> Functionally, a 'flag of convenience' can be defined as the flag of any country allowing the registration of foreign-owned and foreign-controlled vessels under conditions which,

be provided before a vessel's intended arrival into Singapore. The latest (2017) revision of the PAN (pre-arrival notification) requires a declaration of the vessel's certificate of registry (cl 4.2.2.1) – see MPA Port Marine Circular No 19 of 2017 ('Revision to the Pre-arrival Notification (PAN)') – and has been modified to incorporate reporting the use of compliant fuel in accordance with the IMO 2020 Fuel Oil Sulphur Limit (MPA Port Marine Circular No 19 of 2019).

[26] Denmark, France, Germany, Greece, Italy, Japan, Netherlands, Norway, Sweden, USSR, USA.

[27] Board of Trade, 'Committee of Inquiry into Shipping' (Cm 4337, 1970) [166].

[28] FOCs. See, eg, 'Review of Maritime Transport 1972–1973' (UNCTAD, 1975) 40; SG Sturmey, *British Shipping and World Competition* (Liverpool, Liverpool University Press, 2018) 177.

[29] Although created in 1917, Law 8 of 1925 (Panama) removed restrictions regarding nationality and residence of shipowners: see F Piniella, JI Alcaide and E Rodríguez-Díaz, 'The Panama Ship Registry: 1917–2017' (2017) 77 *Marine Policy* 13, 14.

[30] See RP Carlisle, *Sovereignty for Sale* (Annapolis, Naval Institute Press, 1981) ch 7; *Linsen International Ltd v Humpuss Sea Transport Pte Ltd* [2011] EWHC 2339 (Comm), [2011] 2 Lloyd's Rep 663 [38].

[31] Carlisle, *Sovereignty* (1981) 14.

[32] See *Mortensen v Peters* (1906) 14 SLT 227.

[33] See LFE Goldie, 'Recognition and Dual Nationality – A Problem of Flags of Convenience' (1963) 39 *British Yearbook of International Law* 220, 224; BN Metaxas, 'Flags of Convenience' (1981) 5 *Marine Policy* 52.

[34] 'Study on the expansion of the flags of convenience fleets and on various aspects thereof'.

[35] TA Mensah, 'Flags of Convenience: Problems and Promises' in MQ Mejia Jr (ed), *Selected Issues in Maritime Law and Policy: Liber Amicorum Proshanto K Mukherjee* (New York, Nova Science Publishers Inc, 2013) 25, 28.

> for whatever reasons, are convenient and opportune for the persons who are registering the vessels … The laws of these countries on the registration of merchant vessels are not only very liberal, but also – a decisive consideration – afford the shipowners who are registering their vessels under them very attractive financial advantages. These advantages are clearly what make [these] flags so convenient.[36]

The essential features were further elaborated in the Rochdale Report in 1970,[37] which highlighted certain features, such as the country of registry allowing ownership and/or control of its merchant vessels by non-citizens; weak governmental control over companies; easy access to the registry, such as at a consul's office abroad; tax breaks on shipping, together with an annual registry fee based on tonnage; and the manning of vessels by non-nationals.[38]

Following the establishment of the United Nations Conference on Trade and Development (UNCTAD) in 1964,[39] international attention turned to flags of convenience. In 1981[40] it suggested reasons why the observance of safety standards were less stringent amongst open registry states. Among the most relevant were that the real owners of a vessel were not readily identifiable and were in a position to take risks, contrasted with shipowners in so-called 'normal' registries, and who could change their entities by manipulating brass plate companies. There was also no national trade union representing the interests of seamen onboard vessels owned by shipowners who had economic links with the flag state and such shipowners could suppress any signs of militancy among crews by virtue of their freedom to change nationalities of crews at whim. Finally, the enforcement of standards was 'basically inconsistent with the operation of a registry with the sole aim of making a profit'.

B. Reaction

Concerns about open registries led to the development of the 'genuine link' requirement in the Geneva Convention on the High Seas 1958.[41] Three decades later the ill-fated[42] United Nations Convention on Conditions for Registration of

[36] BA Boczek, *Flags of Convenience: An International Legal Study* (Harvard, Harvard University Press, 1962) 2.

[37] Board of Trade, 'Committee of Inquiry into Shipping' (Cm 4337, 1970).

[38] ibid [184].

[39] See I Haji, 'UNCTAD and Shipping' (1972) 6 *Journal of World Trade* 58; ML McConnell, '"… Darkening Confusion Mounted Upon Darkening Confusion": The Search for the Elusive Genuine Link' (1985) 16 *Journal of Maritime Law and Commerce* 365; A Behnam and P Faust, 'Shipping' in 'Beyond Conventional Wisdom in Development Policy: An Intellectual History of UNCTAD 1964–2004' (UNCTAD, 2004) 77.

[40] 'Action on the Question of Open Registries' TD/B/C.4/220 (UNCTAD, 1981).

[41] Art 5(1). See now art 91 of the Law of the Sea Convention 1982; Tanaka (ch 1).

[42] The Convention is not in force and is unlikely ever to come into force; art 19.1 provides that this will occur '12 months after the date on which not less than 40 States, the combined tonnage of which amounts to at least 25 per cent of world tonnage, have become Contracting Parties to it'. There are currently 15 signatories (UN Treaty Collection).

Ships 1986 set out to 'promote the orderly expansion of world shipping as a whole'. Article 1 stated that the objective was:

> For the purpose of ensuring or, as the case may be, strengthening the genuine link between a State and ships flying its flag, and in order to exercise effectively its jurisdiction and control over such ships with regard to identification and accountability of shipowners and operators as well as with regard to administrative, technical, economic and social matters, a flag State shall apply the provisions contained in this Convention.

This is not the place to analyse the principles enshrined in the Convention[43] or the reasons why it never succeeded. Suffice to say, however, that most states have simply ignored it:[44] indeed, there is no incentive whatsoever to ratify.[45] An indication of the opposition that the Convention faced was readily apparent in the negotiations leading to its enactment, when the US noted that:

> We believe strongly that every country has the right to set its own economic conditions over the registration of ships flying its flag, so long as it practices effective control and operates ships complying with generally accepted international rules and standards … We do not accept that economic links of a mandatory nature between a flag state and the ship of registry are necessary to produce the control needed to restrict the activities of substandard operators. We can support no Convention which includes them.[46]

Notwithstanding this lack of cohesion internationally, the International Transport Workers Federation (ITF)[47] has organised a concerted campaign against open registries for decades. This currently includes 35 states, including prominent flags such as the Bahamas, Liberia, Malta, the Marshall Islands and Panama.[48] Other flag states in this list are of much more doubtful standing, but all are listed because the ITF seeks to protect the position of seamen who suffer low wages, poor onboard conditions, inadequate food and clean drinking water, and long periods of work without proper rest, leading to stress and fatigue. The position has been exacerbated during the COVID-19 pandemic. The ITF encourages shipowners to enter into agreements with the crew to pay 'fair wages' and, if agreed, the shipowner will have made an ITF Standard Agreement with its crew and is issued with a certificate of compliance, an ITF Blue Certificate or ITF Blue Card.[49] Not all open registries originally on the ITF's list have remained there; a classic example is the Singapore flag which, when established in the mid-1960s, was regarded as an open registry.[50]

[43] See SG Sturmey, 'The United Nations Convention on Conditions for Registration of Ships' [1987] *LMCLQ* 97; ML McConnell, 'Business as Usual: An Evaluation of the 1986 United Nations Convention on Conditions for Registration of Ships' (1987) 18 *Journal of Maritime Law and Commerce* 435.

[44] It has been described as a 'relic': Watt (n 1) [3.24].

[45] Churchill and Lowe, *Law of the Sea* (1999) 260.

[46] Cited by McConnell, 'Business as Usual' (1987) 440.

[47] www.itfglobal.org/en/sector/seafarers/flags-of-convenience.

[48] UNCTAD (n 1) 44.

[49] A vessel will not be unseaworthy if it does not carry an ITF Blue Card: see *Alfred C Toepfer Schiffahrtsgesellschaft GmbH v Tossa Marine Co Ltd (The Derby)* [1984] 1 Lloyd's Rep 635.

[50] See below, VI(D).

C. Sub-standard Shipping

Open registries have been vilified as representing a disregard of safety standards, with critics pointing to the over-representation of such flags among major shipping casualties, including major pollution incidents involving the *Amoco Cadiz*,[51] *Exxon Valdez*,[52] *Braer*,[53] *Erika*[54] and *Prestige*,[55] among others. Although the contrast between these flag states and older flags has often been that the latter are 'subject to stringent conditions and involve far-reaching obligations' many leading open registry states have also integrated the major IMO Conventions into their national law[56] and perform well in the published White Lists of the Paris MOU[57] and Tokyo MOU.[58] Conversely, certain flags do not perform so well in the lists[59] nor in the United States Coast Guard's (USCG) list of Targeted Flag Administrations.[60] Even flags which perform well on these lists do not have unblemished records in every respect. A study published in 2015 revealed that the most prominent flags involved in the 100 largest oil spills were Liberia (33.7 per cent), Greece (18.3 per cent), Panama (5.8 per cent), Cyprus (4.8 per cent), Malta (4.85 per cent), and Spain and Italy (2.9 per cent).[61] A later study, published by INTERCARGO, identified 39 bulk carrier total losses in the period 2010 to 2019, 18 of which were with the Panamanian flag, while Cyprus, Korea, Liberia and Malta each had two to three casualties. Among these was the *MV Stellar Daisy*, a South Korean-owned VLOC which sank on 31 March 2017 off the coast of Uruguay while on a voyage between Brazil and China.[62] The investigation report, published eventually

[51] *The Amoco Cadiz* [1984] 2 Lloyd's Rep 304 (unseaworthy vessel and inadequately trained crew).

[52] This incident led to the Oil Pollution Act 1990 (OPA). See, eg, C de la Rue and CB Anderson, *Shipping and the Environment*, 2nd edn (London, Informa, 2009) 864 ff.

[53] See the Report of the Chief Inspector of Marine Accidents: assets.publishing.service.gov.uk/media/54c11606e5274a15b3000015/MAIBReport_Braer-1993.pdf.

[54] This led to various steps by the EU, notably the 'Erika I', 'Erika II', and 'Erika III' packages. See, generally, V Power, *EU Shipping Law*, 3rd edn (London, Informa, 2019) ch 26.

[55] See, eg, A-JE Corres and AA Pallis, 'Flag State Performance: An Empirical Analysis' (2008) 7 *WMU Journal of Maritime Affairs* 241; DD Miller, K Tooley and UR Sumaila, 'Large-scale Oil Spills and Flag-use Within the Global Tanker Fleet' (2015) 42 *Environmental Conservation* 119.

[56] Though not all. See ICS, *Performance Table* (2021).

[57] www.parismou.org/detentions-banning/white-grey-and-black-list.

[58] www.tokyo-mou.org/doc/Flag%20performance%20list%202019.pdf.

[59] Current 'Black List' countries (Paris MOU) (above, n 57) are Tunisia, Cook Islands, Mongolia, Belize, Ukraine, Moldova, Togo, Albania and Comoros. For the Tokyo MOU these are Togo, Mongolia, Democratic People's Republic of Korea, Niue, Barbados and the Federated States of Micronesia (Tokyo MOU) (above n 58). Tanzania, Sierra Leone, Palau, and Saint Kitts and Nevis appear on *both* Black Lists. The Tokyo MOU also has a 'Grey List', which currently includes 19 flags.

[60] See www.dco.uscg.mil/Our-Organization/Assistant-Commandant-for-Prevention-Policy-CG-5P/Inspections-Compliance-CG-5PC-/Commercial-Vessel-Compliance/Foreign-Offshore-Compliance-Division/Port-State-Control/targetedflags. A convenient summary is provided in ICS, *Performance Table* (2021) 9.

[61] Miller, Tooley and Sumaila, 'Large-scale Oil Spills' (2015) 123 *cf* www.intercargo.org/bulk-carrier-casualty-report-2019/, referred to in the next sentence.

[62] See, eg, MT Lin, 'Intercargo Calls for *Stellar Daisy* Probe', *Lloyd's List* (6 April 2017); I Walia, '*Stellar Daisy* Accident Investigation Continues as Search Operations Halted', *Lloyd's List* (17 July 2017).

on 19 April 2019,[63] determined that the likely direct cause of the casualty 'was a rapid list to port following a catastrophic structural failure of the ship's hull that resulted in a loss of buoyancy and uncontrolled flooding'.[64] In 2020, losses included the *MV Wakashio* and the *Gulf Livestock I*. The *MV Wakashio*, a bulk carrier, ran aground on a coral reef off Mauritius on 25 July 2020.[65] The results of a preliminary investigation indicated that the vessel diverted because its crew was seeking internet connectivity and a mobile phone connection to contact families.[66] A second casualty, the *Gulf Livestock I*, a livestock carrier, sank during Typhoon Maysa 100 nautical miles west of Amami Ōshima Island in south-west Japan on 2 September 2020.[67]

These losses nevertheless have to be placed within the context of a 70 per cent decline in losses during the last decade.[68] Accordingly, the response today to sub-standard shipping has become much more nuanced. As one noted maritime economist has commented:

> This trend towards open registries has now gained support from important entities such as banks, lawyers and, of course, the IMO, and it shows no sign of slowing. Shipping now operates in a world where open registries have an absolute majority. But with majority comes responsibility, and the role of open registries has changed dramatically since the dark days of the 1980s. It is an excellent example of how shipping institutions have adapted, in the quest to balance profit against safety and service.[69]

IV. Choices for Shipping Enterprises: Other Types of Registers

The development of open registries and their success in cornering shipping tonnage opened up a yawning gap between such registers and traditional registers. However, the landscape is no longer entirely bifocal, between open registers and traditional registers. Indeed, the success of open registries has forced traditional registers to adopt some of the strategies associated with

[63] See N Bakhsh, 'Will *Stellar Daisy* Lessons Be Learned Too Late?' (2019) 33 *Maritime Risk International* 24.

[64] See 'Stellar Daisy Casualty Investigation Report' (Republic of the Marshall Islands Maritime Administrator, 2019) 9, available at www.register-iri.com/wp-content/uploads/Republic-of-the-Marshall-Islands-Office-of-the-Maritime-Administrator-STELLAR-DAISY-Casualty-Investigation-Report.pdf.

[65] E Watkins, 'Panama Vows "full co-operation" Over Grounded Vessel', *Lloyd's List* (12 August 2020).

[66] A Corbett, 'Panama Confirms *Wakashio* Diverted for Internet Connection During Birthday Celebrations', *TradeWinds* (9 September 2020).

[67] A Corbett, 'Multiple Failings Likely to be Uncovered in Panama Probe into Livestock Carrier Loss', *TradeWinds* (6 October 2020).

[68] 'Safety and Shipping Review 2020' (Allianz, 2020) 4.

[69] Martin Stopford, quoted in S Bergeron, 'Ship Registry Performance is Not Academic' *Lloyd's List* (5 July 2011).

open registers; in some notable cases opening up international registers, or second registers. In other cases, traditional registers have embraced tonnage tax schemes or other incentives.

A. Traditional Registers

Traditional ship registers such as the UK, Denmark, France, Germany, Greece, Italy, Japan, Netherlands, Norway, Sweden and the USA quickly lost ground to open registers. In their heyday, such traditional registers could be assured that nationals and companies would register with the 'home' flag and crew their vessels with nationals of that state. But this is self-evidently no longer the case, partly because of the success of open registers, but also because of the emergence of second registers ('international registers'). Among the states which dominated the shipping world prior to World War II, today the highest ranked are Greece and Japan,[70] followed by the USA, UK, Italy, Germany and the Netherlands.[71]

B. Offshore Registers / International Registers

As indicated earlier, some traditional registers responded to the haemorrhage of tonnage to the open registries by establishing offshore or international registers offering many of the advantages of the open registers, such as low cost, while retaining the link between beneficial ownership or management and the national flag. These include Denmark (the Danish International Register of Shipping), France (RIF), Germany (GIS), Italy, Norway (the Norwegian International Ship Register) and Portugal.[72] Indeed, the Danish International Register and the Norwegian International Ship Register have done particularly well.[73] As one commentator has written:

> The retention of the national flag preserves the jurisdiction of the maritime power over vessels owned by its nationals – important for regulatory, fiscal, and strategic reasons – and mitigates the need for the subsidies and other forms of financial assistance to the shipping sector which have traditionally characterised maritime policy in developed nations. From the operator's perspective, the principal benefit of the international registers is the ability to employ foreign seafarers without being tied to national wage scale or onerous collective agreements.[74]

[70] 9th and 10th, respectively.

[71] UNCTAD (n 1) 44.

[72] Both the RIF and GIS are also on the ITF list of FOCs: see www.itfglobal.org/en/sector/seafarers/flags-of-convenience.

[73] Around 45% of the Danish-owned fleet and 27.4% of the Norway-owned fleet is registered with the international register in each of those countries: UNCTAD (n 1) 41.

[74] N Ready, 'Nationality, Registration, and Ownership of Ships' in DJ Attard (gen ed), *The IMLI Manual on International Maritime Law*, vol 2 (Oxford, Oxford University Press, 2016) 36.

C. Bareboat Registers

For many shipowning enterprises, the flexibility to bareboat charter[75] the fleet is attractive.[76] Often known as 'flagging out' (and 'flagging in') or 'parallel registration', this permits a vessel registered in one state (State X) to fly the flag of a second state (State Y), usually for an agreed fixed period. During the bareboat charterparty with State Y, registration with State X is cancelled or suspended and becomes effective only after the charterparty comes to an end. Bareboat chartering enables ship operators to take advantage of lower crewing costs and, for emerging maritime countries, training and employment for local seafarers and foreign exchange. The principal objection, however, includes the risk of confusion or legal ambiguity as to the rights of the shipowner and charterer at any time and also the potential for overlapping jurisdiction by two states.[77] Not all flag states permit the practice and some states only permit one of the practices, not the other.[78] The difficulty caused by flagging out may be illustrated by the notorious *Prestige* incident in November 2002, when significant oil pollution was caused after the tanker broke in two and sank 130 miles off the north-west coast of Spain.[79] At the time of the incident the vessel was flagged-out to the Bahamas, although she had previously been flagged with Liberia and Greece. Her owners were a Liberian-registered company, Mare Shipping Inc, but her operating managers were Universe Maritime, a Greek company,[80] and her charterers, a Swiss-based entity, Crown Resources AG.[81]

[75] *The Guiseppe di Vittorio* [1998] 1 Lloyd's Rep 136, 156–57; *Ship Hako Endeavour* v *Programmed Total Marine Services Pty Ltd* [2013] FCAFC 21, (2013) 211 FCR 369 [53]–[61]; *The Chem Orchid* [2014] SGHC 50, [2015] 2 Lloyd's Rep 666 [66]–[67]; *Silverburn Shipping (IOM) Ltd v Ark Shipping Co LLC (The Arctic)* [2019] EWCA Civ 1161, [2019] 2 Lloyd's Rep 603 [6]. Art 2 of the 1986 Convention defines bareboat charter as 'a contract for the lease of a ship, for a stipulated period of time, by virtue of which the lessee has complete possession and control of the ship, including the right to appoint the Master and crew of the ship, for the duration of the lease'.

[76] See A Odeke, 'An Examination of Bareboat Charter Registries and Flag of Convenience Registries in International Law' (2005) 36 *Ocean Development & International Law* 339; Watt (n 1) ch 5; Ready, 'Nationality' (2016) 36. See also A Odeke, *Bareboat Charter (Ship) Registration* (Boston, Kluwer Law International, 1998).

[77] See, eg, *The Stolt Loyalty* [1995] 1 Lloyd's Rep 598, 599–600 (CA); *BP Exploration Operating Co Ltd v Chevron Shipping Co (The Chevron North America)* [2001] UKHL 50, [2003] 1 AC 197 [5]–[6].

[78] *cf* art 12 of the 1986 Convention which only refers to chartering-in.

[79] See 'Report of the investigation into the loss of the Bahamian registered tanker 'Prestige' off the northwest coast of Spain on 19th November 2002' (Bahamas Maritime Authority, November 2004), available at www.bahamasmaritime.com/wp-content/uploads/2015/08/Prestige-Report-November-2002.pdf.

[80] Now defunct. The actual owners of the *Prestige* were allegedly beneficiaries of a foundation set up by the late John Coulouthros: see H Papachristou, '*Prestige* Operator Closes After Litigation Wraps Up' *TradeWinds* (20 March 2015).

[81] For some of the background, see *Crown Resources AG v Vinogradsky* (QBD, 14 November 2001) [3].

D. Fraudulent Registration and Registers

In 2017 the Democratic Republic of the Congo (DRC) proposed that the Legal Committee of the IMO consider the issue of fraudulent registration after having identified 73 vessels using its flag fraudulently.[82] This was not, however, a new or even unique phenomenon.[83] In due course, similar issues were identified with the Federated States of Micronesia, Fiji, the Maldives, Samoa and Tanzania, and also fake or illegal ship registries, the Nauru Maritime Administration International Ship Registry and the Vanuatu International Ship Registry.[84] A combination of tactics were identified as being used to achieve this purpose: (i) vessels continuing to fly the flag of a state after the vessel's registration had expired or been terminated; (ii) the submission of fraudulent documentation to the IMO, without the knowledge of the state, in order to obtain IMO documentation and ship identification numbers; (iii) broadcasting falsified AIS data so as to materially alter the vessel's identifying data or broadcasting false data.[85] At the end of 2019, the IMO adopted Resolution A.1142(31)[86] setting out a new procedure for the communication of information to the IMO on registries of ships in the contact points module in its Global Integrated Shipping Information System (GISIS). Whether these measures will put a stop to such fraudulent activity remains, however, to be seen.

V. Nationality Issues for Shipping Enterprises: Choosing the Flag

As noted earlier, the choice of flag is multifactorial. No shipping enterprise, whether large or small, makes such decisions on a whim. In a larger organisation, the decision is a high-level one and will be made on a vessel-by-vessel basis. For a one ship company, the decision will hone in on the specific features of the vessel and the intended trading patterns of the vessel.[87] Some registries are known to specialise in particular vessel types; the *Review of Maritime Transport* indicates

[82] Report of the Legal Committee on the Work of its 104th session, LEG 104/15 (10 May 2017) para 1.6. See also, MW Bockmann, 'An inconvenient truth: Flags failing' *Lloyd's List* (5 February 2021).

[83] See G Dixon, 'Mysterious Vessel Named Rustbucket' *TradeWinds* (15 March 2001).

[84] See F Kenney, 'Fraudulent Registries and their Impact' (5 March 2020) 3; www.imo.org/en/OurWork/Legal/Pages/Registration-of-ships-and-fraudulent-registration-matters.aspx; A Adamopoulos, 'IMO confronts fraudulent vessel registrations' *Lloyd's List* (13 March 2019); Gary Dixon, 'At least 300 ships flagged with rogue registries' *TradeWinds* (28 October 2019).

[85] See www.imo.org/en/OurWork/Legal/Pages/Registration-of-ships-and-fraudulent-registration-matters.aspx.

[86] Measures to Prevent the Fraudulent Registration and Fraudulent Registries of Ships (4 December 2019), A 31/Res.1142.

[87] Below, V(B).

that 21.6 per cent of the world's dry bulk carrier fleet is registered in Panama.[88] This may be contrasted with 17.1 per cent of the oil and gas tanker fleet which is registered in the Marshall Islands, and 26 per cent of ferries and passenger ships which are registered in the Bahamas. Around 17.9 per cent of the container ship fleet is registered in Hong Kong.[89]

Beyond these considerations, shipping enterprises also make decisions for political reasons, such as ensuring a supply of skilled labour. Increasingly, this has also become a public relations exercise because of close scrutiny by financial institutions.

Some of the issues that shipping enterprises consider are now considered in greater detail.[90] The bottom line is often economics. In broad terms there are four categories of cost which shipping enterprises must keep in mind:

- capital costs, covering the depreciation of the ship over its economic life, as well as interest payments on any financing of the ship;
- operating costs, comprising the variable costs associated with the sailing of the ship, such as manning costs and stores;
- voyage costs, which extends to the variable costs associated with the sailing of the ship, such as bunkers, port charges, and canal dues; and
- cargo-handling costs, which are the costs associated with the loading and discharging of the ship's cargo.[91]

A. Control

It may be prudent for a shipowner to register its company holdings in a different jurisdiction, particularly if the fleet is registered with multiple flags; indeed, many shipowners decouple control and management, with management of the fleet in a separate jurisdiction.[92] The issue of control – restrictions as to the nature, type and nationality of the shipowner who can register a vessel – is a foremost consideration, together with the question as to whether the vessel can be owned by a foreign, non-resident, company. If the flag state insists on a locally incorporated or resident company or resident agent,[93] the shipping enterprise needs to consider this

[88] UNCTAD (n 1) 45.

[89] ibid.

[90] See S Hartley, 'Flag Choice – A Comparative Study' [1998] *International Journal of Shipping Law* 12; Watt (n 1) ch 6.

[91] AS Bergantino and P O'Sullivan, 'Flagging Out and International Registries: Main Developments and Policy Issues' (1999) 26 *International Journal of Transport Economics* 447, 456; K Mitroussi and P Marlow, 'The Impact of Choice of Flag on Ship Management' in C Th Grammenos, *The Handbook of Maritime Economics and Business*, 2nd edn (London, Lloyd's List, 2010) 579.

[92] See, eg, *Porr v Shaw, Johnson & Holden (The Marabu Porr)* [1979] 2 Lloyd's Rep 331, 332 (CA).

[93] See, eg, Panama (below, VI(A)(i)), Liberia (below, VI(B)(i)) and the Marshall Islands (below, VI(C)(i)).

together with any restrictions on the nationality or residence of the shareholders and the directors of the company.

B. Operational Matters

In practice, operational considerations are diverse and, often, pivotal. The starting point is labour (crewing) costs and this extends to both the direct and the indirect costs of crewing the vessel.[94] Annual crewing costs, particularly those associated with traditional 'closed' registers, can be double or even four times those of the crewing costs in an open register[95] and represents a significant chunk of the total operating costs for a vessel.[96] Whether the proposed flag state imposes restrictions on the nationality or qualifications of the crew will also feature high on the list of considerations. A degree of harmonisation has been achieved by the requirements for employment and working conditions for seafarers on board ships following the enactment and coming into force[97] of the Maritime Labour Convention (MLC) 2006.[98] For some shipping enterprises, whether the flag is regarded by the ITF as a flag of convenience[99] and what impact this will have, particularly where the ITF boycott campaign has been effectively pursued,[100] can be a matter of some sensitivity. For those countries which have established themselves as crew-suppliers,[101] employment on a ship represents a significant advantage, particularly because the foreign exchange earned is remitted home. The reverse side of the coin is, of course, only too well known: exploitation of seafarers, egregious non-payment of wages, failure to repatriate, abandonment, and worse.[102]

Another set of operational questions is concerned with the proposed trading of the vessel. If a vessel registered under a particular flag is unable to trade for political or other reasons, this could be unsustainable for the shipping enterprise. The ability to trade worldwide, without concerns about sanctions, embargoes

[94] This is made up of basic salaries and wages, social insurance, pensions, overtime payments, supplementary payments, efficient service and certificate payments, special work payments, leave pay, leave subsistence, medical expeses, training and maintenance allowances, standby pay, union payments, and cadet training: Bergantino and O'Sullivan, 'Flagging Out and International Registries' (1999) 456.

[95] FJM Llácer, 'Open Registers: Past, Present and Future' (2003) 27 *Marine Policy* 513, 520. In 1990, a UK government report established that crewing costs for a UK-registered tanker with a British crew were not far short of US$1m, whereas the same in Hong Kong was US$396,000: see Watt (n 1) [6.12].

[96] See Myburgh (ch 3) I.

[97] 20 August 2013. The MLC has been ratified by 97 states: see www.ilo.org/dyn/normlex/en/f?p=NORMLEXPUB:11300:0::NO::P11300_INSTRUMENT_ID:312331.

[98] Further amendments (2014) came into force on 18 January 2017.

[99] Above, III(B).

[100] For example, Australia and Scandinavia: Watt (n 1) [6.23].

[101] Notably India, Korea, Pakistan, Philippines, Poland and Sri Lanka: ibid [6.14].

[102] See, eg, M Kabai, 'The Maritime Labour Convention and Open Registries, Hand in Glove or Chalk and Cheese?' (2015) 30 *International Journal of Marine and Coastal Law* 189. See also www.ilo.org/dyn/seafarers/seafarersBrowse.list; Myburgh (ch 3) I.

or boycotts, such as those involving Iran, the Russian Federation and Israel,[103] is likely to be very important. The intended trading routes and patterns of the vessel may dictate a clear preference for one flag over another, as will the question whether the proposed flag is acceptable to potential charterers and insurers of the vessel.

A further group of factors concerns the technical and practical issues connected with the very ship. The first of these concerns the type of vessel capable of being registered under the particular flag. The type of vessel and its age (or size) may preclude registration with the intended flag. A second factor is whether the technical, safety and management requirements imposed by the flag state are suitable for the shipowners' business, although these factors are not likely to be dissimilar where the major IMO Conventions have been implemented. If the vessel is a new one, the impact of the chosen flag on the technical specification and the cost of the vessel will be a factor. It may also be preferable to hedge against political strife or industrial action in a given state by dividing the fleet between different flag states, as is the case with each of the top major liner shipping operators, including Maersk,[104] MSC,[105] COSCO,[106] CMA CGM[107] and Hapag-Lloyd.[108]

A final component of the operating costs associated with the vessel includes repairs, maintenance, stores, supplies and lubricating oils, although these are more likely to be influenced by the age, type and condition of the ship, not particular ship registries. That said, the safety and maintenance standards of a particular flag might exercise some influence on these choices.[109]

C. Financing

The attractiveness of the flag to potential financiers is an important and unavoidable consideration, the more so as traditional sources of ship finance have fallen away.[110] Some of the key questions financiers may be concerned about may be the safety record of vessels registered under the flag and the flag's general reputation. More importantly, such financiers will want assurance that the rules of the flag state relating to the validity and enforceability of mortgages are acceptable.

[103] And, in the distant past, South Africa. See, for example, *Shell International Petroleum Co Ltd v Gibbs (The Salem)* [1983] 1 Lloyd's Rep 342 (HL).
[104] maersktankers.com/fleet.
[105] www.msc.com/lca/about-us/our-fleet.
[106] lines.coscoshipping.com/home/Services/ship/0.
[107] www.cmacgm-group.com/en/group/at-a-glance/fleet/ships.
[108] www.hapag-lloyd.com/en/products/fleet/vessel.html.
[109] Bergantino and O'Sullivan (n 91) 459.
[110] See S Girvin, 'Aspects of Ship Finance: The Market, Ship Mortgages and their Enforcement' NUS Centre for Maritime Law Working Paper 19/05, August 2019, available at law.nus.edu.sg/cml/wp-content/uploads/sites/8/2020/04/015_2019_StephenGirvin.pdf.

Registries located in well-established onshore or offshore financial centres[111] may be very attractive to lending institutions who value the familiarity of these centres and also the presence of a sophisticated and trustworthy legal system.[112]

D. Taxation and Fees

Taxation and fees are usually an important consideration for shipping enterprises; registering a vessel in a traditional maritime jurisdiction may involve the ship-owning enterprise being exposed to the fiscal regime in force in that country. In the case of open registries, the shipowner will need to be appraised whether there are any nationality requirements for the shipowner and, if so, whether this impacts on the tax treatment of the shipowners' profits. Domestic corporation tax, if payable, may have a significant impact on the shipping enterprise's bottom line. If there are tax implications for the shipowner, these may be offset if there are double taxation treaties between the flag state and any other state.[113] Multinational corporations use base erosion and profit shifting (BEPS) to erode the corporate tax base.[114] If the intended flag state has a tonnage tax regime – as many now do – this may tilt the balance.[115] If it is possible to obtain rebates or reductions in tonnage taxes and registration fees if a certain number of vessels or a certain amount of tonnage is registered, this will be important information for the shipping enterprise.[116]

Control over annual and recurring costs means that it is important to establish the level of fees payable, both initially and also annually, particularly if a company also has to be incorporated in the flag state. Finally, the cost of registering a mortgage over the vessel is required information.

VI. Nationality Issues for Shipping Enterprises: Particular Flags

We now consider how the considerations discussed above play out in particular ship registers.

[111] Such as Singapore, Hong Kong, the Cayman Islands, the British Virgin Islands (BVI) and the Isle of Man.

[112] See, eg, Watt (n 1) [6.15].

[113] See, eg, Panama (below, VI(A)(v)).

[114] See SM Kim and J Kim, 'Flags of Convenience in the Context of the OECD BEPS Package' (2018) 49 *Journal of Maritime Law and Commerce* 221.

[115] See, eg, the Marshall Islands (below, VI(C)(v)), Singapore (below, VI(D)(v)), Denmark (DIS) (below VI(E)(v)) and the UK (below, VI(F)(v)).

[116] See, eg, Panama (below, VI(A)(v)) and Singapore (below, VI(D)(v)).

A. Panama

The Panama Ship Registry[117] has led the world's maritime flags for two decades[118] and the *Review of Maritime Transport* confirms that Panama continues as the largest flag state, with 16 per cent of the world's total dead-weight tonnage.[119] The principal offices of the registry are in Panama, Busan, Dubai, Houston, Imabari, Istanbul, London, Manila, Miami, Seoul, Shanghai, Singapore and Tokyo, but shipowners are also able to draw on a substantial network of Panamanian consulates worldwide. Certain documents and certificates have, since October 2017, been available online, using an online resource and unique QR code shown on each electronic certificate.[120]

Panama is on the Paris MOU White List (effective from 1 July 2020)[121] and the Tokyo MOU White List (effective 1 July 2020)[122] and also meets the flag criteria for a Low Risk Ship for the Tokyo MOU (effective to 30 June 2021).[123] Panama is a category (a) state member of the Council of the IMO.[124]

i. Law and Regulation

Ship registration in Panama is regulated by Law No 57 of 2008.[125] This specifies that a Panamanian-registered vessel may be owned by 'any individual or legal entity … without any special requirement as to nationality or domicile'.[126] The absence of any nationality restrictions is a clear advantage and explains, at least in part, why the Panamanian flag continues to perform so well compared with its major competitors. Allied with this, Panama permits bareboat charter registration both by way of flagging in[127] and flagging out.[128] Foreign shipowners are required to appoint a resident agent[129] who is an attorney or a firm of attorneys

[117] panamashipregistry.com. See Watt (n 1) ch 21; N Price, 'Registering the Ship – Panama' in J Clegg and J Ward (eds), *Shipping Finance*, 4th edn (Horsell, Globe Law & Business Ltd, 2018) 489.

[118] See 'Review of Maritime Transport 2001' (UNCTAD, 2001) 33. For the history and background, see Llácer, 'Open Registers' (2003) 514; Piniella, Alcaide and Rodríguez-Díaz, 'The Panama Ship Registry' (2017).

[119] UNCTAD (n 1) 44. See also 'Top 10 flag states 2019', *Lloyd's List* (3 December 2019).

[120] Merchant Marine Circulars MMC-347 and MMC-355.

[121] www.parismou.org/detentions-banning/white-grey-and-black-list.

[122] www.tokyo-mou.org/doc/Flag%20performance%20list%202019.pdf.

[123] www.tokyo-mou.org/inspections_detentions/NIR.php. Note that Panama is on the United States Coast Guard's (USCG) list of Targeted Flag Administrations. See www.dco.uscg.mil/Our-Organization/Assistant-Commandant-for-Prevention-Policy-CG-5P/Inspections-Compliance-CG-5PC-/Commercial-Vessel-Compliance/Foreign-Offshore-Compliance-Division/Port-State-Control/targetedflags.

[124] www.imo.org/en/About/Pages/Structure.aspx#2.

[125] General de Marina Mercante (in force 6 February 2009). See amp.gob.pa/normatividad/general-de-marina-mercante.

[126] Art 3 of Law No 57.

[127] ibid, arts 70–79.

[128] ibid, arts 80–87.

[129] Defined in art 168(1) of Law No 57.

qualified to practise their profession in Panama.[130] If the shipowner chooses to register a company in Panama, two subscribers are required at the time of incorporation,[131] but thereafter just one shareholder is required.[132] Although bearer shares[133] are permitted in Panama corporations[134] these are subject to custodial restrictions.[135]

ii. Operation – Vessel Eligibility and Age

The Panama Ship Registry permits any 'vessel' to be registered. This includes:

> Any vessel engaged in the transportation of cargo or persons; pontoons, dredgers, floating docks, oil drilling platforms or any other hulls engaged in or which may engage in maritime trade, as well as any other structure recognised as a vessel by the Panama Maritime Authority.[136]

There is no formal restriction on vessel age, but the General Directorate of the Merchant Marine may decline to register a vessel, after taking into account its 'condition, age, previous record and its activities'.[137]

iii. Operation – Crew

There was formerly a legal requirement that at least 10 per cent of a vessel's crew had to be Panamanian, but because of the difficulty in recruiting sufficient numbers of seafarers, this was not enforced.[138] This requirement was, however, substituted by Law Decree 8 of 1998 in favour of a general obligation to give preference to Panamanian crew members.[139] However, following the entry into force of the Maritime Labour Convention 2006, Law 41 of 14 June 2013 reduced the requirement to fishing vessels and cabotage in Panamanian waters.

Every officer serving onboard a registered ship of over 200 gross tons is required to hold a Certificate of Competency (CoC) issued by the Directorate General of Merchant Marine although the Directorate General recognises CoCs issued by

[130] ibid, art 102.
[131] Law No 32 of 1927 (on Corporations), art 1.
[132] Decree Law No 5 of 2 July 1997, art 33 (amending art 249 of the Code of Commerce).
[133] For critique, see eg, 'Ownership and Control of Ships' (OECD, 2003) [32].
[134] See, eg, art 28 of Law No 32.
[135] Law No 47 of 2013, as amended by Law No 18 of 2015.
[136] Art 168(7) of Law No 57.
[137] ibid, art 5(3).
[138] Watt (n 1) [21.18].
[139] Art 4 states that: 'Every owner or shipping company of a Panamanian ship engaged in international service shall endeavour, under equal conditions and capacity, to give preference to crew members of Panamanian nationality and foreigners married to Panamanian or with Panamanian children residing in Panama. Associations of shipowners or shipowners flying the Panamanian flag shall award scholarships and facilitate training courses to crew or cadets, Panamanians or foreigners married to nationals or with Panamanian children. The competent authorities both in Panama and abroad shall faithfully comply with the provisions of this article'.

national maritime organisations of countries which are on the IMO's STCW 1978 White List.[140] CoCs issued to non-nationals by the Maritime Administrations of Belize, Honduras, Cook Islands, Samoa, Dominica, the Federated States of Micronesia, Vanuatu and Indonesia are not recognised.[141]

iv. Operation – Safety

Panamanian law stipulates that 'each vessel registered with the Merchant Marine shall submit to an annual safety inspection, with the aim of verifying its compliance with international and domestic laws currently in force'.[142]

v. Taxation and Fees

Non-resident Panamanian companies are not liable to pay any income or other taxes in Panama, apart from an annual government corporation tax. Panama also has double taxation treaties with a number of countries, including Singapore.[143] A detailed schedule of fees is available.[144] In addition to registration fees, fees are payable for the issuance of certain documents and certificates, an annual consular fee, an annual safety inspection fee, and annual rate for casualty investigations. There are also fee discounts for newly built vessels[145] and for vessels in the same economic group.[146]

B. Liberia

The Liberian Register[147] is outsourced to a US-owned and globally operated company, the Liberian International Ship & Corporate Registry (LISCR LLC) in Dulles, Virginia (outside Washington DC). The registry also maintains offices around the world: Bergen, Buenos Aires, Cyprus, Dubai, Guangzhou, Hamburg, Imabari,[148] Hong Kong, Houston, Istanbul, Leer, London, Luxembourg, Monrovia, New York, Ningbo, Oslo, Panama City, Piraeus, Qingdao, Rio de Janeiro, Seoul, Shanghai, Singapore, Taipei, Tianjin, Tokyo and Zurich.[149] The Marshall Islands

[140] Merchant Marine Circular MMC-343.
[141] Merchant Marine Circular MMC-344.
[142] Art 117 of Law No 57.
[143] See, eg, www.iras.gov.sg/IRASHome/uploadedFiles/IRASHome/News_and_Events/Singapore-Panama%20DTA%20(Not%20in%20Force)%20(18%20Oct%202010).pdf.
[144] Merchant Marine Circular MMC-343.
[145] Art 149 of Law No 57.
[146] ibid, Arts 150–51.
[147] www.liscr.com; Watt (n 1) ch 17; H Nam and MS Timpone, 'Registering the ship – Liberia' in Clegg and Ward, *Shipping Finance* (2018) 433; K Ladas, 'The Structure and Operations of the Liberian Registry' (5 March 2020), available at www.imo.org/en/OurWork/Legal/Pages/Registration-of-ships-and-fraudulent-registration-matters.aspx. See also J Reed, 'Ship Registry: Steady Source of Funds' *Financial Times* (7 December 2011).
[148] See M Coyne, 'Liberian Register Opens New Office in Japan', *TradeWinds* (10 October 2019).
[149] Watt (n 1) 193–96.

briefly took over from the Liberian register as Panama's major competitor but, as confirmed in the latest *Review of Maritime Transport*, Liberia is once more the second largest flag state, with 13 per cent of the world's total dead-weight tonnage.[150] Liberia is on the Paris MOU White List (effective from 1 July 2020)[151] and the Tokyo MOU White List (effective 1 July 2020),[152] also meeting the flag criteria for a Low Risk Ship for the Tokyo MOU (effective to 30 June 2021).[153]

i. Law and Regulation

Ship registration is regulated by the Liberian Maritime Law, Title 21 (as amended) of the Liberian Code of Laws 1956.[154] Liberia permits bareboat charter registration both by way of flagging in[155] and flagging out.[156] Registration of vessels engaged in foreign trade, wherever built, must be owned by a 'citizen or national'[157] of Liberia.[158] A waiver may, however, be given where an owner or bareboat charterer 'qualifies for, secures and maintains registration in the Republic of Liberia as a foreign maritime entity and appoints a qualified registered agent in the manner prescribed by law'.[159]

The procedure for registration as a foreign maritime entity (FME) is laid down by the Business Corporation Act (as amended), part of Title 5, Associations Law, of the 1976 Liberian Codes of Laws Revised.[160] The principal eligibility provision states that:

> A foreign entity whose indenture or instrument of trust, charter or articles of incorporation, agreement of partnership or other document recognised by the foreign State of its creation as the basis of its existence, which document directly or by force of law of the State of creation comprehends the power to own or operate vessels, and which confers or recognises the capacity under the law of the State of creation to sue and be sued in the name of the entity or its lawful fiduciary or legal representative, may apply to the Registrar or the Deputy Registrar to be registered as a foreign maritime entity. The burden of establishing the capacity to sue and be sued shall be upon the applicant for such registration.[161]

[150] UNCTAD (n 1) 44.
[151] www.parismou.org/detentions-banning/white-grey-and-black-list.
[152] www.tokyo-mou.org/doc/Flag%20performance%20list%202019.pdf.
[153] www.tokyo-mou.org/inspections_detentions/NIR.php. Note that Liberia is on the United States Coast Guard's (USCG) list of Targeted Flag Administrations (although not targeted during the past year). See www.dco.uscg.mil/Our-Organization/Assistant-Commandant-for-Prevention-Policy-CG-5P/Inspections-Compliance-CG-5PC-/Commercial-Vessel-Compliance/Foreign-Offshore-Compliance-Division/Port-State-Control/targetedflags.
[154] www.liscr.com/sites/default/files/RLM-107%20Series%202018%20-%20Final.pdf.
[155] See §§85–89 of the Liberian Maritime Law.
[156] ibid, §§90–94.
[157] This includes 'corporations, trusts, foundations, partnerships, limited partnerships, limited liability companies and other entities of Liberia having legal personality and the capacity to own a ship': ibid, §29(2).
[158] ibid, §51(1).
[159] ibid, §51(5)(c).
[160] www.wto.org/english/thewto_e/acc_e/lbr_e/WTACCLBR5_LEG_6.pdf.
[161] §13.1(1) of the Business Corporation Act.

Once granted, a registered FME has the following powers:

> (a) To own and operate vessels registered under the Laws of the Republic of Liberia provided all requirements of the Maritime Law are met; (b) To do all things necessary to the conduct of the business of ownership and operation of Liberian-flag vessels and, for that purpose, to have one or more offices in Liberia and to hold, purchase, lease, mortgage and convey real and personal property, subject to the organic law of the Republic of Liberia.[162]

Every domestic corporation or foreign corporation authorized to do business in Liberia or FME is required to 'designate a registered agent in Liberia upon whom process against such corporation or foreign maritime entity or any notice or demand required or permitted by law to be served may be served'.[163]

ii. Operation – Vessel Eligibility and Age

Any seagoing vessel of more than 500 net tons engaged in the foreign trade, wherever built, is eligible for registration in Liberia.[164] Vessels will not, however, be eligible if on 1 January of the year in which initial documentation or redocumentation is sought, such vessels are over 20 years of age, computed from completion of first construction.[165] The 20-year maximum age limitation may be waived when: (a) a vessel meets, or there is waived … all other applicable requirements; and (b) it has been satisfactorily demonstrated that there is a genuine need for such waiver.[166]

iii. Operation – Crew

Liberia has no nationality restrictions. Manning requirements are set out in detail in the Liberian Maritime Law[167] and are in compliance with the STCW Conventions, to which Liberia is a party. Liberian seafarers desiring the relevant licence or certificate are required to 'pass such written, oral and physical examinations as shall from time to time be required by the Commissioner or Deputy Commissioner to whom application is made'.[168] Provision is however made for the granting of equivalent licences or certificates:

> A person holding a valid license or certificate issued by a State fully applying the provisions of the International Convention on Standards of Training and Watchkeeping currently in force, as amended, and who is not otherwise disqualified in the opinion of the Commissioner or Deputy Commissioner to whom application is made shall be

[162] ibid, §13.2.
[163] ibid, §3.1(1)(a).
[164] §51(2) of the Liberian Maritime Law.
[165] ibid, §51(4).
[166] ibid, §51(6).
[167] ibid, ch 10.
[168] Liberian Maritime Regulations, reg 1.17(3).

eligible for an equivalent Liberian License, Certificate or Endorsement, subject to proof of physical fitness.[169]

iv. Operation – Safety

There are no requirements for physical inspection of a ship by the Maritime Administrator prior to registration, or the issue of provisional and final certificates of registration.[170] The Act does, however, provide that:

> In order to promote the safety of life and property at sea, vessels registered under this Title shall be required to undergo inspection and shall at all times carry on board such proof of inspection as may be required by Law or Regulation.[171]

Supplementary provisions stipulate that such safety inspections are carried out annually.[172]

v. Taxation and Fees

A company which does not have a place of business in Liberia is exempt from tax in Liberia, unless the income is generated in or remitted to Liberia or more than 25 per cent of the shares are owned by Liberian residents.[173] An annual tonnage tax is, however, payable by all vessels.[174] The office of the Deputy Commissioner of Maritime Affairs provides a detailed schedule of fees.[175] The registry has a self-service electronic platform for seafarer documents (the SEA System) and since 2006 permits electronic vessel certificates. The registry uses WayPoint, a web-based interface 'that provides clients with secure, convenient, real-time, 24/7 access to view their fleet'.[176]

C. Marshall Islands (IRI)

The Marshall Islands,[177] a small Pacific Island nation, has (like Liberia) outsourced and decentralised its international ship register, International Registries Inc (IRI).

[169] ibid, reg 1.17(1).
[170] An initial safety inspection will, however, be required upon registration (if in lay-up upon reactivation), upon re-registration resulting in both change of ownership and management, prior to resuming service at the end of a lay-up period in excess of six months or following any substantial structural alteration: cl 1, Marine Notice INS-001 (06/12).
[171] §190 of the Liberian Maritime Law.
[172] Cl 2, Marine Notice INS-001 (06/12).
[173] Watt (n 1) [17.18].
[174] §54(1) of the Liberian Maritime Law. For the amount of tax payable, see Marine Notice ADM-003 (04/18).
[175] See Marine Notice, ibid.
[176] www.liscr.com/waypoint.
[177] www.register-iri.com. See Watt (n 1) ch 19; N Gaudio, A Maimis and J Stratakis, 'Registering the Ship – Marshall Islands' in Clegg and Ward (n 117) 459; ES Bouchard, 'The Structure and

This is headquartered in Virginia in the US[178] with main offices in Hong Kong, London, New York and Piraeus. Other offices are maintained in Baltimore, Busan, Dalian, Dubai, Ft Lauderdale, Geneva, Hamburg, Houston, Imabari, Istanbul, Long Beach, Manila, Mumbai, Rio de Janeiro, Roosendaal, Seoul, Shanghai, Singapore, Taipei, Tokyo and Zurich.[179] This global network of offices and local representatives has been a very successful strategy in propelling the register up the rankings; indeed, for a while, the Marshall Islands overtook Liberia as the second largest register. The *Review of Maritime Transport* confirms that its share of dead-weight tonnage stands at 13 per cent.[180] Certain of its documents and certificates have, since 2017, been available online, using a quick response code and unique tracking number.[181]

Like Panama, the Marshall Islands is on the Paris MOU White List (effective from 1 July 2020)[182] and the Tokyo MOU White List (effective 1 July 2020),[183] and also meets the flag criteria for a Low Risk Ship for the Tokyo MOU (effective to 30 June 2021).[184]

i. Law and Regulation

Registration of ships in the Marshall Islands is governed by The Maritime Act 1990 (as amended)[185] and the supplementary Maritime Regulations.[186] Bareboat flagging in[187] and flagging out[188] is permitted. In order to be eligible to register a vessel, a shipowner must be either a citizen or national of the Republic, a Marshall Islands corporation, partnership, limited partnership or limited liability company or a foreign maritime entity, such as a corporation, partnership or trust which is registered in the Marshall Islands as such an entity.[189] The ownership requirement specified in the Act may be waived at the discretion of the Maritime Administrator and may be documented or redocumented where: (i) the vessel meets all other applicable requirements for registration; and (ii) it has been satisfactorily demonstrated that there is an absolute and genuine need for such waiver.[190] If a foreign

Operation of the Marshall Islands Registry', available at www.imo.org/en/OurWork/Legal/Documents/IMLIWMUSYMPOSIUM/8%20Panel%203_Bouchard.pdf.

[178] §113 of the Maritime Act 1990 also provides that: 'Insofar as it does not conflict with any other provisions of this Title or any other law of the Republic, the non-statutory general maritime law of the United States of America is hereby declared to be and is hereby adopted as the general maritime law of the Republic'.

[179] Watt (n 1) 214–15.

[180] UNCTAD (n 1) 44.

[181] MN 1-109°1 and the authentication facility at verify.register-iri.com.

[182] www.parismou.org/detentions-banning/white-grey-and-black-list.

[183] www.tokyo-mou.org/doc/Flag%20performance%20list%202019.pdf.

[184] www.tokyo-mou.org/inspections_detentions/NIR.php.

[185] www.register-iri.com/forms/upload/MI-107.pdf.

[186] www.register-iri.com/forms/upload/MI-108.pdf.

[187] §§260–64 of the Maritime Act 1990.

[188] ibid, §§270–74.

[189] ibid, §203(a).

[190] ibid, §203(g).

owner wishes to incorporate a company in the Marshall Islands, this can be achieved under the Business Corporations Act.[191] A Marshall Islands corporation, partnership, limited partnership, LLC or foreign maritime entity must maintain a registered agent in the Marshall Islands;[192] for non-resident entities, the registered agent is mandated to be the Trust Company of the Marshall Islands Inc.[193]

ii. Operation – Vessel Eligibility and Age

Any seagoing vessel 'engaged in foreign trade' is eligible for registration. This effectively means 'any vessel not exclusively operated or engaged in coastwise trade or transportation between atolls, islands and/or ports within the waters of the Republic'.[194] Apart from commercial cargo vessels, private yachts, passenger yachts, and commercial yachts, may also be registered,[195] as may fishing vessels[196] and vessels under construction.[197] A vessel must be less than 20 years old on 1 January of the year when registration is sought[198] but this may be waived at the discretion of the Maritime Administrator and may be documented or redocumented where: (i) the vessel meets all other applicable requirements for registration; and (ii) it has been satisfactorily demonstrated that there is an absolute and genuine need for such waiver.[199] It is said that, in practice, a preregistration inspection will be required before a waiver of the age limit will be issued and that this will only be granted if an approved classification society has issued a certificate of confirmation of class and confirmed that it is prepared to issue all necessary statutory certificates to the vessel.[200]

iii. Operation – Crew

There are no nationality restrictions in the Marshall Islands. The STCW 95 and its amendments are fully implemented in the Marshall Islands and the law affecting merchant seafarers is set out in detail in the 1990 Act (as amended).[201] All officers and ratings who serve on Marshall Islands-registered vessels are required to hold a Certificate of Competence (CoC) issued by or on behalf of the Maritime Administrator.[202]

[191] www.wipo.int/edocs/lexdocs/laws/en/mh/mh004en.pdf.
[192] §20 of the Business Corporations Act.
[193] ibid, §20(2).
[194] §112(10) of the Maritime Act 1990 (as amended).
[195] verify.register-iri.com.
[196] §§279–80 of the Maritime Act 1990 (as amended).
[197] ibid, §203(f) and §112(11).
[198] ibid, §203(e).
[199] ibid, §203(g).
[200] Watt (n 1) 207.
[201] ch 8.
[202] See reg 7.47 of the Maritime Regulations (MI-108) (rev Sep/2020).

iv. Operation – Safety

Although there are no requirements for physical inspection of a ship by the Maritime Administrator prior to registration,[203] an initial safety inspection must be carried out within 60 days of registration (90 days for mobile offshore units) and the issuance of a Provisional Certificate of Registry.[204] An annual safety inspection is required.[205]

v. Taxation and Fees

No tax is payable in the Marshall Islands on income earned by non-resident entities. The Marshall Islands is not party to any double tax treaties.[206] A detailed schedule of fees is provided[207] and this includes initial registration fees, annual tonnage taxes, and an annual Marshall Islands International Participation (MIIP) fee. Various discounts are also available. These include a discount of one-third on the initial registration fee for registration of a vessel, five years of age or less, from date of first construction or which has undergone a major conversion within the past five years. The same discount is available for simultaneous registration of three or more vessels, 15 years of age or less, or with an irrevocable written commitment to register three or more such vessels within a calendar year. This discount will be increased to 50 per cent for an owner registering 10 or more vessels, 15 years of age or less, at the same time or by submitting an irrevocable written commitment to register 10 or more such vessels within a calendar year. There are the usual miscellaneous fees.

D. Singapore

When the Singapore Registry of Ships (SRS)[208] was established in 1966, one year after independence,[209] it was considered a flag of convenience[210] until the law was changed imposing restrictions on ownership to Singapore registered nationals or companies. The SRS permits bareboat charter registration both by way of

[203] Save for bulk carriers 15 years of age or more, which are required to undergo a pre-registration inspection prior to registration: reg 5.34.8 of the Maritime Regulations (MI-108) (rev Sep/2020).
[204] ibid, reg 5.34.2.
[205] ibid, reg 5.34.3.
[206] Watt (n 1) 211.
[207] See MN-1-005-1.
[208] www.mpa.gov.sg/web/portal/home/singapore-registry-of-ships. See also Watt (n 1) ch 22; C Jarraw and J Tan, 'Registering the Ship – Singapore' in Clegg and Ward (n 117) 511. For the background, see Mansell, *Flag State Responsibility* (2009) [7.6]; S Tenold, 'A Most Convenient Flag – The Basis for the Expansion of the Singapore Fleet 1969–82' (2003) 30 *Maritime Policy & Management* 255.
[209] 9 August 1965.
[210] See, eg, 'OECD study on flags of convenience' (1972) 4 *Journal of Maritime Law and Commerce* 231.

flagging in[211] and flagging out.[212] The office of the SRS is in Singapore.[213] The *Review of Maritime Transport* places the flag fifth among flags of registration by total dead-weight tonnage, with a seven per cent market share worldwide.[214] Singapore is on the Paris MOU White List (effective from 1 July 2020)[215] and the Tokyo MOU White List (effective 1 July 2020),[216] also meeting the flag criteria for a Low Risk Ship for the Tokyo MOU (effective to 30 June 2021).[217] Singapore is also a category (c) state member of the Council of the IMO.[218]

i. *Law and Regulation*

Ship registration is regulated by Part II of the Merchant Shipping Act 1995[219] and the Merchant Shipping (Registration of Ships) Regulations 1996.[220] The SRS only permits citizens of Singapore[221] and bodies corporate incorporated in Singapore to apply for registration.[222] In the case a ship which is owned wholly or partly by a company, the minimum paid-up capital is S$50,000.[223] Foreign owned companies[224] may, however, apply to establish a place of business or carry on business in Singapore[225] but under the SRS no foreign-owned vessel may be registered unless fitted with 'mechanical means of self–propulsion' and of 'not less' than 1,600 gross tons.[226]

ii. *Operation – Vessel Eligibility and Age*

No vessel which is above 17 years old may be registered 'unless the Registrar is satisfied that the ship is in a satisfactory condition in all respects'.[227] All ships, including tugs and barges, can be registered,[228] this being further defined in s 2(1) of the Merchant Shipping Act 1995 as meaning

[211] Merchant Shipping (Registration of Ships) Regulations, reg 24.
[212] ibid, reg 31.
[213] Watt (n 1) 193.
[214] UNCTAD (n 1) 41.
[215] www.parismou.org/detentions-banning/white-grey-and-black-list.
[216] www.tokyo-mou.org/doc/Flag%20performance%20list%202019.pdf.
[217] www.tokyo-mou.org/inspections_detentions/NIR.php.
[218] www.imo.org/en/About/Pages/Structure.aspx#2.
[219] ss 7–45.
[220] See also 'Guide to the Registration of Ships in Singapore' (9 July 2014), available at www.mpa.gov.sg/web/wcm/connect/www/c7290236-12d8-4a2e-b396-552ebca1fc50/english-version.pdf?MOD=AJPERES.
[221] This includes permanent residents: Merchant Shipping (Registration of Ships) Regulations, reg 2.
[222] ibid, reg 3.
[223] ibid, reg 5(1).
[224] ie a company, corporation, society, association or other body incorporated outside Singapore: Companies Act 2006, cap 50, s 4(1).
[225] See the detailed provisions in the Companies Act, Pt XI.
[226] Merchant Shipping (Registration of Ships) Regulations, reg 8(1).
[227] ibid, reg 8(2).
[228] ibid, reg 5(2).

any kind of vessel used in navigation by water, however propelled or moved and includes –

(a) a barge, lighter or other floating vessel; and
(b) an air-cushion vehicle, or other similar craft, used wholly or primarily in navigation by water; and
(c) an off-shore industry mobile unit.[229]

iii. Operation – Crew

Singapore has no nationality restrictions, but Singapore is a signatory to the STCW Conventions and so crew members must hold current certification.[230] Valid foreign certificates of competency (COCs) are recognised, provided that they are issued in accordance with the STCW.[231]

iv. Operation – Safety

Unless exempted, the Merchant Shipping Act 1995 specifies that every ship 'shall be surveyed or inspected in the manner provided in this Act'[232] and this is elaborated in detailed requirements laid down in subsidiary legislation.[233]

v. Taxation and Fees

Profits derived from the operation of Singapore registered ship are exempt from Singapore income tax but an annual tonnage tax is payable by all vessels.[234] A demand for payment of the tax may be sent 'to any person appearing as a mortgagee in the ship's register'.[235] A range of schemes to promote the SRS are in operation, including the Block Transfer Scheme (BTS),[236] the Green Ship Programme (GSP),[237] and the Annual Administrative Fee scheme.[238] The fee

[229] This is further defined in Merchant Shipping Act 1995, s 2(1).
[230] See the Merchant Shipping (Training, Certification and Manning) Regulations 1998 (rev ed 2001) (as amended).
[231] ibid, reg 9.
[232] Merchant Shipping Act 1995, s 99.
[233] Merchant Shipping (Safety Convention) Regulations 1984 (rev ed 1999) (as amended).
[234] Merchant Shipping Act 1995, s 14(2)(3). See also the Merchant Shipping (Fees) Regulations 1995 (rev ed 1997).
[235] Merchant Shipping (Registration of Ships) Regulations 1996, reg 36.
[236] The BTS gives an 80% discount over the initial registration fee (IRF) to shipowners who register ships which fulfil the BTS criteria. Under the BTS, the vessel will be registered at the rate of S$0.50 per NT subject to a minimum of S$1,250 for 2,500 NT and maximum of S$20,000 for 40,000 NT. See www.mpa.gov.sg/web/portal/home/singapore-registry-of-ships/register-with-srs/incentives-schemes.
[237] This is intended to encourage Singapore-flagged ships to reduce carbon dioxide and sulphur oxides (SOx) emissions. See ibid.
[238] This is for the payment of a non-refundable, flat fee of S$600 per ship (inclusive of GST) for each calendar year, for applicable registration and crewing-related services provided by MPA to their ships. See ibid.

payable on initial registration is S$2.50 per net ton, subject to a minimum of S$1,250 and a maximum S$100,000.[239] Other fees are set out in delegated legislation.[240]

E. Danish International Register (DIS)

Denmark permits vessels to be registered in the Register of Shipping or the Danish International Register of Shipping,[241] both of which are under the control of the Danish Maritime Authority, located in Korsør. The DIS permits bareboat charter registration both by way of flagging in[242] and flagging out.[243] The *Review of Maritime Transport* ranks the Danish International Register 14th among flags of registration by dead-weight tonnage, with a one per cent market share worldwide.[244] Denmark is on the Paris MOU White List (effective from 1 July 2020)[245] and the Tokyo MOU White List (effective 1 July 2020),[246] also meeting the flag criteria for a Low Risk Ship for the Tokyo MOU (effective to 30 June 2021).[247] Like Singapore, Denmark is a category (c) state member of the Council of the IMO.[248]

i. Law and Regulation

The registration requirements may be found in the Consolidated Merchant Shipping Act[249] and the Consolidated Act on the Danish International Register of Shipping.[250] Ships can be admitted to DIS if a Danish shipping company has control over the foreign company, such as having a significant direct or indirect holding in the foreign company and, by reason of that holding, having a significant influence in the form of voting rights or similar.[251] The foreign company must also have appointed a representative in Denmark. Ships owned by a foreign company

[239] Merchant Shipping Act 1995, s 14(1).

[240] See the Merchant Shipping (Fees) Regulations 1995 (rev ed 1997).

[241] www.dma.dk/SynRegistrering/SkibsregistreringAfgifter/DIS/Sider/default.aspx. For the position in Norway, see T Falkanger, HJ Bull and L Brautaset, *Scandinavian Maritime Law: The Norwegian Perspective*, 4th edn (Oslo, Universitetsforlaget, 2017) ch 2.

[242] Consolidated Act on the Danish International Register of Shipping, s 11a.

[243] ibid, s 11c.

[244] UNCTAD (n 1) 44.

[245] www.parismou.org/detentions-banning/white-grey-and-black-list.

[246] www.tokyo-mou.org/doc/Flag%20performance%20list%202019.pdf.

[247] www.tokyo-mou.org/inspections_detentions/NIR.php.

[248] www.imo.org/en/About/Pages/Structure.aspx#2.

[249] Consolidated Act No 75 of 17 January 2014, available at www.dma.dk/Vaekst/Rammevilkaar/Legislation/Acts/The%20merchant%20shipping%20act%20%28consolidation%29.pdf.

[250] Consolidated Act No 68 of 17 January 2014, available at www.dma.dk/Vaekst/Rammevilkaar/Legislation/Acts/Consolidated%20act%20on%20the%20Danish%20International%20Register%20of%20Shipping.pdf.

[251] Consolidated Act on the Danish International Register of Shipping, s 1(2), available at www.dma.dk/SynRegistrering/SkibsregistreringAfgifter/DIS/OptagelseUdenlandskeSkibe/Sider/default.aspx.

can also be admitted to register in DIS if the ship is operated from Denmark and fulfils requirements relating to activity and establishment.[252]

ii. Operation – Vessel Eligibility

Ships which may be admitted to the DIS include 'barges, lighters, dredgers, floating cranes and similar', but not 'floating docks, cable drums, floating containers and other similar equipment'.[253]

iii. Operation – Safety

Maritime safety is regulated by the Consolidated Act on Safety,[254] which applies to Danish ships.[255] The principal obligation falling on the shipowner is to ensure that the provisions of the Act are observed, inter alia that 'the ship is subjected to the mandatory surveys and is provided with the necessary certificates'.[256] If there are 'faults or defects in hull, machinery, safety equipment, placing of ballast and cargo, manning or other reasons', the Danish Maritime Authority may detain the ship.[257] The Danish Maritime Authority may also detain the ship if it 'does not have the prescribed certificates, documents or equipment or if it is defective'.[258]

iv. Taxation and Fees

The DIS offers a tonnage tax regime as an incentive to shipowners, the Tonnage Tax Act (consolidation).[259] This Act specifies that companies which carry out shipping activities 'may opt to calculate their taxable income from the shipping activity according to the provisions of this Act'.[260] The fee levied by the DIS is laid down in legislation[261] and, for vessels over 500 gross tons, is DKK 2,400.[262]

[252] ibid.
[253] ibid, s 1(3).
[254] Consolidated Act No 1629 of 17 December 2018, available at www.dma.dk/Vaekst/Rammevilkaar/Legislation/Acts/Consolidated%20act%20on%20safety%20at%20sea%20(no.%201629).pdf.
[255] ibid, s 1.
[256] ibid, s 9.
[257] ibid, s 14.
[258] ibid, s 14(2).
[259] Consolidated Act No 945 of 6 August 2015, available at www.dma.dk/Vaekst/Rammevilkaar/Legislation/Acts/Consolidated%20act%20on%20taxation%20of%20shipping%20activities%20(the%20tonnages%20taxation%20act).pdf.
[260] ibid, s 1.
[261] Act no 139 of 28 February 2018. Order no 1258 of 5 November 2013 provides that 'an annual fee for the registration of ships … shall be payable to the Danish Maritime Authority, which shall – prior to the date of payment determined in section 15b(4) of the Merchant Shipping Act – forward a fee invoice giving the time allowed for payment'. See www.dma.dk/Vaekst/Rammevilkaar/Legislation/Orders/Order%20on%20an%20annual%20fee%20for%20ships%20registered%20in%20the%20Danish%20register%20of%20shipping.pdf.
[262] www.dma.dk/SynRegistrering/Skibsregistret/afgifter/Sider/default.aspx.

F. United Kingdom

The UK Ship Register (UKSR)[263] is currently ranked 22nd in the *Review of Maritime Transport* by total dead-weight tonnage.[264] The UKSR previously only permitted bareboat charter registration by way of flagging in[265] but since 'exit day'[266] it is possible to flag-out.[267] The UK flag is on the Paris MOU White List (effective from 1 July 2020)[268] and the Tokyo MOU White List (effective 1 July 2020),[269] also meeting the flag criteria for a Low Risk Ship for the Tokyo MOU (effective to 30 June 2021).[270] It is likely that the UKSR will feel some negative impact after the UK's departure from the EU and there have already been signs of departure from the flag.[271] Like Panama, the UK is a category (a) state member of the Council of the IMO.[272]

i. *Law and Regulation*

The requirements for registration on the UK flag are governed by the Merchant Shipping Act 1995, Part II, and The Merchant Shipping (Registration of Ships) Regulations 1993,[273] as amended.[274] Under The Merchant Shipping (Registration of Ships) Regulations 1993, as amended, only the following are qualified to be owners of ships registered on Part I[275] of the register:

- British citizens or non-UK nationals exercising their right of freedom of movement of workers or right of establishment;
- British Dependent Territories citizens;
- British Overseas citizens;

[263] www.ukshipregister.co.uk. See Watt (n 1) ch 24; P Sharratt, 'Registering the ship – United Kingdom' in Clegg and Ward (n 117) 529.

[264] UNCTAD (n 1) 44.

[265] The Merchant Shipping (Registration of Ships) Regulations 1993, SI 1993/3138, Pt X. See also Merchant Shipping Act 1995, s 17.

[266] Ie the day on which the UK exited the EU. See The European Union (Withdrawal) Act 2018 (Exit Day) (Amendment) (No 3) Regulations 2019, SI 2019/1423.

[267] SI 2019/509, reg 23. This implements a new Part 10A into the principal regulations.

[268] www.parismou.org/detentions-banning/white-grey-and-black-list. See also D Osler, 'UK Ship Register Tops Paris MoU Performance White List' *Lloyd's List* (2 July 2020).

[269] www.tokyo-mou.org/doc/Flag%20performance%20list%202019.pdf.

[270] www.tokyo-mou.org/inspections_detentions/NIR.php.

[271] See, eg, UNCTAD(n 1) 44, which indicates a change from the 18th position held in 2019 ('Review of Maritime Transport 2019' (UNCTAD, 2019) 40); R Meale, 'UK Flag Abandons Growth Targets as Brexit Wipes Out 30% of Tonnage' *Lloyd's List* (19 June 2019); J Porter, 'ACL Chief Does Not Rule Out UK flag Return as Ships Move to Malta', *Lloyd's List* (3 September 2020). See, generally, R Coles and A Serdy, 'Ship Registration and Brexit' (2019) 43 *Tulane Maritime Law Journal* 289; Power, *EU Shipping Law* (2019) ch 48.

[272] www.imo.org/en/About/Pages/Structure.aspx#2.

[273] SI 1993/3138.

[274] By SI 1994/541, SI 1998/1915, SI 1998/2976, SI 1999/3206, SI 2017/879, and SI 2019/509.

[275] Part I of the register is for vessels which are not fishing vessels or small ships: reg 2(1).

- persons who are British subjects;[276]
- persons who under the Hong Kong (British Nationality) Order 1986 are British Nationals (Overseas);
- Commonwealth citizens;
- citizens of a listed country;
- non-UK nationals who are settled in the UK;
- bodies corporate incorporated in a Commonwealth state;
- bodies corporate incorporated in a listed country;[277]
- bodies corporate incorporated in a Member State;
- bodies corporate incorporated in any relevant British possession and having their principal place of business in the UK or in any such possession;
- European Economic Interest Groupings.[278]

If these criteria are not satisfied, a person may be qualified if a 'majority interest' in the ship[279] is owned by persons who are qualified.[280] If a majority interest is also not fulfilled then a ship may only be registered if a 'representative person'[281] is appointed in relation to the ship.[282] If a body corporate is in a British possession then that body corporate may only be registered if it has a place of business in the UK or, failing this, a representative person is appointed.[283]

ii. Operation – Vessel Eligibility and Age

There are no restrictions on the type of ship which can be registered on the UKSR, although fishing vessels and small ships[284] are registered in a different section of the register. The Registrar may refuse to register if he considers that it would be inappropriate to do so

> taking into account any requirement of the Merchant Shipping Acts … relating to the condition of the ship or its equipment so far as it is relevant to its safety or to any risk of pollution or to the safety, health and welfare of persons employed or engaged in any capacity on board the ship.[285]

[276] Under the British Nationality Act 1981.

[277] This and the four categories immediately above it were inserted by SI 2019/509. Schedule 6 ('listed country') is inserted by reg 32 and includes among others Panama, the Marshall Islands, Liberia, and China.

[278] SI 1994/541; The Merchant Shipping (Registration of Ships) Regulations 1993, reg 7(1) (as amended).

[279] The Merchant Shipping (Registration of Ships) Regulations 1993, reg 8 (as amended).

[280] ibid, reg 7(2).

[281] ie an individual resident or a body corporate incorporated in a member State and having a place of business in the UK: ibid, reg 18(2).

[282] ibid, reg 8(3).

[283] ibid, reg 8(4)(b).

[284] ie those less than 24m in length: ibid, reg 1(2). As to registration of such vessels, see Pt XI.

[285] ibid, reg 36(5).

There is no formal age limit for ships on the register, but vessels over 15 years old require approval from the Registry's technical experts before they can be registered.[286]

iii. Operation – Crew

Part III of the Merchant Shipping Act 1995 is concerned with 'Masters and Seamen' but manning and certification requirements are set out in detail in the Merchant Shipping (Standards of Training, Certification and Watchkeeping) Regulations 2015.[287] These Regulations give effect to requirements of the STCW Convention and also implement, in part, Directive 2012/35/EU[288] which amended Directive 2008/10/EC on the minimum level of training of seafarers.[289] The Regulations specify mandatory standards of competence and training and certification requirements for seafarers serving on board merchant ships and impose duties on owners and others responsible for the operation of ships in relation to the certification and training of the seafarers working on their ships and also make provision to ensure the safe manning of vessels in UK waters.

iv. Operation – Safety

The Merchant Shipping Act 1995 lays down a range of safety requirements. Among the most important is s 42 which implies an obligation on shipowners of UK ships charging the owner, master and every agent concerned with '(i) the loading of the ship, (ii) the preparing of the ship for sea, or (iii) the sending of the ship to sea' to use 'all reasonable means to ensure the seaworthiness of the ship for the voyage at the time when the voyage commences and to keep the ship in a seaworthy condition for the voyage during the voyage'. Part IV of the Act is concerned with 'Safety and Health on Ships' more generally.

v. Taxation and Fees

Shipowning enterprises registered in the UK are subject to corporation tax where either registered as a limited company or as a foreign company with a UK branch or office. Taxable profits include 'trading profits', investments and selling assets for greater than their cost ('chargeable gains'). The rate of corporation tax is 19 per cent for the financial year beginning 1 April 2020.[290] Following a report, 'Independent Enquiry into a Tonnage Tax', which recommended introducing a system of tonnage tax for shipping enterprises, legislation was introduced in the

[286] Sharratt, 'Registering the ship' (2018) 531.
[287] SI 2015/782 (as amended by SI 2019/630).
[288] Directive 2012/35/EU, [2012] OJ L343/78.
[289] Directive 2008/106/EC, [2008] OJ L323/33.
[290] Finance Act 2020, s 5.

Finance Act 2000.[291] In order to take advantage of this, an election to pay tonnage tax[292] has to be made and, once made, lasts for 10 years.[293] Such an option is open to a 'qualifying' company or group[294] and a commitment has to be made with the Department for Transport to train a specified number of seafarers annually.[295] Comprehensive guidance on the fees payable is offered by the UKSR.[296]

VII. Conclusions

Shipping enterprises preparing for the delivery of a newbuild, the acquisition of second-hand tonnage, or actively considering whether to reflag a vessel (or the entire fleet), will undertake a detailed review of a range of factors in order to survey the available options. In most flag states, registration is the essential first step in being able to fly the flag. Before registration, however, shipping enterprises undertake careful scrutiny of the available options. In the absence of any international regime, the options open to shipping enterprises are overwhelmingly commercial ones.

Although they have lost ground over the past 40 years, traditional shipping registers have not disappeared and continue to attract tonnage. But they have had to be nimble in adapting to the new reality of an increasingly diverse availability of open registers. Many shipping enterprises are still attracted to affiliation with the home flag. Traditional flags offer a range of incentives, including tonnage taxes, to encourage registration, Singapore being a classic example of a former open registry which has been remarkably successful in fulfilling its aspiration to be one of the leading flags.

Some traditional flags have actively engaged with the open registry model by the formation of second registers. The Scandinavian flags have been particularly successful in encouraging the development of this alternative model.

As this chapter emphasises, open registries continue to attract the lion's share of shipping enterprises. The three leading registers surveyed here, Panama, Liberia and the Marshall Islands, continue to perform extraordinarily well, together accounting for more than 40 per cent of total dead-weight tonnage.[297] As the

[291] Finance Act 2000, s 82 and Sch 22. This is only open to 'qualifying' ships (seagoing ships of 100 tons or more gross tonnage) – Sch 22, para 19(1). See also the *Tonnage Tax Manual*, available at www.gov.uk/hmrc-internal-manuals/tonnage-tax-manual; L Butcher, 'Shipping: Tonnage Tax', House of Commons Library SN/BT/603 (22 February 2010), available at commonslibrary.parliament.uk/research-briefings/sn00603; E Selkou and M Roe, 'UK Tonnage Tax: Subsidy or Special Case?' (2002) 29 *Maritime Policy & Management* 393.

[292] Finance Act 2000, Sch 22, para 4 for the method of calculation.

[293] ibid, Sch 22, para 13(1).

[294] ie is within the charge to corporation tax, operates qualifying ships, and those ships are strategically and commercially managed in the UK: ibid, Sch 22, para 16(1).

[295] ibid, Sch 22, Pt IV.

[296] www.ukshipregister.co.uk/useful-information/fee-indicator/cargo.

[297] UNCTAD (n 1) 44.

above discussion indicates, however, even between these reputable flags, there are formal requirements which distinguish each from the other. These flags, along with others, also attract attention for the wrong reasons, including shipping casualties and poor treatment of crew. It is evident, however, that there is a yawning gap between these registers and other registers on the ITF list, which fall well short of having respectable standards, the ability to enforce them, or the wherewithal to offer protection in times of trouble.[298]

Labels may be a confusing distraction, but the choices open to shipping enterprises give great scope for making decisions based on a rather hard-nosed commercial bottom line. Legal, political and moral considerations may feature, but these are not, ultimately, pivotal in the flagging decisions that shipping enterprises make.

[298] See, eg, M Grey, 'A Question of Convenience' *Lloyd's List* (9 November 2011).

3

Private International Law Strategies in Ship Management and Crewing Arrangements

PAUL MYBURGH*

I. Introduction

International maritime employment arrangements exhibit two fundamental characteristics. First, even more so than their land-based counterparts, they are paradigmatically asymmetrical legal relationships, with shipowners/employers exerting significant power and control over seafarers/employees.[1] Although this power imbalance has been measurably reduced by the activism and collective bargaining efforts of international maritime unions,[2] the regulatory interventions of international organisations[3] and the sheer economic realities of the current

* Deputy Director, Centre for Maritime Law, Faculty of Law, National University of Singapore. The author gratefully acknowledges NUS Grant R-241-000-143-133 (Maritime Private International Law) that supported the research for this chapter.

[1] This is due to a number of factors, including social isolation for long periods of time, insufficient annual and shore leave, fatigue, stress, mental health and addiction issues, being forced to live and work in confined conditions under the exclusive and direct control of the employer, a general lack of job stability or permanent contracts and vulnerability to criminalisation and abandonment. See generally H Sampson, N Ellis, I Acejo, N Turgo and L Tang, *The Working and Living Conditions of Seafarers on Cargo Ships in the Period 2011–2016* (Seafarers International Research Centre, Cardiff University, 2018), available at www.sirc.cf.ac.uk/Seafarers'_Working_and_Living_Conditions.aspx; G Exarchopoulos, P Zhang, N Pryce-Roberts and M Zhao, 'Seafarers' Welfare: A Critical Review of the Related Legal Issues under the Maritime Labour Convention 2006' (2018) 93 *Marine Policy* 62, 66 ff; A Mellbye and T Carter, 'Seafarers' Depression and Suicide' (2017) 68 *International Maritime Health* 108; P Zhang, *Seafarers' Rights in China: Restructuring in Legislation and Practice Under the Maritime Labour Convention 2006* (Switzerland, Springer International Publishing, 2016) ch 4.

[2] Most notably, the International Transport Workers' Federation (ITF): see generally ITF, *Solidarity: The First 100 Years of the International Transport Worke' Federation* (London, Pluto Press, 1996); L Fink, *Sweatshops at Sea: Merchant Seamen in the World's First Globalized Industry, from 1812 to the Present* (Chapel Hill, The University of North Carolina Press, 2011).

[3] See VI below on the work of the International Labour Organization (ILO).

shortage of skilled and experienced seafarers,[4] seafarer exploitation, abuse and abandonment nonetheless remains a very serious issue within the global maritime industry.[5] This power imbalance, together with the fact that crew costs outweigh other criteria in the maritime market,[6] has created an incentive for unscrupulous shipowning and management interests to attempt to circumvent minimum labour standards in the interest of cutting corners and costs.

Secondly, international maritime employment may be seen as a 'testing ground for the globalisation process'.[7] The nineteenth-century model of ships as floating quasi-extensions of national territory, and therefore, as a corollary, floating national workplaces entirely staffed by nationals from the flag state and regulated by the employment law of the flag state, has long since vanished. The rise of open ship registries[8] (and the corresponding rise of crews of convenience)[9] has effectively resulted in an international free market of ship flagging and employment.[10] The increased popularity of flagging out, together with the waning of cabotage restrictions and nationality requirements for crewing, has resulted in a hyper-globalised international maritime labour force, with 80–90 per cent of commercial ships' crews now being multinational.[11] All of these factors have, in turn, significantly weakened and blurred the connections between national legal regulation and maritime employment issues.

This chapter examines the strategic use of private international law strategies by shipowning interests in their ship management and crewing arrangements to achieve their economic ends, and analyses some of the private and public international law responses to such strategies at a national, regional and international level.

[4] International Chamber of Shipping, 'Global Supply and Demand for Seafarers' at www.ics-shipping.org/shipping-facts/shipping-and-world-trade/global-supply-and-demand-for-seafarers.

[5] If anything, instances of abandonment of seafarers have increased drastically in recent years: see the International Maritime Organisation (IMO) statistics at www.imo.org/en/OurWork/Legal/Pages/Seafarer-abandonment.aspx. Roughly a third of all abandonment cases recorded on the IMO/ILO joint database involve vessels flagged in Panama (99 instances), followed by St Vincent and the Grenadines (29) and Liberia (28).

[6] ŞE Kartal, Ö Uğurlu, M Kaptan, Y Arslanoğlu, J Wang and S Loughney, 'An Analysis and Comparison of Multinational Officers of the Watch in the Global Maritime Labor Market' (2019) 46 *Maritime Policy & Management* 757, 773; Girvin (ch 2) V(B).

[7] L Carballo Piñeiro, *International Maritime Labour Law*, Hamburg Studies on Maritime Affairs 34 (Berlin, Springer, 2015) 1.

[8] More pejoratively referred to by maritime unions as 'flags of convenience'. On open registries, see Girvin (ch 2) III.

[9] Typically understood as meaning crews recruited from less developed labour-supplying states, who have no nationality or residence connection to the flag state, and who represent a source of significantly cheaper labour for shipowning interests.

[10] Or, perhaps more accurately, forum shopping for the cheapest law of the flag: this is not a '[h]ealthy competition between legal systems': Carballo Piñeiro, *International Maritime Labour Law* (2015) 2. But see ER DeSombre, 'Globalization, Competition, and Convergence: Shipping and the Race to the Middle' (2008) 14 *Global Governance* 179 for the argument that the economic and regulatory picture is rather more nuanced than that.

[11] Kartal, Uğurlu, Kaptan, Arslanoğlu, Wang and Loughney, 'Multinational Officers of the Watch' (2019) 776.

II. The Law of the Flag

The traditional private international law approach to individual employment contracts, in Anglo-Common Law systems at least, is that – as with other contracts – they are governed by the law expressly or impliedly chosen by the parties or, failing that, the proper law of the contract, that is, the system of law with which the contract has its closest and most real connection.[12] The law of the habitual place of work or *lex loci laboris* will tend to be a major factor in the determination of the objective proper law,[13] not least in cases involving a globalised mobile workforce, where the application of employment laws linked to individual workers' domiciles, habitual residences or places of engagement could lead to overwhelming complexities and inefficiencies for employers and employees.[14] For seafarers and other offshore workers, the *lex loci laboris* has traditionally been deemed to correspond to that of the law of the port of registration of the ship (in other words, the law of the ship's flag).[15] The fictional application of the law of the ship's flag, as opposed to the law where the ship happens to be physically situated at any given time, avoids the absurdity of a *lex loci laboris* that changes as the ship travels through different territorial waters, or disappears while the ship is on the high seas.[16]

This private international law approach mirrors the applicable public international law regime. Article 94 of the United Nations Convention on the Law of the Sea 1982 (UNCLOS) sets out the duty of the flag state to 'effectively exercise its jurisdiction and control in administrative, technical and social matters over ships flying its flag'[17] and to 'take such measures for ships flying its flag as are necessary to ensure safety at sea with regard … to … the manning of ships, labour conditions and the training of crews, taking into account the applicable international instruments'.[18] In particular, art 94(2)(b) of UNCLOS requires the flag state to 'assume jurisdiction *under its internal law* over each ship flying its flag and its master, officers and crew in respect of administrative, technical and social matters concerning the ship'.[19]

[12] *Compagnie d'Armement Maritime SA v Compagnie Tunisienne de Navigation SA* [1971] AC 572 (HL); *Sayers v International Drilling Co NV* [1971] 1 WLR 1176, 1180–81 (CA).

[13] Carballo Piñeiro (n 7) 189 ff.

[14] See *Sayers v International Drilling Co NV* [1971] 1 WLR 1176, 1184 (Salmon LJ): 'He could not have believed that his contractual rights would be governed by a different law from that of his fellow employees, still less that there would be five different laws governing the contractual rights of, say, five different employees. If it were so, it would be awkward for the employers, awkward for their employees, and difficult to give the contracts ordinary business efficacy'. However, in the context of crews of convenience, *dépeçage* of the proper laws of individual seafarers' SEAs may be deliberate or unavoidable where, say, officers are sourced from European jurisdictions and ratings from less developed labour-supplying states.

[15] See generally W Tetley, 'The Law of the Flag, "Flag Shopping", and Choice of Law' (1993) 17 *Tulane Maritime Law Journal* 139.

[16] Carballo Piñeiro (n 7) 191 ff.

[17] Article 94(1) of UNCLOS.

[18] Article 94(3)(b) of UNCLOS.

[19] Emphasis added. See also arts 5 and 10(1)(b) of the Convention on the High Seas 1958 (adopted 29 April 1958, entered into force 30 September 1962); L Carballo Piñeiro, 'Port State Jurisdiction

However, as already alluded to, although the use of the law of the flag, both as a default connecting factor in private international law and as a public international law regulation mechanism, may have made perfect sense in the nineteenth century as a means of extending national employment regulations and protections to cover offshore employment arrangements, the failure of public international law to police the 'genuine link' requirement between vessels and flag states in any real or effective sense[20] and the rise in popularity of open and second registries,[21] has meant that the application of the law of the ship's flag, rather than extending the reach of national employment regulation, may be – and is – now utilised as a mechanism to minimise or evade those same regulatory costs and effects.[22]

III. (Ab)use of Party Autonomy

The starting point in private international law is that maritime employers and employees have autonomy to choose any law to govern their maritime employment contracts, provided their choice of law is 'bona fide and legal, and provided there is no reason for avoiding the choice on the ground of public policy'.[23] In the context of the highly asymmetrical maritime employment relationship, however, the application of this legal test to the facts will not always be entirely straightforward. For example, if the seafarer employment agreement (SEA) simply defaults to the law of the ship's flag,[24] that is clearly not objectionable in and of itself,

over Labour Conditions: A Private International Law Perspective on Extra-territoriality' (2016) 31 *International Journal of Marine and Coastal Law* 531, 534–35. See Tanaka (ch 1), text at n 5.

[20] See art 5 of the Convention on the High Seas 1958; art 91(1) of UNCLOS. The United Nations Convention on Conditions for Registration of Ships (done at Geneva, 7 February 1986), which would have imposed a more stringent national link for ship ownership (art 8) and crewing (art 9), has never entered into force. See Tanaka (ch 1), text at n 65 ff.

[21] ie, international registries which offer many of the advantages of an open register, but nonetheless retain some link between beneficial ownership or management and the national flag: see E Watt, *Ship Registration: Law and Practice*, 3rd edn (London, Informa, 2018) para 4.37 ff; Girvin (ch 2) IV(B).

[22] See eg *Walker v Wallem Shipmanagement Ltd* (2020) UKEAT/0236/18/LA, [2020] IRLR 257 (CMI652): the Equality Act 2010 (UK) and the Equality Act (Work on Ships and Hovercraft) Regulations 2011 (UK) do not apply to protect workers against sex discrimination in respect of recruitment in England to work on foreign-registered vessels outside Great Britain. The Tribunal noted at [7] that 'the Regulations were being enacted within the constraints of the UK's obligations under the United Nations Convention on the Law of the Sea (10 December 1982) ("UNCLOS") which restricts the ability of states to apply their legislation to ships flying a different flag (see articles 92 and 94, within the General Provisions section (section 1) of Part VII, entitled High Seas'.

[23] *Vita Food Products Inc v Unus Shipping Co Ltd* [1939] AC 277, 290 (PC: Lord Wright). See eg the BIMCO CREWMAN A and B 2009 and SHIPMAN 2009 standard agreements, which include the following dispute resolution options: (a) LMAA arbitration and English law (default); (b) US arbitration and US law; (c) 'This Agreement shall be governed by and construed in accordance with the laws of the place mutually agreed by the parties and any dispute arising out of or in connection with this Agreement shall be referred to arbitration at a mutually agreed place, subject to the procedures applicable there'; or (d) mediation.

[24] See eg the Ethiopian Maritime Training Institute SEA, cl 23.1: 'Unless otherwise agreed, this Contract is governed by the laws of the Vessel's country of flag as defined in Part A'.

but may become a contentious issue where the ship has been deliberately flagged out to an open registry with lower employment standards and conditions than those which pertain in the coastal state in which the vessel is operating, or in the labour-supplying state from where the seafarer originates.[25]

This tension between competing employment standards and conditions is likely to be exacerbated where shipowning interests couple a choice of foreign flag law (or another foreign choice of law) with a foreign choice of forum clause, thereby strategically attempting to exclude any oversight or adjudication by other states with a legitimate vested interest in the relevant maritime employment. These may include a coastal state affected by the vessels' operations in its territorial waters, exclusive economic zone (EEZ) or continental shelf, and hence concerned about accidents or pollution caused by poor employment practices, or a labour-supplying state which will have to bear the brunt of its seafaring national's repatriation, medical treatment and rehabilitation costs.

The practice of insulating maritime workplaces from employment regulation by coastal and labour-supplying states is particularly prevalent in the cruise ship industry[26] and in the fishing and offshore sectors, where chartered fishing vessels or offshore units will operate, sometimes on a long-term or permanent basis, in the territorial waters or EEZ or over the continental shelf of State A, but whose workers' employment contracts will be governed and overseen, purportedly exclusively, by the law and forum of State B (usually a jurisdiction and legal system that favours the employer).[27]

The private international law position potentially becomes even more complex when third parties, such as recruitment or placement agencies or ship management companies, are involved in the seafarer employment relationship.[28] It has become typical for such third parties to include choice of law and forum clauses

[25] China, the Philippines, Indonesia, the Russian Federation and Ukraine are estimated to be the five largest labour-supplying countries for all seafarers (officers and ratings).

[26] See eg *Cvoro v Carnival Corp*, 234 F Supp 3d 1220, 2017 AMC 812 (SD Florida 2017); *Navarette v Silversea Cruises Ltd*, 169 F Supp 3d 1314, 2016 AMC 660 (SD Florida 2016); *Johnson v NCL (Bahamas) Ltd*, 163 F Supp 3d 338 (ED Louisiana 2016); *Escobar v Celebration Cruise Operator Inc*, 805 F 3d 1279 (11th Cir 2015); LM Anderson, 'Mandatory Arbitration Within Cruise Ship Employment Agreements: Without Global Change, the Disparity of Power Continues to Expand' (2015) 12 *Loyola Maritime Law Journal* 335; RD Peltz, 'Buffering the Collision between the Historical Protections for Seamen and the Increasing Use of International Arbitration Agreements (2015) 40 *Tulane Maritime Law Journal* 1.

[27] See eg *Udovenko v Karelrybflot*, HC Christchurch AD90/98 (24 May 1999); *Karelrybflot AO v Udovenko* [2000] 2 NZLR 24 (CA): fishing vessels owned by a Russian company, Karelrybflot AO, and chartered to a New Zealand operator (Abel Fisheries Ltd). The SEAs were governed by the Russian Labour Code, which provided for payments below that of the New Zealand minimum wage. The seafarers complained that Karelrybflot falsified the logbooks recording the number of hours they had worked, failed to pay them wages for more than five months and, contrary to the SEA, would only offer them payment of their wages in Russia and in roubles.

[28] These agreements between shipowners and agencies will typically also contain their own forum and governing law provisions: see, eg, Manning Agreement between Höegh LNG Colombia SAS and Höegh Fleet Services Philippines Inc, 1 September 2016, available at www.sec.gov/Archives/edgar/data/1603016/000114420417019310/v461838_ex4-23.htm (London arbitration and English law clause).

in the service agreements that they enter into with seafarers, which raises the possibility of seafarers' employment arrangements being governed by at least two distinct contracts, an 'umbrella' service agreement and a ship-specific employment contract, which may be governed by different legal systems and dispute resolution processes. This can place further obstacles in the way of seafarers when they seek compensation for breaches of their employment contracts.[29]

Finally, the labour-supplying state may also become involved in the employment process. The most prominent example of this practice is the Philippines, where art 18 of the Labor Code[30] bans direct hiring of Filipina/o workers for overseas employment 'except through the Boards and entities authorized by the Secretary of Labor'. The effect of this is that all Filipina/o seafarers must sign up to the standard terms of the Philippine Overseas Employment Administration Standard Employment Contract (POEA SEC)[31] in addition to any individual employment or collective bargaining agreement. The POEA SEC, together with the Philippines' ratification of the Maritime Labour Convention, which has attracted the rather overblown soubriquet of the 'Magna Carta of Filipino seafarers',[32] is designed to protect workers from foreign exploitation. Section 29 of the POEA SEC provides as follows:

> In cases of claims and disputes arising from this employment, the parties covered by a collective bargaining agreement shall submit the claim or dispute to the original and exclusive jurisdiction of the voluntary arbitrator or panel of voluntary arbitrators. If the parties are not covered by a collective bargaining agreement, the parties may at their option submit the claim or dispute to either the original and exclusive jurisdiction of the National Labor Relations Commission (NLRC), pursuant to Republic Act (RA) 8042 otherwise known as the Migrant Workers and Overseas Filipinos Act of 1995, as amended, or to the original and exclusive jurisdiction of the voluntary arbitrator or panel of arbitrators. If there is no provision as to the voluntary arbitrators to be appointed by the parties, the same shall be appointed from the accredited voluntary arbitrators of the National Conciliation and Mediation Board of the Department of Labor and Employment.

[29] See *Mobil Oil New Zealand Ltd v The Ship 'Rangiora' (No 2)* [2000] 1 NZLR 82: seafarers employed on individual employment contracts based on the terms of a collective employment contract (CEC), an ITF special agreement and ship's articles. The CEC which provided for redundancy payments was between the employer, South Pacific Shipping Ltd, and the New Zealand Seafarers Union. Fisher J held that the specific ship's articles did not contain sufficient detail to amount to an employment contract, and because the CEC was in the nature of a general services agreement that did not identify specific ships, there was an insufficient contractual nexus to warrant a wages maritime lien. But *cf Canadian Imperial Bank of Commerce v Le Chêne No 1 (The)* [2004] 1 FCR 120, [2003] FC 873 [29]–[30] where Snider J held on similar facts that 'the right to a maritime lien is not contingent on the nature of the seaman's contractual arrangements'.

[30] Presidential Decree No 442 of 1974 (1 May 1974).

[31] See www.poea.gov.ph/memorandumcirculars/2010/10.pdf; Jean Ver Pugal Pia, '"nangangamuhan": An Analysis of the Standard Employment Contract (POEA-SEC) for Filipino Seafarers' (PhD thesis, Cardiff University, 2016) especially ch 5, available at core.ac.uk/display/82967550.

[32] See www.congress.gov.ph/legisdocs/basic_17/HB04360.pdf.

> The Philippine Overseas Employment Administration (POEA) shall exercise original and exclusive jurisdiction to hear and decide disciplinary action on cases, which are administrative in character, involving or arising out of violations of recruitment laws, rules and regulations involving employers, principals, contracting partners and Filipino seafarers.

In addition to this exclusive arbitration clause, s 31 provides that any 'unresolved dispute, claim or grievance arising out of or in connection with this contract including the annexes thereof, shall be governed by the laws of the Republic of the Philippines, international conventions, treaties and covenants to which the Philippines is a signatory'.

While the POEA SEC does arguably achieve its aim of affording basic minimum employment protections to Filipina/o seafarers, the imposition of a compulsory dispute resolution regime in the Philippines has distinct disadvantages for seafarers[33] in terms of delays to redress, wrangling over medical evidence,[34] the de facto exclusion of an direct action *in rem* against the ship,[35] and a fixed compensation tariff for personal injuries incurred in the course of employment which may be significantly lower than comparable compensation available in other countries.[36]

IV. Mandatory Rules and Extraterritorial Application

Some coastal states have responded to concerns over the negative effects of shipowning interests' (ab)use of party autonomy and flagging out to states with lower

[33] So too Pia, 'nangangamuhan' (2016) vi, who argues that the 'experience of the seafarers on-board the ship suggests that the contract cannot intercede in a beneficial way and falls short as a legal document to protect Filipino seafarers.' But *cf* Gard Insight, 'Crew Claims in the Philippines – When the Contract is Not Enough', 16 January 2013, available at www.gard.no/web/updates/content/20734098/crew-claims-in-the-philippines-when-the-contract-is-not-enough for the argument that the Philippines seafarer dispute resolution system is too 'labourer friendly'.

[34] See 'Litigious Culture Hangs Over Manning', *Lloyd's List* (28 November 2008).

[35] See eg *The Rainbow Joy* [2005] SGCA 36, [2005] 3 SLR(R) 719 where the plaintiff's *in rem* claim for personal injury was dismissed by the Singapore Court of Appeal on the (dubious) basis of *forum non conveniens*. See also Anderson, 'Mandatory Arbitration' (2015) for the US cases.

[36] See s 32 of the POEA SEC. See further *The Rainbow Joy* [2005] SGCA 36, [2005] 3 SLR(R) 719; but *cf Paquito Lima Buton v Rainbow Joy Shipping Ltd Inc* [2008] HKCFA 30, [2008] 4 HKC 14 [25] where the Hong Kong Court of Final Appeal refused to stay proceedings on the basis of the compulsory arbitration clause in the POEA SEC, on the ground that it was considerably less advantageous to the seafarer than the Hong Kong Employees' Compensation Ordinance (ECO): 'Pursuant to … the Philippine contract, loss of his eye entitles the appellant to compensation in the sum of US$20,900. However, under the ECO which is applicable under the Hong Kong contract, compensation payable for such an injury to an employee of the appellant's age is in the sum of US$67,284 … Secondly, … the Hong Kong contract preserves the employee's right to claim common law damages over and above any sums recovered under the ECO. In contrast, … the Philippine contract stipulates that payment of US$20,900 by way of compensation covers all claims arising from or related to the appellant's employment both under Philippine law and the laws of any other country.'

employment standards by extending the application of their mandatory minimum national labour standards beyond their own territorial waters and home-flagged vessels to cover foreign vessels and offshore units or installations operating in their EEZ or continental shelf. This exercise of extraterritorial jurisdiction is generally rationalised by a (broad and contested) reading of coastal states' UNCLOS rights under arts 56 (EEZ) and 77 (continental shelf).[37]

So, for example, in New Zealand, s 103A(7) of the Fisheries Act 1996 provides that any foreign vessels granted an exemption to operate in New Zealand fisheries waters[38] are subject to the mandatory overriding provisions of the Minimum Wage Act 1983 (NZ) and the Employment Relations Act 2000 (NZ). Section 103A(7)(g) of the Fisheries Act 1996 further provides that 'the Employment Relations Authority and the Employment Court may exercise jurisdiction in respect of any employment relationship that arises [on a foreign-owned fishing vessel in New Zealand fisheries waters] as if it were a lawful employment relationship subject to New Zealand law'. These provisions extending New Zealand's internal employment law to all foreign fishing vessels operating in its EEZ were introduced after a number of well-publicised scandals involving Russian-registered fishing vessels chartered to New Zealand operators.[39]

Section 7 of the Continental Shelf Act 1964 (NZ) contains a similar, albeit clumsier, mechanism that deems 'every act or omission which takes place on or under or above or about any installation or device (whether permanent or temporary) constructed, erected, placed, or used in, on, or above the continental shelf in connection with the exploration of the continental shelf or the exploitation of its natural resources' to have taken place in New Zealand and authorises 'every court in New Zealand which would have jurisdiction (whether civil or criminal) in respect of that act or omission if it had taken place in New Zealand' to exercise jurisdiction. This would seem to have the effect of extending mandatory national employment legislation to offshore workers in New Zealand on the basis of the statutory fiction that the employment occurred within the territory of New Zealand.[40]

[37] See *Fair Work Ombudsman v Pocomwell Limited (No 2)* [2013] FCA 1139, (2013) 218 FCR 94 [35]–[36] for the argument (which was rejected by the Court) that the coastal state's rights and interests in the EEZ are limited to the management and exploitation of natural resources and do not extend to seafarer employment issues.

[38] New Zealand fisheries waters are defined in s 2(1) of the Fisheries Act 1996 as meaning: '(a) all waters in the exclusive economic zone of New Zealand: (b) all waters of the territorial sea of New Zealand: (c) all internal waters of New Zealand: (d) all other fresh or estuarine waters within New Zealand where fish, aquatic life, or seaweed that are indigenous to or acclimatised in New Zealand are found.'

[39] See n 27 above. See further *Hartono v Ministry for Primary Industries* [2018] NZSC 17, [2018] 1 NZLR 857, discussed in P Myburgh, 'Fisheries, Forfeiture Relief and Admiralty' [2018] *LMCLQ* 322; J Devlin, 'Modern Day Slavery: Employment Conditions for Foreign Fishing Crews in New Zealand Waters' (2009) 23 *Australian and New Zealand Maritime Law Journal* 82.

[40] See *Teddy v Police* [2014] NZCA 422, [2015] NZAR 80; *Sembawang Salvage Pte Ltd v Shell Todd Oil Services Ltd* [1993] 2 NZLR 97. For the position in Dutch law, see CP Verwer, 'The Law Applicable on the Continental Shelf and the EEZ', available at www.ejcl.org/143/art143-21.pdf.

Likewise, in Australia, the mandatory application of the Fair Work Act 2009 (Cth) is extended by s 33(1) to the Australian EEZ and continental shelf for Australian ships, fixed platforms, offshore supply and service vessels, and ships operated or chartered by an Australian employer and using Australia as a base. This provision was analysed in detail in *Fair Work Ombudsman v Pocomwell Ltd (No 2)*[41] which involved Filipino painters working in Australia's EEZ on two drilling rigs, the *Nan Hai VI* and the *Maersk Discoverer*. The drilling rigs were operated by Maersk Drilling Australia Pty Ltd, a corporation incorporated within Australia. Each of the drilling rigs was also registered as a ship: the *Nan Hai VI* in the People's Republic of China and the *Maersk Discoverer* in Singapore. The painters were employed by Pocomwell Ltd, a corporation incorporated in Hong Kong. By the terms of the contract of employment between the painters and Pocomwell Ltd entered into in the Philippines and governed by the law of the Philippines, each painter was engaged to work for 28 days at 12 hours per day at the rate of US$ 900. The hourly rate of pay for each painter was therefore about A$ 2.68. Under the National Minimum Wage Order that applied under the Fair Work Act 2009 (Cth), a worker doing the work performed by the painters was entitled to be paid A$ 14.31 per hour.

Barker J held that, while s 33(1)(b) of the Fair Work Act 2009 (Cth) and reg 1.15E of the Fair Work Regulations 2009 (Cth) on their proper construction extend to, or are capable of extending to, a drilling rig if it is a 'fixed platform' or a ship which is a 'majority Australian-crewed ship', in this case neither drilling rig was a fixed platform or a majority Australian-crewed ship. The workers' claims therefore failed.

In *Fair Work Ombudsman v Transpetrol TM AS*[42] Rares J had to decide whether a Norwegian corporation, Transpetrol TM AS, the employer of a crew on board an oil and chemical tanker, *MT Turmoil*, had contravened the Fair Work Act 2009 (Cth) by underpaying seafarers. Although s 33(3) of the Fair Work Act 2009 (Cth) and reg 1.15E of the Fair Work Regulations 2009 (Cth) extended the application of the Act to vessels sailing in Australia's EEZ under a temporary licence issued under the Coastal Trading (Revitalising Australian Shipping) Act 2012 (Cth), Rares J found that Transpetrol had complied with its obligations to pay the crew under the Maritime Labour Convention 2006 (MLC),[43] the law of the flag (Panama) and the relevant national employment laws of the seafarers (India and the Philippines), and had a 'blue certificate' issued by the ITF. Transpetrol had been unaware that one of its sub-charterers had applied for a temporary licence to operate in Australian waters and had agreed to top up its workers' payments to the required levels when advised of its contraventions by the Fair Work Ombudsman. In the circumstances, Rares J refused to

[41] *Fair Work Ombudsman v Pocomwell Ltd (No 2)* [2013] FCA 1139, (2013) 218 FCR 94. See also *Fair Work Ombudsman v Devine Marine Group Pty Ltd (No 2)* [2015] FCA 370, (2015) 234 FCR 122.

[42] *Fair Work Ombudsman v Transpetrol TM AS* [2019] FCA 400.

[43] See VI below.

award civil pecuniary penalties against the employer and required the Fair Work Ombudsman to pay half of the costs.

These cases illustrate the complexity of the interaction between national and international labour regimes for seafarers, and the snares involved in extending the extraterritorial reach of national employment legislation to the EEZ and continental shelf. Although Rares J accused the Fair Work Ombudsman of 'overreaching'[44] her authority in *Fair Work Ombudsman v Transpetrol TM AS*, that allegation might more appropriately be laid at the door of the Australian legislature for extending its national mandatory employment legislation to ships temporarily operating in coastal trade, which arguably amounts to an assertion of extraterritorial jurisdiction that is exorbitant on even the most charitable reading of the relevant UNCLOS provisions.

V. Protective Augmentation of Party Autonomy

The EU has taken a different approach to regulating (ab)use of party autonomy in the maritime employment context in the form of art 8 of the Rome I Regulation,[45] which applies to individual employment contracts[46] in all Member States of the EU except for Denmark. The paramount principle of party autonomy still prevails,[47] but the nature of individual employment contracts as involving systemic power imbalances is expressly recognised by the proviso that the choice of law may not have the result of depriving the employee of the protection afforded by provisions that cannot be derogated from by agreement under the law that, in the absence of the parties' choice of law, would have been applicable pursuant to the objectively applicable law identified by the conflicts rules contained in arts 8(2), 8(3) or 8(4):

> 2. To the extent that the law applicable to the individual employment contract has not been chosen by the parties, the contract shall be governed by the law of the country in which or, failing that, from which the employee habitually carries out his work in performance of the contract. The country where the work is habitually carried out shall not be deemed to have changed if he is temporarily employed in another country.
> 3. Where the law applicable cannot be determined pursuant to paragraph 2, the contract shall be governed by the law of the country where the place of business through which the employee was engaged is situated.

[44] *Fair Work* (n 42) [132]. The original judgment read 'overreacted'.

[45] Regulation (EC) No 593/2008 of the European Parliament and of the Council of 17 June 2008 on the law applicable to contractual obligations (Rome I), [2008] OJ L177/6. See generally AAH van Hoek, 'Private International Law: An Appropriate Means to Regulate Transnational Employment in the European Union?' (2014) 3 *Erasmus Law Review* 157.

[46] The Regulation does not cover collective bargaining agreements.

[47] See art 8(1) of the Regulation: 'An individual employment contract shall be governed by the law chosen by the parties in accordance with Article 3'.

4. Where it appears from the circumstances as a whole that the contract is more closely connected with a country other than that indicated in paragraphs 2 or 3, the law of that other country shall apply.

The aim of this scheme is clearly to protect the employee, but its application may prove problematic in the case of employment of seafarers and offshore workers, as is illustrated by the *Voogsgeerd* case.[48] Voogsgeerd, a Dutch marine engineer, entered into an employment contract with Navimer, a Luxembourg company, at the headquarters of Naviglobe NV, an undertaking established in Antwerp, Belgium. The parties chose Luxembourg law to apply to the contract. Voogsgeerd served as chief engineer on two of Navimer's ships. When he was dismissed, Voogsgeerd commenced proceedings in the Labour Court of Antwerp, arguing that the more favourable mandatory rules of Belgian employment law were applicable, despite the parties' express choice of Luxembourg law. He claimed that he was bound by his employment contract to Naviglobe rather than to Navimer, and that he had principally carried out his work from the port of Antwerp in Belgium, where he was obliged to report for boarding, where he received instructions from Naviglobe and to where he returned after each voyage.[49]

The Court held that the relevant private international law factors must be interpreted in a strictly hierarchical fashion, with the primary factor of the habitual place of work being taken into consideration first. Only if a habitual place of work cannot be determined should the secondary factor of the law of the country where the place of business through which the employee was engaged is situated be taken into consideration.[50] Where the employee works in more than one Member State, the habitual place of work will nonetheless be that state with which the work has a significant connection; that is, in which or from which the employee carries out work activities or, if there is no centre of activities, where the majority of the work activities are carried out:[51]

> Therefore, in the light of the nature of work in the maritime sector … the court seised must take account of all the factors which characterise the activity of the employee and must, in particular, determine in which State the place is situated from which the employee carries out his transport tasks, receives instructions concerning his tasks and organises his work, and the place where his work tools are to be found.

The most peculiar aspect of the *Voogsgeerd* case is that the Court completely ignored the law of the flag of either vessel on which the claimant worked as a factor in determining his habitual place of work.[52] If this factor had been considered, it would probably have swung the centre of gravity away from Belgium

[48] *Voogsgeerd v Navimer SA*, Case C-384/10, [2011] ECR I-13275, ECLI:EU:C:2011:842. The case was based on art 6 of the Rome Convention, the predecessor to art 8 of the Rome I Regulation. For the Rome Convention, see [1980] OJ L266/1.

[49] ibid, paras 12, 28.

[50] ibid, paras 32–35.

[51] ibid, paras 36–40.

[52] This point was apparently not argued by counsel. See van Hoek, 'Private International Law' (2014) 160 fn 33. But see *Helsinki HO 14/09/2015* 1282 (CMI948), available at finlex.fi/fi/oikeus/ho/2015/

and towards Luxembourg.[53] Even on the (non-typical) facts of this case, which appeared to have involved relatively short return voyages to the North Sea, the vast majority of Voogsgeerd's work would have been carried out in the places 'in which' he habitually worked – Luxembourg-flagged and -owned vessels – rather than his home base of Antwerp 'from which' he worked.[54] *Voogsgeerd* is unlikely, therefore, to represent the last word on the interpretation of the art 8(2) objective applicable law factor of the Rome I Regulation in the maritime context.[55] It is difficult to see how the law of the flag can be entirely disregarded as a factor in respect of maritime employment contracts involving longer international voyages, or in respect of workers stationed offshore for longer periods of time, particularly when the plain wording of art 8(2) explicitly prioritises the law of the country 'in which' the work is performed. It is, of course, possible that the CJEU could reject the fiction of the law of the flag altogether as outdated or problematic in an open registry age,[56] but that would arguably significantly undermine the test of the place *in which* the habitual work is undertaken in the maritime employment context and give undue significance to the law of the place of mustering or port of boarding *from which* the maritime work was undertaken, which may be entirely fortuitous for 'fly in, fly out' crews without a European land-based office or centre of operations.[57]

helho20151282 where the Helsinki Court of Appeal refused to apply the law of the ship's flag to determine seafarer's employment rights and obligations, on the basis that 'There are no provisions of applicable law in Articles 91 or 94 of the Convention or in any other article. According to the flag State principle enshrined in Article 94 of the Convention on the Law of the Sea, the State is required to exercise jurisdiction over the ship's crew in accordance with its domestic law. However, this does not mean that the employment contract between the seafarer and his employer is governed by the law of the flag State or that the flag State principle determines the place of employment. … The provisions of UNCLOS relating to the high seas thus primarily govern the rights and obligations of states, including the flag state, on the high seas. It cannot be inferred from the purpose, scope and substance of the Convention that the obligations imposed on the state by art 94 of the Convention contain private international law rules which are directly binding on the parties to the contract of employment.' (author's translation).

[53] The Court mentions in passing at [10] that Voogsgeerd served on the *MS Regina* and the *Prince Henri*, both of which were owned by Navimer. It appears that both vessels were registered in Luxembourg at the relevant time.

[54] This would also seem to seem to be at odds with the CJEU's ruling in *Weber v Universal Ogden Services Ltd*, Case C-37/00, [2002] ECR I-2013, [2002] QB 1189 that the habitual place of work (here for the purposes of establishing jurisdiction under art 5(1) of the Brussels Convention) of a cook employed on various vessels and offshore installations 'is, in principle, the place where he spends most of his working time engaged on his employer's business' over the whole employment term.

[55] But see U Grušić, 'Should the Connecting Factor of the "Engaging Place of Business" Be Abolished in Private International Law?' (2013) 62 *ICLQ* 173, 181, who declares that 'this debate has now been resolved'.

[56] See Grušić (ibid), 180–81 for the argument that use of the law of the flag in the context of art 8(2) of the Rome I Regulation would be inappropriate because 'there is no guarantee that the country of the flag of the ship will be sufficiently closely connected with the employment contract. Moreover, this connecting factor is determined unilaterally by the employer'. On the facts of *Voogsgeerd*, however, Navimer's establishment of its business operations and its flagging did align, and it seems highly artificial to ignore both of these factors.

[57] cf *Weber v Universal Ogden Services Ltd*, Case C-37/00, [2002] ECR I-2013, [2002] QB 1189 [48]: 'Mr Weber did not have an office in a Contracting State that constituted the effective centre of his working activities or from which he performed the essential part of his duties *vis-à-vis* his employer'.

Regardless of the role of the law of the flag in determining the place of habitual work, it must presumably also play a role in the 'escape clause' of art 8(4), although this will depend on the actual extent of the law of the flag's connection with the reality of the seafarer's employment experience in any given case.[58] Where the employment contract includes an express choice of the law of the flag, an exclusive jurisdiction or arbitration clause pointing to the flag state and refers expressly to employment remedies available in the flag state, it is difficult to see how this factor can be discounted altogether, although it must be conceded that giving effect to it may undermine the protective function of art 8 of the Rome I Regulation, particularly where the vessel is flagged out to an open registry.[59]

The effect of *Voogsgeerd* and other CJEU cases relating to transport workers[60] is to emphasise and interpret expansively the art 8(2) objective applicable law factor and to de-emphasise strongly the art 8(3) factor of the law of the country where the place of business through which the employee was engaged is situated. This seems sensible, particularly in the context of maritime employment, where it is common practice nowadays for seafarers to be recruited by third parties in labour-supplying states and then to be flown to their first port of engagement. In such circumstances, the law of the place of engagement (say, China, Indonesia or the Philippines) may have no connection with the reality of these seafarers' day-to-day employment. Given the socio-economic realities of the situation, the application of the law of the place of engagement is also unlikely to perform any protective function in respect of seafarers recruited from less developed labour-supplying states. Finally, the law of the country where the place of business through which the employee was engaged is situated may be difficult to determine and apply where the recruitment or placement agency or ship management company is established in a third country or countries and sends its representatives in to labour-supplying states to source seafarers.[61]

VI. International Regulation

In addition to measures adopted at the national and regional level to attempt to impose minimum or most favourable regulation standards and to limit the abuse of party autonomy in maritime employment contracts, international regulation has come to the fore in the twenty-first century as the 'only factor that can balance the scales of global competition in its race to the bottom'.[62] The most notable

[58] See J Basedow, *The Law of Open Societies: Private Ordering and Public Regulation in the Conflict of Laws* (Amersfoort, Brill/Nijhoff, 2015) paras 674–76.

[59] The POEA SEC would be a classic example of this: see III above. *cf Schlecker v Boedeker*, Case C-64/12, [2014] QB 320; van Hoek (n 45) 161–64.

[60] See generally van Hoek (n 45).

[61] Grušić, 'Engaging Place of Business' (2013) 187; Carballo Piñeiro, Port State Jurisdiction (2016) 543, 545.

[62] Carballo Piñeiro (n 7) 41.

international instrument in this regard is the Maritime Labour Convention 2006 (MLC), developed under the auspices of the International Labour Organisation (ILO).[63] A detailed examination of the MLC framework falls outside the scope of this chapter.[64] It suffices to highlight that the MLC builds on the public international law concepts of flag and port state control and enforcement reflected in the international law of the sea[65] to attempt to ensure 'decent' employment standards and conditions for seafarers[66] in ships registered in, or visiting the ports of, contracting states to the Convention.

The definition of ships[67] to which the MLC applies is reasonably broad, but excludes non-seagoing vessels, ships of traditional build (eg dhows and junks), warships, ships not ordinarily engaged in commercial activities (which presumably would exclude workers on most superyachts from protection)[68] and, most disappointingly, fishing vessels, which are covered by the much less successful instrument, the Work in Fishing Convention 2007.[69] This is a serious omission as the fishing industry is notorious for its exploitative practices.[70] The drafters of the MLC could also not agree on whether to include offshore units or installations within the ambit of the MLC and therefore decided that the Convention should remain silent on this issue. As a result, offshore workers are now left in something of a limbo – whether they will enjoy MLC coverage will depend on whether the law of the relevant coastal state in whose EEZ or on whose continental shelf they are situated deems their unit or installation to be a 'ship' for the purposes of national law.[71] National legal practices in this regard are uneven and sometimes unclear.

[63] Maritime Labour Convention 2006 (adopted by the International Labour Conference at its 94th (Maritime) Session, 23 February 2006, entered into force 20 August 2013). The official text and *travaux préparatoires* of the MLC are available at www.ilo.org/global/standards/maritime-labour-convention/lang--en/index.htm. The MLC has been amended three times, in 2014 (entered into force 18 January 2017), 2016 (entered into force 8 January 2019) and 2018 (entered into force 26 December 2020).

[64] On the MLC, see further Carballo Piñeiro (n 7), ch 2.5; J Lavelle (ed), *The Maritime Labour Convention 2006: International Labour Law Redefined* (Abingdon, Informa, 2014); ML McConnell, D Devlin, and C Doumbia-Henry, *The Maritime Labour Convention, 2006: A Legal Primer to an Emerging International Regime* (Leiden, Martinus Nijhoff Publishers, 2011).

[65] See UNCLOS arts 94, 217, 218.

[66] Which is defined broadly as 'any person who is employed or engaged or works in any capacity on board a ship to which this Convention applies': see MLC art 2(1)(f).

[67] See MLC art 2(1)(i), 2(4).

[68] R Neate, 'Life and Death on a Superyacht: "If Something Goes Wrong, They can just Raise the Anchor and Leave"', *The Guardian* (26 May 2018).

[69] Convention Concerning Work in the Fishing Sector 2007 (adopted by the International Labour Conference at the 96th ILC session, 14 June 2007, entered into force 16 November 2017): for the official text see www.ilo.org/dyn/normlex/en/f?p=NORMLEXPUB:12100:0::NO::P12100_ILO_CODE:C188. At the time of writing only 14 countries have ratified this Convention.

[70] See generally L Carey, 'The Maritime Labour Convention 2006: The Seafarer and the Fisher' (2017) 31 *Australian and New Zealand Maritime Law Journal* 14.

[71] So eg in Singapore the Merchant Shipping (Maritime Labour Convention) (Definition of Ship) Order 2014 excludes Mobile Offshore Drilling Units (MODUs) from the ambit of the MLC's application.

In addition to flag and port state responsibility, the MLC attempts to make labour-supplying states accountable for recruitment and placement services operating in their countries, requiring them to 'ensure the implementation of the requirements of this Convention regarding the recruitment and placement of seafarers as well as the social security protection of seafarers that are its nationals or are resident or are otherwise domiciled in its territory'.[72] This is an important aspect to international regulation of maritime employment, as the use of recruitment and placement services is both ubiquitous and subject to serious abuse.[73] The details of the requirements placed on labour-supplying states are rather underwhelming, however: they are obliged to establish an effective inspection and monitoring system for licensing and operational breaches by recruitment and placement services, but are not obligated to police the substantive terms and conditions being negotiated by those services. Guideline B5.3 provides the aspirational advice that:

> Private seafarer recruitment and placement services established in the Member's territory and securing the services of a seafarer for a shipowner, wherever located, should be required to assume obligations to ensure the proper fulfilment by shipowners of the terms of their employment agreements concluded with seafarers.

A cynic might reasonably ask: required by whom, and how ensured, given that both the shipowner and the relevant vessel is likely to be overseas and have no connection with the labour-supplying state?

Although the MLC is conceptually linked to private international law norms, primarily via the use of the connecting factor of the law of the flag state, it must be borne in mind that the MLC is designed to regulate public international relationships between states: unlike the examples of national and regional regulatory responses discussed above, the emphasis here is not on the enforcement of private law employment contracts between shipowners and seafarers.[74] Rather, the aim of the MLC is to achieve minimum standards in these employment relationships indirectly, via public international law control and enforcement on the part of flag, port and labour-supplying states. As a result, the effectiveness of the MLC framework depends on a number of factors:

(1) The willingness of the international maritime community to ratify the Convention. By this measure, the MLC is undoubtedly a resounding success. Its coverage of approximately 91 per cent of global tonnage is impressive,[75]

[72] MLC reg 5(3)(1).

[73] See I Urbina, 'Tricked and Indebted on Land, Abused or Abandoned at Sea', *New York Times* (9 November 2015).

[74] Fink, *Sweatshops at Sea* (2011) 197: 'the MLC notably stopped short of empowering the seafarers *on their own behalf*. To be sure, this was a bigger problem than the MLC – or even the ILO – itself.'

[75] At the time of writing, 93 states have ratified the MLC. Implementation of the MLC amendments is patchier. Carballo Piñeiro (n 19) 551 suggests that flag states are incentivised to ratify the MLC to avoid port state interventions legitimated by the Convention. It may also be argued that the minimum labour obligations and standards imposed by the MLC are hardly onerous for reasonable flag states or their shipowning interests.

with most flag states having ratified the Convention, with the exceptions of the open registry states of Bolivia, Cambodia, Moldova and Vanuatu, as well as the US.[76]

(2) The effectiveness of domestic implementation and enforcement, which is undoubtedly still uneven, particularly in respect of less developed countries, which may also be major open registry or labour-supplying states.[77]

(3) The ability to update minimum standards and conditions in a timely fashion to respond to changes in the maritime employment landscape. There is a regular updating process for the MLC,[78] and a subcommittee of the Joint Maritime Commission (JMC) of the ILO meets periodically to establish minimum wages through tripartite negotiations. The last meeting of the JMC was in 2018. It determined that the minimum monthly wage of able-bodied seafarers should increase from US$ 614 to US$ 618 as of 1 July 2019, US$ 625 as of 1 January 2020 and US$ 641 as of 1 January 2021, representing an overall increase of 4.5 per cent. However, this is well below the inflation rates of key labour-supplying states such as the Philippines and India.[79]

(4) Whether the MLC provisions can be seen, in private international law terms, as providing non-derogable or mandatory overriding rules. This is important because national and regional legal regimes often use the mechanism of non-derogable or overriding mandatory rules[80] to ensure minimum employee protection and avoid a 'race to the bottom' through party autonomy. In this regard, the MLC may be a victim of its own success. In aiming to achieve widespread ratification through 'a considerable degree of flexibility in the way Members implement [MLC] rights and principles',[81] the MLC divides itself

[76] See Lavelle, *The Maritime Labour Convention 2006* (2014) para 6.92: 'The international community is not holding its breath to see whether the USA ratifies the MLC'. See further United States Coast Guard, 'Navigation And Vessel Inspection Circular (NVIC) No 02-13', 30 July 2013, 2, available at www.regulations.gov/document?D=USCG-2012-1066-0034: 'As of the effective date of this NVIC, the United States has not ratified the MLC. Until such time that the United States ratifies the MLC, the Coast Guard cannot mandate enforcement of its requirements for U.S. vessels or for foreign vessels while operating on the navigable waters of the United States. However, Article V, Paragraph 7, of the Convention contains a "no more favorable treatment clause" that requires ratifying governments to impose Convention requirements on all vessels – even those from a non-ratifying government – when calling on their ports. As a result, U.S. vessels that cannot demonstrate compliance with the MLC may be at risk for Port State Control actions, including detention, when operating in the port of a ratifying nation.'

[77] ML McConnell, 'The Maritime Labour Convention, 2006 – Reflections on Challenges for Flag State Implementation' (2011) 10 *WMU Journal of Maritime Affairs* 127.

[78] See MLC arts 14 and 15.

[79] S Chambers, 'AB Pay Set to Rise by Just $27 over the Next Three Years' *Splash* (2 November 2018).

[80] See eg arts 8(1) and 9 of the Rome I Regulation; *Republik Griechenland v Nikiforidis*, Case C-135/15, ECLI:EU:C:2016:774 (also reported as *Hellenic Republic v Nikiforidis* [2017] ICR 147) on the restrictive interpretation to be given to the term 'overriding mandatory provisions' in the employment context, as derogating from the primary principle of party autonomy.

[81] MLC Explanatory Note to the Regulations and Code of the MLC, art 7. See also art 9: 'The second area of flexibility in implementation is provided by formulating the mandatory requirements of many provisions in Part A in a more general way, thus leaving a wider scope for discretion as to the precise

into Part A (mandatory standards) and Part B (non-mandatory guidelines). Some of the Part A mandatory standards, such as the minimum employment age, number of work and rest hours, the right to a seafarer employment agreement (SEA), repatriation and safety, health protection and hygiene rules are sufficiently detailed and concrete as to operate effectively as mandatory overriding legal rules.[82] Others, however, may not be. So, for example, the standard on wages simply provides for wages to be paid at least monthly and requires mechanisms to be put in place for wage remittances. The devil is always in the detail, and here the detail regarding the methods of calculation of wages and overtime, the setting of wage rates and minimum wages are all dealt with in Guideline B2(2), which is expressly stated to be non-mandatory.[83] Given this two-tiered structure of the MLC text, it is certainly not safe to assume that national courts – particularly courts of states that have not ratified the MLC – will necessarily characterise its provisions as mandatory overriding rules.[84] If they do not, such standards can conceivably be circumvented by choosing a legal system to govern the SEAs that prescribes a lower minimum wage or has no minimum wage at all.

Although the MLC has undoubtedly been successful in improving seafarers' employment conditions, enforcement difficulties for individual seafarers remain. Because the MLC is a public international law instrument designed to harmonise substantive employment standards and conditions, it does not address either choice of law or jurisdiction issues.[85] There is also no official public international forum for the adjudication of breaches of the MLC, although the instrument appears to be gaining some indirect relevance in UNCLOS disputes before the International Tribunal of the Law of the Sea (ITLOS).[86] However, where no potential breaches of UNCLOS are involved (for example, in cases of shipowners' underpayment or non-payment of wages) ITLOS will obviously have no jurisdiction to intervene.

action to be provided for at the national level. In such cases, guidance on implementation is given in the non-mandatory Part B of the Code.'

[82] So too Carballo Piñeiro (n 19) 548.

[83] Fink (n 2) 196–97: 'Whereas underage employment, inadequate food or drinking water, and repeated violation of work hours or non-payment of wages were singled out in the guidelines as potential justification for the detention in port of an offending ship, the document drew no such specific attention to rates of pay and/or benefits. … Thus, even as prospects for the MLC held out hope for a minimal, protective flooring for the welfare of the third-world seafarer, its power to affect living standards was likely to be severely limited. Most assuredly, it could do nothing by itself to harmonize the wage levels of the older seafaring supplier nations with those of more recent years.'

[84] Carballo Piñeiro (n 19) 549.

[85] Title 5(4) MLC: 'The provisions of this Title shall be implemented bearing in mind that seafarers and shipowners, like all other persons, are equal before the law and are entitled to the equal protection of the law and shall not be subject to discrimination in their access to courts, tribunals or other dispute resolution mechanisms. The provisions of this Title do not determine legal jurisdiction or a legal venue.' See Carballo Piñeiro (n 19) 537.

[86] See eg *The M/T 'San Padre Pio' Case (Switzerland v Nigeria), Provisional Measures*, ITLOS Case No 27, Order of 6 July 2019 [26], [49]–[50], [69], [89], [109].

VII. Jurisdiction and Forum

There are significant obstacles in the path of seafarers wishing to bring *in personam* actions against their employers. Although in most jurisdictions seafarers are in theory entitled to bring actions where the defendant shipowner is incorporated, the prevalent use by shipowners of offshore corporate entities and complex corporate 'webs' typically render this option practically impossible. Similarly, although seafarers are in theory entitled to complain to the flag state, 'due to the popularity of open registries, it has become difficult for seafarers to access the jurisdictions of Flag States, such as those in Panama, Bahama or Liberia'.[87] In Europe, the position is slightly more advantageous to seafarers, as the Brussels I Regulation (Recast), arts 21–23 allow the habitual place of work or place of engagement as alternative connecting factors, allow claims against non-EU employers and police jurisdiction clauses.[88] However, the Brussels I Regulation (Recast) does not cover compulsory arbitration clauses, such as those contained in the POEA SEC and in most cruise ship employment contracts.[89]

The access to an *in rem* action against the vessel and the power to arrest the ship for unpaid wages (broadly construed), personal injury or death under either national legislation or the Arrest Conventions remains the seafarer's most powerful remedy. This remedy has been supplemented by the 2014 MLC amendments, which came into effect in 2017, and require shipowners to provide financial security for four months' worth of unpaid wages. The P&I clubs have agreed to provide coverage for this obligation under the MLC Extension Clause 2016.[90] However, there are a number of obvious difficulties with this scheme. First, many cases of non-payment of seafarers' wages drag on for considerably longer than four months.[91] Secondly, it is difficult to see how P&I clubs can be forced to provide this cover where the shipowner is already insolvent (which will typically be the underlying cause of non-payment of wages). Thirdly, if P&I clubs do pay the seafarers' wages, are they thereby entitled (by subrogation or by assignment)

[87] See G Chen and D Shan, 'Seafarers' Access to Jurisdictions over Labour Matters' (2017) 77 *Marine Policy* 1, 2, who cite the example of Chinese seafarers working on a Panamanian-registered vessel. China has no diplomatic relationship with Panama, which makes enforcement of flag state responsibility under the MLC impracticable.

[88] See generally Lavelle (n 64) ch 9; U Grušić, 'Jurisdiction in Employment Matters under Brussels I: A Reassessment' (2012) 61 *ICLQ* 91. For the Brussels I Regulation (Recast), see [2012] OJ L351/1.

[89] See Y Farah and S Hourani, 'Recasting *West Tankers* in the Deep Water: How *Gazprom* and Recast Brussels I reconcile Brussels I with International Arbitration' (2018) 14 *Journal of Private International Law* 96.

[90] See O Fotinopoulou Basurko, 'El Abandono de la Gente de Mar y el Recurso al Aseguramiento Privado Vía P&I: Una Visión desde España' (2018) 10 *Cuadernos Derecho Transnacional* 409; R Petrinovića, I Lovrića, and T Perkušić, 'Role of P&I Insurance in Implementing Amendments to Maritime Labour Convention 2014' [2017] *Transactions on Maritime Science* 39; E Cheng, 'The Effectiveness of the Maritime Labour Convention's Financial Security Certificates in Resolving Claims for Unpaid Seafarers' Wages' [2021] *LMCLQ* 124.

[91] The global scale of this issue is alarming. ITF inspectors assisted seafarers to recover US$ 37.8 million in owed wages in 2018, and US$ 15.5 million in the first five months of 2019: see ITF Seafarers Maritime News, 'ITF wins $38m in back pay for crew', 7 June 2019.

to enforce the seafarers' wages maritime lien against the relevant vessel? The legal position on this last issue is far from clear.

The advantage to the seafarer of ship arrest and the wages maritime lien in particular is that it allows the *forum arresti* to assert jurisdiction over the ship directly and slice through the Gordian knot of corporate ownership and management. As discussed above, however, the use of compulsory jurisdiction and arbitration clauses in SEAs and the use of generic service agreements that are not linked to specific ships may erode the protective function of ship arrest and the availability of wage maritime liens for seafarers.[92]

VIII. Extra-contractual Claims

Breaches of maritime employment contracts will often also give rise to claims in tort/delict, particularly in respect of incidents involving the personal injury or death of seafarers. In such cases, seafarers may prefer to characterise their claims as tortious, particularly if this will give rise to a more favourable outcome on the application of relevant private international law principles.

In this regard, an application of the standard *lex loci delicti* rule will tend to default to the law of the ship's flag, at least where the vessel is on the high seas and the tort is internal to the ship.[93] The situation may be different where the vessel on which the seafarer injury or death occurs is in territorial waters[94] or (possibly) within the coastal state's EEZ.[95] Even in the US, where a multifactorial approach to determining the governing law of the tort is adopted,[96] the law of the flag plays

[92] See text at nn 26 and 29 above.

[93] See generally J Basedow, 'Rome II at Sea – General Aspects of Maritime Torts' (2010) 74 *Rabels Zeitschrift für ausländisches und internationales Privatrecht* 118; MP George, 'Choice of Law in Maritime Torts' (2007) 3 *Journal of Private International Law* 137.

[94] See *Union Shipping New Zealand Ltd v Morgan* [2002] NSWCA 124, (2002) 54 NSWLR 690: the Court applied NSW law as the *lex loci delicti* in respect of seafarer personal injury occurring on board an unloading vessel moored in NSW territorial waters, despite all other connecting factors (the law of the ship's flag, the governing law of the seafarer's employment contract, the employers place of establishment, the employee's habitual residence and the performance of the employment contract) pointing to New Zealand.

[95] *CMA CGM SA v The Ship Chou Shan* [2014] FCAFC 90, (2014) 224 FCR 384 [84]–[102]: where a tort occurs in a coastal state's EEZ, its law will not necessarily apply – this is likely to depend on how closely the tort is connected to the coastal state's legitimate interests in its EEZ under UNCLOS and customary international law of the sea.

[96] *Lauritzen v Larsen*, 345 US 571, 1953 AMC 1210 (1953): the *Lauritzen* factors are (1) the place of the wrongful act, (2) the law of the flag, (3) the allegiance or domicile of the injured party, (4) the allegiance of the shipowner, (5) the place of the seaman's employment contract, (6) the accessibility of a foreign forum, and (7) the law of the forum. The Supreme Court in *Hellenic Lines Ltd v Rhoditis*, 398 US 306, 309, 1970 AMC 994, 996 (1970) stated that 'the list of seven factors in *Lauritzen* was not intended as exhaustive' and instructed courts to consider the shipowner's base of operations as an additional factor.

a predominant role.[97] The application of the law of the flag as the deemed *lex loci delicti* may, of course, prove to be inappropriate or artificial for all the reasons that were discussed above in regard to the use of the law of the flag as a connecting factor to determine the *lex loci laboris*.

Whether the *forum arresti* will hear the claim in tort, and how it will be affected by the terms of the SEA, will depend on the *forum arresti*'s views on characterisation of concurrent tortious claims within a contractual framework. Some national courts will undoubtedly defer to the terms of the seafarer's employment contract, depending upon the interpretation of its wording.[98]

IX. Collective Bargaining Agreements and Industrial Action

Although the MLC refers to seafarers' rights of freedom of association and rights to organise, it does not cover collective bargaining agreements (CBAs) directly, thereby leaving workers and maritime unions 'to do the heavy lifting' in this regard.[99] As mentioned above,[100] much of the heavy lifting in the context of international maritime employment has been done by the ITF, which has for many years used a carrot ('blue certificate') and stick ('blacking') approach to improve shipowning interests' behaviour.[101] The ITF enters into CBAs with shipowning companies, who agree to apply the CBA terms to all seafarers working on board their vessels as an overriding addendum to their individual SEAs.

Perhaps because of this bargaining model, the ITF CBAs do not contain express choice of law or forum clauses, which has given rise to choice of law and enforcement issues in conflicts cases.[102] It has been suggested that the ITF should include

[97] *Bilyk v The Vessel Nair*, 754 F 2d 1541, 1545, 1985 AMC 2243, 2248 (9th Cir 1985): '*Lauritzen* … firmly mandates that the law of the flag presumptively controls, unless other factors point decidedly in a different direction'; *Pereira v Utah Transport Inc*, 764 F 2d 686, 689, 1985 AMC 2743, 2746 (9th Cir 1985): 'The second factor, law of the flag, is of "cardinal importance." … The *Lake Mendocino* flew the Liberian flag, and this fact should be accorded great weight in the choice of law analysis.'

[98] See eg *The Rainbow Joy* [2005] SGCA 36, [2005] 3 SLR(R) 719; *Sarabia v Oceanic Mindoro (The)* (1996) 26 BCLR (3d) 143: POEA compulsory arbitration clause covered tortious personal injury claims because the compulsory arbitration clause conferred on the NLRC 'original and exclusive jurisdiction over any and all disputes or controversies *arising out of* or by virtue of this Contract'; but *cf Noble v Carnival Corp* (2006) 80 OR (3d) 392: SEA providing that 'any dispute or claims arising *under this Agreement* shall be brought before the courts in England and governed by the laws of the Flag State, regardless of any other legal remedies which may be available' did not preclude the bringing of a tort claim in Ontario.

[99] Fink (n 2) 196.

[100] See text at n 2 above.

[101] See generally HR Northrup and RL Rowan, *The International Transport Workers' Federation and Flag of Convenience Shipping* (Philadelphia, University of Pennsylvania, 1983).

[102] See eg *Monterosso Shipping Co Ltd v International Transport Workers' Federation (The Rosso)* [1982] 2 Lloyd's Rep 120 (CA): Spanish law held to be the proper law of the ITF agreement.

an express choice of English law in its agreements,[103] but this may cause more problems than it solves, as the seafarers' SEAs are highly unlikely to be governed by English law. Indeed, given the multinational character of modern shipping crews, the outsourcing of labour and the use of third-party recruitment, placement and management agencies, it is highly unlikely that all workers' SEAs on the same vessel will be governed by the same legal system. The exact scope, enforceability and effect of seafarers' CBA cover will therefore tend to mirror the mosaic of the underlying governing laws of the crews' individual SEAs,[104] which presumably goes a long way towards explaining why disparities in wages and conditions between officers and ratings from different countries persist, despite the ITF and ILO's best efforts.

The MLC also does not refer to seafarers' rights to strike or undertake other forms of industrial action. This too is left to national law and may be restricted by the law governing the seafarer's SEA or the law of the flag state.[105] Where strikes or other industrial action do occur on board ships, an application of the *lex loci actus* rule to the loss or damage caused to the ship will typically result in an application of the law of the flag.[106] Where the loss or damage caused by the strike or industrial action is less direct, the law of the flag of the affected vessel will only be a relevant factor in determining the governing law.[107]

X. Conclusions

Despite gains in substantive harmonisation of working conditions through increased public international law regulation by instruments such as the MLC, private international law approaches to maritime ship management and crewing arrangements remain uneven and unsatisfactory. The insistence of private international law in characterising most employment issues as contractual (rather than as, say, a matter of status) inevitably opens up a Pandora's box of party autonomy, which, as well as providing shipowning interests with legitimate benefits of

[103] DM Kloss, 'The Enforceability of Foreign Collective Agreements' (1983) 46 *MLR* 774, 776. The ITF's headquarters is located in London.

[104] But see *Amosin v Mercury Bell (The)* [1986] 3 FC 454, (1986) 27 DLR (4th) 641 [5], where the Canadian Federal Court of Appeal applied the law of the ship's flag (Liberian law) to determine whether the CBA entered into between the shipowner and the ITF was enforceable on the basis that it was the law governing 'the rights of seamen against the owner of the ship on which they are serving'. In the absence of proof of Liberian law, the Court applied the Canada Labor Code, RSC 1970, c L-1.

[105] PJ Bauer, 'The Maritime Labour Convention: An Adequate Guarantee of Seafarer Rights, or an Impediment to True Reforms?' (2008) 8 *Chicago Journal of International Law* 643, 655–57; Carballo Piñeiro (n 7) 231 ff.

[106] Rome II Reg, art 9 (Regulation (EC) No 864/2007 of the European Parliament and of the Council of 11 July 2007 on the law applicable to non-contractual obligations [2007] OJ L199/40) and *DFDS Torline A/S v LO Landsorganisationen i Sverige*, Case C-18/02, [2004] ECR I-1417, [2004] 2 Lloyd's Rep 162, discussed by Basedow (n 93) 131 ff.

[107] ibid, *DFDS Torline A/S* [44].

rationalisation and efficiency, may also result in further exploitation and marginalisation of an already vulnerable workforce. National and regional attempts to counteract the worst excesses of party autonomy in relation to offshore workers through extended extraterritorial application of mandatory overriding rules, or by augmenting party autonomy with alternative applicable legal systems that may be more protective of employees, have produced mixed results.

In the former case, there are limits to what can be achieved beyond territorial waters without contravening UNCLOS provisions or principles of the customary international law of the sea. At public international law, the coastal state's rights in respect of its EEZ and continental shelf are not unlimited. Attempting to provide domestic law equivalent employment protection to workers operating in those zones may result in the assertion of extraterritorial jurisdiction that is considered exorbitant as it infringes on the rights of the flag state of the relevant vessel or other offshore workplace. There is the further issue of the extent and duration of the connection between the offshore workplace and the coastal state that is required before extraterritorial intervention from the coastal state is justifiable.

In the latter case, supplementing party autonomy with additional legal systems, most notably the law of the habitual place of work or at least the law of the 'home base' of the seafarer, has been relatively successful in raising the level of minimum protections. However, this model, which is based on the proximity principle of affording workers ready access to justice where they work or from where they are deployed, is much more difficult to transpose onto offshore workers, who are often recruited by offshore recruitment, placement or management companies in labour-supplying states and flown internationally to service various offshore workplaces. The traditional Savignian private international law model, which seeks to apply appropriate legal systems to legal issues on the basis of ideal connecting factors, struggles to 'localise' maritime crewing issues in a sensible and effective fashion in a hyper-globalised industry.

Significant discrepancies in seafarer wages and employment conditions along national and ethnic lines remain.[108] This gap appears to be gradually narrowing, not merely due to the positive effect of increased public international regulation, but also the economic realities of a shortage of qualified seafarers, despite the downturn in the international shipping industry in recent years. Nonetheless, significant employment abuses that would not be tolerated in land-based workplaces persist, even on board ships consistently certified as MLC compliant.[109] These cases serve

[108] See eg Zhang, Seafarer's Rights in China (2016) 37 fig 2.3 for a comparison of seafarers' wages by selected Asian countries and ranks: 'even on the same ship, it is very common that some Chinese officers earn less than a bosun or AB from other countries'. The wage gulf between seafarers from traditional maritime nations and less developed labour-supplying states is even greater: ibid, 119 ff. But *cf* Jason Jiang, 'Chinese Crew Wages Leap during Covid', *Splash 247.com*, 19 October 2020, at https://splash247.com/chinese-crew-wages-leap-during-covid/.

[109] See M Kabai, 'The Maritime Labour Convention and Open Registries: Hand in Glove or Chalk and Cheese' (2015) 30 *International Journal of Marine and Coastal Law* 189, 196–97.

as a testament to the limitations of both traditional private and public international law models in achieving a fair and decent offshore working environment for seafarers. It remains to be seen what impacts current trends towards greater automation, remote control, outsourcing and digitisation will have on the future of maritime management and crewing arrangements.[110] At the very least, they are likely to make the task of legally defining the maritime workplace and protecting the employment rights of international maritime workers even more complicated and challenging in the future.

[110] See eg *Seafarers and Digital Disruption* (study prepared by the Hamburg School of Business Administration for the International Chamber of Shipping, October 2018) at www.ics-shipping.org/docs/default-source/resources/ics-study-on-seafarers-and-digital-disruption.pdf.

Sustainability Perspectives on Management and Organisation in Shipping

4

Maritime Value Chains and Liability for Work Injuries

VIBE ULFBECK*

I. Introduction

Over the past decade, global value chains have increasingly attracted attention. Thus, for big and powerful companies, typically based in the Global North, outsourcing of production to the Global South has become a common business model. Outsourcing takes place through various company structures or through contract. Thus, a global value chain may consist of parent companies outsourcing tasks to both subsidiaries and contractual partners. The outsourcing model has drawn attention to the conditions under which the supplies and services are provided and to the environmental consequences of the production. In other words, the *production methods* used in the global value chain have attracted attention and revived an interest in the concept of corporate social responsibility (CSR), sometimes through major disasters, such as the one in Bangladesh in 2013, where a factory building collapsed, killing over 1,000 people.[1] This case drew attention to the question of the possible liability of the outsourcing company for work injuries in the value chain.

While several studies have focused on production value chains and the possible liability of the buyer for acts and omissions of the suppliers of the goods, the logistical side of the global value chain seems to have attracted less attention. However, companies outsourcing production to the Global South do not only need to contract for the production of the goods but also for the transport of the goods to warehouses or shops in the Global North. Thus, shipowners may form part of the global value chains of major, commercial actors. In addition, shipowners

* Professor of Law; Director, Centre for Private Governance (CEPRI), Faculty of Law, University of Copenhagen.

[1] On the Bangladesh disaster, see for instance www.pbs.org/newshour/world/5-years-after-the-worlds-largest-garment-factory-collapse-is-safety-in-bangladesh-any-better.

have their own value chains. For instance, shipowners enter into contracts for the supply of *goods* such as ships, spare parts for ships and ship supplies, such as food and clothing for crew, often through ship management companies. Shipowners also contract for a number of *services*. A shipowner may subcontract the task of carrying goods from one place to another wholly or partly to another shipping company or to a road carrier under multimodal transport contracts and shipowners may charter ships for the purpose of performing the sea transport. Shipowners also contract for harbour services in connection with loading and discharge, make repair contracts with shipyards and contracts for recycling of ships that have reached the 'end of life' stage.

The maritime industry was a latecomer to the CSR area.[2] This was so even though the maritime sector has always been exposed to CSR risks. For instance, the shipping industry is responsible for a fair percentage of the global carbon emissions and poor working conditions for seafarers has time and again been identified as a widespread problem. Today there is also in the maritime sector an increased awareness of the need of focus on production methods in the value chains.[3] Thus, shipowners are associated with their value chains and criticisable production methods may have negative reputational consequences and thereby imply commercial risks. In the same way, retailers and cargo owners may be associated with the maritime part of the value chain and working conditions on board vessels.

This chapter focuses on the way in which shipowners are organised in global value chains and the the way in which these are 'managed'. The purpose of the chapter is to examine the extent to which shipowners and cargo owners may incur liability for acts and omissions in the value chain giving rise to work injuries. In this connection, the chapter examines whether ways of organising the value chain, through either company structures or contracts may have an impact on liability issues and whether self-governing measures such as company codes of conduct may influence the assessment. The chapter focuses on the question of liability for work injuries as a consequence of poor working conditions.[4] Terminologically, the term 'value chain', rather than 'supply chain', is used to signify that it is the broader question of the possible liability for not only suppliers but also other contractual partners that is investigated.

[2] See for instance, J Skovgård, 'Responses to Institutional Processes: A Study of Corporate Social Responsibility in Danish Shipping Companies' in LL Froholdt (ed), *Corporate Social Responsibility in the Maritime Sector* (Cham, Springer International Publishing AG, 2018) 279.

[3] This is reflected in the codes of conduct that are today adopted by shipping companies. See further below, IV.

[4] In some jurisdictions, seafarers and other victims of industrial injuries are covered by special social schemes in case they suffer work injuries. However, this is far from always the case. Moreover, to the extent a social scheme is in place, the scheme may not cover the entire loss and the injured party will need to sue a liable party for damages under ordinary tort law in order to obtain full coverage. In the following, the focus is on ordinary tort law. The possible, obtainable compensation under various social schemes is not dealt with.

II. Regulatory Framework

The Maritime Labour Convention (MLC)[5] lays down public law requirements with regard to health and safety onboard ships. The requirements must be observed by shipowners. States that have ratified the convention must implement measures to meet these requirements. This may involve specifying both the concept of the 'ship owner',[6] the 'employee'[7] and the duties of the shipowner. Moreover, the Convention only concerns the responsibility with regard to seafarers.

However, today various international instruments are concerned with the duty of private companies to respect human rights, including workers' rights not only in their own businesses, but also in companies with which they do business. These instruments are relevant for maritime actors to the same extent as they are relevant for all other commercial parties. The UNGPs[8] require that business enterprises must carry out human rights due diligence (HRDD) in order to live up to their responsibilities to respect human rights. According to UNGP 15, HRDD should 'identify, prevent, mitigate and account for' actual or potential adverse human rights issues a company may be involved in through its own activities or business relationships. Also the ILO Tripartite Declaration of Principles concerning Multinational Enterprises and Social Policy,[9] the OECD Guidelines for Multinational Enterprises[10] and the OECD Guidance on Responsible Business Conduct[11] contain expectations of HRDD. All of these principles are not directly binding on companies and can therefore be categorised as 'international soft law'. With regard to hard law HRDD requirements, so far mainly reporting requirements for companies have been introduced. At EU level, the Non-Financial Reporting Directive[12] is an example of this. The Directive does not impose any HRDD duties on companies. It only requires reporting on what the company has actually done. Also at national level, an increasing number of reporting requirements are being introduced. The so-called 'Modern Slavery Acts' are examples of this.[13]

[5] The Maritime Labour Convention 2006. For a brief overview see J Constantino Chagas Lessa, 'The Maritime Labour Convention: An Overview' (2016) 22 *JIML* 379.

[6] ibid, 384.

[7] ibid, 385.

[8] See www.ohchr.org/Documents/Publications/HR.PUB.12.2_En.pdf.

[9] ILO Tripartite declaration of principles concerning multinational enterprises and social policy, adopted by the Governing Body of the International Labour Office at its 204th Session 8 Geneva, November 1977) and amended at its 279th (November 2000), 295th (March 2006) and 329th 8 March 2017) Sessions (ILO MNE Declaration).

[10] See www.oecd.org/corporate/mne.

[11] See mneguidelines.oecd.org/OECD-Due-Diligence-Guidance-for-Responsible-Business-Conduct.pdf.

[12] Directive 2014/95/EU of the European Parliament and of the Council of 22 October 2014 amending Directive 2013/34/EU as regards disclosure of non-financial and diversity information by certain large undertakings and groups.

[13] See UK Modern Slavery Act 2015, Australian Modern Slavery Act 2018, New Zealand Transparency in Supply Chains Bill 2017, California Transparency in Supply Chains 2010.

Some of the Modern Slavery Acts are particularly relevant to the maritime industry. For example, this is true of the UK Modern Slavery Act,[14] which entered into force in 2015. According to the Act, it is an offence to knowingly hold another person 'in slavery or servitude',[15] to make them 'perform forced or compulsory labour'[16] or to 'arrange or facilitate the travel of another person'[17] with a view to their being exploited. For the maritime industry, the Act creates awareness towards working conditions on board ships ('slavery'), but also towards ships as facilitators of human trafficking ('travel of another person'). However, the Act has a much broader reach, obliging companies to take an interest not only in their own companies but also in their supply chains. Thus, according to the Act, companies with a turnover over a certain threshold must publish an annual 'slavery and human trafficking statement' explaining the steps taken during the year to avoid slavery and human trafficking in any parts of its supply chains (goods and services) and any parts of its own businesses. The Act applies to any company 'carrying on business or part of a business in the UK' and has a turnover of £36 million or more. The interpretation of the term 'carrying on business in the UK' is uncertain. It may not apply to shipping companies who merely call at ports in the UK but it may likely apply if the shipping company has a branch office in the country. Such shipping companies are obliged to report the steps taken to avoid slavery and human trafficking in the supply chain. In addition, shipping companies may themselves form part of supply chains led by other companies (for example cargo-owners) who are subject to reporting requirements under the Act regarding their supply chains. In this way, shipping companies may also indirectly come under a reporting requirement through a 'cascading effect' of the Act. By indirectly imposing reporting requirements with regard to companies in the supply chain not necessarily based in the UK, the Act can be seen as having 'extraterritorial effect'.[18] The Act does not contain any provisions establishing tort liability for non-reporting. In this way, the reporting requirements too are a 'softer way' of approaching the responsibility of companies to respect human rights. However, both international soft law and reporting requirements may indirectly have an impact in a liability case.

Thus, as a reflex of internal soft law principles, reporting requirements and legislation with extraterritorial effect – many shipping companies and other actors in the maritime industry choose to develop codes of conduct and internal

[14] UK Modern Slavery Act 2015.

[15] ibid, s 1(1)(a).

[16] ibid, s 1(1)(b).

[17] ibid, s 2(1).

[18] With regard to human trafficking, the Act provides for special sanctions. Thus, if a person connected to the shipowner is convicted of a trafficking offence, the courts may order the forfeiture of the ship involved. This sanction is available if the convicted person is the owner of the ship or a director, secretary or manager of the company that owns the ship, if the person is in possession of the ship under a hire-purchase agreement, if the person is a charterer of the ship or acting as a captain of the ship. If the convicted person is not the owner itself, forfeiture is only available as a sanction if the owner knew or ought to have known of the intention to use the ship for trafficking purposes.

company policies concerning sustainability requirements in a broad sense, including workplace conditions, and the observance of these policies is made a condition for doing business with the company. As will be explained in what follows, such 'self-governance instruments' may indirectly impact liability.

To date, the French law on Vigilance[19] and the Dutch Child Labour Due Diligence Act[20] are the only examples of hard law mandatory HRDD requirements. However, at EU level, the European Commission has announced its intention to propose a directive on mandatory HRDD requirements in 2021.[21] Such legislation will also impact the maritime industry and emphasise the need to consider how to organise supply chains and networks in the sector in order to be able to control and contain liability exposure.

III. Some Starting Points

In the relationship between the shipowner and the voyage or time charterer it is the shipowner who is responsible for the working conditions on board the ship. As a starting point, this is the case also if the daily running of the ship has been outsourced to a management company.[22] This means that shipowners can be held liable if a crew member suffers a work injury on board the ship and there is sufficient basis for liability under the relevant national rules according to applicable choice of law rules, most often the law of the flag state.[23] If the carriage is subcontracted to another shipowner (the performing carrier), the 'other shipowner' (the performing carrier) will be liable for work injuries on board.

The value chain liability discourse raises the question whether the shipowner may be liable for work injuries in a wider extent than this and whether shipowners could become a liability to others.

In particular, one might ask whether shipowners could incur liability for work injuries suffered by employees of other employers when shipowners subcontract for the carriage of goods or other services and when they enter into contracts for the supply of goods or for the supply of ships. Some of these services and goods may be provided either through subsidiaries of the shipowner or through other companies with which the shipowner contracts. One question is whether the shipowner can be held liable for injuries to workers employed by such subsidiaries or contractual partners. Another question is whether the cargo owner may be

[19] Law no 2017-399 of 27 March 2017 on the 'Duty Vigilance of Parent Companies and Ordering Companies'.

[20] The Dutch Child Labour Due Diligence Act, 2019, Kamerstukken I, 2016/17, 34 506, A.

[21] As a basis for this, see 'Study on due diligence requirements through the supply chain' (EU Commission, 2020).

[22] If the management company is also the employer of the crew, the primary liability for working conditions may rest on the company; see for instance the Norwegian Ship Labour Act § 2-2.

[23] On choice of law rules in this regard, see Myburgh (ch 3).

held liable for work injuries suffered by employees of the shipowner happening on board the ship.

Theoretically, two different legal constructions can be thought of as a basis for liability: direct liability; and vicarious liability.

IV. Direct Liability

A. General Principles

In establishing direct liability in a supply chain context, the basic question is whether the shipowner owes a duty of care towards more 'distant plaintiffs' such as injured workers in the chain.

Until now, only a relatively small number of value chain liability cases have been brought before the courts. Although they have not concerned maritime value chains, the general principles expressed in the cases will also be relevant in the maritime context. Most cases have concerned parental liability for subsidiaries in the value chain, but some cases have also concerned liability for contracting parties.

With regard to parental liability, under company law the starting point is that the parent company is not liable for the acts and omissions of the subsidiary. This follows from the basic company law principle of separate entities and limited liability. According to company law, piercing of the corporate veil is only permitted in few and limited circumstances. However, over the past decade, direct tort law liability seems to have challenged these principles.[24]

The groundbreaking case in Europe in this regard was the much-discussed UK case *Chandler v Cape Plc.*[25] In this case, the parent company was held liable for work injuries sustained by workers employed by the subsidiary on the basis that the parent company – in the circumstances – had 'assumed responsibility' for these workers. Thus, the court emphasised the fact that the parent company and the subsidiary where in the same business but the parent company had superior knowledge on relevant aspects of health and safety, that the parent company knew or ought to have known that the workplace was unsafe and that the employees of the subsidiary could reasonably rely on the parent company to use its superior knowledge to protect them. With regard to the element of reliance on the part of the employees, the court noted that

> it is not necessary to show that the parent is in the practice of intervening in the health and safety policies of the subsidiary. The court will look at the relationship between the

[24] On the general topic of foreign direct liability (FDR), see L Enneking, *Foreign Direct Liability and Beyond – Exploring the Role of Tort Law in Promoting International Corporate Social Responsibility and Accountability* (The Hague, Eleven International Publishing, 2012); CA Witting, *Liability of Corporate Groups and Networks* (Cambridge, Cambridge University Press, 2017).

[25] *Chandler v Cape Plc* [2012] EWCA Civ 525, [2012] 1 WLR 3111.

companies more widely. The court may find that the element [of reliance] is established where the evidence shows that the parent has a practice of intervening in the trading operations of the subsidiary, for example production and funding issues.[26]

In other words, overall, the court focuses on the criteria of 'superior knowledge' and a 'practice of intervening' in establishing that the parent company has assumed responsibility for the employees of the subsidiary.

A later and recent Supreme Court decision *Lungowe v Vedanta Resources Plc*,[27] concerning environmental damage caused in Zambia, has confirmed the possibility of holding parent companies liable for damage caused by a subsidiary, emphasising that the specific criteria used in *Chandler* for finding an 'assumption of responsibility' were merely examples of how a liability case could be established according to ordinary principles of tort law. In the words of Lord Briggs:

> [T]here is nothing special or conclusive about the bare parent/subsidiary relationship, it is apparent that the general principles which determine whether A owes a duty of care to C in respect of the harmful activities of B are not novel at all[28] … the *Chandler indicia* are no more than particular examples of circumstances in which a duty of care may affect a parent … Although this if anything imposed an unnecessary straightjacket, both upon the claimants and the judge, it did not lead to the identification of a wider basis in law for the recognition of the relevant parental duty of care than that which, in my view, the law actually provides, by reference to basic principle.[29]

In this way, *Vedanta* has simplified the liability test concerning the parent/subsidiary relation.[30] Both cases show that the company law doctrine of separate entities is not a barrier to the application of the ordinary tort law principle of fault based liability.[31]

The role of company group policies in establishing liability was also addressed in *Vedanta*, where Lord Briggs concluded:

> I regard the published materials in which Vedanta may fairly be said to have asserted its own assumption of responsibility for the maintenance of proper standards of environmental control over the activities of its subsidiaries, and in particular the operations at the mine, and not merely to have laid down but also implemented those standards by training, monitoring and enforcement, as sufficient on their own to show that it is well arguable that a sufficient level of intervention by Vedanta in the conduct of operations at the mine may be demonstrable at trial, after full disclosure of the relevant internal documents of Vedanta an KCM, and of communications passing between them.[32]

[26] ibid, [80].

[27] *Lungowe v Vedanta Resources Plc* [2019] UKSC 20, [2019] 2 WLR 1051.

[28] ibid, [54].

[29] ibid, [56].

[30] Also in the case *AAA v Unilever plc* [2018] EWCA Civ 1532, [2018] BCC 959 it was emphasised that ordinary principles of tort law apply when assessing whether a parent company can be held liable for the acts of its subsidiary. See also the Australian case of *CSR Ltd v Wren* (1997) 44 NSWLR 463, applying ordinary tort law principles.

[31] One might ask whether or not tort law principles on vicarious liability for independent contractors could be used as an alternative to company law principles, see below, V(B).

[32] *Lungowe v Vedanta Resources Plc* (n 27) [61].

This shows that company policies and the enforcement of these policies can contribute to establishing an 'assumption of responsibility' on the part of the parent company for the activities carried out by its subsidiary.

The above cases concern parental liability for the acts of subsidiaries, not liability for contractual partners. However, it has been argued that since the cases are based on pure tort law reasoning, the liability principles must be applicable also in cases where the supply chain is organised as a contractual chain.[33] So far, only few cases have concerned supply chain liability for contractual partners and in no cases has liability been imposed. However, the Canadian case *Das v George Weston Ltd*[34] concerned a supply chain based on contracts and confirmed, by remaking reference to *Chandler*, that the tort law reasoning applied in the context of parent/subsidiaries can be transferred to supply chains based on contracts. Likewise, in a German case that concerned liability of the discount retailer KIK for work injuries in a supply chain based on contracts, the claimant relied heavily on the reasoning in *Chandler*,[35] but the case was closed on the basis of time limitations. An early US case, *Doe v Wal-mart*,[36] also concerned the possible liability of the US-based company Walmart for the employees of a contractual supplier. In this case, the plaintiffs argued that a duty of care towards the employees existed on the basis of the doctrine of the Good Samaritan according to which someone who undertakes a duty to assist another, assumes a duty to take reasonable care in doing so if a third party relies upon the undertaking. It was argued that Walmart's code of conduct, which had been published in various languages in all of Walmart's factories, contained the required undertaking. However, the court emphasised that there had been no day-to-day control of the factories by Walmart and that finding for the plaintiffs on the basis of their arguments would imply that all businesses would 'be responsible for the employment conditions for their workers and all of their workers employed by their suppliers'.

On the basis of the above, it is assumed that in assessing the possible direct liability of the shipowner for work injuries in the value chain, it is likely that the criteria will be the same whether the value chain is organised in company structures or whether it is based on contract. In both situations, the courts will focus on whether the shipowner knew or ought to have known that the workplace was unsafe and the extent to which the shipowner has intervened and/or exercised some kind of control over the value chain, thereby assuming responsibility for the

[33] P Rott and V Ulfbeck, 'Supply Chain Liability of Multinational Corporations' (2015) 3 *European Review of Private Law* 415, 432; C Terwindt, S Leader, A Yilmaz-Vastardis and J Wright, 'Supply Chain Liability: Pushing the Boundaries of the Common Law? (2018) 8 *Journal of European Tort Law* 261, but *cf* Witting, *Liability of Corporate Groups* (2017) 382 ff suggesting the law of conspiracy to fill the liability gap.

[34] *Das v George Weston Ltd* (2017) ONSC 4129.

[35] See Terwindt, Leader, Yilmaz-Vastardis and Wright, 'Supply Chain Liability' (2017) 261.

[36] *Doe v Wal-mart* (2009) 572 F 3d 677 (9th Cir).

injured party. In contrast, following *Vedanta*, it is not necessarily a requirement for imposing liability that the shipowner and the supplier can be regarded as being in the 'same business' or that the shipowner had 'superior knowledge' with regard to health and safety issues (as mentioned in *Chandler*), although establishing these factors may support an allegation that the shipowner was exercising control in the value chain. Likewise, establishing reliance on the part of the employees may support the view that the shipowner has exercised control of the chain.

As pointed out in *Vedanta*, Codes of Conduct and sustainability reports may be elements in documenting intervention in and control of the chain by the shipowner with regard to production methods. The line of reasoning seems to be that if a party is aware of a workplace problem in the chain and has control over the chain then it may also be possible to argue that this party ought to have taken measures to avoid work injuries, and that consequently, this party will be subject to fault based liability for not having taken the relevant precautions.

B. Shipowner Liability for Work Injuries in the Chain?

The extent to which shipowners exercise control over their value chains varies. Different shipowners may exercise a different amount of control and control may also vary depending on the type of service or product supplied through the chain. A shipowner will not always be the 'lead firm' in a value chain in which it is involved. For example, the terms of a carriage contract between the cargo owner and the shipowner may often in reality be dictated by the cargo owner rather than by the shipowner[37] and the terms in this contract may ripple down in the supply chain if the shipowner chooses to subcontract a carriage to another shipowner. In other chains, for example in chains for the provision of spare parts for the ship or for ships, the cargo owner will not play the same role in the chain, leaving more space to the shipowner. Also, different shipping companies may have different amounts of bargaining power. Research investigating power structures in maritime value chains is generally lacking.[38]

On the basis of these observations and reservations, it is assumed that shipowners can either be forced by cargo owners or other contractual parties to exercise control in the value chain. In addition, as explained above, reporting requirements may also force the shipowner to attempt to gain some kind of insight in and control over the value chain practices. CSR codes of conduct and CSR/sustainability reports from different companies may give some indications of the steps taken in this regard.

[37] RT Poulsen, S Ponte and H Sornn-Friese, 'Environmental Upgrading in Global Value Chains: The Potential and Limitations of Ports in the Greening of Maritime Transport' (2018) 89 *Geoforum* 83 on buyer-driven demands in the maritime supply chain.

[38] See ibid, with references.

For example, Maersk has developed a Supplier Code of Conduct, which is publicly accessible in various different languages.[39] The Code applies a wide 'supplier concept'. Thus, according to the Code, by supplier is meant:

> An entity, organization or individual providing goods or services, or acting or sourcing on behalf of AP Moller-Maersk (including any controlled joint ventures and associated companies) under a contract or otherwise, or as an agent, contractor or distributor.

Amongst other things, the Code addresses health and safety at work, requiring suppliers to provide a 'safe, secure and healthy working environment for all of their workforce'. This requirement is further specified in the Code and the Code is supplemented by guidelines detailing the requirements further.

According to the Code, all suppliers are required to commit to the adherence of the Code and Maersk assesses the supplier's compliance with the Code through audits, self-assessments and documentation reviews. Gaps in the implementation must be addressed by the suppliers and an improvement plan must be worked out in consultation with Maersk. In case of severe violations of the Code, Maersk reserves the right to terminate contracts with the supplier.

Moreover, according to Maersk's sustainability report for 2019, the following is stated:

> Furthermore, we conducted a series of critical risk reviews involving frontline workers in 2019, which resulted in the identification of the top five to seven critical risks of causing fatal and severe injuries across our operational contexts. These include: cargo fires, warehousing operations, dropped objects, mooring operations, man over board and working at height. Tangible, practical critical controls are being implemented to prevent and mitigate consequences, and a framework for the harmonization of critical risk management across the business is being developed.

Other major shipping companies have developed supplier codes of conduct.[40] The examples are an indication that shipowners do focus on their value chains and implement policies and control systems to ensure compliance with the principles in the chain.

As mentioned above, in both *Chandler* and *Vedanta*, the fact that the company had a common company policy with regard to production methods, was used as an argument that the company had assumed liability for the workers of the subsidiary. In other words, the efforts of the company to avoid work injuries in the supply chain may also be used as an argument that the company had the necessary control in the chain to incur liability for the injuries that were not avoided.

[39] See www.maersk.com/about/sustainability/supplier-code-of-conduct.

[40] See for example the supplier code of conduct of Evergreen Marine: www.evergreen-marine.com/tbi1/html/TBI1_SupplierCodeofConduct.pdf?v=1600069600630; APL UK Ltd: www.apllogistics.com/wp-content/uploads/2019/06/APLL-Vendor-Code-of-Conduct_Engl.pdf; and DSV: www.dsv.com/en/about-dsv/corporate-responsibility/policies/supplier-code-of-conduct.

C. Cargo Owner Liability for Work Injuries on Board the Ship?

While the concept of value chain liability may expand the range of employees for whom the shipowner can be regarded responsible, the concept also raises the question whether other actors in the chain could be held liable for work injuries suffered by employees of the shipowner on board the ship.

For cargo owners, sea carriers will constitute part of their value chains. At the same time cargo owners will often be importers of products or raw materials from different places in the world. Importers may be under specific duties to exercise due diligence with regard to production methods in their supply chains. For example, the EU Conflict Minerals Regulation[41] imposes on the importer of conflict minerals a duty to try to ensure that imported minerals due not come from areas in which there is risk that the minerals have been extracted by the use of forced labour. Likewise, the EU Timber Regulation[42] imposes a special obligation on the 'operator' to try to ensure that imported timber has not been harvested in an illegal manner. So far, however, no such rules impose a special obligation on the importer to exercise due diligence with regard to the working environment in the transport sector. However, other regulatory measures may indirectly incite a cargo owner to take an interest in the working environment on board the ship carrying its goods. The UK Modern Slavery Act constitutes an example. The Act imposes on companies carrying out business or part of their business in the UK a duty to report on measures to prevent 'modern slavery' in their supply chains. Although poor working conditions on board ships will only in extreme cases amount to 'modern slavery' ('forced or compulsory labour') the Act forces companies to take an interest in working conditions in their value chains.

Cargo owners may be linked to the shipowner either by a contract of carriage or by a charterparty (or both). Under basic maritime law principles, the owner of the vessel is responsible for the crew under both time charterparties and voyage charterparties.[43] Value chain liability principles may obstruct this clear division of responsibilities by pointing to the cargo owner (charterer) as a potential additional liability subject.[44] According to the principles established in the case law described

[41] Regulation (EU) 2017/821, [2017] OJ L130/1 (Conflict Minerals Regulation). See eur-lex.europa.eu/legal-content/EN/TXT/PDF/?uri=OJ:L:2017:130:FULL&from=EN. A new Conflict Minerals Regulation will enter into force in 2021; see trade.ec.europa.eu/doclib/docs/2017/march/tradoc_155423.pdf.

[42] Regulation (EU) No 995/2010, [2010] OJ L295/23 (Timber Regulation). See eur-lex.europa.eu/legal-content/EN/TXT/PDF/?uri=CELEX:32010R0995&from=EN.

[43] See for instance T Falkanger, HJ Bull and L Brautaset, *Scandinavian Maritime Law: The Norwegian Perspective*, 4th edn (Oslo, Universitetsforlaget, 2017) 315.

[44] This aspect has recently surfaced in Australia where the vessel *Unison Jasper* was detained for violations of the MLC 2006. The issue of a possible responsibility of the cargo owner has been brought up; see www.newcastleherald.com.au/story/6858758/ship-seized-on-newcastle-wharf-over-alleged-crew-underpayment-and-bullying.

above, such liability could be imposed if it is possible to show an 'assumption of responsibility' on the part of the cargo owner for work conditions on board the ship. Cargo owners often have a considerable amount of bargaining power vis-à-vis shipowners and may be able to insist on the shipowners' adherence to the cargo owner's code of conduct. Consequently, it cannot be excluded that a cargo owner could be seen as having assumed responsibility for workplace conditions on board a ship in particular if the relationship between the cargo owner and the shipowner is a long-term, collaborative relationship.

D. The Dilemma of Control

As explained above, direct liability of maritime actors rests on the concept of 'assumption of responsibility'. This raises the question whether maritime actors can avoid liability by *not* taking control. Most often, neither shipowners nor cargo owners will be under any obligation to contract which means that liability can be avoided by avoiding contracts with companies that have problematic workplace conditions. For instance, a cargo owner can decide not to contract with a shipowner renowned for sailing under flags of convenience for the purpose of evading burdensome regulatory requirements[45] and a shipowner can refuse to transport cargo which has been produced under workplace conditions that are substandard.

Yet, in other situations, avoiding responsibility may be more difficult. Firstly, as explained, various reporting requirements and reputational concerns may in reality force maritime actors to take some amount of control. Secondly, although the cited case law suggests that companies incur liability because they (voluntarily) assume liability it seems unlikely that shipowners and cargo owners can avoid liability by 'turning a blind eye' to workplace conditions that they could potentially impact in an ongoing relation or when entering into a contract.[46]

E. Conclusion

This analysis has shown that value chain liability for shipowners and other maritime parties cannot be excluded. On the one hand, this liability hinges on the extent to which the maritime actors intervene and take control in the chain.

[45] On the strategic use of flag state rules, see Girvin (ch 2).

[46] For discussions concerning the possible difference between 'actual control' and 'potential control' see P Gilliker, *Vicarious Liability in Tort: A Comparative Perspective* (Cambridge, Cambridge University Press, 2010) 67 referencing van Gerven, Lever and Larouche: 'the focus of the [control] test is no longer on the fact of instructing the employee how to do his job but the *possibility* of being able to control the employee's actions'; A Sanger, 'Crossing the Corporate Veil. The Duty of Care Owed by a Parent Company to the Employees of its Subsidiary' (2012) 71 *CLJ* 478, 480. See also Witting (n 24) 380: 'When the exercise of control is absent, negligence law does not provide a remedy'.

On the other hand, it can hardly be assumed that liability can always be avoided by deliberately not taking control. In any case, in order to succeed with a fault based claim, the plaintiff must show that the company had both knowledge of the unsafe working conditions and the power to do something about it. Most often, lifting this burden of proof for fault-based liability is not easy. This raises the question whether a claim could instead be based on notions of vicarious liability.

V. Vicarious Liability for Independent Contractors?

A. General Rule on Vicarious Liability

By vicarious liability is meant liability for the acts of others. Vicarious liability is a form of strict liability. For the plaintiff it has the advantage that it is not necessary to prove fault on the part of the employer. The starting point in most legal systems is that vicarious liability only applies in the context of employers and employees.[47] Thus, an employer can be held liable for the acts of an employee, but normally not for the acts of an independent contractor. The basic reason for this is that the independent contractor is not subject to the instructions of the employer and not under the control of the 'employer' in the same way as employees. However, there are exceptions to this rule.

B. General Exceptions

Different legal systems have developed the same or similar exceptions to the general rule that excludes liability for independent contractors. Firstly, liability may be imposed on the employer if it in reality retains control over the work performed by the independent contractor. Another exception states that it is generally not possible to escape liability for injuries incurred by the performance of services that involve a 'peculiar risk'. Finally, common law systems recognise the doctrine of 'non-delegable duties'.

In the supply chain context, these exceptions, which will be dealt with further below, may seem to have limited application. Firstly, it could be argued that they cannot apply to all types of suppliers. Thus, an independent contractor is someone who is given the task of performing some kind of service. Consequently, a mere seller of products cannot be regarded an independent contractor.[48] The view may be challenged if it is in fact the buyer ordering and defining the product to be

[47] S Galand-Carval, 'Comparative Report on Liability for Damage Caused by Others (Part 1)' in J Spier (ed), *Unification of Tort Law: Liability for Damage caused by Others* (The Hague, Kluwer Law international, 2003) 306.

[48] G Williams, 'Liability for Independent Contractors' (1956) 14 *CLJ* 180.

delivered, in particular if the supplier delivers the products to the buyer on a long-term basis and under the instructions of the buyer.[49] However, some suppliers of products may fall outside the definition of independent contractors. Secondly, it may also be argued that the rules establishing vicarious liability for independent contractors cannot apply if the supplier is a subsidiary providing products or services to the parent company because the imposition of vicarious liability would amount to a piercing of the corporate veil which, as a general rule, is not allowed.[50] Also this argument may be challenged. If it is recognised that the company law doctrine of separate entities is not a barrier for imposing fault-based liability on the parent company for the acts of the subsidiary (see above), why should the doctrine then prevent the imposition of vicarious liability?[51]

The most general exception to the rule excluding vicarious liability for independent contractors concerns 'retention of control'.[52] Thus, to the extent the employer in reality retains control over the independent contractor, liability may be imposed. In the US case *Abdur Rahaman v JC Penny Corporation Inc*,[53] this test was applied as a basis for denying liability of a buyer towards the injured employees of a supplier. Thus, the court found that no proof of 1) active control of manner and method of performing the work contract; 2) a voluntary undertaking to implement safety measures; or 3) retention of control over the premises during work. In the maritime context, this rule invites the same considerations with regard to the possible impact of codes of conduct as does the discussion on direct liability as explained above. In general, it must be assumed that the level of control required to satisfy the test for imposing vicarious liability is higher than the level required in order to establish an assumption of responsibility as an element of fault-based liability. Presumably, it will most often be difficult to establish this kind of control with suppliers or other contracting parties on the part of the shipowner. Likewise, cargo owners will not normally have the required amount of control with shipowners to trigger vicarious liability for the acts and omissions of the shipowner.

The other exception, which may be considered, concerns the notion of 'non-delegable duties' in common law systems. The essence of the concept is that some duties cannot be delegated and if they are the person delegating remains

[49] V Ulfbeck and A Ehlers, 'Direct and Vicarious Liability in Supply Chains' in V Ulfbeck, A Andhov and K Mitkidis (eds), *Law and Responsible Supply Chain Management* (Abingdon, Routledge, 2014) 101.

[50] Along this line, see Witting (n 24) 401, 412.

[51] For a more in-depth analysis of this argument, see Ulfbeck and Ehlers, 'Direct and Vicarious Liability' (2014) 98 ff, V Ulfbeck, 'Vicarious Liability in Groups of Companies and in Supply Chains – Is Competition Law Leading the Way?' (2019) 3 *Market and Competition Law Review* 107, 121.

[52] For a fuller explanation of the content of this principle, see Ulfbeck and Ehlers (n 49) 102. The control test is also widely used to determine whether an individual is to be regarded an employee of the employer. In this regard, the test has also been criticised for being too narrow, see Gilliker, *Vicarious Liability in Tort* (2010) 60.

[53] CA No N15C-07-174 MMJ [2016].

liable towards the injured party.[54] A well known non-delegable duty is the duty of the employer to ensure that reasonable care is taken to provide employees with a safe system of work. Shipowners often choose to delegate 'crewing matters' to a ship management company. The duties of the ship management company are determined on a contractual basis and may vary. The ship management company may have undertaken to organise training seminars and deliver safety instruction courses for crew members.[55] It must be assumed that, according to the doctrine of non-delegable duties, the shipowner remains liable should crew members employed by the shipowner be misinstructed during the course of such training programmes. It seems arguable that this should also be the case if the crew members are (technically) employees of the ship management company.[56] However, in general, the doctrine of non-delegable duties does not render liable the shipowner for injuries suffered by employees of *other* employers, for instance employees of a trucking company or a shipyard.[57] Consequently, the doctrine of non-delegable duties can only be relevant to a limited extent as a basis for imposing liability on the shipowner for work injuries in the value chain. Likewise, the doctrine will not constitute a basis for imposing liability on the cargo owner for work injuries on board the ship since the cargo owner does not (attempt to) delegate workplace responsibility by entering into a contract with the shipowner.

The last general exception to be considered is the 'peculiar risk' doctrine. This doctrine is particularly clearly formulated in the US in Restatement (Third) of Torts, sections 58 and 59:

> Section 59. An actor who hires an independent contractor for an activity that the actor knows or should know poses a peculiar risk is subject to vicarious liability for physical harm when the independent contractor is negligent as to the peculiar risk and the negligence is a factual cause of any such harm within the scope of liability.

The peculiar risk must be inherently dangerous. The principle has also been recognised in English law[58] and in Scandinavian law.[59] Most of the activities which shipowners subcontract can hardly be considered as posing 'peculiar risks' or as

[54] Technically, non-delegable duties are not seen as establishing vicarious liability, but a form of fault-based liability, but see Gilliker (n 46) 117: 'The operation of this doctrine greatly resembles that of vicarious liability'; and P Morgan, 'Recasting Vicarious Liability' (2012) 71 *CLJ* 615, 640: 'Non-delegable duties are often resorted to and adopted as a response to perceived inadequacies in vicarious liability'.

[55] A-P Pollalis, *Third Party Ship Management Companies and their Legal Relationship with their Principals* (2009) 7, available at thesis.eur.nl/pub/33339.

[56] See for this purpose the BIMCO standard contract CREWMAN B; S Gault and SJ Hazelwood (gen eds), *Marsden and Gault, Collisions at Sea*, 14th edn (London, Sweet and Maxwell, 2016) 550.

[57] ibid, 553 which mentions examples of shipowner liability for injuries sustained by its own employees in connection with bareboat chartering and repair contracts.

[58] WV Horton Rodgers, 'Liability for Damage Caused by Others under English Law' in Spier, *Unification of Tort Law* (2003) 76.

[59] V Hagstrøm and A Stenvik, *Erstatningsrett*, 2nd edn (Oslo, Universitetsforlaget, 2019) 274; B von Eyben and H Isager, *Lærebog i Erstatningsret*, 9th edn (Copenhagen, DJØF Forlag, 2019) 193, 196.

involving 'abnormally dangerous' activities. For example, a sea carriage or a road carriage which has been contracted out cannot be said to involve a peculiar risk that is inherently dangerous or an abnormally dangerous activity. In contrast, it is well known that work performed in the course of ship-breaking may involve dangers when it is done at unauthorised facilities. However, in these situations, shipowners do not technically hire an independent contractor to carry out the work. Rather, the ship is sold at a low price to a third party who in turn delivers it for ship-breaking, typically at a beach. Although this may be regarded an indirect way of hiring an independent contractor, it seems doubtful whether the principle can be used for the imposition of liability for work injuries on the part of the shipowner.[60] Likewise, although work conditions on board ships are known to be at times problematic, cargo owners can typically not be regarded as outsourcing inherently dangerous work by contracting with a sea carrier.

In conclusion, the imposition of vicarious liability in the maritime supply chain on the basis of the general exceptions described is far from straightforward.

C. Special Rule on Vicarious Liability in Nordic Maritime Law

In the Nordic Maritime Codes, an extended version of the concept of vicarious liability is applied. This rule could become relevant if the injury happens in the Nordic countries or onboard a ship sailing under a Nordic flag. According to the rule, the shipowner is liable not only for the acts of employees but also for someone who provides work 'in the service of the ship'. Taking the Danish Maritime Code as an example, § 151 reads: 'The shipowner (reder) shall be liable to compensate damage caused in the service by the fault or negligence of the master, crew, pilot, tug or others performing work in the service of the ship.'[61] This means that vicarious liability covers not only employees, but also certain independent contractors. This dramatically broadens the scope of the classical rule on vicarious liability.[62]

It is important to note, however, that the work must have been performed in the service of the *ship*, not in the service of the *shipowner*. It is generally assumed that, for instance, independent contractors loading, discharging or towing the vessel are covered by the provision so that the shipowner incurs vicarious liability for damage caused by these independent contractors.[63] This applies if a third party is injured. However, it must also apply to work injuries suffered by an employee of the independent contractor due to poor working environment

[60] For environmental law implications, see Glinski (ch 5). For background knowledge on shipbreaking, see M Galley, *Shipbreaking: Hazards and Liabilities* (Cham, Springer, 2014).

[61] There are parallel provisions in the Norwegian Maritime Code § 151, the Swedish Maritime Code (1994:1009), ch 7, § 1 and the Finnish Maritime Code (15.7.1994/674) ch 7, § 1.

[62] In contrast, it is the clear general rule in English law that the shipowner is only liable for its employees, not independent contractors, see Gault and Hazelwood, *Marsden and Gault* (2016) 551.

[63] Falkanger, Bull and Brautaset, *Scandinavian Maritime Law* (2017) 200.

conditions for which the independent contractor as an employer is responsible.[64] It follows directly from the wording of the provision that pilots are also covered, whether the use of these is voluntary or mandatory.[65] The rule applies although there is no contract between the shipowner and the independent contractor causing the injury. The classical example is a charterer who hires a stevedore company to take care of loading/discharging and the stevedore company hires longshoremen to do the job.[66] If damage or injuries are caused by one of the longshoremen, the shipowner is liable. The reason is that the longshoreman is working in the service of the ship. The shipowner may even incur vicarious liability for public authorities such as harbours to the extent the work performed is in the service of the ship.[67]

As will be apparent, the concept of working 'in the service of the ship' is a rather broad one. It does have its limits, however. Activities that cannot be characterised as 'typical shipowner activities' fall outside the scope of the concept.[68] Classical examples are icebreakers and salvors.[69] This means that a shipowner that contracts out tasks to an icebreaker or a salvor does not become vicariously liable for damage caused by these actors, including work injuries. The rationale is that a shipowner should not be able to avoid liability by contracting out a task that could have been carried out by the shipowner itself. The question is to what extent the provision can be used for establishing supply chain liability of the shipowner.

As explained, subcontracting is widespread in the maritime sector. It is most likely that shipowners cannot be held liable for work injuries on board subcontracted ships under § 151. Thus, the subcontracted ship can hardly be said to be in the service of the (other) ship; rather, it is in the service of the carrier/shipowner.[70] This applies all the more if a different type of carrier – for instance, a road carrier – is subcontracted by the shipowner to perform part of the carriage. As a general rule, a trucker cannot be seen as being in the service of the ship, but of the carrier.

In contrast, a shipyard that repairs the ship must be seen as working in the service of the ship. However, the extent to which the shipowner may be held vicariously liable for damage caused by the shipyard depends on the type of repair carried out and possibly also the circumstances under which it has been carried out. It is normally assumed that major repair works are not covered by § 151.[71] The reason for this is that carrying out a major repair cannot be characterised as a typical

[64] As an example, see RT 1931.788 concerning work injuries.

[65] The same is the case in English law, see Gault and Hazelwood (n 56) 554.

[66] Falkanger, Bull and Brautaset (n 43) 200.

[67] As an illustration see ND 1984.122 NSC (Norwegian Supreme Court).

[68] Falkanger, Bull and Brautaset (n 43) 207.

[69] ibid.

[70] For the same reason a shipping company which charters a ship on time charter or voyage charter from another shipping company cannot be held liable for work injuries on board the ship under § 151. This would also obstruct the basic division of labour between shipowner and charterer.

[71] Falkanger, Bull and Brautaset (n 43) 207.

shipowner activity. In contrast, smaller repairs that could have been carried out by the shipowner itself might fall under the provision. In addition, under a lengthy stay at a shipyard, the shipyard may end up taking over tasks that would normally have been carried out by the shipowner.[72] However, there are no cases confirming the vicarious liability of the shipowner in this situation. On the contrary, an early case seems to reach the opposite result with regard to work injuries.[73]

In running the ship, shipowners also contract with a number of suppliers of various products, such as clothing for seafarers, food for voyages, spare parts for the ship, etc. Such purchases are often made through ship management companies and on the basis of long-term contracts.[74] Probably, such purchases must be considered a typical shipowner activity. However, it seems doubtful whether selling supplies to a ship can be seen as providing a service of the ship. Even if it is argued that the distinction between supplying goods and services is to some extent arbitrary in particular in the case of long-term contracts (see above), § 151 expressly states that it applies to damage caused by someone performing work in the service of the ship. Consequently, it must be assumed that it would not be possible to hold the shipowner vicariously liable under § 151 for injuries which have taken place at the workplace of this type of supplier.

Shipyards also act as suppliers of shipowners when they on the order of a shipowner build and sell ships to the owner. In these situations, the ship itself is the product that is supplied to the shipowner. If workers have suffered injuries or been exposed to a damaging health environment while building the ship, the question arises whether the shipowner can be held liable for such work injuries.[75] Quite clearly, § 151 would not establish a basis for liability in this situation. By providing a ship, the shipyard is not performing work in the service of the ship itself.

When a ship is to be scrapped it is typically sold for demolition. Thus, the shipowner enters into a sales contract with the buyer. An example of a contractual standard term is the BIMCO form Demolishcon 2003. According to cl 17 of the contract, the IMO Guidelines regarding environmental aspects of the scrapping must be observed both by the buyer and the seller. In addition, the seller has the right to visit the ship recycling facility 'to ascertain that safe and environmentally sound practices are being conducted'. The buyer of the ship for demolishing cannot be regarded as acting in the service of the ship. The same goes for the recycling facility even though it carries out work. In addition, demolition cannot be regarded a typical shipowner activity. Consequently, § 151 cannot be used as a basis for liability in this situation.

[72] ibid.

[73] See Rt 1931.788 NSC ORWELL.

[74] Pollalis, *Third Party Ship Management Companies* (2009) 8–9.

[75] A recent case in Denmark concerned the possible responsibility of the buyer (the Danish Defense Ministry), of a ship which turned out to have been constructed by prison workers from North Korea, see shippingwatch.com/carriers/article9898697.ece.

D. Conclusion

On the basis of the above, it can be concluded that notions of vicarious liability will most often not be applicable as the basis of liability for work injuries in the value chain. The clear general rule is thus that there is no liability in tort for independent contractors. Even in the Nordic jurisdictions, which recognise a much broader concept of vicarious liability of the shipowner, this special notion will most often not be applicable as a basis for value chain liability since it is a requirement that the tortfeasor has acted in the service of the ship. This limits the reach of the rule.

VI. Limitation of Liability

As explained above, although there is no general rule establishing vicarious liability of the shipowner or other maritime actors for the acts and omissions of business partners, it cannot be ruled out that it would be possible to establish direct liability of a maritime actor towards employees in the value chain. This raises the question as to what extent maritime actors will be able to limit liability for such claims. As a general rule, shipowners have the right to limit liability under the global limitation rules, notably the Convention on Limitation of Liability for Maritime Claims (LLMC 1976).[76] According to art 3(e) of the LLMC 1976, claims of the servants of the shipowner may be excluded from limitation. Although the employees of the shipowner are to some extent protected under this rule, the rule does not protect employees of other actors in the maritime value chain. In a claim against the shipowner, such claims could be subject to limitation under art 2.1(a) concerning personal injury claims in general. However, the shipowner's right to limit liability under this rule is limited to injury 'occurring on board or in direct connexion with the operation of the ship'. Oftentimes, injuries happening at other workplaces in the value chain will not be considered as occurring 'in direct connexion with the operation of the ship'. Consequently, to the extent the shipowner can be held liable for work injuries in the value chain, the global limitation rules will most often not be applicable and the injured party will be entitled to full compensation.

Conversely, should a charterer be held liable for work injuries on board the ship, it must be assumed that the charterer will have the right to limit its liability under the global limitation rules. According to art 1(2), the charterer belongs to the group of actors who has the right to limit,[77] and crew members will not

[76] And the LLMC Protocol 1996.

[77] See, eg, Falkanger, Bull and Brautaset (n 43) 214–215, mentioning that this right to limit may for instance be relevant for a time charterer or a voyage charterer if a bill of lading imposes liability on the charterer as carrier just as it may be relevant if the shipowner files a recourse action against the charterer. For English law, *cf CMA CGM SA v Classica Shipping Co Ltd (The CMA Djakarta)* [2004] EWCA Civ 114, [2004] 1 Lloyd's Rep 460.

be protected against this right if they are employees of the shipowner and not the charterer.[78] Consequently, the general rule in art 2.1(a) concerning personal injury will apply and give the charterer (voyage or time charterer) the right to limit liability. This means that crew members will not necessarily be entitled to full compensation in a claim against the charterer. In contrast, a cargo owner, who is not at the same time a charterer, will not have the right to limit liability under the LLMC 1976 since the cargo owner itself does not belong to the group of actors who have this right.

These differences with regard to the right to limit liability may be difficult to justify.The examples illustrate how a traditional building block in the maritime liability system may come under pressure if the new notion of value chain liability becomes a reality also in the maritime sector.

VII. Conclusions

The notion of value chain liability has recently begun to attract attention. It focuses on the possible liability of those commercial actors who drive global value chains and have leverage in the entire chain to the extent that they can influence and sometimes in reality even dictate terms of contracts and thereby also indirectly influence workplace conditions in the chain. So far, it is mainly production chains that have been under scrutiny. However, transport and logistics are closely connected to the production process and shipowners form part of global value chains and also form their own value chains. While discussions of liability for work injuries in shipping have so far mainly focused on the shipowner's liability for work injuries on board the ship, the value chain liability discourse raises the question whether shipowners may in reality be subject to a more far-reaching liability for work injuries, namely for work injuries taking place in the value chain which they form part of. It equally raises the question whether other maritime actors, such as cargo owners, could be held liable for work injuries taking place in the maritime part of the chain on board the ship.

Value chains may be organised through subsidiaries or on the basis of contract. From a liability perspective, it seems that the means of organisation does not matter. In assessing the possible liability of the shipowner for work injuries in the chain, the same criteria apply whether the chains are organised through subsidiaries or contractually. As a general rule, shipowners and other maritime actors are not vicariously liable for acts and omissions in the chain. This also applies under Nordic law, despite the more far reaching rules on liability for independent contractors in the maritime sector in these legal systems. In contrast, case law supports the view that maritime actors may incur fault-based liability for work

[78] See, eg, Falkanger, Bull and Brautaset (n 43) 219.

injuries in the value chain to the extent the actor – for instance through codes of conduct – has intervened in and taken control over workplace conditions in the chain.

At first glance, this may be seen as putting the maritime actor in a control dilemma with regard to management of the value chains. Thus, it might seem that the more control is taken to avoid injuries, the greater the exposure to liability. However, in reality this may be a false dilemma. Firstly, reporting requirements often force companies to take an interest in what goes on in the chain. This forced interest will be strengthened if mandatory due HRDD requirements are imposed on companies in the EU. Secondly, from a tort law perspective it already seems doubtful whether it would be possible to escape liability by deliberately not taking control over something that could be controlled. In conclusion, it seems that shipowners should take into consideration the risk that in the future their liability for work injuries will not only concern injuries taking place on the board the ship but may be much more far-reaching and not limited by flag state rules or global limitation rules. Likewise, cargo owners should be aware that their liability for work injuries may extend to injuries that take place on board ships and only if they are also charterers may they have the right to limit liability.

At the more general level, the notion of value chain liability may have the potential to partly obstruct the traditional distribution of risks and liabilities between parties in a maritime value chain, just as the system of limitation of liability may prove not be aligned with new liability considerations. This may in turn give rise to new insurance issues that must be handled as part of the implications of the development for the management of maritime value chains in the future.

5

Sustainable Shipping: The New Governance Approach to Ship Recycling

CAROLA GLINSKI*

I. Introduction

The issue of sustainable ship recycling has gained new currency with the entry into force of Regulation (EU) No 1257/2013 on ship recycling[1] for vessels sailing under an EU flag. This Regulation is meant to pre-implement the new regulatory approach of the Hong Kong International Convention for the Safe and Environmentally Sound Recycling of Ships.[2] The Ship Recycling Regulation has introduced specific product responsibility for ships, and allows for recycling only in authorised facilities.

This chapter analyses the new governance approach, its differences to and inconsistencies with general waste shipping regimes, and the potential consequences for the management of ship recycling. After a short overview of the current practice of ship dismantling, the chapter outlines the main requirements of the international and European waste shipment regime, the difficulty of applying them in practice, and the new approach of the Hong Kong Convention and the European Ship Recycling Regulation. The chapter compares the levels of protection, control and enforcement of the two regimes before analysing the resulting collision of regimes, coverage and applicability and the concrete impact this has on the decisions made by shipowners. It concludes that the coexistence and applicability of the two differing regimes on the dismantling of ships has the potential for improving ship recycling conditions in the foreseeable future.

* Associate Professor, Centre for Private Governance, Faculty of Law, University of Copenhagen.

[1] [2013] OJ L330/1. In force 31 December 2018.

[2] Adopted on 15 May 2009 but not yet in force. On the Hong Kong Convention, see MN Tsimplis, 'The Hong Kong Convention on the Recycling of Ships' [2010] *LMCLQ* 305.

II. The Problem of Ship Dismantling

A. Ship Dismantling in Practice

Dismantling of the vast majority of ships still takes place under highly unsafe, unhealthy and environmentally problematic conditions. In the first half of the last decade, more than 1,000 large ocean-going vessels, such as tankers, container ships, and cargo and passenger ships were sold for dismantling every year.[3] Since 2015, the figures have dropped to 862 in 2016 and 674 in 2019.[4] Nevertheless, these numbers are still high.

For 2019, the NGO Shipbreaking Platform reported that almost 90 per cent of the gross tonnage dismantled globally was broken down on only three beaches in Bangladesh, India and Pakistan.[5] Beaching is highly unsafe, and it leads to many accidents; in 2019, according to the NGO Shipbreaking Platform, 26 workers were killed breaking ships and at least another 34 seriously injured.[6] Beaching is also very unhealthy for neighbouring communities and environmentally disastrous as often highly toxic parts or substances are broken out or extracted from the wreck and dumped or burned on the spot. This practice has irreparable consequences for human health and local ecosystems, in particular coastal zones and the maritime environment.[7] The remaining ships were mainly dismantled in China and Turkey, where better infrastructure and procedures allow for cleaner and safer practices, if applied correctly.[8] High-standard facilities, which are primarily used by some European and US ship recycling companies, face difficulties competing with cheap ship recycling in South Asia. The price paid per lightweight tonne of an end-of-life ship varies considerably and is twice as high in India, Pakistan and Bangladesh than in China or Turkey.[9] The consequence is that very few shipowners ensure and monitor the clean and safe recycling of their end-of-life ships.[10]

[3] See P Heidegger, I Jenssen, D Reuter, N Mulinaris and F Carlsson, 'What a difference a flag makes: Why ship owners' responsibility to ensure sustainable ship recycling needs to go beyond flag state jurisdiction' (Brussels, NGO Shipbreaking Platform, 2015), available at www.shipbreakingplatform.org/wp-content/uploads/2019/01/FoCBriefing_NGO-Shipbreaking-Platform_-April-2015.pdf.

[4] See 'The Toxic Tide: 2019 Shipbreaking Records' (Brussels, NGO Shipbreaking Platform, 2019), available at www.offthebeach.org.

[5] NGO Shipbreaking Platform, 'What a difference a flag makes' (2015).

[6] ibid.

[7] For details, see 'Ship Recycling: Reducing Human and Environmental Impacts', available at ec.europa.eu/science-environment-policy (European Commission, 2016) 3. See also UD Engels, *European Ship Recycling Regulation* (Berlin, Springer, 2013) 15. On the question of whether beaching should be prohibited, see MN Tsimplis, 'Recycling of EU Ships: From Prohibition to Regulation?' [2014] *LMCLQ* 415, 426.

[8] Eight Turkish facilities are now listed by the European Commission as compliant with the Ship Recycling Regulation (EU) No 1257/2013; see below, section III(C)(ii). China has banned the import of waste, including vessels, with effect from January 2019; see I Jensen, M Mørk and N Mulinaris, 'Recycling Outlook: Decommissioning of North Sea Floating Oil & Gas Units' (2019) 22, available at www.shipbreakingplatform.org/wp-content/uploads/2019/09/Shipbreaking-OG-Report.pdf.

[9] See NN, 'Seatrade Found Liable for Shipbreaking Practices', available at www.maritime-executive.com/article/seatrade-found-liable-for-shipbreaking-sale.

[10] See European Commission, 'Green Paper on Better Ship Dismantling', COM(2007) 269, 5.

B. European Ownership and Flags of Convenience

At the same time, there is a significant discrepancy between the 25 largest flag states in general and the 25 largest flag states of end-of-life ships.[11] This discrepancy is caused by the frequent use of so-called 'flags of convenience'.[12] Often ships are reflagged at the end of their life into ship registries of countries with relatively low legal standards, a poor record of implementing international legislation and weak enforcement mechanisms.[13] According to UNCTAD, less than 27 per cent of the world's fleet is flagged in the country of the vessel's beneficial ownership, and around 40 per cent of all ships beached in South Asia were imported under flags of convenience.[14]

Currently, European shipowners control over 40 per cent of the world's merchant fleet, with Greece being the top shipowning country globally. However, only 22 per cent of vessels fly the flag of an EU Member State during their operational life, and only seven to nine per cent still have an EU flag when they reach their end of life.[15] European shipowners account for around one-third of the ships which were beached for dismantling. In 2014, 32 per cent of all beached ships by gross tonnage were under EU ownership and only 7.7 per cent were still registered under an EU flag. German and Greek owners beached 74 per cent and 87 per cent of their disposed vessels respectively. The EU is the single largest market sending end-of-life ships for dirty and dangerous ship breaking.[16]

III. The Legal Framework

A. Overview

Traditionally, the Basel Convention on the Control of Transboundary Movements of Hazardous Wastes of 1989[17] covers (or at least should cover) the problem of ship dismantling under poor health and safety and environmental conditions

[11] See Engels, *European Ship Recycling Regulation* (2013), 173.

[12] See Girvin (ch 2) III.

[13] The NGO Shipbreaking Platform in Heidegger, Jenssen, Reuter, Mulinaris and Carlsson, 'What a difference a flag makes' (2015) names Palau, Comoros and St Kitts and Nevis for flags that are typical end-of-life flags and barely used for ships in operation.

[14] See Heidegger, Jenssen, Reuter, Mulinaris and Carlsson (n 3) 1. See also European Commission, 'Ship recycling' (2016) 3.

[15] Moreover, the EU-flagged fleet is relatively young compared to other flags, which reduces the relevance of the EU Regulation. See Transport and Environment and NGO Shipbreaking Platform, *EU-listed Yards Can Handle the Recycling Demand of EU-flagged Ships, Implementation of the EU Ship Recycling Regulation No 1257/2013 (EU SRR)*, September 2018, www.transportenvironment.org/sites/te/files/publications/2018_09_Shipbreaking_report_final.pdf.

[16] Heidegger (n 3) 1. See also European Commission (n 7) 3. For detailed figures for 2019, see NGO Shipbreaking Platform (n 3).

[17] Ratified by 187 parties. See www.basel.int/TheConvention/Overview/TextoftheConvention/tabid/1275/Default.aspx.

abroad. The Convention generally aims at minimising or prohibiting transboundary movements of hazardous waste and is based on self-sufficiency, proximity and polluter pays principles, high environmental standards and the particular protection of the interests of developing countries. The Convention requires that the parties minimise the generation of hazardous waste and ensure the availability of sufficient facilities for the environmentally sound management of this waste within their borders. Any shipment has to be based on prior informed consent procedures between the exporting and the importing state.[18] The importing country has to approve each shipment of waste on the basis that the waste will be treated in an environmentally sound manner in accordance with certain minimum standards.

In addition, the Basel Ban Amendment[19] of 1995 established a ban on the export of hazardous waste from OECD member countries to non-OECD countries, so as to strengthen the protection of developing countries. This amendment entered into force, as article 4A of the Basel Convention, on 5 December 2019.[20]

The EU implemented the Basel Convention in 1993 and the Ban Amendment in 1997[21] and the current regime is Regulation (EC) No 1013/2006 on shipments of waste (Waste Shipment Regulation).[22] Consequently, since 1998, shipments of hazardous waste from EU and also EFTA States to non-OECD states have been generally prohibited.[23] As nearly all ships contain considerable quantities of hazardous materials, such as oils and oil sludge, asbestos, glass wool, PCB, TBT, heavy metals in paints and others,[24] end-of-life ships must, in principle, be regarded as hazardous waste. Any transfer of an end-of-life ship from Europe to a non-OECD state has been prohibited since that time.

However, as the numbers above show[25] and as will be outlined below, the application of the waste shipment regime to ships has always been disputed de jure, while its implementation de facto has proved difficult. As a consequence, departing from this approach to target transboundary movements, Regulation (EU) No 1257/2013 on ship recycling (the Ship Recycling Regulation)[26] has reopened the lawful possibility of the transfer of end-of-life vessels sailing under an EU flag to non-OECD countries. However, these ships may only be recycled at authorised facilities. The Ship Recycling Regulation thereby pre-implements the regulatory

[18] Arts 4 and 6.

[19] Decision III/1: Amendment to the Basel Convention (28 November 1995), UN doc UNEP/CHW.3/35.

[20] See www.basel.int/Countries/StatusofRatifications/BanAmendment/tabid/1344/Default.aspx.

[21] Regulation (EEC) No 259/93 on the supervision and control of shipments of waste within, into and out of the European Community, [1993] OJ L30/1 and its amendment by Regulation (EEC) No 120/97, [1997] OJ L22/14. For an overview, see C Glinski, 'Umweltqualität' in H-W Micklitz and N Reich, *Europäisches Verbraucherrecht*, 4th edn (Nomos, Baden-Baden, 2003) 939, 984.

[22] [2006] OJ L190/1.

[23] Waste Shipment Regulation, arts 34 and 36.

[24] See European Commission, 'An EU Strategy for Better Ship Dismantling', COM(2008) 767, 3.

[25] See above, section II(A).

[26] [2013] OJ L330/1.

approach of the Hong Kong Convention with the aim of facilitating the early ratification of that Convention, not only by EU Member States, but also by third countries. This will be promoted by initiating the increased installation of proper recycling capacities and by applying proportionate controls over ships flying other flags and calling at a port or anchorage of an EU Member State.[27] This approach is also accompanied by a product responsibility and life-cycle perspective for vessels because hazardous materials built into a ship must be reduced and documented. In this way, the Ship Recycling Regulation has introduced higher standards than the Hong Kong Convention concerning ship recycling facilities as well as in relation to hazardous materials in ships.[28] The success of the new approach will be ensured through surveys, certification and notification requirements, in particular between the shipowner and the flag state, and between the recycling facility and the recycling state.

B. Challenges to the International and European Waste Shipment Regime

Ships are per se moving assets and the prohibition of the *shipment of ships* highlights this inherent tension. This applies both to the categorisation of ships as waste as well as to the navigation between flag and port State responsibilities.

i. Ships as Waste?

The shipping industry and others who are opposed to the application of the Waste Shipment Regulation to end-of-life ships have argued that ships should not be characterised as hazardous waste because shipbreaking creates economic benefits for the recycling states, such as jobs and the reuse of steel. It is further argued that the responsibility for the related social and environmental standards lies with recycling states and that a ship under its own power and/or a ship that is still used for transportation, even on its last journey, does not constitute waste.[29] These arguments, however, depart from established waste law doctrine.[30]

[27] See recital (5) of the Ship Recycling Regulation.

[28] See below, section III(C)(i) and (ii).

[29] See the arguments of the defence in the criminal proceedings against the directors of Seatrade in the District Court of Rotterdam, 15/3/2018, Case no 10/994550-15, ECLI:NL:RBROT:2018:2108, at 4.1. Doctrinally this was either incorrectly based upon art 1(4) of the Basel Convention, which exempts waste *from* ships but not ships themselves, see District Court of Rotterdam, at 4.3.4.1., or on the argument that an interpretation to the contrary could only be based upon a revised logic concerning the interplay between the definition of hazardous properties laid down in art 1 of the Basel Convention and the requirement of disposal as laid down in art 2 of the Basel Convention.

[30] For detailed analysis, see S Claußen, *Die Abwrackung von Seeschiffen in Nicht-OECD-Staaten* (Hamburg, Dr Kovač, 2009). See also T Ormond, 'Enforcing EU Environmental Law Outside Europe? The Case of Ship Dismantling' (2009) *elni Review* 13, 16.

The Basel Convention defines waste as a substance or object that is disposed of, intended to be disposed of, or required to be disposed of.[31] Disposal means any operation specified in Annex IV (read with article 2(4)) including, for example, operations which lead to resource recovery such as reclamation of metals.[32] Article 1(4) exempts waste *from* ships from the scope of the Convention. This definition is also relevant for implementing acts and is in principle identical to that of the Waste Shipment Regulation. Whether waste is considered as hazardous either depends on the dangerous categories listed in Annex I to the Basel Convention or is subject to definition by the exporting, importing or transit state.[33] Although intended to be disposed of, neither the fact that a product or vessel can still be used nor economic benefits resulting from the disposal are valid arguments against the application of waste law. The latter is explicitly reflected in Annex IV of the Basel Convention, which includes the recovery of substances in the list of disposal activities.

The applicability of the Basel Convention to ships has been confirmed by decisions and practice under the Convention. In 2004, the Conference of the Parties to the Basel Convention explicitly acknowledged its applicability to ships, including ships still under their own motive power.[34] Within the EU, this is confirmed by recital 35 of the Waste Shipment Regulation, which clarifies that a ship may become waste as defined in article 2 of the Basel Convention and at the same time still be defined as a ship under other international rules.[35]

Nevertheless, the concrete characterisation of a ship as waste and, in particular, the exact moment when the ship becomes waste, is in fact difficult to determine. As legal obligations to dispose of a ship are rare, the subjective criterion of the *intention* to dispose of a ship is crucial. Although the Basel Convention itself does not specify whose intention it refers to, general waste law and implementing laws such as article 3(1) of the European Waste Framework Directive 2008/98/EC[36] refer to the waste-holder, which in this regard can only mean the shipowner.[37]

In order to determine from the perspective of the port state the subjective *intention* of a shipowner to dispose of a ship, this intention must be deduced from objective factors in accordance with established waste law doctrine.[38] Such factors could be seen in a contract with a dismantling facility or in preparatory acts such as deletion from the registry, predeinstallations for dismantling, the sale to a cash

[31] Art 2(1).

[32] Annex IV, B.R4.

[33] Art 1(1).

[34] Doc UNEP/CHW.7/33, VI. B. with Annex VII/26. Environmentally sound management of ship dismantling: '*Noting* that a ship *may* become waste as defined in article 2 of the Basel Convention and that at the same time it may be defined as a ship under other international rules'.

[35] See also District Court of Rotterdam (n 29) 4.3.4.2.

[36] [2008] OJ L312/3.

[37] See R Lagoni and J Albers, 'Schiffe als Abfall?' (2008) 30 *Natur und Recht* 220, 224.

[38] See ECJ, 12/12/2013, Joined Cases C-241/12 and C-242/12 *Shell Nederland Verkoopmaatschappij BV* and *Belgian Shell NV*, ECLI:EU:C:2013:821.

buyer, and renaming, reclassification and reflagging into open registers in poorly regulated jurisdictions.[39]

Even where decisions and preparatory acts are started within European ports, the intentions of the shipowner can be difficult to identify and to prove.[40] This can arise where the shipowner denies his intention to dispose of the ship and asserts another use. It is difficult to prove an existing intention before any concrete dismantling preparations actually start and also before the last journey.[41] Finally, there is the argument that it is normally not the original shipowner who sells a ship, but the cash buyer who decides on further use or dismantling.[42]

ii. Exporting State?

A problem concerns the identification of the exporting state which is responsible for the control of transboundary movements and the proper execution of the PIC procedure. Article 2(10) of the Basel Convention defines the exporting state as the state from which a transboundary movement is planned or initiated, whereas a transboundary movement is defined in article 2(3) as a movement from an area under the national jurisdiction of one state to or through an area under the national jurisdiction of another state, which includes marine areas.[43] Some authors and some parties to the Basel Convention consider the flag state to be relevant as this would be in line with customary law and the United Nations Convention on the Law of the Sea 1982 (UNCLOS).[44] Moreover, even applying the waste law principle of producer responsibility, the flag state could be regarded as relevant. By contrast, the wording 'state party from which a transboundary movement is planned or initiated' rather points in the direction of territorial jurisdiction. As the territorial jurisdiction of a state is, however, not limited to persons of its own nationality or flag but also to others – here, waste generators – on its territory, the port state in which the ship turns into waste (before its last or penultimate journey) can be regarded as the exporting state.[45] Again, given uncertainty as to when exactly a ship turns into waste, there are at least two potential states of export, either the EU Member State where a shipowner decides to dispose of the ship and to sell it to a cash buyer or a state elsewhere where the cash buyer prepares the ship for its last journey.

[39] See G Ulfstein, 'Legal Aspects of Scrapping of Vessels: A Study for the Norwegian Ministry of Environment' (1999) 8. See also CIEL, 'Shipbreaking and the Basel Convention: Analysis of the Level of Control Established under the Hong Kong Convention' (2011) 20, available at www.shipbreaking platform.org/wp-content/uploads/2018/11/CIEL-on-Basel-IMO-compairson.pdf.

[40] See also Engels (n 7) 175; Ormond, 'Enforcing EU Environmental Law Outside Europe?' (2009) 18.

[41] See also Engels (n 7) 128.

[42] See Lagoni and Albers, 'Schiffe als Abfall?' (2008) 224 ff.

[43] Art 2(9).

[44] See Engels (n 7) 175.

[45] See S Bhattacharjee, 'From Basel to Hong Kong: International Environmental Regulation of Ship Recycling Takes One Step Forward and Two Steps Back' (2009) 1 *Trade, Law and Development* 193, 215; CIEL, 'Shipbreaking and the Basel Convention' (2011) 20.

Thus, European port state responsibility does in fact not apply when European shipowners sell their ships on the second-hand market before the ship has reached recycling age[46] or when they take their decision and start preparatory acts outside European waters.

iii. Compatibility with UNCLOS

Beyond the immediate interpretation of the Basel Convention, legal uncertainty has been further fuelled by discussions concerning potential conflicts of norms between the Basel Convention and maritime freedoms as codified in UNCLOS. Some writers have suggested that port states might interfere with the freedom to navigate as laid down in article 78 of UNCLOS, when applying the Basel Convention incorrectly.[47] This might even be the case while applying the Basel Convention correctly, as article 219 of UNCLOS on prohibitions to navigate does not refer to the Basel Convention but only to the seaworthiness of a ship.[48]

iv. Application in Practice

Although the general applicability of the waste shipment regime to ships has been clarified in the affirmative, its concrete application faces enormous legal and factual difficulties. As can be seen from the numbers above, this is equally true with a view to the application of the European waste shipment ban. There is a widespread practice both among European and other shipowners to sell, rename, reclassify and reflag their ships and hand them over to cash buyers in a non-OECD port from where the last journey (often still with cargo) starts.[49]

Nevertheless, only a few cases, such as the *Blue Lady* (formerly *SS Norway*), have gained public attention. When the ship left the port of Bremerhaven, its declared destination was Port Klang (Malaysia) where it was supposed to be used as a hotel and training ship. German authorities found no evidence that this was not true. On its way to Asia, it was decided to dismantle the ship in Alang (India).[50] A similar case involved the Danish vessel, *Kong Frederik IX*, where the

[46] It is assumed that this is a widespread practice. In 2009, 14% of the world merchant fleet was older than 25 years old whilst only 9% of the German merchant fleet was older than 16 years old. See Engels (n 7) 173.

[47] See Lagoni and Albers (n 37) 224. See also Engels (n 7) 129; G Moncayo, 'International Law on Ship Recycling and its Interface With EU Law' (2016) 109 *Marine Pollution Bulletin* 301, 303.

[48] Lagoni and Albers (n 37) 224; Engels (n 7) 129.

[49] For details, see Engels (n 7) 17, 69. In rare cases, the ship is directly sold to a recycling company engaging a shipbroker. Interestingly, the price per ship mainly relates to the relevant price for steel, whereas the amount of hazardous substances built into the ship is basically irrelevant – which again shows the irrelevance of proper, socially and environmentally sound recycling.

[50] See TG Puthucherril, *From Shipbreaking to Sustainable Ship Recycling* (Leiden, Martinus Nijhoff, 2010) 86.

owner claimed that the dismantling decision and preparatory acts were only taken outside European waters.[51]

In the past, European administrations or courts have issued very few orders prohibiting shipowners from transferring and dismantling ships abroad. One prominent case was the French (asbestos-containing) aircraft carrier *Le Clemenceau* (2005), which was sent to India for dismantling and then ordered back to France after a decision of the Conseil d'Etat found a breach of the EU Waste Shipment Regulation.[52] In 2002, the Dutch authorities denied the vessel *Sandrien* permission to sail to India for dismantling.[53] In both cases, the existence of a contract with a facility in India was proof of the fact that the ship had already become waste before it left French or Dutch waters respectively.[54] In 2018, the Scottish Environment Protection Agency detained three vintage oil rigs for suspected illegal export to Alang, where two other rigs have already been scrapped.[55]

The recent case of *Seatrade* may provide evidence of a shift towards stronger enforcement practices. In that case, the directors of *Seatrade* were held criminally liable by the District Court of Rotterdam[56] for having breached the waste shipment ban in four cases. Four ships had been shipped from the ports of Rotterdam and Hamburg to beaches in India, Bangladesh and Turkey for scrapping. The prosecution was based on email evidence showing negotiations about the scrap value of the ships and the evidence of crew members who bore witness that they were ordered to carry out preparatory measures. Thus, one suggestion for better enforcement is to trace European ships which have entered beaching yards in India, Bangladesh or Pakistan back to their scrapping decisions in Europe.[57] Currently, the Norwegian National Authority for Investigation and Prosecution of Economic and Environmental Crime is investigating a case against a Norwegian shipowner who allegedly sold the vessel *Harrier* for beaching in Pakistan.[58]

Low adherence to the European export ban was reinforced by the fact that recycling options for European shipowners in line with the Waste Shipment Regulation were effectively restricted to the existing British and Turkish facilities, which did not have the capacity to meet the demand of EU shipowners.[59] At the same time, most recycling countries – with the notable exception of Turkey – proved

[51] ibid, 77.
[52] ibid, 81. See also Ormond (n 30) 20.
[53] Dutch Council of State, 19/6/2002, ECLI:NL:RVS:2002:AE4310, available at www.raadvanstate.nl/@10535/200105168-2 (in Dutch). See also Engels (n 7) 172.
[54] See CIEL (n 39) 18.
[55] See Jensen, Mørk and Mulinaris, 'Recycling Outlook' (2019) 19, and NGO Shipbreaking Platform, 'BBC exposes dirty and dangerous scrapping of oil and gas units in India' (18 March 2020), available at www.shipbreakingplatform.org/bbc-disclosure-diamond-offshore.
[56] District Court of Rotterdam (n 29).
[57] See, eg, www.nortonrosefulbright.com/en/knowledge/publications/f686f825/seatrade-a-new-approach-to-violations-of-regulations-on-ship-recycling-in-the-european-union.
[58] See Jensen, Mørk and Mulinaris (n 8) 5, and NGO Shipbreaking Platform, 'The controversial case of the Harrier', available at www.shipbreakingplatform.org/spotlight-harrier-case.
[59] Engels (n 7) 172.

reluctant to use the Basel Convention procedure of notification and consent for ships imported for scrapping.[60]

The *Otapan* case of 2007 illustrates the importance of the recycling state's attitude. Here, the ship was correctly defined as waste and the PIC procedure was initiated. However, Turkey as the importing state did not allow the ship to enter Turkish waters because it had more asbestos on board than set out in the notification.[61] Also, the Supreme Court of Bangladesh has declared the import of ships containing hazardous materials illegal in several cases,[62] such as the *North Sea Producer* which was beached in Chittagong after it had left the UK on false documents. Importantly, the Supreme Court of Bangladesh excluded the shipyard from further dismantling and directed the competent authority to claim compensation from the yard for having violated Bangladeshi environmental law.[63]

The generally weak implementation of the waste shipping regime in the maritime sector has led to the perception that the waste shipping regime is unsuitable to meet the problem of ship dismantling.[64] In particular, the concept of the 'exporting state' was regarded as too broad for its proper application to ships and an 'impediment to effective control and enforcement'.[65] This was in fact a major reason to justify the development of the Hong Kong Convention and, subsequently, the EU Ship Recycling Regulation.[66]

C. The EU Ship Recycling Regulation

The EU Ship Recycling Regulation applies to vessels sailing under an EU flag.[67] Warships, small ships of less than 500 gross tonnage, and ships which only sail in the territorial waters of the flag state are exempt under article 2(2), which follows articles 3.2 and 3.3 of the Hong Kong Convention.[68] At the same time, according to article 27 and recital 10, ships to which the Ship Recycling Regulation applies are exempt from the scope of application of the Waste Framework Directive 2008/98/EC and of the Waste Shipment Regulation. The idea is to exempt ships

[60] See European Commission, 'An EU Strategy' (2008) 3. For an example, see the case of the US waste vessel *Horizon Trader* as described by NGO Shipbreaking Platform, 'Dead US Ship on Four-Month Tow Ends on Indian Beach' (25 January 2016), available at www.shipbreakingplatform.org/dead-u-s-ship-on-four-month-tow-ends-on-indian-beach.

[61] See CIEL (n 39) 19.

[62] An early case was the case of the *MT Enterprise*. See International Federation of Human Rights, 'High Court Halts Deadly Shipbreaking on the Beaches of Bangladesh' (18 March 2009), available at www.fidh.org/en/region/asia/bangladesh/High-Court-Halts-Deadly.

[63] See NGO Shipbreaking Platform, 'NGOs win FPSO North Sea Producer case' (19 November 2019), available at www.shipbreakingplatform.org/north-sea-producer-judgement.

[64] See, eg, R Wolfrum and N Matz, *Conflicts in International Environmental Law* (Berlin, Springer, 2003) 115. See also European Commission (n 24) 3.

[65] See Engels (n 7) 145.

[66] See CIEL (n 39) 21.

[67] Art 2.

[68] For critique, see Bhattacharjee, 'From Basel to Hong Kong' (2009) 222.

from the applicability of general waste law and to create a specific waste regime for ships. In this respect, and differing from waste law, 'recycling' means dismantling of a ship in order to recover components and materials and includes storage and treatment of components on site.[69]

i. Requirements for Ships

The requirements for ships are based on a product responsibility and life-cycle perspective with hazardous materials built into a ship to be reduced and documented. According to article 4, the installation or use of hazardous materials such as asbestos and PCBs on ships will be prohibited or restricted. Here, the Ship Recycling Regulation goes slightly beyond the requirements of the Hong Kong Convention because it has listed more hazardous materials.[70]

New ships – and existing ships as far as practicable – must have an updated inventory of hazardous materials on board,[71] again with slightly more substances to be included in the inventory than the Hong Kong Convention requires.[72] The European Maritime Safety Agency (EMSA) has published a guidance document, 'EMSA's Best Practice Guidance on the Inventory of Hazardous Materials',[73] which is based on relevant IMO guidelines but takes into account the specifics of the EU Ship Recycling Regulation.[74] The document also covers surveys on inventory and enforcement issues.

Shipowners must ensure that ships are only recycled in facilities which are included in the European List of ship recycling facilities (the 'European List').[75] Prior to recycling, shipowners have to minimise residues, wastes and remaining fuel oil, provide the recycling facility with all relevant information (on the basis of which the facility develops a recycling plan) and notify the intended recycling with all relevant information within a given timeframe to the competent administration of the flag state/Member State. The shipowner remains responsible for the ship until the recycling facility has accepted responsibility. The facility may decline to accept the ship if the ship does not correspond to the relevant certificates, in particular the inventory of hazardous materials.[76]

[69] Art 3.1(6).

[70] In particular perfluorooctane sulfonic acids (PFOS): see Ship Recycling Regulation, Annex 1. See also Moncayo, 'International Law on Ship Recycling' (2016) 307; J Falke, 'Neue Entwicklungen im Europäischen Umweltrecht' [2012] *Zeitschrift für Umweltrecht* 383, 385.

[71] Art 5.

[72] In particular brominated flame retardants (HBCDD), see Ship Recycling Regulation, Annex 2. For details of that inventory, see S Claußen, 'Schiffsrecycling – der europäische Weg' [2016] *Recht der Transportwirtschaft* 201, 202.

[73] See www.emsa.europa.eu/implementation-tasks/environment/ship-recycling/items.html?cid=150&id=2874.

[74] ibid, 4.

[75] See below, section III(C)(ii). Different from the Hong Kong Convention, recycling includes 'preparation for re-use' which rules out the possibility to have a first round of dismantling activities in a non-compliant facility, see Tsimplis, 'Recycling of EU Ships' [2014] 433.

[76] See Arts 6 and 7.

The competent authority of the flag state/Member State or a recognised organisation on their part have to carry out several surveys on the ships, from the initial survey over a renewed survey to the final survey. The surveys include the inventory of hazardous substances and the recycling plan,[77] which are completed with inventory and/or ready for recycling certificates.[78] These certificates are also subject to port state control.[79] In addition, the requirement to have an inventory of hazardous materials on board also applies to ships flying the flag of a third country when calling at a port or anchorage of a Member State.[80]

ii. Requirements for Recycling Facilities

Of crucial importance for the Ship Recycling Regulation is the European List of ship recycling facilities (the 'European List'), which the Commission has to establish and to update regularly[81] and which was last updated on 11 November 2020.[82] The inclusion of a ship recycling facility is valid for a maximum of five years and renewable, and the date of the expiry of the inclusion must be indicated in the European List.[83]

In order to be included in the European List, ship recycling facilities must be authorised by the competent authorities of the recycling state, to be designed, constructed and operated from built structures in a safe and environmentally sound manner.[84] The latter rules out the widely used 'beaching' method and goes further than the Hong Kong Convention which does not contain explicit minimum standards in this regard.[85]

The relevant provisions and guidelines of the International Maritime Organisation (IMO), the Basel Convention and the Stockholm Convention on Persistent Organic Pollutants and also of the International Labour Organization (ILO) have to be 'tak(en) into account' – but they are not explicitly mandatory. Sound management and monitoring procedures preventing adverse environmental effects and health risks for workers and neighbours must be in place, as must a sound management of hazardous materials and wastes, emergency plans, health and safety training for workers and a record of incidents; requirements which again go beyond the Hong Kong Convention.[86]

[77] Art 8.

[78] Arts 9 and 10.

[79] Art 11.

[80] Art 12.

[81] See Arts 16(1) and 16(4).

[82] Commission Implementing Decision (EU) 2020/1675, [2020] OJ L378/5.

[83] See Art 16(3).

[84] Art 13(1).

[85] See Claußen, 'Schiffsrecycling' (2016) 203. See also Moncayo (n 47) 307; Falke, 'Neue Entwicklungen' [2012] 385. On the respective requirements in the Hong Kong Convention, see Tsimplis (n 7) 422.

[86] Art 13(1). Tsimplis (n 7) 436 argues that these stricter general requirements for foreign recycling facilities pose problems under international law as they render the Hong Kong standards irrelevant and lead to a problematic preferential treatment of Turkish and Chinese facilities.

Whereas authorities in Member States have to authorise their ship recycling facilities and inform the Commission,[87] ship recycling facilities located in third countries need to apply to the Commission for inclusion in the European List. This must be done on the basis of detailed information, including authorisation by the competent authorities of the recycling state, a certification by 'an independent verifier with appropriate qualifications', and the acceptance of 'site inspections by the Commission or agents acting on its behalf'.[88]

Currently, the European List contains seven facilities in Norway, six in Denmark, four each in France and in Lithuania, three each in the Netherlands and the UK, and one each in Finland, Belgium, Italy, Spain, Portugal, Latvia and Estonia. Outside Europe, the list contains eight facilities in Turkey and one in the USA.

iii. Procedures

In terms of procedure, the operator of the recycling facility has to develop a ship recycling plan which has to be tacitly or explicitly approved by the competent authority of the recycling State.[89] The approved recycling plan must be sent to the shipowner and the administration of the flag state/Member State or a recognised organisation. In addition, a 'ready for recycling' statement as well as a statement of completion have to be sent to the administration of the flag state/Member State.[90]

Member States are required to send the Commission reports containing a list of ships for which a ready for recycling certificate has been issued, and/or a statement of completion has been received, and also any information regarding illegal ship recycling.[91]

iv. Entry into Force

The Ship Recycling Regulation entered into force on 30 December 2013 but, pursuant to article 32, has a graded applicability. Various preparatory requirements were already applicable from 31 December 2014,[92] but the main requirements governing the safe and environmentally sound recycling of ships applied from 31 December 2018 when the necessary recycling capacity was reached.[93] The required dates

[87] Art 14.
[88] Art 15.
[89] Art 7.
[90] Art 13(2).
[91] Art 21.
[92] See, in particular, those concerning requirements for recycling facilities in arts 13–16.
[93] In June 2019, the Commission decided to commence infringement procedures against Croatia, Cyprus, Germany, Greece, Italy, Portugal, Romania, Slovenia, and Sweden as they had not fully implemented the Ship Recycling Regulation. In particular, these countries had failed to implement key obligations relating to the designation of competent authorities, administrations and contact persons and to the establishment of national legal provisions relating to the enforcement of these EU rules and the applicable penalties, as required, by 31 December 2018.

also vary in the case of the duty to have an inventory of hazardous substances in place; these apply from 31 December 2018 for ships sailing under the flag of an EU Member State, but only from 31 December 2020 for ships flying the flag of a third country.

IV. Differences between the Waste Law and the Ship Recycling Approaches

As the new ship recycling regime is meant to provide a cure for the Basel Convention's shortcomings and improve the situation of ship recycling, this chapter now analyses relevant differences in the approaches and the potential consequences of these differences for shipowners.

The Open-Ended Working Group of the Basel Convention has laid down criteria for a comparison of the protection level of the Basel Convention and the Hong Kong Convention, namely scope and applicability, control and enforcement, as well as coordination and exchange of information amongst state parties.[94] When compared, there are many shortcomings. A particular criticism is that the strict Basel approach, which aims at a minimisation or even prohibition of transboundary movements of waste between OECD and non-OECD states, has been abdicated, while the loopholes of the old regime with regard to control and enforcement have not been closed but increased.[95]

A. Scope and Level of Protection

The Hong Kong Convention has been criticised for its renunciation of the clear environmental focus of the Basel Convention and its aim of protecting developing countries from hazardous waste with economic interests.

It has been argued that the Hong Kong Convention's life-cycle approach to prohibit or strictly control a number of listed substances is less stringent than the general substitution principle of the Basel Convention.[96] The Hong Kong Convention has a narrower coverage of dangerous substances with the listing of additional substances also based on economic considerations.[97] Many of the hazardous substances that are relevant to ship dismantling and that are listed in Appendix B of the Technical Guidelines to the Basel Convention[98] are neither

[94] Decision IX/30: 'Dismantling of ships' (27 June 2008), UN-doc. UNEP/CHW.9/39, 56.

[95] For detailed analysis, see Engels (n 7) 137. See also CIEL (n 39) 28, 41.

[96] CIEL (n 39) 44.

[97] Regulation 6.4.1.1.4 of the Annex to the Hong Kong Convention.

[98] Basel Convention Technical Guidelines for the Environmentally Sound Management of the Full and Partial Dismantling of Ships, UNEP/CHW.6/23.

prohibited nor subject to control,[99] nor are they included in Appendix 2 of the Hong Kong Convention as relevant for the inventory. Although the EU Ship Recycling Regulation lists more hazardous materials in both respects,[100] the latter list is incomplete. As a consequence, the inventory of hazardous substances requires less substances to be listed than the Basel movement document[101] that has a similar purpose when it comes to recycling.[102]

As the inventory has to be on board throughout the lifetime of the ship, this might nevertheless strengthen shipowner responsibility from early on. At the same time, the life-cycle approach of the Hong Kong Convention is not entirely new. Article 4.2(a) of the Basel Convention clearly requires 'that the generation of hazardous wastes … is reduced to a minimum'. In this regard, the Technical Guidelines 'consider the implementation of "clean" ship design practices'.[103] Ship inventories of hazardous materials as well as precleaning measures have already been addressed in these Guidelines.[104]

In addition, the Basel requirement in article 4.2(b) 'that adequate disposal facilities, for the environmentally sound management of hazardous wastes' should be available within each state party was meant to further strengthen product responsibility 'from cradle to grave' from an international perspective. This has further been reinforced with the Basel Ban Amendment and the EU Waste Shipment Regulation, which prohibit hazardous waste shipments to non-OECD countries.

Compared with the Basel Convention, the Hong Kong Convention has not included mandatory minimum standards for the authorisation of recycling facilities; indeed, it only provides for the voluntary application of standards and guidelines for the environmentally sound treatment of end-of-life ships.[105] The same applies, in principle, to the EU Ship Recycling Regulation.[106] Further, both the Hong Kong Convention and the EU Ship Recycling Regulation have not included downstream waste treatment facilities in the control regime.[107]

Turning to recycling standards, the beaching method used to be a major source of concern under the Basel Convention and its Technical Guidelines.[108] By contrast, a large number of ship recycling facilities which use the beaching method

[99] Hong Kong Convention, App 1.
[100] See above, III(C)(i).
[101] Basel Convention, art 4.7(c).
[102] See also CIEL (n 39) 44.
[103] Basel Convention Technical Guidelines (n 98) 24.
[104] ibid, 9, 11. It has been argued that the new shipowner responsibility for pre-cleaning and decontamination is even less clear than under the Basel Convention: see CIEL (n 39) 44, 53.
[105] Reg 3 of the Annex to the Hong Kong Convention only requires the parties to take the standards and guidelines of the Basel Convention and the ILO into account. See also CIEL (n 39) 47.
[106] See above, III(C)(ii).
[107] CIEL (n 39) 46.
[108] See Basel Convention Technical Guidelines (n 98) 29.

have already been certified by classification societies as being compliant with the Hong Kong Convention.[109]

From a European legal perspective, the fact that the EU Ship Recycling Regulation rules out the beaching method does not change much as this method has not been used in OECD countries and exports to non-OECD states used to be prohibited.

In conclusion, while the substantive requirements for ships and ship recycling have not been raised significantly, the relatively broad approach of the waste shipment regime has been narrowed down. But, on the other hand, the approach has been concretised and thus potentially given more teeth.

B. Control and Enforcement

An important aim of the new ship recycling regime was to better address the shipping-specific needs and requirements and to avoid the weaknesses and loopholes of the Basel Convention with a view to control and enforcement. However, a number of shortcomings have also been identified.

State control under the Hong Kong Convention is considered to be less tight than under the Basel Convention, as states only have the possibility of prohibiting the recycling, but not the import and export of the end-of-life ship as such. Next, in contrast to the Basel Convention, which requires explicit approval of each individual waste shipment based on proof that the waste can also be handled environmentally sound by downstream facilities, the Hong Kong Convention considers a *tacit* authorisation of the ship recycling plan to be sufficient. Further, there is no duty of the exporting state to reimport ships that are not authorised for recycling, which might lead to the dumping of ships. Finally, the Hong Kong Convention does not rule out trade with non-parties and therefore leaves territorial loopholes, where insufficient facilities could be run.[110]

In contrast, the regular ship surveys as well as the certification of completion under the Hong Kong Convention and the Ship Recycling Regulation go beyond the standards of the Basel Convention. The Hong Kong Convention, however, only provides for transit state responsibility over controlling the inventory certificate,[111] not the authorisation or denial of port entry.[112] In this regard, article 11(3) of the EU Ship Recycling Regulation gives port states the opportunity to reject ships which fail to submit valid certificates from their ports. As the EU requirement to

[109] See, eg, ClassNK, Ship Recycling Convention, available at www.classnk.or.jp/hp/en/activities/statutory/shiprecycle/index.html. For critique, see the Special Rapporteur on the implications for human rights of the environmentally sound management and disposal of hazardous substances and wastes; Tuncak, quoted by E Daems and G Goris, 'Behind the Hypocrisy of Better Beaches' (2019), available at www.shipbreakingplatform.org/wp-content/uploads/2019/01/Final-Report-PE.pdf, 31.

[110] On differences in this regard, see also Tsimplis (n 7) 423 ff.

[111] Hong Kong Convention, art 8.

[112] CIEL (n 39) 44.

have an inventory on board also applies to ships flying the flag of a third country from 31 December 2020, European port state control under the amended Port State Control Directive 2009/16/EC[113] can, in fact, strengthen the product responsibility of shipowners globally.

In terms of enforcement, the Hong Kong Convention only requires 'adequate sanctions', whereas the Basel Convention criminalises infringements.[114] The European implementation has, however, made no distinction in that both the Waste Shipment Regulation and the Ship Recycling Regulation require effective, proportionate and dissuasive penalties.[115] The Waste Shipment Regulation, however, requires a number of accompanying inspections in order to prevent circumvention.

Overall, a criticism is that the new control approach is based on two particularly weak pillars, namely flag state and recycling state responsibility. Flag state responsibility for the inventory of hazardous substances as well as for the final oversight of proper recycling can easily be circumvented as the new approach has not included a prohibition of or any other safeguards against reflagging prior to dismantling. The waste shipment regime at least applies from the moment of the decision to dispose of the ship.

The weakness of recycling state responsibility for the proper installation and running of recycling facilities[116] has basically been a justification of the waste shipment regime, as such, with the aim of minimising and prohibiting waste shipments.

The protection of developing countries in this regard was one of the major aims of the Basel Convention. Although the general requirements for technical assistance[117] under the Hong Kong Convention are regarded as generally equivalent to the Basel Convention, the Hong Kong Convention has no explicit concern for developing countries and neither provides for regional competence centres, training, funding and technology transfers nor for a prohibition on export.[118] It must, however, be recognised that the Hong Kong Convention has triggered numerous projects to support the efforts of shipyards in developing countries to meet the requirements of the Convention.[119]

Although the EU Ship Recycling Regulation requires recycling facilities in third countries to be approved and listed by the European Commission and considerably strengthens and complements state control of recycling facilities abroad when compared to the Hong Kong Convention, this new approach nevertheless rules

[113] [2009] OJ L131/57. See also EMSA (n 73) 22 and EMSA, 'Guidance on Inspections of Ships by the Port States in Accordance with Regulation (EU) 1257/2013 on ship recycling', available at www.standard-club.com/media/3167946/guidance-on-inspections-of-ships-by-the-port-states-in-accordance-with-regulation-eu-12572013-on-ship-recycling.pdf.

[114] Hong Kong Convention, art 10. See also Bhattacharjee (n 45) 224; CIEL (n 39) 52.

[115] See Waste Shipment Regulation, art 50; Ship Recycling Regulation, art 22.

[116] See also Bhattacharjee (n 45) 225.

[117] Hong Kong Convention, art 13.

[118] CIEL (n 39) 53, 55.

[119] For one example, see IMO, 'Safe and Environmentally Sound Ship Recycling in Bangladesh', available at www.imo.org/en/OurWork/PartnershipsProjects/Pages/Ship-recycling.aspx.

out the existing European ban of shipments of hazardous wastes from EU and also EFTA states to non-OECD states.

C. Private Governance

The private governance mechanisms enshrined in the new approach might, however, be powerful supplements for achieving a more effective governance mechanism than the Basel Convention has demonstrated in practice.

Private governance comes in several forms. Firstly, recognised organisations, which in practice are mainly classification societies,[120] can be involved in the ship survey, the certification of the inventory of hazardous materials and the recycling plan. That certification, however, only replaces flag state control and thus does not provide added value. The same applies to certification of recycling facilities on behalf of the recycling state.

Secondly, an independent verifier with appropriate qualifications has to certify recycling facilities in third countries. This clearly provides for an additional safeguard and is the basis for European Commission approval of these facilities. Experience with other industries involving transnational certification activities shows that the reliability of these certificates depends on – or at least can be strengthened considerably by – a number of factors.[121]

On the administrative side, these include a clear and precise legal framework with clearly defined standards, clear structural and procedural requirements for certification bodies (ideally with mandatory inclusion of stakeholders in auditing processes), the direct recognition of certification bodies by the European Commission, and the possibility of controlling their activities. These factors not only reduce the likelihood of infringements and insufficient audits but also reduce competition and the likelihood of a race to the bottom among certification bodies. In this regard, the possibility of having European Commission agents carry out on-site inspections clearly strengthens the reliability of certificates and the control framework.

On the private control side, it is important to strengthen stakeholders and to enable private enforcement, for example through the possibility of holding certification bodies liable for damage caused as a consequence of the issue of a certificate that did not meet the relevant requirements.[122]

[120] See, for example, RINA, 'Green Ship Recycling Certification', available at www.rina.org/en/green-ship-recycling.

[121] For biofuels, see C Glinski, 'Certification of the Sustainability of Biofuels in Global Supply Chains' in P Rott (ed), *Certification – Trust, Accountability, Liability* (Berlin, Springer, 2019) 163. For classification societies, see V Ulfbeck and A Møllmann, 'Public Function Liability of Classification Societies' in Rott (ibid) 213.

[122] For the relevance of tort law as a complement to the public law framework, *cf*, eg, C Glinski and P Rott, 'Regulating certification bodies in the field of medical devices: The PIP breast implants litigation and beyond' [2019] *European Review of Private Law* 403.

The inclusion of private actors in the governance system envisaged in article 23 of the Ship Recycling Regulation is of particular interest. Article 23 entitles natural or legal persons affected or likely to be affected or having a sufficient interest in environmental decision-making to request the European Commission to take action with a view to breaches or imminent threats of a breach of the provisions concerning ship recycling facilities. The provision is particularly geared at environmental organisations.

What has not survived the legislative process is the provision on access to justice. According to article 25 of the proposal for the Ship Recycling Regulation,[123] Member States should ensure that the persons referred to in article 24(1) have access to a court or other independent and impartial public body competent to review the procedural and substantive legality of the decisions, acts or failure to act of the competent authority under this Regulation. This idea has no equivalent in the final Ship Recycling Regulation.

V. Interaction of the Regimes and Consequences for the Management of Ship Recycling

The waste shipment regimes of the Basel Convention and the EU Waste Shipment Regulation and the ship recycling regimes of the Hong Kong Convention and the Ship Recycling Regulation deal with the same issue, namely the shipment of end-of-life ships and their safe and sound recycling. As, however, the approach in these instruments is procedurally and substantially different, in practice their interplay is not easy to predict.

The state parties to the Basel Convention could not reach an agreement as to whether the Hong Kong Convention establishes an equivalent level of control and enforcement,[124] and no clear demarcation between the scope of application of the Basel Convention and the Hong Kong Convention was made.[125] The Hong Kong Convention has also not yet entered into force. For this reason, the Basel Convention remains applicable and still provides for the relevant international framework on the subject matter.

[123] COM(2012) 118 final.

[124] On the basis of the criteria outlined and discussed at D: see Decision IX/30: 'Dismantling of Ships' (27 June 2008), UN-doc. UNEP/CHW.9/39, at 56. The relevant decision COP X/17 reads as follows: '1. Notes that, while some parties believe that the Hong Kong International Convention for the Safe and Environmentally Sound Recycling of Ships provides an equivalent level of control and enforcement to that established under the Basel Convention on the Control of Transboundary Movements of Hazardous Wastes and Their Disposal, some parties do not believe this to be the case; 2. Encourages parties to ratify the Hong Kong Convention to enable its early entry into force; 3. Acknowledges that the Basel Convention should continue to assist countries to apply the Basel Convention as it relates to ships.' For further detail, see CIEL (n 39) 29; Engels (n 7) 147. The main conflict in this regard was that the Hong Kong Convention does not rule out the beaching method: see Tsimplis (n 7) 425.

[125] Tsimplis (n 7) 425 argues that both remain applicable and recycling states could rely on both in accordance with their needs.

The application of the EU Ship Recycling Regulation therefore faces legal and practical challenges. Legally, the Ship Recycling Regulation could constitute an unlawful deviation from the Basel Convention[126] and its implementation, the Waste Shipment Regulation.[127] The consequence is that Member States and shipowners would still be bound by the Basel Convention requirements. However, the potential invalidity of the Ship Recycling Regulation cannot be held against shipowners following the new regime.[128]

Even if applied as provided for, the Ship Recycling Regulation does not rule out the Basel Convention requirements outside Europe. The consequence of this is that importing states outside Europe would or could still require the different Basel Convention notifications and documentation, including export permits, from Member State authorities.[129]

Within Europe, the new system would cover all ocean-going ships of a minimum 500 gross tons flying the flag of an EU Member State. This does not only hold true for European ships located within the EU but applies equally to European ships outside European waters when dismantling is prepared.

In contrast, non-European ships, and in particular ships which have been flagged out before its end-of-life, would still come under the regime of the Basel Convention and the Waste Shipment Regulation. For ships anchored in a European port when end-of-life decisions are taken, this would still imply that shipment to dismantling facilities abroad is prohibited.

Thus, as the Ship Recycling Regulation does not provide for any safeguards against reflagging, owners of ships that currently fly under the flag of an EU Member State have a choice. They can use a listed facility, or they can reflag their ship and bring it outside European waters before its end-of-life and avoid the Ship Recycling Regulation. The differences in the costs of using a listed facility and of 'beaching' remain significant and may point towards the latter.

If, however, a shipowner reflags the ship or sells it to a cash-buyer and sends it to a non-OECD state at a time when they already have the intention of disposing of the ship, the Waste Shipment Regulation applies. Breach of the Regulation can lead to administrative and criminal proceedings, as occurred in

[126] See the discussion by L Krämer, 'The Commission Proposal for a Regulation on Ship Recycling, the Basel Convention and the Protection of the Environment: A Legal Analysis' (2012), available at www.shipbreakingplatform.org/wp-content/uploads/2018/11/Legal-Analysis-of-EC-proposal_Ludwig-Kramer_FINAL-1.pdf; Moncayo (n 47) 307; CIEL, 'Legality of the EU Commission Proposal on Ship Recycling' (2013), available at www.shipbreakingplatform.org/wp-content/uploads/2018/11/CIEL-legal-opinion-on-EU-Ships-Proposed-Regulation-12-Dec-2012.pdf, 7; Tsimplis (n 7) 428.

[127] As the EU is a party to the Basel Convention; see, eg, P-T Stoll, T P Holterhuis and H Gött, *Investitionsschutz und Verfassung* (Tübingen, Mohr Siebeck, 2017) 81.

[128] Such as criminal proceedings for having breached the shipment ban. See, eg, ECJ, 26/11/1996, Case C-168/95 *Criminal Proceedings against Luciano Arcaro*, ECLI:EU:C:1996:363, [42].

[129] See Gorrissen Federspiel, 'Legal landscape After the Entry of the EU Ship Recycling Regulation' (4 September 2019), available at gorrissenfederspiel.com/viden/nyheder/legal-landscape-after-the-entry-of-the-eu-ship-recycling-regulation.

the *Seatrade* case. This case demonstrates that the risk of detection of an unlawful shipment to a non-EU State, such as India, Bangladesh or China, has increased significantly. In that sense, it can be assumed that the Ship Recycling Regulation provides shipowners with a safe way out of the shipment ban of waste law and the possibility of using a proper facility even outside OECD countries in the foreseeable future.[130]

The European Commission has considered the introduction of financial incentives to compensate shipowners for the higher costs of using the system of the Ship Recycling Regulation. Relevant considerations have been foreseen in article 29 of the Ship Recycling Regulation and the European Commission has published its view in its Report of 8 August 2017 on the feasibility of a financial instrument that would facilitate safe and sound ship recycling.[131] The system favoured by the European Commission and supported by NGOs is a ship recycling licence.[132] This has been heavily criticised by shipowners' organisations who have argued, among other things, that the EU would have no competence to administer an EU ship recycling scheme. This would also be incompatible with UNCLOS, with World Trade Organisation rules, and the principle of common but differentiated responsibilities.[133] The European Commission intends to clarify the legal situation and, at the same time, to monitor the use of the facilities of the European List in order to see whether additional financial incentives are necessary at all.[134]

A practical problem is that owing to the relatively strict procedures for recycling facilities to be included into the European List, only eight facilities from the main shipyards in Turkey were approved. None of the facilities of the other major recycling states, namely India, Pakistan and Bangladesh, have been included in the European List. There are, however, efforts to be approved and so the situation may change over time, although there still seems some way to go.[135]

VI. Conclusions

Some authors have predicted that the new regime is less likely to lead to the environmentally sound recycling of ships than 'more complicated considerations and procedures for shipowners to navigate through'.[136] This chapter suggests,

[130] See Claußen (n 72) 203. Tsimplis (n 7) 437, however, states that without financial incentives or coercion, the Ship Recycling Regulation does not contain any incentives for shipowners to use a European flag.

[131] COM(2017) 420 final.

[132] For details, see ibid, 4.

[133] ibid, 6. For details, see H Jessen, 'Safe and Environmentally Sound Ship Recycling: Obligations under EU Law and Public International Law' in Piraeus Bar Association (ed), '9th International Conference of Maritime Law' (Nomiki Bibliotiki, 2018) 149.

[134] On the difficulties relating to different financial systems, see also Tsimplis (n 7) 437.

[135] See ECSA, 'Indian ship recycling facilities far from the EU list' (7 May 2019), available at safety4sea.com/ecsa-indian-ship-recycling-facilities-far-from-the-eu-list; Jensen (n 8) 22.

[136] See Gorrissen Federspiel (n 129). See also CIEL (n 39).

nevertheless, that the coexistence and applicability of the two differing regimes on the dismantling of ships may in fact lead to an improvement of ship recycling conditions in the foreseeable future. While the new regime supports the availability of a greater number of better ship recycling facilities, the continuing applicability of the waste shipment regime, including the ban on shipment of hazardous waste to developing countries, and the increased threat of sanctions for non-adherence, may well provide an additional incentive for European shipowners to actually use the new system.

Challenges in Shipping Management and Organisation Stemming from the Financial Market

6

Ship Arrest and the Hanjin Bankruptcy: Lessons for Ship Management

JINGCHEN XU*

I. Introduction

On 31 August 2016, Hanjin Shipping Co Ltd (Hanjin) filed an application for rehabilitation proceedings in the Korean Bankruptcy Court, causing shock to the international shipping industry and causing worldwide disruption to the supply chain.[1] Hanjin participated in several strategic alliances with other shipping lines, through which ships owned or operated by Hanjin often carried a mixture of cargo belonging to some or all of the alliance members.[2] These alliance partners encountered problems in handling the Hanjin cargo loaded on their ships as well as their own cargoes loaded on Hanjin's ships.[3] In addition, ship-chartering and container-leasing companies faced the problem of recovering their chartered vessels, leased containers and overdue payments from Hanjin.[4] In view of the stay order issued by the Korean Bankruptcy Court preventing creditors from enforcing their claims against Hanjin in Korea, the collapse of Hanjin immediately sparked a scramble to initiate arrest proceedings against ships in other worldwide jurisdictions. Some ships belonging to Hanjin were instructed to slow steam and delay entering ports in order to avoid the potential risk of arrest. Other Hanjin ships

* Associate, Helmsman LLC; formerly Postdoctoral Fellow, Centre for Maritime Law, Faculty of Law, National University of Singapore.

[1] J Lee and SY Lee, 'Hanjin Shipping Files for Receivership, As Ports Turn Away Its Vessels', Reuters (31 August 2016), available at in.reuters.com/article/hanjin-shipping-debt-idINL3N1BC18V.

[2] Hanjin was a member of the CKYHE Alliance, consisting of Cosco Container Lines Co Ltd, Kawasaki Kisen Kaisha Ltd (K Line), Yang Ming Marine Transport Corp (Yang Ming), Hanjin and Evergreen Line. Under the terms of the Alliance's vessel-sharing agreement, member carriers were permitted to share vessels, charters and slots on each other's ships, and enter into cooperative arrangements. In 2017, the CKYHE Alliance ceased to operate and K Line and Yang Ming joined the THE Alliance: www.chinadaily.com.cn/newsrepublic/2016-11/21/content_27446932.htm.

[3] EYC Wong, JCK Yeung and L Chen, 'Modified Universalism and the Proposed Adoption of the UNCITRAL Model Law on Cross-Border Insolvency in Hong Kong – From the Hanjin Shipping Bankruptcy Case' (2019) 50 *Journal of Maritime Law and Commerce* 21, 38.

[4] ibid.

were stranded at sea and were refused entry into ports by port operators who feared that Hanjin would not be able to pay the relevant port fees.[5]

The purpose of this chapter is to focus on the challenges in shipping industry stemming from the financial market with a specific interest on the insolvency of shipping enterprises, which have had a pronounced impact on shipping enterprises, particularly those engaged in liner trades. Hanjin's insolvency was one of the largest and most significant insolvencies in the container shipping industry. It followed a series of shipping insolvencies, including those of Korea Line Corporation,[6] Sanko Steamship[7] and STX Pan Ocean.[8] The chaos caused by Hanjin's bankruptcy attracted the attention of ship managers to the conflict between the regimes of maritime law and cross-border insolvency. Among other concerns, a major issue for shipowners was whether a stay order under the universalist cross-border insolvency regime protected shipowner-debtors from admiralty *in rem* proceedings brought by local maritime claimants, enabling shipowner-debtors to carry out an effective reorganisation process without incurring unnecessary expense.

This chapter will analyse four decisions on the recognition of Hanjin's rehabilitation proceedings in four leading countries which have adopted the Model Law on Cross-Border Insolvency (the Model Law) developed by the United Nations Commission on International Trade Law. Each of these decisions focuses on an important underlying issue, namely whether *in rem* actions can be exempted from insolvency stay orders. Section II examines the collapse of Hanjin and the problem of conflicts between the cross-border insolvency and maritime regimes. Section III provides an overview of the different underlying theories when dealing with the problems of cross-border insolvency and the basic mechanisms of the Model Law. Section IV examines the recognition application initiated by Hanjin's administrator in four leading Model Law countries – Australia, Singapore, the UK and the US – and analyses the differing approaches in these jurisdictions when applying the Model Law in the maritime context. Section V analyses the different factors

[5] T Hals, 'Hanjin Shipping gets US court order, cash to unload ships', Reuters (10 September 2016), available at www.reuters.com/article/us-hanjin-shipping-debt-usa-bankruptcy-idUSKCN11F2DV.

[6] Korea Line Corporation filed for a receivership in the Korean Bankruptcy Court in 2011. Korea Line used to be the second largest dry bulk shipping company in Korea. When Korea Line filed for bankruptcy, it operated about 140 vessels. See 'Updated 1-Korea Line says in court receivership', Reuters (15 February 2011), available at www.reuters.com/article/korealine-court/update-1-korea-line-says-in-court-receivership-idUSTOE71E03I20110215.

[7] Sanko Steamship filed for bankruptcy in Japan in 2012. Sanko Steamship was one of the oldest shipping firms in Japan. Before it filed for bankruptcy, it managed a fleet of 185 ships, which included 46 tankers and 27 dry bulk carriers. See 'Japan's Sanko Steamship Declares Bankruptcy', Maritime Executive (18 December 2012), available at www.maritime-executive.com/article/japan-s-sanko-steamship-declares-bankruptcy#gs.7a9l8NY.

[8] STX Pan Ocean filed for bankruptcy in Korea in 2013. STX Pan Ocean was the largest bulk shipping group in Korea and also the largest bulk shipping company in the world. When STX Pan Ocean filed for bankruptcy, it had more than 340 vessels, including 270 bulk carriers. See 'Valemax Operator STX Pan Ocean Applies for Court Receivership', Maritime Executive (7 June 2013), available at www.maritime-executive.com/article/Valemax-Operator-STX-Pan-Ocean-Applies-For-Court-Receivership-2013-06-07#gs.B=jiTjk. See also *Fibria Celulose S/A v Pan Ocean Co Ltd* [2014] EWHC 2124 (Ch), [2014] Bus LR 1041.

that may influence the scope and effect of automatic stay orders and the preventative measures which the shipping industry should consider in order to avoid another Hanjin crisis. Finally, section VI concludes that the conflicts that arise between the cross-border insolvency and maritime law regimes are difficult, and that the outcome depends on individual cases.

II. The Collapse of Hanjin and the Rise of Conflicting Proceedings

Prior to its bankruptcy, Hanjin was the largest container shipping line in Korea and the seventh largest in the world.[9] Its earlier success benefitted from the rapid globalisation of the world's economy, the enormous growth in the entire container shipping industry, and the supporting policy of the Korean Government.[10] At the time of its bankruptcy, Hanjin operated approximately 60 container lines, with approximately 140 vessels and a capacity of approximately 630,000 20-foot equivalent units (TEUs).[11]

However, Hanjin was seriously affected by the 2008 financial crisis and experienced a 'deep deterioration' in both its financial performance and standing.[12] Between financial years 2011 and 2015, Hanjin reported a loss in its financial performance in each of these years and a negative cash flow in four out of these five years. In addition, in the same period, the value of total assets owned by Hanjin shrunk by almost 50 per cent.[13] The main reason for this deterioration was that Hanjin failed to correctly estimate the market. More specifically, Hanjin had entered into chartering agreements in 2010 when charter rates were fixed at a relatively high level, close to the pre-2008 level.[14] However, as shipping demand and freight prices continued to fall, Hanjin's charter rates remained high, quickly eroding its revenues. By the end of June 2016, Hanjin was approximately US $5.5 billion in debt.[15] As part of the requirement for receiving additional loans from its lenders, Hanjin proposed a self-rescue programme. This required a capital contribution of US $4.5 billion by Hanjin's creditors over two years in order to allow

[9] MT Lin, 'South Korea's History of Shipping Bankruptcies', *Lloyd's List* (2 September 2016). But *cf* 'Review of Maritime Transport 2015' (UNCTAD, 2015) 37, where Hanjin was reported as the eighth largest liner shipping company.

[10] TP Myers, 'Hung Up on Hanjin: Universalism and Bareboat Charter Hire Purchase Agreements Leave Maritime Lienholders Adrift' (2017) 42 *Tulane Maritime Law Journal* 195, 198–99.

[11] See P Fitzgerald, 'South Korea's Hanjin Shipping Files for US Bankruptcy Protection', available at www.wsj.com/articles/south-koreas-hanjin-shipping-files-for-u-s-bankruptcy-protection-1473002745.

[12] ibid. See also C Neame, G Eddings and M Wilmshurst, 'Hanjin Insolvency Set to be Significant Event for Market' (2016) 30 *Maritime Risk International* 10.

[13] See Hanjin Shipping Ltd Financial Statements (2011–2015), available at www.hanjinkal.co.kr/kr/contentsid/412/index.do. See also Wong, Yeung and Chen, 'Modified Universalism' (2019) 37.

[14] See 'South Korean shipping giant Hanjin to enter receivership', *BBC News* (31 August 2016), available at www.bbc.com/news/business-37227560.

[15] ibid.

Hanjin to survive as a going concern and until freight rates began to increase.[16] However, one of Hanjin's main creditors, the state-run Korea Development Bank, refused to further extend any further credit line and rejected Hanjin's proposed plan.[17]

Owing to a lack of support from its main creditors, Hanjin had no option but to file for rehabilitation protection under the Korean Debtor Rehabilitation and Bankruptcy Act 2006.[18] Korean rehabilitation proceedings are similar to US Chapter 11 proceedings and allow the debtor to retain its assets and continue in operation while paying creditors over an extended period of time.[19] As one of the major international shipping companies, Hanjin's insolvency affected most parties in the supply chain. Its creditors were spread across the globe and included, but were not limited to, bank mortgagees, shippers and consignees, freight forwarders, stevedores, container-leasing companies, crew members on ships, shipping companies that had entered into slot-chartering agreements with Hanjin and shipping companies that had time chartered and/or demise chartered their vessels to Hanjin.[20] In February 2017, after finding that Hanjin's liabilities vastly outweighed its assets, the Korean Bankruptcy Court terminated Hanjin's rehabilitation proceedings and converted the proceedings to liquidation proceedings.[21]

Hanjin's collapse inevitably raised issues of cross-border insolvency because of the worldwide dispersal of its assets and creditors. In the area of cross-border insolvency, the Model Law calls for assisting courts in other countries to cooperate with the courts in the home country of the debtor's insolvency proceedings and prevent any claimants from commencing or continuing any actions against the debtor in the assisting countries.[22] Thus, in order to avoid potential ship arrests by enjoying the automatic stay protections provided by the Model Law, Hanjin immediately applied to have its Korean rehabilitation proceedings recognised in various jurisdictions that had adopted the Model Law, including Australia, Singapore, the UK and the US.[23]

[16] See N Papadopoulos, 'Dealing with Problem Loans' (Norton Rose Fulbright, 2017), available at www.nortonrosefulbright.com/knowledge/publications/146792/dealing-with-problem-loan.

[17] I-S Nam, 'Hanjin Shipping Nears Bankruptcy After Creditors End Support', available at www.wsj.com/articles/hanjin-shipping-moves-closer-to-bankruptcy-1472532479.

[18] ibid. *cf* Torm, a Danish-based shipping company which reached an out-of-court agreement with its major creditors in order to obtain new capital when it was in severe financial difficulties, avoiding the filing of insolvency proceedings. See Bang-Pedersen (ch 7).

[19] Ministry of Justice, Republic of Korea, 'Special Rehabilitation Proceedings for MSMEs', available at www.uncitral.org/pdf/english/workinggroups/wg_5/51stWG5/MSMEs_Rehabilitation_Proceedings_Korea_20170505.pdf.

[20] Wong, Yeung and Chen (n 3) 39.

[21] 'Hanjin Shipping – Korean Rehabilitation (Converted to Bankruptcy) Proceedings (Update)', available at www.nepia.com/industry-news/hanjin-shipping-korean-rehabilitation-converted-to-bankruptcy-proceedings-update.

[22] Model Law, art 20. See M Davies, 'Cross-Border Insolvency and Admiralty: A Middle Path of Reciprocal Comity' (2018) 66 *American Journal of Comparative Law* 101.

[23] See, eg, *In re Hanjin Shipping Co Ltd* No 16-27041 (JKS), 2016 WL 6679487, 2016 AMC 2126 (Bankr New Jersey 20 September 2016); *Tai-Soo Suk v Hanjin Shipping Co Ltd* [2016] FCA 1404;

Maritime law has established a relatively independent and unified regime when a shipowner is in default or suffers financial difficulties – an *in rem* action. Such an action allows affected creditors to arrest the vessels of debtors and satisfy their claims against the vessels regardless of any insolvency proceedings, wherever they might be, against the shipowners. Thus, once Hanjin's rehabilitation protection was filed in Korea, creditors around the world tried their best to locate and arrest Hanjin's vessels in order to realise their claims, outside the Korean insolvency proceedings.

When Hanjin's ships were arrested under *in rem* actions in a country that adopted the Model Law, the Model Law called for the courts in that country to release the vessels and required maritime creditors to participate in Hanjin's insolvency proceedings in Korea. However, maritime law allowed creditors to proceed with their *in rem* actions against Hanjin and to realise their claims from the proceeds of the judicial sale of ships, regardless of Hanjin's insolvency proceeding in Korea. Thus, the most controversial issue following the collapse of Hanjin was the question whether an automatic stay order provided by the Model Law protected shipowner-debtors from *in rem* actions brought by local maritime claimants. This issue will now be discussed in detail.

III. Overview of Cross-Border Insolvency and the Model Law

A. Universalism and Territorialism

Historically, '[insolvency] has been one of the most parochial and nationalistic areas of the law' because it has often been seen as the last chance to get value from a business that is about to be liquidated.[24] Each nation follows a 'grab rule' approach, collecting debtors' assets physically within its territory and distributing the assets to local claimants under its local insolvency rules, without regard to the international group as a whole.[25] This is known as territorialism. However, territorialism has obvious drawbacks. It leads to the piecemeal disposition of the debtor's assets and an inconsistent and territory-based distribution of assets to local creditors; this, in turn, frustrates a unified restructuring of a multinational business because of the inconsistent and uncoordinated insolvency rules in different jurisdictions.[26]

In the Matter of Hanjin Shipping Co Ltd and in the Matter of Cross-Border Insolvency Regulations 2006 No CR-2016-005448 (Chancery Division, 6 September 2016); *Re Taisoo Suk (as foreign representative of Hanjin Shipping Co Ltd)* [2016] SGHC 195, [2016] 5 SLR 787.

[24] E Warren, JL Westbrook, K Porter and J Pottow, *The Law of Debtors and Creditors: Text, Cases, and Problems*, 7th edn (New York, Wolters Kluwer, 2014) 885.

[25] ibid.

[26] LM Clark and K Goldstein, 'Sacred Cows: How to Care for Secured Creditors' Rights in Cross-Border Bankruptcies' (2011) 46 *Texas International Law Journal* 513, 518.

The increasing trend, however, towards economic integration requires a global default.[27] There is a strong and growing trend towards universalism, mandating a cooperative and centralised administration of the debtor's assets in one single proceeding.[28] In other words, the fundamental principle of universalism is 'one law, one court', where all bankruptcy assets and claims should be administrated in a single forum. The main court will have full jurisdiction over all the debtor's assets across the world and distribute those assets to creditors under the law of that forum.[29] By entrusting the insolvency to a single proceeding, this avoids the costs of duplication of multiple concurrent proceedings, maximising the value of the debtor's company, and ensuring the equal treatment of all creditors on a global basis.[30] However, in order for universalism to work effectively, it requires the assisting forum to transfer authority over the assets within their jurisdiction or to enforce judgments rendered in the main insolvency proceedings.[31]

A significant majority of scholars agree that universalism is the future for international insolvency, but the ultimate goal may take time to achieve.[32] Thus, as an interim or transitional solution, modified universalism has emerged as the dominant theory. As Adams and Fincke have explained: 'Modified universalism embraces universalism's core belief of co-operation, but maintains the primacy of local courts' power to exercise discretion with respect to "the fairness of the home country procedures" and with respect to protecting the interests of local creditors'.[33] Because of its pragmatic flexibility, modified universalism 'provides the best fit with the problem presented by the current patchwork of laws in the global market, and because it will foster the smoothest and fastest transition to true universalism'.[34] The Model Law, discussed below, represents a typical attempt to impose a modified universalism approach.

[27] J Westbrook, 'Global Solution to Multinational Default' (2000) 98 *Michigan Law Review* 2276, 2287.

[28] B Wessels, B Markell and J Kilborn, *International Cooperation in Bankruptcy and Insolvency Matters* (Oxford, Oxford University Press, 2009) 49; Westbrook (ibid) 2287.

[29] F Tung, 'Is International Bankruptcy Possible?' (2001) 23 *Michigan Journal of International Law* 31, 40.

[30] ES Adams and J Fincke, 'Coordinating Cross-Border Bankruptcy: How Territorialism Saves Universalism' (2009) 15 *Columbia Journal of European Law* 43, 49.

[31] See E Gerber, 'Not All Politics Is Local: The New Chapter 15 to Govern Cross-Border Insolvencies' (2003) 71 *Fordham Law Review* 2051, 2052.

[32] See, eg, Westbrook, 'Global Solution' (2000) 2328; Adams and Fincke, 'Coordinating Cross-Border Bankruptcy' (2009) 48–49; EH Biery, JL Boland and JD Cornwell, 'A Look at Transnational Insolvencies and Chapter 15 of the Bankruptcy Abuse Prevention and Consumer Protection Act of 2005' (2005) 47 *Boston College Law Review* 23, 57; A Guzman, 'International Bankruptcy: In Defense of Universalism' (2000) 98 *Michigan Law Review* 2177, 2198; H Buxbaum, 'Rethinking International Insolvency: The Neglected Role of Choice of Law Rules and Theory' (2000) 36 *Stanford Journal of International Law* 23, 26.

[33] Adams and Fincke (n 30) 50.

[34] Westbrook (n 27) 2277.

B. The Model Law

The Model Law was developed to assist enacting states to equip their insolvency laws and to promote a fair and efficient administration of cross-border insolvency.[35] Respecting the differences between national insolvency laws, the Model Law does not attempt a 'substantive unification of insolvency law', but is designed to provide a framework for the 'modest but significant' development towards greater cooperation in international insolvencies and aims to harmonise the approaches of national legal systems in how to deal with international insolvencies.[36] In other words, the goal of the Model Law is to overcome judicial and administrative barriers, rather than to unify the substantive law of insolvency. Thus, the Model Law is essentially procedural in nature.[37]

In UNCITRAL terms, 'a model law is a legislative text that is recommended to states for incorporation into their own national law'.[38] The Model Law is not binding in itself. Thus, it is designed in a way that ensures that it may be easily adopted by any state that is interested in doing so.[39] The Model Law provides the enacting state with the flexibility to adopt and modify the text for the needs of the state, prior to its enactment. Nevertheless, the intention of the drafter of the Model Law is that, 'a state should stay as close as possible to the text of the Model Law to ensure a degree of certainty and predictability'.[40] By July 2019, 46 states had adopted the Model Law, including major shipping countries such as Australia, Canada, Greece, Japan, Korea, Singapore, South Africa, the UK and the US.[41]

The Model Law encourages international judicial cooperation and the efficient administration of cross-border insolvencies – courts in each assisting country will recognise the insolvency proceeding in the main country and cooperate with each other, bringing all claims together in a single forum.[42] Generally, all bankruptcy assets and claims are expected to be administrated in the debtor's centre of main interests (COMI) and distributed under the law of COMI, subject to appropriate coordination procedures or local public policy exceptions.[43] The recognition

[35] UNCITRAL Secretariat, 'Cross-Border Insolvency Law with Guide to Enactment and Interpretation' (United Nations Office at Vienna, 2014) 19.

[36] ibid. See also Westbrook (n 27) 2315.

[37] UNCITRAL Secretariat, 'Cross-Border Insolvency Law' (2014) 24.

[38] ibid.

[39] MS Wee, 'Lessons for the Development of Singapore's International Insolvency Law' (2011) 23 *Singapore Academy of Law Journal* 932, 942–43.

[40] Wessels, Markell and Kilborn, *International Cooperation* (2009) 202. See also UNCITRAL Secretariat (n 35) 25.

[41] 'Status: UNCITRAL Model Law on Cross-Border Insolvency (1997), available at uncitral.un.org/en/texts/insolvency/modellaw/cross-border_insolvency/status.

[42] Westbrook (n 27) 2315.

[43] Model Law, arts 2, 6, 28; UNCITRAL Secretariat (n 35) 19. The Model Law does not define the term COMI, but only provides a presumption that, absent proof to the contrary, the centre of a debtor's main interests is the state where the debtor's registered office or habitual residence is located. Model Law, art 16(3).

procedure provided by the Model Law is relatively straightforward and easy to comply with. Unless the public policy exception is triggered, there is little room left for local courts to exercise any discretion to refuse to grant a recognition application if all the documentary requirements are met.[44] Nevertheless, the Model Law intends the public policy exception to be strictly interpreted.[45]

Among all the provisions of the Model Law, the most important and relevant provision for ship management is article 20. Article 20(1) of the Model Law provides that a stay order will be automatically issued upon the recognition of a foreign main proceeding,[46] freezing all claims in the local forum from commencing or continuing any action against the insolvent debtor's assets, rights, obligations or liabilities. The assets of the insolvent debtor outside of the foreign main proceeding are therefore protected from being seized by local creditors in the assisting states. However, the Model Law is procedural in nature and does not intend to alter the substantive insolvency laws of the recognising countries.[47] Thus, article 20(2) of the Model Law suggests that enacting states are allowed to modify the scope and effect of stay orders by introducing exceptions and limitations that already exist under the domestic insolvency laws of the enacting states.[48] Accordingly, article 20(2) deliberately leaves assisting states to decide on the scope and effect of stay orders, including the issue of whether secured creditors should be an exception to stay orders.[49]

IV. Different Approaches by Different Countries

In the case of Hanjin's bankruptcy, maritime creditors opposed the debtor's application for recognition on the grounds that they were secured creditors and should, therefore, be exempted from the automatic stay mechanism provided by the Model Law. However, different countries have different approaches when applying the Model Law in the maritime context. This is because different countries have different enactments of article 20(2) when adopting the Model Law and different countries have different local insolvency rules with regard to the exception of stay orders. This part examines key decisions made in the US, Australia, the UK and Singapore respectively regarding the recognition of Hanjin's rehabilitation proceedings and its subsequent stay order, focusing on the main underlying issue, namely, whether shipowners can utilise the Model Law regime as a measure

[44] ibid, art 17(1).

[45] ibid, art 6. For the interpretation of the public policy exception, see UNCITRAL Secretariat (n 35) 26, 52; Wessels (n 28) 215.

[46] A foreign main proceeding is the proceeding commenced in the state where the debtor has its COMI: ibid, art 2(b).

[47] UNCITRAL Secretariat (n 35) 19; Wee, 'Lessons' (2011) 943.

[48] Model Law, art 20(2); Wessels (n 28) 217.

[49] ibid, art 20(2). See also J Xu, *Maritime Cross-Border Insolvency under the UNCITRAL Model Law Regime: Commonwealth and US Perspectives* (Oxford, Hart Publishing, 2020) ch 4, pt III.

of protection to avoid ship arrests initiated by maritime creditors in insolvency proceedings.

A. United States

i. US Enactment of the Model Law

The US enacted the Model Law in 2005 as a new chapter of the US Bankruptcy Code – Chapter 15.[50] The stated purpose of Chapter 15 is to 'provide an effective mechanism for foreign representatives of foreign insolvency proceedings to obtain the recognition and assistance of the US bankruptcy courts to protect or administer assets within the US'.[51] In interpreting Chapter 15, the US courts are instructed to consider the international origin of Chapter 15, and the need to promote universalism in the area of cross-border insolvency.[52]

Section 1520(a)(1) provides that, if the foreign proceeding is recognised as a foreign main proceeding, an automatic stay will be triggered to prevent creditors from commencing or continuing any proceedings against the debtor's assets, rights, obligations and liabilities within the US.[53] Specifically, the scope and effect of the automatic stay will be the same as the protection and limitations for creditors that are set out in § 362 of the US Bankruptcy Code.[54] Since the US Bankruptcy Code has traditionally been deemed as very 'pro-debtor', the scope of automatic stay orders under § 362 is quite broad.[55] The stay applies to, 'any act to create, perfect, or enforce against the property of the debtor any lien to the extent that such lien secures a claim that arose before the commencement of the case'.[56] Thus, all creditors will be stayed upon the insolvency proceedings being filed, whether secured or unsecured and whether in liquidation or reorganisation proceedings. Although courts may grant creditors relief from the stay under certain circumstances, upon the application of creditors, relief to lift the § 362 automatic stay is usually hard to obtain.[57] Accordingly, by referring to § 362 in its enactment of the Model Law, the US actually mandates a stay upon the recognition of a foreign main proceeding.[58] In the maritime context, such relief could include a stay order preventing creditors from arresting and selling the vessels of shipping companies.[59]

[50] GF Seitz, 'Interaction between Admiralty and Bankruptcy Law: Effects of Globalisation and Recurrent Tensions' (2009) 83 *Tulane Law Review* 1339, 1343–44.
[51] 11 USC § 1501(a).
[52] ibid, § 1508.
[53] ibid, § 1520(a)(1).
[54] ibid, §§ 362, 1520(a)(1).
[55] ibid, § 362. See also G McCormack, *Secured Credit and the Harmonisation of Law: The UNCITRAL Experience* (Cheltenham, Edward Elgar, 2011) 183.
[56] ibid, § 362(a)(5).
[57] ibid, §§ 362(d), 1520.
[58] ibid, §§ 362(a)(5), 1520(a)(1). See also Davies, 'Cross-Border Insolvency and Admiralty' (2018) 109.
[59] ibid, § 1520.

ii. In re Hanjin Shipping Co Ltd

a. Petition for Recognition

On 2 September 2016, immediately after its application for Korean insolvency proceedings, the administrator of Hanjin filed a petition for recognition under Chapter 15 of the US Bankruptcy Code in the United States Bankruptcy Court for the District of New Jersey, seeking an automatic stay order to suspend any action from commencing or continuing against Hanjin's vessels.[60] The Court held the hearing on 6 September 2016.

In order to support its arguments, Hanjin noted that, at the time of the hearing, 13 of its ships were outside of US territorial waters, unable and/or unwilling to enter the US ports because of the fear of being arrested by maritime lienholders. Maritime lienholders, especially bunker suppliers of Hanjin, argued that their maritime liens deserved sufficient security under US maritime law, such as bonds or cash deposits, and therefore that the automatic stay should not apply in the absence of these securities.[61] Maritime lienholders explained that their rights of maritime liens under US law were far superior to those rights recognised in Korea. If the claims of the maritime lienholders were going to be subject to the Chapter 15 stay order, they had to file their claims under Hanjin's Korean rehabilitation proceeding, and they argued that their rights under US law would be severely prejudiced.[62]

Given the extremely short notice, the court granted an interim order to recognise Hanjin's Korean rehabilitation proceeding as a foreign main proceeding and granted a temporary stay order to prevent Hanjin's vessels from being arrested if they entered US ports to deliver cargo. The vessels were not permitted to depart the US until a further hearing on Hanjin's petition was completed.[63] The purpose of this interim order was to allow Hanjin's vessels to enter the relevant ports and discharge cargo, minimising the negative impact on the supply chain because of the non-delivery or delayed delivery of cargo. Nevertheless, the court 'carved out' the arrest of the *M/V Hanjin Montevideo* from the temporary stay because it was arrested before Hanjin's Chapter 15 petition had been filed.[64] The issue as to whether maritime lienholders could be exempted from the stay order was scheduled to be decided in a subsequent hearing three days later.

However, contrary to what the Court expected, none of Hanjin's ships entered any of the US ports during the three days between the hearings because of the threat of arrest to enforce maritime liens by maritime lienholders. In fact, one of the vessels had turned around.[65]

[60] *In re Hanjin Shipping Co Ltd* No 16-27041 (JKS), 2016 WL 6681169, 2016 AMC 2113 (Bankr New Jersey 16 September 2016).

[61] ibid, 2.

[62] ibid.

[63] ibid.

[64] See *World Fuel Services Inc v M/V Hanjin Montevideo* No 2-16-cv-06584 (CD California 2016).

[65] *Hanjin Shipping* (n 60) 2.

In the subsequent hearing, in addition to the arguments made by Hanjin's administrator and the maritime lienholders, several parties in the supply chain argued that the impasse caused imminent negative financial consequences for them.[66] For example, the beneficial cargo owners, whose cargo was stranded at sea, in warehouses and port facilities, argued that the stay order should be granted without carving out the maritime claimants because their business would otherwise be financially harmed due to the non-delivery or delayed delivery of their cargo. In addition, the operators of port facilities and warehouses claimed that any arrests would lead to valuable docks and storage spaces being occupied by Hanjin's ships, containers and cargo.[67] Thus, showing an awareness of the negative impact that the immobilisation of cargo would have on these parties, the Court held that the stay order extended to maritime liens claims and that the vessels would be allowed to leave the US port after docking and discharging.

b. Motion for Reconsideration

The maritime lienholders promptly filed a motion for reconsideration of the Court's decision. However, the Court dismissed the motion for reconsideration and held that the automatic stay must extend to ship arrests so as to allow Hanjin's ships to enter US ports under the protection of the stay.[68]

The Court explained that the goal of universalism was to direct creditors and assets to the foreign main proceeding for the orderly and fair distribution of assets, avoiding the piecemeal seizure of assets by creditors operating outside the jurisdiction of the foreign main proceeding.[69] Although the Court noted that maritime lien claimants, especially suppliers of necessaries, were in a better position in the US than they were in Korea,[70] it held that any enforcement of maritime lien claims against vessels would violate Chapter 15's 'clear directive' and would signal the embrace of territorialism.[71] Thus, the Court adhered to the universalist approach under Chapter 15 and refused to grant relief exceptions for maritime lien claimants.[72]

In addition, the Court held that preventing maritime lienholders from enforcing their lien rights did not violate the bankruptcy code or US public policy.[73]

[66] ibid.

[67] ibid.

[68] *In re Hanjin Shipping Co Ltd* No 16-27041 (JKS), 2016 WL 6679487, 2016 AMC 2126 (Bankr New Jersey 20 September 2016).

[69] ibid, 4 (citing *In re ABC Learning Centres Ltd* 728 F 3d 301 (3rd Cir 2013), 306–07).

[70] ibid, 3; see also 46 USC § 31342. Korean Law only provides claimants with maritime liens when the claims are against the registered owner of the ship. As discussed in section V of this chapter, most of Hanjin's operating vessels were not owned by Hanjin, but chartered from third parties and, therefore, the claimants did not have maritime liens in Korea: *Hanjin Shipping* (n 68) EFC No 85. See also HI Kim, 'An Overview of Korean Maritime Law' (2012) 10 *Asian Business Lawyer* 35, 58.

[71] *Hanjin Shipping* (n 68) 3.

[72] ibid.

[73] ibid, 6.

In reaching this conclusion, the Court weighed the interests of all the parties involved and the practicalities, and eventually granted a general stay order without carving out maritime claimants. The Court reasoned that

> if the debtor's vessels were not allowed to dock, unload their cargo, and depart under the protection of a stay, they would potentially avoid ports in the United States, leaving delivery of their cargo in limbo and causing [cargo owners], port operators and others harm.[74]

Thus, with the interests of Hanjin and all global creditors in mind, the Court dismissed the maritime lienholder's motion for reconsideration.

Nevertheless, the Court confirmed the 'carve out' of the *M/V Hanjin Montevideo* from the stay protection. The Court reasoned that the purpose of an automatic stay was to preserve the status quo at the time of the stay and to provide debtors with a 'breathing spell'.[75] The timing of the status quo in *Hanjin Shipping* was at the time when the automatic stay was granted. Thus, the lien claims against the *M/V Hanjin Montevideo* were mature and enforceable when the issue was before the court; this was because the *M/V Hanjin Montevideo* was arrested before Hanjin's Chapter 15 petition had been filed.[76]

In the US, the overall goal of Chapter 15 is to promote a single, orderly and fair distribution of assets and to avoid the seizure of assets by local creditors. This provides shipping companies with protection through automatic stays over any enforcement actions against the debtors' assets.[77] Creditors will have no option but to seek relief in the foreign main proceeding. However, the carve out of the *M/V Hanjin Montevideo* may at least indicate some leeway that automatic stay orders are not applied to vessels that have already been arrested before recognition orders are granted.[78]

B. Australia

i. Enactment of the Model Law

Australia adopted the Model Law entirely in its 'standalone' Cross-Border Insolvency Act 2008 (Cth) (CBIA). In enacting the Model Law, Australia chose to preserve the exceptions and limitations to article 20 regarding automatic stays, by referring to its own domestic insolvency laws, namely, the Corporations Act 2001 (Cth) and the Bankruptcy Act 1966 (Cth). Section 16 of the CBIA provides that:

> For the purposes of paragraph 2 of Article 20 of the Model Law (as it has the force of law in Australia), the scope and the modification or termination of the stay or suspension

[74] ibid, 7.
[75] ibid, 6.
[76] ibid.
[77] 11 USC § 1520.
[78] *cf Evridiki Navigation Inc v Sanko SS Co* 880 F Supp 2d 666, 2012 AMC 1817 (D Maryland 2012).

referred to in paragraph 1 of that Article, are the same as would apply if the stay or suspension arose under:

(a) the Bankruptcy Act 1966; or
(b) Chapter 5 (other than Parts 5.2 and 5.4A) of the Corporations Act 2001;[79]

This section provides that the scope and effect of the stay order are identical to the stay provisions as if the case had arisen under Australian domestic insolvency proceedings.[80] In other words, whether secured creditors may be permitted to proceed with their rights against debtors will be decided by the same stay provisions applicable to Australian local insolvency proceedings that the foreign proceedings 'most closely resemble'.[81] However, in practice, article 20(2) can become 'beguilingly ambiguous', because the Corporations Act 2001 has various stay provisions that 'differentially affect the position of secured creditors, sometimes at different points in the same overall process'.[82] The local stay provisions in Australia depend on the type of insolvency proceedings:

(1) Part 5.1 (scheme of arrangement) – no stay applies.
(2) Part 5.3A (voluntary administration) – ss 440A–440JA provide for stays.
(3) Part 5.4/Part 5.4B (court-ordered liquidation) – ss 467, 471B and 471C provide for stays.

….[83]

Secured creditors can be exempted from stay orders. In court-ordered liquidation proceedings, secured creditors are allowed to proceed with their claims against the debtor regardless of the stay order.[84] In voluntary administration proceedings, however, enforcement actions by secured creditors will usually be suspended unless either consent can be obtained from the administrator or the court grants relief. The reason is so that the corporate debtor can still have some 'breathing space' and the prospect of surviving its insolvency.[85] In Australia, therefore, if the foreign main proceeding resembles proceedings for a court-ordered liquidation, secured claimants are exempted from an automatic stay of proceedings and the suspension of the enforcement process. If, however, the foreign main proceeding resembles a voluntary administration, secured claimants are not exempted from an automatic stay order, but are prevented from commencing or continuing any enforcement action against the debtor, unless they obtain the consent of the administrator or relief from the court.[86] Secured creditors may apply for the

[79] CBIA, s 16.
[80] See, eg, *Hur v Samsun Logix Corp* [2009] FCA 372; *Aker v Deputy Commissioner of Taxation* [2014] FCAFC 57; *Yu v STX Pan Ocean Co Ltd* [2013] FCA 680, (2013) 233 FCR 189; *Kim v Daebo International Shipping Co Ltd* [2015] FCA 684, (2015) 232 FCR 275. See also S Rares, 'Ship Arrests, Maritime Liens and Cross-Border Insolvency' [2018] *LMCLQ* 398, 409.
[81] *Suk v Hanjin Shipping Co Ltd* [2016] FCA 1404, [21].
[82] *Hur* (n 80) [21].
[83] *Suk* (n 81) [20].
[84] Corporations Act 2001 (Cth), s 471C.
[85] ibid, s 440D.
[86] ibid, ss 440D, 471C. See also CBIA, s 16; *Yu* (n 80) [40].

court's permission to be exempted from the administration proceeding, but such relief depends on individual cases.

ii. Suk v Hanjin Shipping Co Ltd

On 23 September 2016, Hanjin's administrator applied, on an ex parte basis, to have its Korean rehabilitation proceedings recognised as a foreign main proceeding under the CBIA in New South Wales. The Court found that Hanjin's Korean proceeding met all the elements and requirements laid out in articles 2 and 17 of schedule 1 of the CBIA and therefore recognised Hanjin's rehabilitation proceeding as a foreign main proceeding, granting a stay order preventing maritime creditors from arresting the vessels owned or operated by Hanjin.[87]

Jagot J was asked to identify the specific stay provisions of the Corporations Act that would apply to the foreign proceedings if they were taking place in Australia.[88] The reason for this identification was that, as secured creditors, the treatment of maritime lien claimants would be different under the different types of proceedings. The plaintiff argued that rehabilitation proceedings were more akin to voluntary administration proceedings under part 5.3A of the Corporation Act, and therefore the stay provisions should not exclude any actions regarding maritime liens held against Hanjin's assets.[89] Jagot J explained that under article 20(2) of the Model Law and section 16 of the CBIA, the Court had a duty to determine the type of proceedings that the foreign proceeding most closely resembled.[90] The Court would compare the nature of the foreign proceedings with the nature of the proceedings under the relevant parts of the Corporations Act and the scope of the stay order would be the same as that provided for those types of proceedings in the Corporations Act.[91] After examining the evidence submitted by Hanjin's administrator, the Court found that the Korean rehabilitation proceeding more closely resembled an Australian voluntary administration proceeding under part 5.3A of the Corporations Act. This provided that secured creditors were subject to an automatic stay rather than a scheme of arrangement, where no automatic stay would apply. The Court held that the automatic stay order did not harm the interests of maritime lienholders, because maritime lienholders could always apply for relief to proceed with their *in rem* actions simultaneously.[92] If the relief was granted, maritime lienholders would be in the same position as they would have been if the stay did not apply to their claims.[93] The Court therefore concluded that no proceedings to enforce maritime liens could be initiated or continued against

[87] *Suk* (n 81) [16].
[88] ibid, [21].
[89] ibid.
[90] ibid, [22].
[91] ibid, [24].
[92] ibid, [51]–[58].
[93] ibid, [57].

vessels owned or chartered by Hanjin unless they were with the debtor's written consent or with the relief of the Court.

By identifying the Korean rehabilitation proceeding as akin to a voluntary administration proceeding, the Court was able to issue a wide stay order, preventing maritime creditors from enforcing their claims to further the objective of the Korean rehabilitation proceeding. The stay extended to all vessels owned or chartered by Hanjin, without carving out any pre-arrested vessel. One additional issue is that, after Hanjin's Korean rehabilitation proceeding was converted to a liquidation proceeding and the administrator lost his status as a foreign representative, Jagot J vacated the recognition order and lifted the stay order the Court had earlier granted.[94] The reason for this termination was that Hanjin's administrator failed to comply with his obligation under article 18 of the Model Law to inform the court of a substantial change in the status of the foreign proceeding.[95] The Court took the initiative to terminate the previous recognition order. It is therefore important for foreign representatives to respect their notification obligations under article 18 of the Model Law, keeping the Court updated, so that it can modify the recognition order or stay order accordingly.

C. United Kingdom

i. Enactment of the Model Law

The UK took an active role in the development of the Model Law and brought it into force on 4 April 2006 by means of the Cross-Border Insolvency Regulations 2006 (CBIR 2006).[96] However, the CBIR 2006 applies to Great Britain only.[97] Article 20(1) of schedule 1 to the CBIR 2006 provides that once a foreign proceeding is recognised as a foreign main proceeding, an automatic stay will be triggered to protect the debtor's assets, rights, obligations and liabilities.[98] Following the 'Guide to Enactment and Interpretation' of the Model Law,[99] the CBIR 2006 limits the scope and effect of the stay order in article 20(2):

> 2. The stay and suspension referred to in paragraph 1 of this article shall be—
>
> (a) the same in scope and effect as if the debtor, in the case of an individual, had been adjudged bankrupt under the Insolvency Act 1986 or had his estate sequestrated

[94] *Suk v Hanjin Shipping Co Ltd* [2017] FCA 404.

[95] ibid, [11]. *cf Yakushiji v Kaisha (No 2)* [2016] FCA 1277 where the debtor brought an application under art 18 after its change of ownership in the Korean rehabilitation proceedings and the court vacated the original recognition order.

[96] SI 2006/1030. See IF Fletcher, 'Better Late than Never: The UNCITRAL Model Law Enters into Force in Great Britain' (2006) 19 *Insolvency Intelligence* 86, 86, available at www.iiiglobal.org/sites/default/files/media/076A_Better_late_by_Fletcher.pdf.

[97] Northern Ireland has parallel legislation implementing the Model Law, the Cross-Border Insolvency Regulations (Northern Ireland) 2007, SI 2007/115, which came into force on 12 April 2007.

[98] CBIR 2006, sch 1, art 20(1).

[99] UNCITRAL Secretariat (n 35).

under the Bankruptcy (Scotland) Act 1985, or, in the case of a debtor other than an individual, had been made the subject of a winding-up order under the Insolvency Act 1986; and

(b) subject to the same powers of the court and the same prohibitions, limitations, exceptions and conditions as would apply under the law of Great Britain in such a case,

and the provisions of paragraph 1 of this article shall be interpreted accordingly.

3. Without prejudice to paragraph 2 of this article, the stay and suspension referred to in paragraph 1 of this article, in particular, does not affect any right—

(a) to take any steps to enforce security over the debtor's property; …[100]

In other words, in the UK the scope and effect of the automatic stay is limited to the same extent as if the case had arisen in a comparable case under the Insolvency Act 1986.[101] In *Cosco Bulk Carrier Co v Armada Shipping SA*, the Court explained that article 20(2) clearly identified English domestic insolvency law as the primary source with regard to the effect and scope of the automatic stay upon the recognition of a foreign main proceeding.[102] As is the case also in Australia, the court will compare the nature of the foreign proceedings with the local insolvency proceedings and apply the stay provisions applicable to the most comparable local insolvency proceedings.[103] Although article 20(3)(a) provides that the automatic stay or suspension does not affect a creditor's right to enforce its security over the debtor's property, article 20(3) needs to be subject to article 20(2).[104] Therefore, whether secured creditors can be exempted from automatic stay orders under CBIR 2006 depends on the English domestic stay provisions that apply to the local insolvency proceedings that the foreign proceedings most closely resemble.

In domestic insolvency proceedings, upon the commencement of a compulsory winding up or an administration proceeding, an automatic stay will be imposed against creditors. No action or proceeding will be proceeded with or commenced against the debtor or its property.[105] Nevertheless, it is well settled that the automatic stay provision has no effect on the secured creditors in winding-up proceedings.[106] On the contrary, in administration proceedings, secured creditors

[100] CBIR 2006, sch 1, art 20(2).

[101] ibid, art 20(2)(a). See also UNCITRAL Secretariat (n 35) 85.

[102] *Cosco Bulk Carrier Co v Armada Shipping SA* [2011] EWHC 216 (Ch), [2011] 2 All ER (Comm) 481, [45].

[103] ibid.

[104] ibid. See also LC Ho, *A Commentary on the UNCITRAL Model Law*, 4th edn (London, Globe Law and Business, 2017) 240.

[105] Insolvency Act 1986, s 130(2).

[106] ibid, ss 183(1), (2)(a). See, eg, W Tetley, *Maritime Liens and Claims*, 2nd edn (Montreal, Editions Yvon Blais, 1998) 1133; B Leonard, 'Getting the Deal Through – The Restructuring and Insolvency' (Law Business Research, 2017) 151; N Meeson and J Kimbell, *Admiralty Jurisdiction and Practice*, 5th edn (Abingdon, Informa, 2018) 115; IF Fletcher, *The Law of Insolvency*, 5th edn (London, Sweet & Maxwell, 2017) 703.

are not exempted from the stay order, but are prevented from enforcing their securities against the company without first obtaining the consent of the administrator or the leave of the court.[107]

ii. In the Matter of Hanjin Shipping Co Ltd *and* In the Matter of Cross-Border Insolvency Regulations 2006

Hanjin's rehabilitation proceeding was recognised as a foreign main proceeding by an order made by Nugee J on 6 September 2016, in accordance with article 17 of schedule 1 to the CBIR 2006.[108] Finding that Hanjin's proceeding more closely resembled administration proceedings, Nugee J granted a wide automatic stay to suspend all creditors from enforcing any mortgage, lien or other security rights against Hanjin as if it had been entered into administration in the UK:

> Save for the proceedings identified in the Schedule to this Order, which are permitted to continue to the content identified in the Schedule, no legal process may be instituted or continued against the Company or its property except with the consent of the Administrator or the permission of the Court.[109]

In other words, the stay order issued by the English High Court was a wide automatic stay to prevent all parties from enforcing any mortgage, lien or other security over Hanjin's assets except with the consent of the administrator or the permission of the Court.[110] However, in the schedule to the order, the Court did allow several arbitrations against Hanjin that had already been initiated before the commencement of Hanjin's Korean rehabilitation proceeding or had been given consent by Hanjin's administrator to continue, up to the extent of the specific purposes identified in the schedule to the order.[111] The Court emphasised that the claimants were not allowed to take any further steps in those arbitrations or to seek to enforce any arbitration award against Hanjin.[112]

Similarly to Australia, maritime creditors were prevented from arresting Hanjin's vessels *in rem* to enforce their maritime claims in the UK. Since Hanjin's proceeding was similar to English administration proceedings, this wide stay order granted by Nugee J was in compliance with the CBIR 2006 and the Insolvency Act 1986.

[107] Insolvency Act 1986, sch B1, para 43. See Leonard (ibid) 154; Fletcher (ibid) 516–17; Meeson and Kimbell (ibid) 119.

[108] *In the Matter of Hanjin Shipping Co Ltd* No CR-2016-005448 (Chancery Division, 6 September 2016).

[109] ibid, para 2(3).

[110] *Hanjin Shipping* (n 108). See Insolvency Act 1986, sch B1, para 43.

[111] *Hanjin Shipping* (n 108) sch, paras 1–3.

[112] ibid.

D. Singapore

i. Enactment of the Model Law

At the time of Hanjin's application to have its Korean rehabilitation proceeding recognised, Singapore had not formally adopted the Model Law. Nevertheless, the High Court recognised Hanjin's rehabilitation proceeding in accordance with its inherent power under the common law.[113] In order to strengthen Singapore as an international debt restructuring hub, Parliament passed the Companies (Amendment) Act 2017 ('the Act') on 10 March 2017, and this came into force on 23 May 2017.[114] The Act formally embraced modified universalism by adopting the Model Law, abolishing the traditional ringfencing rule in the winding up of foreign companies.[115] The aim of the Act was to enhance the restructuring legal framework, create a restructuring friendly ecosystem and addressing the perception gap.[116] Since July 2020, the bulk of Singapore's insolvency legislation now appears in the Insolvency, Restructuring and Dissolution Act 2018 (IRDA), with the Model Law adopted by way of the 3rd Schedule.[117]

Article 20(1) of the 10th Schedule to the Act provides that once a foreign proceeding is recognised as a foreign main proceeding an automatic stay will be triggered to protect the debtor's assets, rights, obligations and liabilities. Article 20(2)–(3) limits the scope and effect of the automatic stay, providing that:

> 2. The stay and suspension mentioned in paragraph 1 of this Article are —
>
> (a) the same in scope and effect as if the debtor had been made the subject of a winding-up order under this Act; and
>
> (b) subject to the same powers of the Court and the same prohibitions, limitations, exceptions and conditions as would apply under the law of Singapore in such a case,
>
> and the provisions of paragraph 1 of this Article are to be interpreted accordingly.
>
> 3. Without prejudice to paragraph 2 of this Article, the stay and suspension mentioned in paragraph 1 of this Article do not affect any right —
>
> (a) to take any steps to enforce security over the debtor's property;
>
> ...[118]

[113] *Re Taisoo Suk (as foreign representative of Hanjin Shipping Co Ltd)* [2016] SGHC 195, [2016] 5 SLR 787.

[114] I Rajah, 'Enhancing Singapore as an International Debt Restructuring Centre for Asia and Beyond', available at app.mlaw.gov.sg/files/NoteonDebtRestructuring.pdf.

[115] Companies Act, cap 50 (2006 rev ed), s 377(3)(c). The ringfencing rule in Singapore requires that in the event of a liquidation a company registered under the Companies Act must pay its debts and liabilities incurred in Singapore first before transmitting the balance to the liquidator of the foreign company's principal place of liquidation. The ringfencing rule has now been abolished by the Companies Act 2017. See Rajah (ibid).

[116] 'Report of the Committee to Strengthen Singapore as an International Centre for Debt Restructuring' (20 April 2016), available at www.mlaw.gov.sg/files/news/public-consultations/2016/04/Final%20DR%20Report.pdf.

[117] For ease of reference, this chapter refers to the provisions of the Companies Act, notwithstanding that some of these provisions have been repealed.

[118] Companies Act, sch 10, arts 20(2), (3).

Article 20(2) expressly refers to local insolvency proceedings with regard to the scope and effect of the automatic stay orders.[119] In other words, when applying article 20, courts will look into the nature of the foreign insolvency proceedings and identify the type of local insolvency proceedings under the Act that the foreign insolvency proceedings most closely resemble.[120] The scope and effect of the automatic stay imposed by article 20(1) of the 10th Schedule to the Act will be the same as that in local insolvency law in Singapore.[121] In addition, without prejudice to article 20(2), the scope and effect of the automatic stay are further curtailed by article 20(3), which specifically points out that the stay and suspension 'do not affect any right to take any steps to enforce security over the debtor's property'.[122] Nevertheless, since article 20(3) provides that it is 'without prejudice to paragraph 2 of this article' it is merely declaratory and does not operate as an exception to article 20(1)–(2).

ii. Re Taisoo Suk

In *Re Taisoo Suk*, the High Court incorporated the Model Law-type of concepts into Singapore's common law and embraced a universalist approach in its inherent power under the common law.[123] Relying on O 92 r 4 of the Rules of Court, the Court granted the recognition and stay order to restrain all pending, contingent or fresh proceedings against Hanjin, its Singapore subsidiaries or any of their assets.[124] However, the stay order did not apply to the *M/V Hanjin Rome*, a vessel that had been arrested before Hanjin's administrator applied for recognition. This 'carve-out' arose out of a concession by Hanjin's administrator.[125]

In granting the order, the High Court relied on the Court of Appeal decision in *Beluga Chartering GmbH (in liquidation) v Beluga Projects (Singapore) Pte Ltd (in liquidation)*,[126] where the Court recognised the benefits of a universalist approach in winding-up proceedings and noted that courts in Singapore could render assistance to foreign winding-up proceedings in certain circumstances.[127] In *Re Taisoo Suk*, the High Court extended *Beluga*'s approach to other forms of insolvency proceedings, including restructuring and rehabilitation proceedings.[128]

[119] ibid, art 20(2).
[120] See *Cosco Bulk Carrier* (n 102).
[121] ibid.
[122] Companies Act, sch 10, art 20(3).
[123] *Re Taisoo Suk* (n 113).
[124] ibid, [14].
[125] ibid, [35].
[126] *Beluga Chartering GmbH (in liquidation) v Beluga Projects (Singapore) Pte Ltd (in liquidation)* [2014] SGCA 14, [2014] 2 SLR 815.
[127] *Re Taisoo Suk* (n 113) [15].
[128] ibid, [16].

The High Court listed three factors in determining whether recognition of foreign rehabilitation proceedings should be granted:

(a) the connection of the company to the forum in which the rehabilitation proceedings are taking place and to the place of rehabilitation;
(b) what the rehabilitation process entails, including its impact on domestic creditors and whether it is fair and equitable in the circumstances; and
(c) whether there are any strong countervailing reasons against recognition of the foreign rehabilitation proceedings.[129]

The Court was satisfied with all three factors. First, Hanjin's common law centre of main interest was in Korea, which provided a strong connecting factor between Hanjin and the Korean Court.[130] Second, the Korean rehabilitation process would treat all creditors in the same class fairly and equitably, whether local or foreign creditors.[131] Third, there were no strong countervailing reasons against recognition of the foreign rehabilitation proceedings.[132]

Hanjin's creditors argued that granting the recognition would infringe the High Court's exclusive admiralty jurisdiction and would have a possible adverse impact on the admiralty creditors who sought to arrest Hanjin's vessels in Singapore.[133] The High Court rejected these arguments. It explained that the High Court (Admiralty Jurisdiction) Act did not carve out ship arrests as being exclusive to admiralty jurisdiction, and thus, the Court could properly order a stay over the arrests.[134] In addition, the Court was of the view that 'the inability of individual creditors to obtain security was a necessary consequence of universal collection and marshalling of assets'.[135] Therefore, the Court held that both the imperative for orderly rehabilitation and the need to protect Hanjin's assets provided sufficiently strong grounds for granting the recognition and the stay order.[136]

This stay order was later tested before the registrar of the Supreme Court when the arrest of the *M/V Hanjin New York* was sought on 6 October 2016. The registrar allowed the arrest despite the stay order freezing the actions of creditors against Hanjin issued by the High Court, on the grounds that the registered owner of the *M/V Hanjin New York* was a Panamanian entity, not Hanjin. Nevertheless, the vessel was released from arrest following a settlement between the parties, and proceedings were discontinued.[137]

In Singapore, although the Court in its inherent jurisdiction approved Hanjin's application of recognition for the benefit of all Hanjin's creditors, the stay order

[129] ibid, [18].
[130] ibid, [19].
[131] ibid, [21].
[132] ibid, [22]–[31].
[133] ibid, [30].
[134] ibid, [25]–[26].
[135] ibid, [31].
[136] ibid, [32].
[137] B Ang, 'Arrest and Cross-Border Insolvency: The Singapore Experience' in P Myburgh (ed), *The Arrest Conventions: International Enforcement of Maritime Claims* (Oxford, Hart Publishing, 2019) 208.

carved out the pre-arrest *Hanjin Rome* on the grounds that arrest occurred before the commencement of the recognition proceeding. This indicates that if maritime claimants take steps early enough to file their *in rem* actions, and do so before the commencement of the recognition petition by foreign trustees or administrators, they will be allowed to proceed with these actions regardless of the subsequent insolvency proceedings. In addition, Singapore has now adopted the Model Law, which will provide it with a more straightforward, comprehensive and predictable framework for cross-border insolvency assistance. However, the Singapore Ministry of Law did not carve out *in rem* proceedings from automatic stays under article 20 of the 10th Schedule to the Act; instead, as in the three other countries discussed above, the Act referred to local insolvency provisions and established case law with regard to the scope and effect of stay orders.[138] The Ministry of Law explained that there was no need to add a new specific exception provision for *in rem* actions in the Act, since the case law was well established regarding when leave would be granted in local insolvency proceedings.[139]

V. Analysis

A. Alternative Relevant Factors

As discussed above, the courts in Australia, Singapore, the UK and the US granted a broad stay order to suspend all the subsequent claims against Hanjin's vessels. This provided a measure of protection for shipowners to have some breathing space to reorganise their business and prevent the potential risk of ship arrest. However, such broad stays may be changed due to the following factors:

i. Secured Status of In Rem *Actions*

Different jurisdictions have different views whether *in rem* actions can be regarded as secured claims, and if so, when *in rem* actions will become secured. This influences the issue whether maritime creditors with rights of actions in rem can be exempted from automatic stay orders granted by bankruptcy courts.

In Anglo common law countries, the issue with regard to the secured status of *in rem* actions can be further divided into the secured status of *in rem* actions based upon maritime lien claims, and the secured status of *in rem* actions based

[138] Ministry of Law, 'Supplementary Response to Feedback Received on Companies (Amendment) Act 2017 to Strengthen Singapore as an International Centre for Debt Restructuring', available at www.mlaw.gov.sg/news/public-consultations/supplementary-response-to-feedback-received-on-companies--amendm. See also JZ Ji, 'Cross-Border Rehabilitation: An Impediment to Ship Arrest in Singapore?', CML Working Paper Series, No 17/04, March 2017, available at law.nus.edu.sg/cml/pdfs/wps/CML-WPS-1704.pdf.

[139] ibid.

upon statutory rights of action *in rem*, respectively. With regard to maritime lien claims, the majority of courts adopt the so-called procedural theory that maritime liens arise and remain inchoate from the moment the claims attach; they are not secured until subsequently perfected by the issuance of a writ *in rem*.[140] Once a maritime lien is perfected by the issuance of a writ *in rem*, the secured interest is retroactive and relates back to the date when the claims arise.[141] However, if the courts adopt a true personification doctrine, as is the case in the US, maritime liens will be treated as substantive property rights that arise and become secured simultaneously from the moment maritime liens attach to the ship, that is, when certain services are rendered to the ship or certain damages are done by the ship.[142]

With regard to statutory rights of action *in rem*, there is no property interest vested in the ship before the arrest.[143] Statutory rights of action *in rem* are not therefore secured claims when they initially arise. The majority view is that they become secured claims once they are perfected by the issuance of writs *in rem*.[144] However, these proprietary consequences are prospective only, which indicates that the proprietary consequences of statutory rights of actions are products of the statutory criteria, plus actions *in rem*, and not because of any pre-existing inchoate liens.[145] In Canada, however, the courts hold that statutory rights of action *in rem* are merely procedural tools and do not create any security interest even if the writs of arrest are issued.[146]

To make matters more complicated, the scope and ranking of maritime liens and statutory rights of action *in rem* vary from jurisdiction to jurisdiction. In the US there are a wide range of maritime liens, with virtually all maritime claims giving rise to maritime liens.[147] In the UK, Australia and Singapore, however, only certain categories of maritime claims are secured by maritime liens and most other maritime claims merely give rise to statutory rights of action in rem.[148] A further issue which complicates the certainty and predictability of the courts' decisions is whether assisting courts would recognise a foreign maritime lien claim and, compared with other domestic insolvency claims, what the ranking of this foreign

[140] *The Bold Buccleugh* (1851) 7 Moo PC 267, 13 ER 884 (PC); *In re Aro Co Ltd* [1980] Ch 196 (CA); *Bankers Trust International Ltd v Todd Shipyards Corp (The Halcyon Isle)* [1981] AC 221 (PC).

[141] *The Halcyon Isle* (n 140); *The Heinrich Bjorn* (1885) 10 PD 44, 54 (CA).

[142] R Force, *Admiralty and Maritime Law*, 2nd edn (Washington DC, Federal Judicial Centre, 2013) 173.

[143] *The Heinrich Bjorn* (n 141) 54.

[144] Courts in the UK, Australia and Singapore take the view that a statutory right of action *in rem* becomes a secured claim upon the issue of a writ *in rem*. See, eg, *In re Aro* (n 140); *Danny Morris v Ship Kiama (Mubum)* [1998] FCA 256, (1998) 16 ACLC 945; *Kuo Fen Ching v Dauphin Offshore Engineering & Trading Pte Ltd* [1999] SGCA 95, [1999] 2 SLR(R) 793.

[145] MJ Hafeez-Baig, 'Navigating the Waters between Admiralty and Cross-Border Insolvency: A Comparison of the Australian, German and French Positions' [2018] *LMCLQ* 97, 115.

[146] *Benson Brothers Shipbuilding Co (1960) Ltd v The Miss Donna* [1978] 1 FC 379.

[147] W Tetley, *International Maritime and Admiralty Law* (Montreal, Editions Yvon Blais, 2002) 483.

[148] ibid.

maritime lien claim should be.[149] Accordingly, as discussed above, the differing views of the secured status of *in rem* actions in different jurisdictions make the scope and effect of the automatic stay order uncertain.

ii. Time of the Ship Arrest

Since most Anglo common law countries hold that actions *in rem* become secured claims upon the issue of writs *in rem*, whether ships are arrested before the foreign proceedings are recognised is another factor that may alter the scope and effect of the stay order. In Hanjin's bankruptcy, courts in the US and Singapore held that the stay did not apply to a ship arrest that had already occurred prior to the courts issuing the initial recognition order.[150] However, courts in the UK and Australia held that the stay orders extended to all the vessels of Hanjin, without carving out any pre-arrested vessel. Accordingly, in certain jurisdictions, if the vessel is arrested early enough, prior to the filing of the application for recognition or even before the filing of a foreign insolvency proceeding, the *in rem* action may be allowed to proceed regardless of the subsequent insolvency proceedings. In addition, if the vessel is arrested before the filing of the application for recognition, the *in rem* claims may be regarded as secured claims, which may also become another reason for courts to exempt maritime creditors from the stay order.

iii. Liquidation or Reorganisation

Even if actions *in rem* are recognised as secured claims in the assisting countries, the type of insolvency proceedings that shipowners file in the foreign main proceedings also influence the scope and effect of the automatic stay. The insolvency proceedings filed by Hanjin in the Korean Court was a reorganisation-like proceeding and, thus, the discussion provided in section IV of this chapter were the circumstances under reorganisation proceedings. If shipowners are in liquidation or winding-up proceedings, the scope and effect of the stay order will be different in certain countries. Since the Model Law is a model legislative text and procedural in nature, countries that adopt the Model Law usually refer to local insolvency stay provisions to decide the scope and effect of the automatic stay order.

[149] The US and Canada take the view that the status of a foreign maritime claim should be decided by the *lex causae*, see, eg, *Ocean Ship Supply Ltd v M/V Leah* 729 F 2d 971, 1984 AMC 2089 (4th Cir 1984); *The Ioannis Daskalelis* [1974] SCR 1248; whereas the UK, Australia and Singapore have adopted a *lex fori* rule, see, eg, *The Halcyon Isle* (n 140); *The Andres Bonifacio* [1993] SGCA 70, [1993] 3 SLR(R) 71; *Reiter Petroleum Inc v The Ship 'Sam Hawk'* [2016] FCAFC 26, [2016] 2 Lloyd's Rep 639. With respect to the issue of ranking of foreign maritime lien claims, it is widely accepted that the *lex fori* governs this issue. See, eg, *The Halcyon Isle* (n 140); *The Sam Hawk*, ibid. See also M Davies, 'Maritime Liens and Choice of Law' (2018) 42 *Tulane Maritime Law Journal* 269, 270–71; W Tetley, 'Maritime Liens in Conflict of Laws' in J Nafziger and S Symeonides (eds), *Law and Justice in a Multistate World: Essays in Honour of Arthur T von Mehren* (Leiden, Brill Nijhoff, 2002) 448.

[150] *Hanjin Shipping* (n 68); *Re Taisoo Suk* (n 113).

Thus, whether the secured creditors can proceed to enforce their claims depends on the local stay provisions that most closely resemble the foreign main proceeding. In the UK and Australia, for example, secured creditors are exempted from the automatic stay order if a shipowner is in liquidation.[151] US stay orders, however, are relatively strong and broad, and secured creditors will be stayed from obtaining possession or exercising control over the assets in either liquidation or reorganisation.[152]

iv. Owned or Chartered

Since most of Hanjin's operating vessels were under a bareboat charter hire purchase (BBCHP) charter agreement, it remains controversial whether vessels chartered by Hanjin can be subject to the stay order. A BBCHP charter party is a convenient and practical method of ship financing in Korea,[153] and is a type of hire purchase agreement in which Hanjin was able to use the vessel for the duration of the BBCHP agreement. At the end of the designated charter period, Hanjin had the option of purchasing the vessel 'at a nominal price'.[154] The parties therefore argued that the chartered vessels were not Hanjin's property, but owned by financial lessors, usually banks. These vessels were not the property of the debtor and should not be subject to the stay. This argument was upheld in Korea,[155] but courts in the other four countries discussed in this chapter granted general stay orders to stay all Hanjin's vessels either chartered or owned by it. While it is uncertain and inconsistent whether BBCHP or bareboat chartered vessels can be regarded as a shipowner's assets, it is undoubtedly the case that time-chartered or voyage-chartered vessels are not assets of the insolvent debtor. This is because time charterers or voyage charterers only have the right to use the carrying capacity of the chartered vessels, but 'no right of property in or to possession of the vessel'.[156] The type of charterparty therefore also alters the scope and effect of the automatic stay.

Subject to various factors, the scope and effect of the stay orders will therefore depend on the specific case. Nevertheless, stay orders are initial orders which could be modified or terminated if creditors apply to and ask for relief from the courts.[157] Whether to grant relief depends on the discretion of each court. For example, the English High Court allowed several arbitrations that had already commenced to continue up to and including the publication of interim final awards by the

[151] *Suk* (n 81); *Hanjin Shipping* (n 108).

[152] See 11 USC §362.

[153] IH Kim, 'Korean Maritime Case Update: 2015/2016' (2017) 48 *Journal of Maritime Law and Commerce* 211, 222.

[154] ibid.

[155] The Changwon District Court in the *M/V Hanjin Xiamen* ordered the return of the chartered vessels to their owner, defeating the aims of all courts which applied protections and issued stays: ibid.

[156] See *Port Line Ltd v Ben Line Steamers Ltd* [1958] 2 QB 146, 163.

[157] Model Law, art 22.

arbitration.[158] However, the High Court did not allow any further steps in those arbitrations or seek to enforce any awards that the claimants might have obtained against Hanjin.[159]

B. Preventative Measures

The Hanjin bankruptcy has been described as a wake-up call to many in the maritime industry.[160] In the aftermath of any bankruptcy, one of the biggest challenges facing individual ocean carriers and ocean carrier alliances is how best to prepare and mitigate the impact of a future insolvency event should one occur.[161] Typically, when shipowners face ship arrests or the potential risk of ship arrests, the shipowners' protection and indemnity club (P&I club) will step in and provide security with a letter of undertaking (LOU) for the release of vessels.[162] However, when shipowners are insolvent, the rulebooks of P&I clubs generally contain a 'cesser' or 'ipso facto' clause which will automatically terminate insurance coverage upon the commencement of any insolvency proceedings.[163] The termination of insurance coverage was an actor which lead to Hanjin's vessels being stranded at sea, causing the interruption of the supply chain.

So as to prevent a repeat of the chaos of a disrupted supply chain arising from the early days of the Hanjin crisis, container shipping lines chose to take proactive measures to establish an insolvency contingency fund in the event of the collapse of any member carrier. This fund could be used to ensure that the supply chain remained uninterrupted, with all cargo onboard offloaded, and the suppliers of necessaries and port operators paid in a timely manner.

This arrangement has been utilised by at least one of the major container shipping alliances, the THE Alliance, which includes former partners of Hanjin from the CKYHE Alliance, and which was severely impacted by the bankruptcy of Hanjin.[164] The THE Alliance will set up a US $50 million insolvency contingency

[158] *Hanjin Shipping* (n 108) sch, paras 1–3.

[159] ibid.

[160] Federal Maritime Commission, 'Statement from Commissioner Maffei on Bankruptcy Amendment to THE Alliance', available at www.fmc.gov/statement-from-commissioner-maffei-on-bankruptcy-amendment-to-the-alliance.

[161] ibid.

[162] Davies (n 22) 114–15; Myers, 'Hung Up on Hanjin' (2017) 218; P Myburgh, 'P & I Club Letters of Undertaking and Admiralty Arrests' (2018) 24 *JIML* 201–02. See also *Belmont Park Investments Pty Ltd v BNY Corporate Trustee Services Ltd* [2011] UKSC 38, [2012] 1 AC 383; *Pan Ocean* (n 8). The US courts have held that the cesser or ipso facto clause is invalid under the US Bankruptcy Code and that the insurance rights of insolvent shipowners continued after their petition for bankruptcy: *In re Probulk Inc* 407 BR 56 (Bankr SDNY 2009).

[163] See, eg, UK P&I Club Rules, available at www.ukpandi.com/fileadmin/uploads/uk-pi/LP%20Documents/2018/RULES/Final_Rulebook_2018.pdf; American P&I Club Rules, available at www.american-club.com/files/files/1819.pdf.

[164] The THE Alliance consists of five container shipping lines: Hapag-Lloyd AG and Hapag-Lloyd (America) LLC (acting as one party); K Line; Mitsui OSK Lines Ltd (MOL); Nippon Yusen Kabushiki

fund in the event one of its members faces financial distress or insolvency. Each carrier member initially contributes US $1 million into a contingency trust fund and a further US $9 million in additional funds or through a letter of credit.[165] The contingency fund can be used to ensure that the affected members continue to make port calls by paying costs, losses or liabilities reasonably incurred by the insolvent member as a result of ship arrest; advance funds or payments related to carriage, handling, storage or delivery of containers carried by an insolvent member; and pay third-party claims that may have a potential risk of ship arrest.[166] Nevertheless, this contingency fund mechanism is still in the early stages and has not yet been applied in practice. Ambiguities remain regarding many detailed and practical issues, such as how to provide sufficient funds in a timely manner in the event of the insolvency or 'material adverse change' of a member.[167] It still has to be determined under what detailed rules the alliance member should distribute the fund, what type of costs or liabilities will be regarded as the payment used for such a purpose, what percentage each shipping company should bear, and how to approve the disbursement of the contingency fund. The THE Alliance is the only alliance that has set up such a fund and its preventative measures have not yet been followed by other alliances. The Ocean Alliance refused to set up such a fund, declaring that the companies in the alliance were financially strong enough not to require such a measure.[168] The influence and practicability of a contingency fund are, therefore, still limited and uncertain.

VI. Conclusions

Hanjin's bankruptcy has given rise to a number of complexities and chaos in the shipping industry. Broadly, shipowners can use the Model Law as general protection. One of the main advantages for shipowners to have their bankruptcy proceedings recognised in the countries which have adopted the Model Law is that, upon such recognition, courts in the assisting countries will issue a stay order to prevent creditors from enforcing their claims against the ships of shipowners

Kaisha (NYK) and Yang Ming. Under the terms of the vessel-sharing agreement, member carriers are permitted to share vessels, charters and slots on each other's ships, and enter into cooperative arrangements. Federal Maritime Commission, 'THE Alliance establishes $50 million insolvency contingency fund', available at www.fmc.gov/the-alliance-establishes-50-million-insolvency-contingency-fund. See Chacón (ch 10), II(A).

[165] ibid.

[166] ibid.

[167] According to THE Alliance's filing with Federal Maritime Commission, the insolvency contingency fund will be used for members in the event of an 'Insolvency Event or Material Adverse Change': ibid.

[168] R Hutchins, 'OOIL: Ocean Alliance's stability doesn't require emergency fund', available at www.joc.com/maritime-news/container-lines/ocean-alliance/ooil-ocean-alliance%E2%80%99s-stability-doesn%E2%80%99t-require-emergency-fund_20170313.html.

when calling at the ports of assisting countries. However, even within the Model Law regime, each country has a distinct approach as to the scope and effect of stay orders and these are subject to various factors and depend on individual cases. Carrying out a maritime cross-border insolvency efficiently is not an easy task. In order to better harmonise the conflicts between cross-border insolvency and maritime regimes the shipping industry needs to build a preventative mechanism through standard practices or mutual agreements in order to ensure that the flow of commerce will continue even when a major company collapses.[169]

[169] Myers (n 10) 219–20.

7

Ship Arrest and Insolvency Proceedings: A European Perspective

ULRIK RAMMESKOW BANG-PEDERSEN*

I. Torm – A Case of Insolvency of a European Shipping Company

Torm is a Denmark-based international shipping company with offices across the world, including Copenhagen and Singapore, and a substantial number of ships. Torm is listed on the Nasdaq Copenhagen and NASDAQ in New York. In 2011 Torm was in severe financial difficulties. The threat of bankruptcy was imminent. Further, Torm faced the risk of creditors arresting its ships, which would mean that those ships would no longer generate any income for the company. The only hope for Torm was to file for reorganisation proceedings to obtain a temporary protection from individual actions from creditors and hopefully to have a reorganisation plan passed by the bankruptcy court. As Torm had its centre of interest in Denmark, filing for reorganisation in Denmark would be the obvious choice. Luckily, the Danish Parliament had recently passed legislation modernising the reorganisation rules in the Danish Bankruptcy Act.[1] But Torm did not file for reorganisation proceedings; nor was it put into bankruptcy proceedings.

In 2019 Torm had an equity capital around EUR 100m, owned more than 100 product tankers,[2] and had more than 3,000 employees.[3] The case of Torm raises many interesting issues. Why did Torm not file for reorganisation proceedings despite the risk of creditors arresting Torms ships? How did Torm overcome its financial difficulties? However, before addressing these questions, it will be useful to make some general observations about ship arrest and insolvency law. Further,

* Professor of Law, Faculty of Law, University of Copenhagen.
[1] See below, III.
[2] www.euroinvestor.dk/nyheder/2019/03/12/torm-plc-aarsrapport-2018/13988704.
[3] www.torm.com/about-torm.

it is necessary to look more closely at international insolvency law and the possibilities for forum shopping.

II. Ship Arrest and Insolvency Law

Many states have ratified the 1952 International Convention for the Unification of Certain Rules Relating to the Arrest of Sea-going Ships (the 1952 Convention) or the 1999 International Convention on Arrest of Ships (the 1999 Convention). These Conventions lay down rules for the arrest of ships. A far larger number of states have ratified the 1952 Convention than the 1999 Convention.[4] The general principle is that a creditor holding a maritime claim in a ship can obtain an arrest of the ship if the ship is in a port in a contracting state. A maritime claim is defined in art 1 of the 1952 Convention as a claim arising from: (a) damage caused by any ship either in collision or otherwise; (b) loss of life or personal injury caused by any ship or occurring in connection with the operation of any ship; (c) salvage; (d) agreement relating to the use or hire of any ship whether by charter-party or otherwise; (e) agreement relating to the carriage of goods in any ship whether by charter-party or otherwise; (f) loss of or damage to goods including baggage carried in any ship; (g) general average; (h) bottomry; (i) towage; (j) pilotage; (k) goods or materials wherever supplied to a ship for her operation or maintenance; (l) construction, repair or equipment of any ship or dock charges and dues; (m) wages of Masters, Officers or crew; (n) Master's disbursements including disbursements made by shippers, charterers or agents on behalf of a ship or her owner; (o) disputes as to the title to or ownership of any ship; (p) disputes between co-owners of any ship as to the ownership, possession employment or earnings of that ship; or (q) the mortgage or hypothecation of any ship. In Denmark, the 1952 Convention has been implemented in the Merchant Shipping Act,[5] §§ 91–96.[6]

The rules on arrest of ships have an important function. Where the owner of the ship has not paid the maritime claim these rules give the holders of maritime

[4] See, for the 1952 Convention, treaties.un.org/pages/showDetails.aspx?objid=08000002801338ba and, for the 1999 Convention, treaties.un.org/Pages/ViewDetails.aspx?src=TREATY&mtdsg_no=XII-8&chapter=12&clang=_en. See also, generally, F Berlingieri, *Berlingieri on Arrest of Ships*, 6th edn (Abingdon, Informa, 2016) and P Myburgh (ed), *The Arrest Conventions: International Enforcement of Maritime Claims* (Oxford, Hart, 2019).

[5] 'Søloven' in Danish. See now Consolidated Act No 1505 (17 December 2018). The English translation of the 2014 version of the Act is downloadable from www.dma.dk/Vaekst/Rammevilkaar/Legislation/Acts/The%20merchant%20shipping%20act%20(consolidation).pdf.

[6] *cf*, for Singapore, the High Court (Admiralty Jurisdiction) Act cap 123 (rev ed 2001), which is derived from the UK Administration of Justice Act 1956 and the UK Senior Courts Act 1981. Singapore is not a formal signatory to the 1952 Convention but implements the Convention in its domestic law.

claims a powerful enforcement mechanism for the enforcement of their claims through the arrest of the ship. This is important because of the mobile nature of a ship and because it is not always clear who is the (ultimate) owner of a ship.[7] As a consequence, the supplier of goods or services that gives rise to a maritime claim does not need to demand cash payment or security as a condition for performance. Putting this another way, the international rules on the arrest of ships make it easier for shipping companies to obtain goods and services on credit. Further, because the rules on maritime claims also apply to claims secured by a mortgage over the ship, the rules on arrest of ships also strengthens the position of mortgagees and may result in easier access to credit through ship mortgaging.

If a debtor, such as a shipping company, becomes insolvent and insolvency proceedings are commenced, the general principles of insolvency law must also be taken into account. By contrast with the law relating to the arrest of ships, there are no international conventions harmonising substantive insolvency law. However, some fundamental principles are common to most insolvency legislation. A general principle of insolvency law is the equal treatment of creditors. A further principle is that the opening of insolvency proceedings results in a stay of actions from individual creditors. The latter principle is necessary in order to maximise the value of the debtor's assets and to make it possible to reorganise the debtors' business. If there is no stay of individual actions the debtors' business is likely to be realised by a piecemeal liquidation. This would lead to a loss of value and often conflict with the principle of equal treatment of creditors as the distribution of assets would be based on a first-in-time principle (the 'race to the court house').

As already noted, most insolvency legislation contains rules which stay actions by individual creditors once insolvency proceedings have commenced. The extent of the stay varies from state to state. Some states exempt certain claims from such stays. Other states limit the insolvency stay in time or provide for the lifting of the stay with respect to creditors who are not adequately protected. However, it is important to note the stay often also applies to secured claims and similar claims, such a maritime claims. Some may view this as a conflict between maritime law and insolvency law. In other words, the insolvency stay of a maritime claim could be seen as conflicting with maritime law, which entitles a holder of a maritime claim to arrest the ship. However, before discussing whether this is a true conflict, it will be useful to look more closely at the interplay between ship arrest and insolvency proceedings.

[7] See, eg, S Chong, 'The Interaction Between Insolvency and Maritime Law' (keynote address at the 2nd meeting of the Judicial Insolvency Network, 2018), available at jin-global.org/content/jin/pdf/2018-sept-jin-keynote-address-new-york.pdf.

III. Effects of Insolvency Proceedings on Ship Arrest in Local Ports – The Example of Danish Law

Generally, as noted, the commencement of insolvency proceedings will result in a stay of individual actions. If Torm had applied for reorganisation proceedings in Denmark, Danish insolvency law would have applied. Consequently, Danish law will be used to illustrate the effect of a stay.

An insolvent debtor, which has its centre of interest in Denmark, may file for reorganisation proceedings according to the Danish Bankruptcy Act.[8] The rules on reorganisation are found in chapters 2–2e of the Danish Bankruptcy Act.[9] Under this Act,[10] the debtors' assets cannot be arrested during reorganisation proceedings. In Danish law, there are two types of arrest: ordinary arrest; and the arrest of ships for maritime claims. It does not follow explicitly from the Danish Bankruptcy Act[11] that the stay applies to both types of arrest. However, the provision must be interpreted as staying both kinds of arrest and is supported by the fact that, in the case of bankruptcy (liquidation), an arrest cannot be made.[12] This provision does not explicitly deal with ship arrest, but is construed as compromising a stay of ship arrest as well.[13]

Under Danish law, reorganisation proceedings can last a maximum of approximately 11 months. Consequently, the reorganisation stay is limited to this period. However, if the reorganisation proceedings fail, the debtor automatically becomes subject to bankruptcy proceedings.[14] During such proceedings arrests, including arrests of ships, are also stayed.[15] It may be noted that a bankruptcy stay in relation to mortgaged assets in practice is often limited to six months. This is because once the bankruptcy proceedings have lasted six months a secured lender holding a claim due for payment can demand that the bankruptcy estate realises the mortgaged asset without undue delay.[16]

The rules in the Danish Bankruptcy Act on stay provide efficient protection of the debtors' assets against actions by individual creditors. This is also true with respect to ships. An insolvent shipping company can obtain protection of its ships from being subject to arrest by initiating reorganisation proceedings. However, in practice, this protection is sometimes only effective with respect to ships in Danish ports or Danish territorial waters. If a ship is located outside Denmark, the stay will not necessarily be upheld by a court in the state where the ship is located.

[8] 'Konkursloven' in Danish.
[9] §§ 10–15 b.
[10] § 12 c, no 1.
[11] ibid.
[12] See the Danish Bankruptcy Act, § 31.
[13] See L Lindencrone Petersen and A Ørgaard, *Konkursloven med kommentarer*, 14th edn (Copenhagen, Karnov Group, 2018) 387–88.
[14] See the Danish Bankruptcy Act, § 15.
[15] ibid, § 31.
[16] ibid, § 86.

On the contrary, the stay is only likely to be enforced if the courts of the state where the ship is located recognise the Danish insolvency proceedings.

IV. Effects of Insolvency Proceedings on Arrest of Ships in Foreign Ports – A European Perspective

A. General Remarks about Extraterritoriality of Insolvency Proceedings

The commencement of insolvency proceedings in a shipping company's home state only provides an effective stay against the arrest of ships and other actions by creditors if the stay has exterritorial effect in the states where a shipping company's ships are located. However, there is no international convention which ensures such exterritorial effects of insolvency proceedings. Whether or not insolvency proceedings in the home state of the shipping company will have effect in another state often depends solely on whether the latter state's national legislation recognises the insolvency proceedings and the effects thereof.

UNCITRAL has enacted a Model Law on Cross-Border Insolvency, which contains rules on the recognition of foreign insolvency proceedings. At present, 44 states have adopted this Model Law.[17] However, this does not mean that these states have identical rules on the recognition of foreign insolvency proceedings. The Model Law is a model law and not a binding international convention. Consequently, a state which wishes to adopt the Model Law can make any changes it desires in its national implementation of the Model Law. Further, even though article 20(1) of the Model Law embodies an important rule that a stay in an insolvency proceeding in the debtor's home country is automatically recognised and given effect to, it follows explicitly from article 20(2) that a state can list modifications and exceptions to the stay in its national implementation of the Model Law. The fact that a state has enacted the Model Law increases the likelihood that it will recognise a stay following from insolvency proceedings in the shipping company's home state. However, whether such recognition of the stay will also apply to ship arrests does not necessarily follow and depends on the way the recognising state has adopted the Model Law. In other words, obtaining extraterritorial effect of the home state insolvency stay will be a state-to-state exercise. An example of this is the insolvency proceedings in Korea concerning Hanjin Shipping Company Ltd and the differing extent to which the stay in the Korean insolvency proceedings was given extraterritorial effect in the states which had adopted the Model Law.[18]

[17] www.uncitral.org/uncitral/en/uncitral_texts/insolvency/1997Model_status.html.

[18] See Xu (ch 6) IV. For this reason, the extraterritorial effect of a stay in states having adopted the UNCITRAL Model Law on Cross-Border Insolvency is not addressed further. Generally on the

In Europe there are two multilateral instruments regulating the recognition and enforcement of insolvency proceedings. First, there is the EU Insolvency Regulation[19] which applies to all EU states, except Denmark.[20] The EU Insolvency Regulation determines which effects an insolvency proceeding opened in an EU state, except Denmark, have in the other EU states, again with the exception of Denmark. Second, there is the Nordic Bankruptcy Convention, which applies to the Nordic states, Denmark, Finland, Iceland, Norway and Sweden.[21] The Nordic Bankruptcy Convention determines which effects an insolvency proceeding opened in a Nordic state has in the other Nordic states. However, as Finland and Sweden are both EU states subject to the EU Insolvency Regulation, the effects of a Finnish insolvency proceeding in Sweden and vice versa are determined by the EU Insolvency Regulation and not by the Nordic Bankruptcy Convention.[22]

B. The Nordic Bankruptcy Convention

The Nordic Bankruptcy Convention only applies to insolvency proceedings that are initiated in the state where the debtor has its corporate seat.[23] Often the corporate seat is in the state where the debtor has its centre of main interests (COMI).

According to article 1 of the Nordic Bankruptcy Convention, a bankruptcy proceeding in one Nordic state is automatically recognised and has effect in the other Nordic states. The general rule is that the insolvency law of the state where the bankruptcy proceedings are opened (the *lex concursus*), determines the effects of the bankruptcy proceedings in the other Nordic states.[24] This rule also applies the effects of the bankruptcy stay on debtors' assets in the other Nordic states.[25] However, with respect to assets subject to a security interest the law of the state where the asset is located (the *lex rei sitae*) determines whether or not the bankruptcy proceedings stay the secured creditor.[26] A maritime claim secured by a mortgage in the ship is a security interest subject to art 5 of the Nordic Bankruptcy

UNCITRAL Model Law on Cross-Border Insolvency and ship arrests, see J Xu, *Maritime Cross-Border Insolvency under the UNCITRAL Model Law Regime* (Oxford, Hart Publishing, 2020); S Rares, 'Ship Arrests, Maritime Liens and Cross-Border Insolvency' [2018] *LMCLQ* 398, M Davies, 'Cross-Border Insolvency and Admiralty: A Middle Path of Reciprocal Comity' [2018] 66 *American Journal of Comparative Law* 101; L Athanassiou, *Maritime Cross-border Insolvency* (London, Routledge, 2018); M Tsimplis, 'Modified Universalism and Cross-Border Insolvency of Shipping Companies' [2020] *JBL* 346.

[19] EU 2015/848. See [2015] OJ L141/19.

[20] See the EU Insolvency Regulation, recital 88. The reason why Denmark is not subject to the European Insolvency Regulation is Denmark's general reservation to the EU Treaty on the Functioning of the European Union [2012] OJ C326/47, art 81, on 'judicial cooperation in civil matters'.

[21] The Nordic Bankruptcy Convention was concluded in 1933 and was revised in 1977 and 1982. In this chapter, references are to the 1982 Nordic Bankruptcy Convention.

[22] See the EU Insolvency Regulation, art 85(1).

[23] See the Nordic Bankruptcy Convention, art 13.

[24] The Nordic Bankruptcy Convention, art 1.

[25] ibid, art 1(2).

[26] ibid, art 5.

Convention. The same is probably true with respect to a maritime claim, if it gives rise to a maritime lien in the ship according to the law of the state where the ship is registered. For the purposes of art 5 of the Nordic Bankruptcy Convention a ship is considered to be located in the state where the ship is registered.[27]

As an example of the practical consequences of these rules, if a Danish shipping company becomes subject to bankruptcy proceedings in Denmark, the bankruptcy stay will prevent arrest of those of the company's ships that are located in Danish ports or Danish territorial waters, regardless of which state the ship is registered in. Due to the Nordic Bankruptcy Convention, the bankruptcy stay will further prevent the arrest of ships located in the other Nordic states, provided that the ships are registered in Denmark. However, if such ships located in the other Nordic states are not registered in Denmark, the bankruptcy proceedings will not necessarily stay the arrest of the ships. If such a ship is registered in another Nordic state, the insolvency law of that state will determine the extent of the bankruptcy stay with respect to that ship.[28] If a ship located in another Nordic state is registered in a non-Nordic state, it is likely that the Nordic Bankruptcy Convention will not regulate whether an arrest of the ship is stayed by the Danish bankruptcy proceedings. Instead, this issue must be considered governed by the national law of the state where the ship is located.

A further complication with respect to the Nordic Bankruptcy Convention is that it is questionable if it applies to all kinds of reorganisation proceedings. Article 15 of the Nordic Bankruptcy Convention merely makes the Convention applicable to proceedings aiming at a compulsory composition. Consequently, a reorganisation proceeding aiming at achieving a transfer of the debtor's business will likely not be governed by the Nordic Bankruptcy Convention. Finally, it should be noted that compulsory composition proceedings in one Nordic state, such as Denmark, merely stays an arrest of a ship located in another Nordic state if that follows from the insolvency law of the latter state (*lex rei sitae*).[29]

C. The EU Insolvency Regulation

The EU Insolvency Regulation applies to insolvency proceedings which are commenced in an EU state (except Denmark), provided that the insolvency proceedings are listed in Annex A to the Regulation.[30]

If insolvency proceedings are commenced in the state where the debtor has its COMI, the insolvency proceeding is automatically recognised and has effects in the other EU states (except Denmark).[31] The general rule is that the effects are

[27] ibid, art 8(2).
[28] ibid, arts 5, 8.
[29] Ibid, art 15.
[30] See the EU Insolvency Regulation, art 1.
[31] ibid, arts 19–20 and art 3.

determined by the *lex concursus* of the COMI state.[32] This rule also applies the effects of the insolvency stay on debtors' assets in the other EU states because article 7(2)(f) explicitly mentions 'the effects of the insolvency proceedings on proceedings brought by individual creditors'. Consequently, the insolvency proceeding opened in the COMI state stays the arrests of ships located in the COMI state or other EU states (except Denmark). However, the insolvency proceedings in the COMI state cannot affect the rights *in rem* of creditors or third parties in respect of assets which are situated within the territory of another EU state at the time of the commencement of proceedings.[33] A maritime claim secured by a mortgage in the ship is a right *in rem* subject to article 8 of the EU Insolvency Regulation. The same is true with respect to a maritime claim, if it gives rise to a maritime lien over the ship according to the law of the state where the ship is registered.[34]

With respect to article 8 of the EU Insolvency Regulation, it should be noted that in the case of 'property and rights, ownership of or entitlement to which is entered in a public register' the asset according to article 2(9) of the Regulation shall be considered to be located in the EU state under the authority of which the register is kept.[35] Consequently, in relation to the EU Insolvency Regulation, a registered ship must be considered to be located in the EU state where the ship is registered.

The effect of the rule in article 8 of the EU Insolvency Regulation is that the insolvency proceedings in the shipping company's COMI state stay arrest of a ship if the ship is registered in the COMI state. If a ship is registered in another EU state than the COMI state, the EU Insolvency Regulation does not give the insolvency stay effect with respect to the holders of mortgages or maritime liens in the ship.[36] Consequently, such a ship is only protected against arrest if the ship is in the ports or territorial waters of the COMI state.

If a ship is not registered in the COMI state, the COMI state insolvency proceedings will not stay holders of mortgages or maritime liens in the ship from arresting the ship if the ship is in a port in an EU state other than the COMI state.

However, such an arrest may be prevented if secondary (local) insolvency proceedings are opened either in the EU state where the ship is in port or in the EU state where the ship is registered. Secondary insolvency proceedings are restricted to the assets of the debtor, which are considered to be situated in the state where the secondary proceeding takes place.[37] As a general rule, the effects

[32] ibid, art 7.

[33] ibid, art 8(1).

[34] ibid, art 8(2)(a) which explicitly mentions liens. See also Athanassiou, *Maritime Cross-border Insolvency* (2018) 202. *cf*, however, Davies, 'Cross-Border Insolvency and Admiralty [2018], who finds that there may be doubt whether a maritime lien is a right in rem under the EU Insolvency Regulation, art 8.

[35] See also Athanassiou (n 18) 204.

[36] ibid, 202.

[37] EU Insolvency Regulation, art 3(2).

of the secondary proceedings in a state, including the extent of a stay, are determined by the (local) insolvency law (*lex concursus*) of that state.[38] Consequently, during such secondary proceedings, the local insolvency law will determine whether an arrest is stayed with respect to ships which are registered in the state where the secondary proceedings takes place. This is because these ships are considered to be located in that state by virtue of article 2(9) of the EU Insolvency Regulation. Further, the local insolvency law of the state where the secondary proceedings takes place will decide whether the insolvency stay applies to ships which are in the ports of that state.[39] Even if the local insolvency law of the state where the secondary proceedings takes place does not prescribe a stay of the arrest of ships, the insolvency practitioner appointed in the COMI state insolvency proceedings has the power to request a stay of realisation of assets in the secondary proceedings.[40]

Secondary insolvency proceedings can only be opened in a state, where the debtor (shipping company) has an establishment.[41] An establishment is defined in article 2(10) of the EU Insolvency Regulation as 'any place of operations where a debtor carries out or has carried out in the three-month period prior to the request to open main insolvency proceedings a non-transitory economic activity with human means and assets'. The fact that a ship happens to be in a port of a state will not in itself be considered sufficient to constitute the shipping company having an establishment in that state. It is questionable whether registration of a ship in a state is sufficient to constitute the shipping company having an establishment in that state. This is because, in general, a ship is not in one place all the time because it sails between ports and often states. The shipping company's activity in the state where the ship happens to be in port is of a transitory nature. It can thus be argued that this does not qualify for an 'establishment' which, by definition, must be a non-transitory activity. However, as mentioned above in relation to the EU Insolvency Regulation, a registered ship is considered to be located in the EU state where the ship is registered.[42] Consequently, it can be argued that in relation to the EU Insolvency Regulation the ship will be considered to be located permanently in the EU state where the ship is registered even if the ship is in a port in another state. If the ship is operated by staff employed by the shipping company, the ship must then be considered a place of operation carried out by the shipping company with assets (the ship) and human means (the employees). In other words, the requirements of article 3(2) of the EU Insolvency Regulation for considering the shipping company to have an establishment in the EU state where the ship is registered will be fulfilled. Of course, even though it is possible to open secondary proceedings in the EU state where the ship is registered in order to

[38] ibid, art 7.
[39] ie, except if the ship is registered in the COMI State. *cf* the discussion above.
[40] See the EU Insolvency Regulation, art 46.
[41] ibid, art 3(2).
[42] ibid, art 2(9).

obtain a stay of arrest of the ship, it should be borne in mind that such proceedings generate costs.

V. Forum Shopping – Shopping for Courts or for Ports?

A. Forum Shopping through Choice of COMI State

As it appears from the above analysis,[43] the rules on cross-border insolvency in the Nordic Bankruptcy Convention and the EU Insolvency Regulation are quite complex. A shipping company facing insolvency may thus consider whether there are any advantages in choosing to file for insolvency proceedings in one European state instead of another. However, the possibilities for such forum shopping are extremely limited. Both the Nordic Bankruptcy Convention and the EU Insolvency Regulation rely on the principle that only an insolvency proceeding commenced in the shipping company's COMI state has effect in other states. Consequently, if the shipping company files for insolvency proceedings in a state which is not the COMI state, the insolvency stay will only protect assets considered to be located in the state where the insolvency proceedings are commenced, against individual actions from unsecured creditors. This is not compatible with keeping the business of the shipping company going, which is a condition for a successful reorganisation.

If a shipping company wishes to reorganise by using the insolvency law system from an EU state other than the company's COMI state, most often the only solution is to change COMI to the state where the shipping company wishes to apply for insolvency proceedings. In practice, however, such forum shopping by a change of COMI is not easy as it requires that the shipping company makes a true change of COMI prior to the filing for insolvency proceedings. In fact, the EU Insolvency Regulation aims at preventing fraudulent and abusive attempts to forum shop through manipulation of COMI.[44] The presumption in the EU Insolvency Regulation that a company's COMI is at the place of the registered office does not apply if the company has moved its registered office within the last three months.[45] The reason why it should not be possible to strategically manipulate a company's COMI, is that the COMI should be ascertainable by third parties and that special consideration should be given to the creditors and to their perception as to where a company conducts the administration of its interests.[46] Forum shopping by a change of COMI is not – and should not be – an option for shipping companies or other debtors.

[43] Above, IV.
[44] See the EU Insolvency Regulation, recital 29.
[45] ibid, art 3(1).
[46] ibid, recital 28.

B. Forum Shopping for Multiple Courts

A further complication is that the commencement of insolvency proceedings in the shipping company's COMI state is not sufficient to protect the shipping company from the arrest of ships by creditors holding a mortgage or maritime lien in a ship. As mentioned above,[47] a stay following from the commencement of insolvency in the shipping company's COMI state is not sufficient to prevent the arrest of ships located outside the COMI state. The Nordic Bankruptcy Convention and the EU Insolvency Regulation merely gives the COMI state insolvency stay exterritorial full effect with respect to ships which are registered in the COMI state. Even with respect to such ships, the exterritorial effect following from the Nordic Bankruptcy Convention and the EU Insolvency Regulation is limited to the Nordic states respectively and the EU states (except Denmark).

If a shipping company with COMI in Europe is to obtain protection against creditors holding a mortgage or maritime liens in ships located outside the COMI state, it is necessary to open additional (secondary) insolvency proceedings in the state where ships are located or – by virtue of article 2(9) of the EU Insolvency Regulation – where they are considered to be located. This will generate costs. Further, this may complicate obtaining a successful reorganisation of the shipping company. Multiple insolvency proceedings result in a need to cooperate in the proceedings.[48] Multiple proceedings may result in complex issues in relation to creditor voting regarding a reorganisation plan because the reorganisation rules are different in the different states where insolvency proceedings are opened. Finally, it should be kept in mind that if the shipping company has its COMI in an EU state, the opening of secondary insolvency proceedings in another EU state is not always possible, as it requires that the shipping company has an establishment in the latter state.[49] In insolvency proceedings governed by the Nordic Bankruptcy Convention it is not possible to open secondary proceedings in another Nordic state, even if the debtor has an establishment there.

As it appears, forum shopping for multiple insolvency proceedings is often not a feasible solution for an insolvent shipping company.

C. Forum Shopping for Ports

An alternative to forum shopping for multiple courts is forum shopping for ports. In other words, a shipping company may consider whether arrest of its ships can be prevented by making sure that the ships are in safe harbours, when insolvency proceedings in the COMI state are opened. In this context, a safe harbour is a port

[47] See above, IV.
[48] See the EU Insolvency Regulation, art 43.
[49] See above, IV(B).

in a state where the arrest of ships is stayed. But as described earlier,[50] if the shipping company is only subject to insolvency proceedings in its COMI state the only true safe ports are the ports in the COMI state.

If the shipping company's ships are registered in the company's COMI state, the ships – during insolvency proceedings in that state – are also be protected against arrest in ports in the EU provided that the COMI is in an EU state (except Denmark), or in ports in the Nordic states, provided the shipping company has its COMI in a Nordic state. Even though such 'shopping' for registration of the ship in the COMI state may expand the safe area, it may have negative consequences for the shipping company as the choice of registration state may have an impact on taxation and employment rules. In any event, if the shipping company has business sailing outside the EU and the Nordic states, registration of the ship in the shipping company's COMI state will not in itself give any protection against arrest of ships in ports outside the EU and the Nordic states.

In practice, shopping for ports is rarely a possible solution for an insolvent shipping company which needs to keep its business going in order to obtain a reorganisation. Having all its ships registered in the state where the shipping company has its COMI is not a solution for a shipping company operating internationally. But, depending on the circumstances, it may be a viable solution for a shipping company with its COMI in the EU (except Denmark) which only operates in the EU or a shipping company with its COMI in a Nordic state and which only operates in the Nordic states. As Sweden and Finland are both subject to the EU Insolvency Regulation and the Nordic Bankruptcy Convention, a shipping company with its COMI in one of these two states may use the registration of all ships in the company's COMI state as a solution even if the company operates both in the EU and the Nordic states.

VI. General Perspectives – Are Maritime Law and Insolvency Law Conflicting Regimes?

As it appears from the analysis earlier,[51] it is very difficult for an insolvent shipping company to obtain an efficient stay against the arrest of its ships. Even though the national insolvency law of the European state where the shipping company has its COMI often prescribes a stay of arrest and other individual creditor actions during insolvency proceedings, this stay is often not given effect in all of the shipping company's ships in the EU and the Nordic states. Generally, the EU Insolvency Regulation and the Nordic Bankruptcy Convention exempt ships registered outside the COMI state from the stay. Further, it is not generally possible to obtain an efficient stay in the EU or the Nordic states through forum shopping. In any

[50] See above, V(A)–(B).
[51] Above, IV–V.

event, forum shopping is not – and should not be – the answer to the problem as one of the fundamental principles of international insolvency is to avoid forum shopping in order to safeguard the legitimate interests and expectations of third parties and creditors.

It must be recognised, however, that the arrest of ships is not efficiently prevented by international insolvency law. On one view, there may be a conflict between maritime law (on arrest of ships) and insolvency law, and that maritime law should prevail in this conflict. Some would say that this is quite right because they consider that the advantages of access to the arrest of ships is more important that the principles of insolvency law.

However, it is arguable that the relation between maritime law and insolvency law should not be viewed as a conflict. This is because insolvency law affects all creditors. It is the nature of insolvency law that the law applies to all creditors and this follows from the fundamental principle of equal treatment of creditors. The stay of individual actions is necessary to maximise the value of the debtors' assets, such as through a sale as a going concern or through a reorganisation. Secured creditors, workers and contracting parties are all subject to insolvency law, including the rules on stay. This does not mean that insolvency law conflicts with the law of secured credit, labour law or contract law. Rather, there is an interplay between insolvency law and other areas of law which seeks at minimising the losses of all creditors to the extent possible. In other words, the application of the insolvency stay to all creditors should be seen as a collective bargain to the benefit of all creditors. The exemption of one class of creditors, such as maritime claimants, from the insolvency stay would be to favour that class of creditors at the cost of all other creditors. Consequently, an application of an insolvency stay to maritime claims should merely be viewed as an example of the principle that insolvency law applies to all creditors regardless of the origin of the claim. Of course, insolvency law should respect mortgages and other rights *in rem* properly created before the insolvency proceedings were commenced, provided that the rights were not granted in a fraudulent or otherwise avoidable manner. However, it ought to be possible to stay the enforcement of such rights during part of the insolvency proceedings.

The problem relating to ship arrests and insolvency proceedings is not that there is a conflict between maritime law and insolvency law. Instead, the problem is that ships often sail internationally, whereas insolvency law in practice often only has effects in the state where the insolvency proceedings are commenced. Even in cases where the insolvency proceedings do have extraterritorial effect according to the EU Insolvency Regulation or the Nordic Bankruptcy Convention, this extraterritorial effect does not apply to the holders of mortgages and maritime liens in ships registered outside the state where the insolvency proceedings are opened. This is not because access to arrest is more important than insolvency law. If that had been the case, insolvency law would generally exempt maritime claims from the insolvency stay also with respect to ships registered in the state where the insolvency proceedings are commenced. Ideally, when a shipping company is subject to insolvency proceedings in its COMI state, the insolvency stay should apply to all the shipping company's ships so that arrest of the ships is prevented, regardless of where the ships are registered or located. Anything else is counterproductive to the success of reorganising an insolvent shipping company. Of course, such a global effect of the insolvency stay should be subject to the condition that the courts in the state where the insolvency proceedings takes place respects rights *in rem* in the ships properly created before the insolvency proceedings were opened.[52] Within the EU and the Nordic states, this condition is satisfied through the rules in article 8 of the EU Insolvency Regulation and article 5 of the Nordic Bankruptcy Convention which protects rights in rem in ships registered in another EU respectively Nordic state than the state where the insolvency proceedings are opened. Consequently, there seems to be no good reason why the EU Insolvency Regulation and the Nordic Bankruptcy Convention exempt rights in rem in ships registered in another EU respectively Nordic state from the insolvency stay.

At present, it is often impossible for an insolvent international shipping company to obtain protection of all its ships against arrest. Even in Europe such protection is not offered by the EU Insolvency Regulation and the Nordic Bankruptcy Convention.

Returning to the case of Torm described earlier,[53] one of the primary reasons why Torm never filed for insolvency proceedings was most likely precisely because such proceedings would not have given Torm sufficient protection against the arrest of its ships. How did Torm overcome its financial difficulties? The answer is that Torm reached an out-of-court reorganisation with its major creditors. The key element in the reorganisation was that the existing shareholders accepted a reduction of their shares. Thereafter, the major creditors – in particular the banks – purchased new shares issued by Torm, thereby ensuring that Torm obtained new capital.[54] Of course, it must be considered a success for Torm and society that Torm was rescued. Some may even say that the case of Torm illustrates that there is no need for rules which give wider protection against ship arrest. However, an out-of-court agreement reached on the basis that the rules on insolvency proceedings do not provide any feasible solution is often not a fair agreement. Some creditors will be able to stay out of the agreement and receive payment in full because they know that other creditors who have more to lose will feel pressured to finance a reorganisation and accept a 'haircut' of their claims. This does not constitute a fair and equal treatment of all creditors. Ship arrest is and should be an enforcement mechanism against the shipping company, but is should not be a toll whereby the holders of maritime claims obtain advantages at the expense of the shipping company's other creditors.

[52] See Davies (n 18), Chong, 'Insolvency and Maritime Law' (2018) and E Göretzlehner, *Maritime Cross-Border Insolvency* (Cham, Springer Nature Switzerland AG, 2019) 147–48. However, see Tsimplis, 'Modified Universalism' (2020) arguing that generally ship arrests should be allowed to proceed despite insolvency proceedings.

[53] Above, I.

[54] maritimedanmark.dk/?Id=16321.

Management and Organisation in a Digitalised Maritime Sector

8

Surrender, Release and Digital PIN Codes

MICHIEL SPANJAART*

I. Introduction

Slowly, but inevitably, the maritime world is making its way towards a paperless future.[1] Bills of lading, sea waybills, (ship's) delivery orders, and most likely all paper documents are ultimately going to be replaced by electronic equivalents.[2] One of these equivalents is already widely used: the digital PIN code for the collection of containers from the terminal in the port of discharge.[3]

An electronic release system basically operates as follows: when a ship arrives at the port of discharge, the carrier notifies the designated receiver, the consignee or notify party, who is in practice often a local forwarding agent acting on behalf of its principal. The forwarder surrenders one original bill of lading to the local ship's agent and, in return, it receives a digital PIN code that gives access to the terminal where the containers have been stored after discharge.

Obviously, such a system is not 100 per cent waterproof. Digital PIN codes can become lost and can be forgotten. But they can also be intercepted, for instance by a third party with bad intentions, and this is what must have happened in the port of Antwerp in the course of 2012.

* Academic Fellow, Centre for Maritime Law, Faculty of Law, National University of Singapore. This chapter was finalised during a period as Visiting Senior Research Fellow at the Centre for Maritime Law. Translations are by the author.

[1] See, Chacón (ch 10).

[2] See Girvin and Ong (ch 9).

[3] Digital PIN codes are for instance in use in the port of Jurong (Singapore), Mussalo (Finland), Rotterdam (The Netherlands), Westports (Malaysia) and, of course, Antwerp (Belgium). In fact, in view of the risks inherent to the use of digital PIN codes, the Port of Rotterdam started a pilot in the summer of 2020 whereby the PIN code is replaced by a digital signal. See www.offshore-energy.biz/port-of-rotterdam-launching-a-blockchain-pilot-project-on-pin-free-container-handling.

II. *Glencore International AG v MSC Mediterranean Shipping Co SA*

On 24 June 2012,[4] the *MSC Katrina* arrived at the port of Antwerp carrying three containers with cobalt briquettes, completing a voyage that had originated with the *MSC Eugenia* in Fremantle (Australia). MSC had issued a bill of lading for the carriage of the cobalt briquettes. This bill of lading was made out 'to order' and named Glencore as the shipper and Steinweg as the notify party. The face of the bill of lading furthermore contained the following provision:

> If this is a negotiable (To Order / of) Bill of Lading, one original Bill of Lading, duly endorsed must be surrendered by the Merchant to the Carrier (together with outstanding Freight) in exchange for the Goods or a Delivery Order.

Steinweg had been Glencore's regular agent in Antwerp for more than 25 years,[5] and it handled this particular shipment as well. Glencore, therefore, sent two originals of the bill of lading to Steinweg with the instruction to arrange for the delivery of goods,[6] and upon arrival of the ship in Antwerp Steinweg surrendered one original of the bill of lading to MSC's Belgian office.

Prior to 2010, the presentation of an original bill of lading by its lawful holder would have caused MSC to issue a so-called 'laat volgen',[7] a one-page document that contains the carrier's instruction to the terminal to release the goods to a specified receiver:[8]

> This is a document by which the sea carrier (or his agent) instructs the terminal to deliver the goods to the cargo-interested party that has surrendered one original of

[4] *Glencore International AG v MSC Mediterranean Shipping Co SA* [2015] EWHC 1989 (Comm), [2015] 2 Lloyd's Rep 508. The case is one of few on digital PIN codes so far, and therefore very welcome in the exploration of these still somewhat unchartered waters: see M Goldby, 'What is Needed to Get Rid of Paper? A New Look at Delivery Orders' (2015) 21 *JIML* 339; M Song and M Tsimplis, 'Innovation and the Law: Legacy v Efficiency and Optimisation' (2017) 17 *Shipping & Trade Law* 11; A Tettenborn, 'Bills of Lading and Electronic Misdelivery' [2017] *LMCLQ* 479; S Rainey, 'Pinning Down Delivery: *Glencore v MSC* and the Use of PIN Codes to Effect Delivery' in B Soyer and A Tettenborn (eds), *New Technologies, Artificial Intelligence and Shipping Law in the 21st Century* (London, Informa, 2019) 47.

[5] Albeit without a specific contract. Apparently, Steinweg would inform Glencore of the rates for the coming year and for the rest their relationship was governed by the forwarder friendly Belgian Freight Forwarders – Standard Trading Conditions: at www.commodycentre.com/assets/b-general-conditions-final.pdf.

[6] The judgment at first instance is not very clear on this point. In his overview of the relevant facts, the judge initially talks about 'copies' instead of originals: 'Glencore sent Steinweg two copies of it and other documentation': see *Glencore* (n 4) [13]. His remark in the same paragraph clarifies that these 'copies' must really have been originals: 'Steinweg lodged with MSC Belgium one of the bills of lading, signed and stamped by itself and Glencore, and paid the handling charges'. This also makes sense, of course, as MSC would never have accepted a mere copy 'in exchange for the Goods or a Delivery Order': see also *Mitsui OSK Lines (Thailand) Co Ltd v Jack Fair Pty Ltd* [2015] FCCA 558, [2015] 1 Lloyd's Rep Plus 55; G Treitel and FMB Reynolds, *Carver on Bills of Lading*, 4th edn (London, Sweet & Maxwell, 2017) [6-075], fn 636.

[7] The Dutch words *laat volgen* (in French: *laissez suivre*) would literally, and as such rather awkwardly, translate as 'let follow'.

[8] E van Hooydonk, *Proeve van het Belgisch Scheepvaartwetboek (privaatrecht), Scheepsagentuur en goederenbehandeling, Zevende Blauwdruk over de herziening van het Belgische scheepvaartrecht*

> the bill of lading to the ship's agent. With the 'laat volgen' the receiver can collect the discharged goods in the port. By signing the 'laat volgen', the receiver confirms receipt of the goods and discharges the carrier.

In practice, the receiver was usually a local haulier acting upon instructions of Steinweg. The driver would present the *laat volgen* to the MSC terminal in order to collect the goods. When everything was in order and the goods had been released, the driver would sign off on the document itself in order to confirm the receipt of the goods.[9]

In the course of 2010, however, the Antwerp Port Authority began to facilitate the use of a digital equivalent, an electronic release system (ERS). The operation of the ERS was described in a 'model covenant' between the carrier and the terminal. Article 1 of this covenant outlined the system:

> (1) the container is released by the shipping company or its ship's agent, to the consignee or the latter's representative, by communicating an electronic release code generated individually for each container, which is also communicated to the terminal operator;
> (2) delivery of the container by the freight handler to the consignee or the latter's representative can only be made once the latter has entered the container number together with the corresponding release code mentioned under (1) above in the terminal operator's ICT system.

The use of the ERS was not in any way imposed by the Antwerp Port Authority, but interested carriers could opt in, and that is exactly what (the Belgian office of) MSC did. MSC informed the Antwerp forwarding community, including Steinweg of course, that it would 'no longer work with Delivery order (Laatvolgen)',[10] and that it would be using the ERS as from January 2011 instead.[11]

This new *modus operandi* meant that MSC would send Steinweg digital PIN codes on a regular basis and it asked Steinweg for an email address. Steinweg indicated that its general email address would probably be best suited for this purpose as all its relevant (15–20) employees would then have access to the same information at the same time.[12] Clearly, MSC did not have any problem with this as it went on to use this email address for the next one and a half years.

Once the ERS was operational, the delivery procedure for the containers with cobalt briquettes went as follows: Steinweg received the bills of lading from Glencore and presented them to MSC while paying the freight and other charges. In return, MSC sent an electronic Release Note with the digital PIN codes to this

(Antwerp, Commissie Maritiem Recht, 2012) 118. This work contains the most recent studies underlying the new Belgium maritime code, see www.zeerecht.be (2012) 118.

[9] Since this description may be a bit abstract, see the sample *laat volgen* (courtesy MH Claringbould) in the appendix to this chapter.

[10] The wording of this notification suggests that a *laat volgen* equals a delivery order, at least in the perception of MSC.

[11] There was also a second 'model covenant', namely to regulate the relation between the carrier and the forwarder, but it was never discussed, let alone concluded, between MSC and Steinweg.

[12] This was also the address to which MSC normally sent its arrival notices.

general email address, and Steinweg then forwarded the codes to a local haulier with the instruction to collect the corresponding containers from the MSC terminal.

This release note came with terms and conditions. First, it stipulated that the PIN codes were only valid for a limited period of time, 'usually of about a month from discharge',[13] but the release note also contained (amongst others) the following conditions:[14]

> All terms and conditions contained in the MSC bill of lading concerned are applicable to subject release note. The addressee of subject release note expressly confirms to have knowledge to these terms and conditions and to accept them unconditionally.
>
> Discharge of the cargo will constitute due delivery of the cargo. After discharge the cargo will remain on the quay at risk and at the expense of the cargo, without any responsibility of the shipping agent or the shipping company/carrier.

Between January 2011 and June 2012 no less than 69 shipments of cobalt briquettes were handled under the new procedure, and this worked perfectly well on each occasion. And then the *MSC Katrina* arrived in Antwerp in June 2012. In line with the procedure followed until then, Steinweg presented the bill of lading, received the release note with the PIN codes by email and forwarded these to a local haulier named Carjo Trans for the collection of the containers.[15] When Carjo Trans arrived at the gate of the MSC terminal, however, it was informed that two of the three containers had already been collected. Apparently, someone else had entered the correct PIN codes, gained access to the containers, taken them from the terminal and disappeared.

III. An Original Bill of Lading in Exchange for the Goods or a Delivery Order

Glencore sued MSC for misdelivery, and its position was very straightforward. An original bill of lading had been surrendered, but the delivery of the goods to its lawful holder had not followed. MSC was therefore liable under the contract of carriage and in bailment since the carrier must deliver the goods against the presentation of an original bill of lading. This is correct, of course, and this presentation rule has often been confirmed over the years.[16]

[13] *Glencore* (n 4) [12].

[14] ibid. The release note furthermore stipulated that it was 'subject to the terms and conditions contained in the Resolution by Alfaport Antwerp dated 3rd of September 2010 concerning electronic release of containers in the port of Antwerp'.

[15] The procedure was sharpened afterwards, and the containers from then onwards could only be released to a specific driver with a specific transport company, who could identify himself and drove a vehicle with a specific registration number: *Glencore* (n 4) [15].

[16] *The Stettin* (1889) 14 PD 142; *Carlberg v Wemyss* (1915) SC 616; *Sze Hai Tong Bank v Rambler Cycle Co* [1959] AC 576 (PC); *Barclays Bank Ltd v Commissioners of Customs and Excise* [1963]

There is another side to this presentation rule as well, one that can be traced back to the sixteenth century.[17] Before that time, there really was no need for any presentation of original bills of lading. The shipper of the goods was also the owner of those goods, and he would travel together with his goods so that he could deliver them to his buyer at the place of destination or make alternative arrangements if that were necessary. Besides, these medieval (rudimentary straight) bills of lading could not be transferred to third parties, and this made it practically impossible for the carrier to deliver the goods to the wrong consignee.

This changed at the end of the Middle Ages. Instead of travelling together with their goods, merchants started to instruct agents and factors in the port of discharge to deal with the goods or their behalf.[18] As a result of this development the identity of the consignee was not always a given, and the bills of lading had to adapt to this new commercial reality as well. The bills of lading would no longer just mention the name of consignee, but they would also allow for the delivery of the goods to his assigns.[19] Over the years, the named consignee 'or his assigns' evolved into the named consignee 'or order or assigns', and ultimately into the named consignee 'or order', or just 'to order'. These bills of lading were easily transferable from one consignee to the next by endorsement and delivery.[20]

Depending on the local custom in the port of loading a bill of lading would usually be issued in three or four originals.[21] The issuance of several originals in combination with their easy transferability could, however, complicate the delivery of goods in the port of discharge. With several original documents in circulation, all of them easily transferable from one consignee to the next, a carrier could find itself confronted with more than one consignee demanding the delivery of the goods in the port of discharge.

At this point, the first rather basic attestation clauses started to appear on bills of lading. These clauses did not explicitly prescribe the surrender of one original

1 Lloyd's Rep 81; *SA Sucre Export v Northern River Shipping Ltd (The Sormovskiy 3068)* [1994] 2 Lloyd's Rep 266; *Kuwait Petroleum Corporation v I & D Oil Carriers Ltd (The Houda)* [1994] 2 Lloyd's Rep 541 (CA); *Motis Exports Ltd v Dampskibsselskabet AF 1912, A/S* [2000] 1 Lloyd's Rep 211 (CA); *Standard Chartered Bank v Dorchester LNG (2) Ltd (The Erin Schulte)* [2013] EWHC 808 (Comm), [2013] 2 Lloyd's Rep 338.

[17] For the development of the bill of lading, see CB McLaughlin, 'The Evolution of the Ocean Bill of Lading' (1926) 35 *Yale Law Journal* 548, 551; WP Bennett, *The History and Present Position of the Bill of Lading as a Document of Title* (Cambridge, Cambridge University Press, 1914); M Bools *The Bill of Lading: A Document of Title to Goods: An Anglo-American Comparison* (London, LLP, 1997) 2; SF du Toit, 'The Evolution of the Bill of Lading' (2005) 11 *Fundamina* 16; A Polak, *Historisch-juridisch onderzoek naar den aard van het cognoscement* (Amsterdam, Gebroeders Binger, 1865) 26.

[18] Bennett (ibid) 12.

[19] *The Andrewe* (1544): RG Marsden, *Select Pleas in the Court of Admiralty*, vol 1 (London, Selden Society, 1894) 126.

[20] This formality had been borrowed from the medieval custom of merchants endorsing their bills of exchange and in due course this became a recognised custom for the transfer of bills of lading as well: Bennett, *Bill of Lading as a Document of Title* (1914) 11; *Lickbarrow v Mason* (1794) 5 TR 683, 686, 101 ER 380, 382; *Goodwin v Robarts* (1875) LR 10 Exch 337, (1876) 1 App Cas 476 (HL).

[21] But in fact any number of originals is possible: see, eg, *Australia Capital Financial Management Pty Ltd v Freight Solutions (Vic) Pty Ltd* [2017] NSWDC 279, where there were eight originals.

bill of lading, but they did protect the carrier to the extent that it could no longer be pursued by subsequent consignees once it had delivered the goods to the first consignee. The delivery to the first consignee ensured that any other original bills of lading in circulation had become void. The bill of lading for iron shipped from Bilbao to London in *The Mary Martyn* is one of the oldest examples of such a clause:[22] 'In wytness of the truythe I the sayde master or the purser for me have firmyd iij bylls of the one tenor the one complyed with and fulfylled the other to stand voyd'.[23] The protection of the carrier against misdelivery claims was the primary objective of the clause, and the courts initially also applied the clause in this (strict) way. The carrier was perfectly free to deliver the goods to any holder of an original bill of lading and its responsibilities ended then and there. Lee CJ held, for instance, in *Fearon v Bowers*:[24]

> That according to usage of trade, the captain was not concerned to examine who had the best right on the different bills of lading. All he had to do was to deliver the goods upon one of the bills of lading, which was done.

This unconditional carrier friendly approach was abandoned in 1882. The House of Lords held that the carrier cannot just deliver the goods to any holder when it is (or could have been aware) of other endorsements of the bill of lading as 'it puts too much power in the master's hands'.[25] Cottam & Co (or their assigns) were the consignees of a shipment of sugar, carried on the *Mary Jones* from Jamaica to London. The bill of lading contained the common clause that 'the master of the ship hath affirmed to three bills of lading, all of this tenor and date, the one of which bills being accomplished, the others to stand void'. In need of a cash advance from its bank, Cottam & Co gave only one original bill of lading,[26] endorsed in blank, to Glyn Mills Currie & Co as security for the loan.[27] When the *Mary Jones* arrived in London, the sugar was discharged at the facilities of East and West India Dock Co awaiting payment of the freight, and only to be released against an original bill of lading. Shortly afterwards, Cottam & Co visited the warehouse to show its (second) original bill of lading.[28] Cottam & Co paid the freight a few days later, and ultimately ensured the release of the sugar to its agent, yet at the expense of the

[22] *The Mary Martyn* (1539); Marsden, *Select Pleas* (1894) 89.

[23] It is remarkable to see how little has changed over the years. Almost 500 years later, albeit with a few obvious changes modernising the wording, the clause is still widely used. See the standard MSC bill of lading: 'IN WITNESS WHEREOF the Carrier or their Agent has signed the number of Bills of Lading stated at the top, all of this tenor and date, and wherever one original Bill of Lading has been surrendered all other Bills of Lading shall be void'.

[24] *Fearon v Bowers* (1753) 1 H BL 365(n), 126 ER 214.

[25] *Glyn Mills Currie & Co v East and West India Dock Co* (1882) 7 App Cas 591 (HL).

[26] Clearly, a prudent banker would have asked for the full set: ibid 603 (Lord O'Hagan); 606–07 (Lord Blackburn). See, more recently, Treitel and Reynolds, *Carver* (2017) [6-077]: 'If a similar situation arose today, the bank would be likely to safeguard its rights against the carrier by insisting on a full set of bills of lading'.

[27] This original stipulated that it was the 'first'.

[28] This original stipulated that it was the 'second', and it was not endorsed.

bank. Glyn Mills Currie & Co sued the East and West India Dock Co for misdelivery and Lord Blackburn held:[29]

> Where he has notice or probably even knowledge of the other indorsement, I think he must deliver, at his peril, to the rightful holder, or interplead. But where the person who produces a bill of lading is one who – either as being the person named in the bill of lading which is not indorsed, or as actually holding an indorsed bill – would be entitled to demand delivery under the contract, unless one of the other parts had been previously indorsed for value to someone else, and the master has no notice or knowledge of anything except that there are other parts of the bill of lading, and that therefore it is possible that one of them may have been previously indorsed, I think the master cannot be bound, at his peril, to ask for the other parts.

This approach has retained its value over the years. In the later Court of Appeal judgment in *Motis Exports Ltd v Dampskibsselskabet AF 1912, A/S*, Stuart-Smith LJ went through the relevant authorities since 1882 and concluded that:[30]

> [I]t has been established for well over a century that under a bill of lading contract a shipowner is both entitled and bound to deliver the goods against production of an original bill of lading, provided he has no notice of any other claim or better title to the goods.

In the course of the proceedings, both Glencore and MSC therefore ended up relying on one side of the presentation rule. Whereas Glencore argued that MSC had failed to deliver the goods against the surrender of an original bill of lading, MSC argued that it was discharged from its obligations under the bill of lading contract when it communicated the PIN codes to the lawful holder, or otherwise at least when the goods were physically delivered to the first presenter of the correct PIN codes at the terminal.

IV. The Digital PIN Code as a Symbol of the Goods

MSC's most ambitious defence was that it had delivered the goods in exchange for an original bill of lading. This was on the basis that the digital PIN code gave access to the goods themselves, and as such operated as a symbol of those goods. Just as the transfer of a 'key which, in the hands of the rightful owner, is intended to unlock the door of the warehouse, floating or fixed, in which the goods may chance to be' could transfer the possession of those goods,[31] the communication of a digital PIN code with the intention to provide access to the terminal where the goods were stored then equalled the delivery of those goods. The fact that the containers had subsequently been collected by someone else was unfortunate,

[29] *Glyn Mills* (n 25) 611.
[30] *Motis Exports Ltd v Dampskibsselskabet AF 1912, A/S* [2000] 1 Lloyd's Rep 211 (CA), [19].
[31] *Sanders Bros v Maclean & Co* (1883) 11 QBD 327 (CA), 341.

but no longer MSC's concern since the delivery to the bill of lading holder had already taken place.

The defence was rejected. At first instance, Andrew Smith J held that delivery required a transfer of possession.[32] In that respect, access to the goods by means of a digital PIN code was really just access at the discretion of MSC since it still had 'the power, albeit not the contractual right as against Glencore and Steinweg, to invalidate them'.[33] On appeal, Sir Christopher Clarke said:[34]

> In the present case, where the parties contemplated either actual delivery against presentation of a bill of lading or in accordance with a delivery order, I do not think that delivery of the code can, itself, constitute delivery. Delivery usually means actual delivery, not delivery of a means of access, and nothing is spelt out in the contract to the contrary.

It is submitted that this is indeed the correct approach. A digital PIN code is really just a number and not a document of title,[35] and the fact the carrier retained the power to invalidate the PIN codes does not help. Still, perhaps the best argument in favour of this approach is that the digitalisation of an existing release procedure should not change the rights and obligations of the parties involved without their express intention.[36] In that respect, it is submitted that the outcome would, and in fact should, have been the same under the operation of the former system whereby MSC would have issued a *laat volgen* instead of an electronic release note with digital PIN codes.

For obvious reasons, there is a lack of English case law on the legal nature of the *laat volgen*[37] but, for those same obvious reasons, the *laat volgen* has surfaced more regularly in Belgian and Dutch case law.[38]

[32] Referring to *Barclays Bank Ltd v Commissioners of Customs and Excise* [1963] 1 Lloyd's Rep 81, 88. See also *Powell v McFarlane* (1979) 38 P & CR 452; *JA Pye (Oxford) Ltd v Graham* [2002] UKHL 30, [2003] 1 AC 419.

[33] *Glencore* (n 4) [18]. That risk would arguably also be present in the case of paper document. See, eg, *Great Eastern Shipping Co Ltd v Far East Chartering Ltd (The Jag Ravi)* [2012] EWCA Civ 180, [2012] 1 Lloyd's Rep 637 [45] (Tomlinson LJ): 'The facts here show a shipowner may attempt to revoke the authority given by a delivery order and may succeed in doing so'.

[34] *Glencore International AG v MSC Mediterranean Shipping Co SA* [2017] EWCA Civ 365, [2017] 2 Lloyd's Rep 186 [31].

[35] *Sanders* (n 31).

[36] See J Delen, *Elektronische handel in het Zeevervoer: Is het Belgische recht voorbereid op de komst van elektronische transportdocumenten?* (Masterproef, Gent, 2014) saying (at 103): 'The notification of the code forms the equivalent of the issuance of a "laat volgen" … in the classic system'.

[37] A search on I-law of 'laat', 'volgen', 'laissez' and 'suivre' produces exactly one hit: *Comptoir d'Achat et de Vente du Boerenbond Belge SA v Luis de Ridder Limitada (The Julia)* [1949] AC 293 (HL).

[38] See for the Belgian cases, eg, Hof van Beroep Antwerpen 19 Juni 1993, ETL 1993, 894; Rechtbank van Koophandel Antwerpen 15 Maart 1983, ETL 1983, 911. See also Van Hooydonk, *Proeve van het Belgisch Scheepvaartwetboek* (2012) 118; Delen, *Elektronische handel in het Zeevervoer* (2014) 102; H Heirbaut 'Het electronisch laat-volgen en cognossement' in I de Weerdt (ed), *Grondbeginselen van het Belgisch Privaatrechtelijk Zeerecht* (Antwerp, ETL, 2003) 188, 191; F Stevens, *Vervoer onder cognossement* (Brussels, Larcier, 2001) 156.

The leading case in the Netherlands on the relation between the issuance of a *laat volgen* and the delivery of the goods is *The Sriwijaya*.[39] The *Sriwijaya* had sailed from Padang (Indonesia), carrying bundles of 'dark red meranti sawn timber' under a bill of lading, and arrived in Rotterdam in October 1989. The bundles were discharged from the ship by a local stevedore, Hanno, and subsequently stored at its premises awaiting collection. Suedex, the lawful holder of this bill of lading, had instructed its local forwarder Betramy to collect the bundles from Hanno. In accordance with these instructions, Betramy presented the bill of lading to Anthony Veder, the carrier's agent in Rotterdam, and against the surrender of the bill of lading Anthony Veder issued a *laat volgen* in November 1989. When Betramy presented the *laat volgen* to Hanno in December 1989, however, a number of bundles had mysteriously disappeared and could not be collected.

Suedex was reimbursed by its insurers, who then turned to Hanno to recover the loss. Hanno rejected all liability and, in particular, relied on the Himalaya clause and the exonerations in the bill of lading.[40] Conversely, Suedex's insurers argued that Hanno was unable to rely on any provisions from the contract of carriage as that contract had already come to a full stop, namely when the *laat volgen* was issued against the surrender of the bill of lading.

Ultimately, the court had to decide whether the issuance of the *laat volgen* was equal to the delivery of the goods. The Court of Rotterdam and the Court of Appeal in The Hague did not think so and held that:

> The delivery of carried goods implies that the receiver can actually dispose of the goods. The issuance of the 'laat volgen' is not the same as the delivery of the goods … It is furthermore irrelevant that … the bill of lading had already been surrendered since that presentation did not lead to any actual disposal of the carried goods on the part of the receiver in this case.[41]

[39] *The Sriwijaya* HR 9 September 1997, NJ 1998, 63 (ann RE Japikse), S&S 1997/121 (Sriwijaya). Also of interest, but for the question whether the acceptance of a *laat volgen* could trigger an accession to the contract of carriage, see Hof 's-Gravenhage, 28 July 2009, S&S 2010/108 (*MSC Claudia*).

[40] It is hereby expressly agreed that no servant or agent of the carrier including every independent contractor from time to time employed by the carrier and every servant or agent of every such independent contractor shall in any circumstances whatsoever be under any liability whatsoever to the shipper, consignee or owner of the goods or to any holder of this bill of lading for any loss, damage or delay of whatsoever kind arising or resulting directly or indirectly from any act, neglect from default on his part while acting in course of or in connection with his employment and, but without prejudice to the generality of the foregoing provisions in this clause, every exemption, limitation, condition and liberty herein contained and every right, exemption from liability, defence and immunity of whatsoever nature applicable to the carrier or to which the carrier is entitled hereunder shall also be available and shall extend to protect every such servant or agent of the carrier acting as aforesaid … The responsibility of the carrier, whether as carrier or as custodian or as bailee of the goods, shall be deemed to commence only when the goods are loaded on the ship and to cease absolutely after they are discharged therefrom and no liability shall attach to the carrier before the said loading and after the said discharge. … all responsibility is to cease as soon as the cargo is lifted from and leaves the ship's deck. Goods in the custody of the carrier or his servants before loading and after discharge … whether awaiting shipment or landed or stored … are in such custody at the sole risk of the shipper and the carrier shall not be liable for loss or damage arising or resulting from any cause whatsoever.

[41] Hof' s-Gravenhage 23 January 1996, S&S 1996/110 (Sriwijaya).

The Supreme Court agreed, and held that:[42]

> Delivery can take place because the carried goods are brought into the actual possession of the person entitled thereto or into the possession of a third party acting on his behalf. Furthermore, it cannot be ruled out that the goods upon arrival at their destination pursuant to a different agreement with the person entitled thereto either remain in the custody of the carrier or in the custody of someone who held the goods on the basis of an agreement with the carrier, and that in these cases the contract of carriage ends at the time that this different agreement enters into force. … The reasoning of the Court of Appeal must apparently be understood in this way that it had agreed with and adopted the decision of the Court that these shipments of timber were only delivered on 11 and 13 December 1989 when they were collected by Betramy on instruction of Suedex. … These decisions do not reveal an incorrect opinion of the law, more in particular not an incorrect opinion of the concept of 'delivery'.

This view of the concept of 'delivery' as applied in *The Sriwijaya*[43] and *Glencore International AG v MSC Mediterranean Shipping Co* SA[44] was also the view adopted by the Hamburg Court of Appeal in a recent German decision on the delivery of containers against digital PIN codes.[45] The facts and circumstances were very much in line with the events in Antwerp, with the difference that the goods were discharged at and subsequently misdelivered from the ECT terminal in Rotterdam. At first instance, the Hamburg Landesgericht held that:[46]

> The loss, caused by the collection of the goods by someone unauthorised thereto, falls within the timeframe between receipt and delivery in accordance with § 498 (1) of the German Commercial Code (GCC). Bringing the time of delivery forward to the moment the container was ready for collection and the PIN had been communicated is barred by the fact that the terminal is an 'extension of the ship' under German law.

On appeal, the Hamburg Senat said that 'the delivery in the sense of § 498(1) GCC requires the carrier to relinquish his possession in an orderly way with the consent of the entitled receiver and to enable him to exercise the possession of the goods'.[47] Further, it held that:

> The terminal is a servant of the carrier in as far as its obligation to deliver the goods to the entitled receiver is concerned. Against this background, it is hard to imagine how a transfer from the care of the carrier to the receiver can be achieved before the terminal has physically handed the goods to the receiver or his authorised agent.

Clearly, neither the issuance of a *laat volgen* nor the communication of a digital PIN code is equivalent to the delivery of the goods under the contract of carriage. They are just means to an end because the concept of delivery requires the carrier

[42] HR 9 September 1997, NJ 1998, 63 (ann RE Japikse), S&S (Sriwijaya).
[43] See above, n 39.
[44] See above, n 4.
[45] Hanseatisch Oberlandesgericht Hamburg 6. Zivilsenat, 4 May 2017, 6 U 133/16.
[46] LG Hamburg 6. Zivilsenat, 10 June 2016, Az: 412 HKO 51/15.
[47] Hanseatisch Oberlandesgericht Hamburg 6. Zivilsenat, 4 May 2017, 6 U 133/16.

to enable the bill of lading holder or his agent to actually exercise the possession of those goods.[48]

V. The Digital PIN Code as a 'Delivery Order'

If the communication of the release note with the PIN codes could not amount to a symbolic delivery of the goods, MSC argued that the release note with the PIN codes qualified as a delivery order. Since the attestation clause allowed the carrier to exchange the bill of lading for the goods *or* a delivery order, the issuance of the release note to Steinweg ensured its compliance with the clause. Andrew Smith J found that a delivery order was used to describe a number of different documents,[49] and held that the correct meaning of 'delivery order' must be interpreted within the context of the bill of lading contract. He then moved on to say, however:[50]

> To my mind, the parties must be taken to be referring to what is commonly called a 'ship's delivery order', an expression used and defined in the Carriage of Goods by Sea Act 1992, section 1(4). It is an essential feature of such a delivery order that it contains an undertaking given by the carrier who is party to it … to a person identified in it to deliver the goods to which it relates to that person. This is required by the statutory definition, and is in accordance with usage before the 1992 Act: … It strikes me as improbable that it would agree to a term whereby the holder of the bill of lading might surrender its rights under it against the carrier without receiving in return either the goods themselves or the benefit of a substitute undertaking from the carrier. There is no need to interpret the B/L so as to have this improbable effect.

The Court of Appeal followed the same line of reasoning,[51] and reached the same conclusion. Sir Christopher Clarke held that:[52]

> The Delivery Order is to be provided by the owners of the ship as an alternative to actual delivery in exchange for the B/L and in substitution for it. It seems to me implicit in those circumstances that the parties intended that the Delivery Order should have the key attribute of a bill of lading, namely an undertaking by the carrier to deliver the goods to the person identified in it, which would, here, have to be Glencore or Steinweg, Glencore's agent. As the judge found, it is improbable that a shipper would agree to a term whereby he might surrender the bill without receipt of either the goods or the benefit of a substitute undertaking in his favour from the carrier.

[48] See, eg, *Barclays Bank Ltd v Commissioners of Customs and Excise* [1963] 1 Lloyd's Rep 81, 88–89; *The Jag Ravi* (n 33) [45].

[49] The judge referred to M Bridge (gen ed), *Benjamin's Sale of Goods*, 9th edn (London, Sweet & Maxwell, 2014) [18-212]. See, however, also Carver (n 6) [8-029]: 'The term "delivery order" is used to describe documents of various kinds'.

[50] *Glencore* (n 4) [19].

[51] Referring to *Waren Import Gesellschaft Krohn & Co v Internationale Graanhandel Thegra NV* [1975] 1 Lloyd's Rep 146; *Colin & Shields v W Weddel & Co Ltd* [1952] 2 Lloyd's Rep 9 (CA); *Cremer GmbH v General Carriers SA (The Dona Mari)* [1973] 2 Lloyd's Rep 366.

[52] *Glencore* (n 34) [194].

It is submitted, however, that it is not very likely that any of the parties involved really had a ship's delivery order in mind. First, this already follows from the ratio behind the document. A ship's delivery order is designed to split bulk shipments into separate parcels to be received by different consignees.[53] In the case at hand, however, there was no need to split the cargo as Glencore was the shipper of these three containers, and, with the help of Steinweg and Carjo Trans, was going to receive these containers in the end as well. Steinweg was just a forwarding agent in this process, not the owner of the goods. If anyone would have wanted to exchange the bill of lading for a ship's delivery order, it surely would have been the owner/shipper, Glencore.[54]

Second, Steinweg presented only one original of the bill of lading to MSC, not the full set. This is relevant because the surrender of one original bill of lading against a ship's delivery order would not have caused the remaining two originals to stand void.[55] A ship's delivery order, according to the Law Commission, is 'really designed to act like a "mini" bill of lading, the main difference being that a ship's delivery order is issued after shipment and is usually issued in respect of a smaller cargo'.[56] This also implies that MSC would never have agreed to it.[57] MSC would only have issued a ship's delivery order in exchange for the full set,[58] because it could never take the risk of (one of) the remaining two original bills of lading being presented afterwards.[59] The term 'delivery order' in the attestation clause on the bill of lading,[60] requiring the surrender of one original in exchange for a delivery order, cannot have meant ship's delivery order.[61]

Third, it is not as 'improbable' as it seems for a bill of lading holder to accept a mere document in exchange for a document of title. Surely, there must have been a time when the lawful holder surrendered an original bill of lading to the master of

[53] *Colin & Shields v W Weddel & Co Ltd* [1952] 2 Lloyd's Rep 9, 17 (CA).

[54] Glencore would not have needed Steinweg if it wanted to split the cargo. As the shipper and lawful holder of the bill of lading, it could simply have surrendered all three original bills of lading to MSC in exchange for delivery orders instead of going through the process of sending only two originals of the bill of lading to Steinweg.

[55] See also *The Dolphina* [2011] SGHC 273, [2012] 1 Lloyd's Rep 304, [139], referring to *Glyn Mills* (n 25) and *Motis* (n 16): '"Accomplished" or "accomplishment", in this context, means completing the performance of the contract of carriage by delivery of the cargo against the surrender of one of the original bills of lading' (Belinda Ang J).

[56] *Rights of Suit in Respect of Carriage of Goods by Sea* (Law Com No 196, Scot Law Com No 130, 1991) [5.29].

[57] The practice is equally 'fraught with danger': see *Glencore* (n 4) [19]; *Noble Resources Ltd v Cavalier Shipping Corp (The Atlas)* [1996] 1 Lloyd's Rep 642, 644. MSC might have taken the chance if Glencore would have offered to provide it with a letter of Indemnity, but there is no mention of this in either of the judgments. See also M Goldby, 'Managing the Risks of Switch Bills of Lading' [2019] *LMCLQ* 457.

[58] P Todd, *Bills of Lading and Bankers' Documentary Credits*, 4th edn (London, Informa, 2007) 70.

[59] *Elder Dempster Lines v Zaki Ishag (The Lycaon)* [1983] 2 Lloyd's Rep 548, 552: 'It seems to me that the whole problem goes back to one single event, namely, the issue of the February bill of lading while the January bill of lading was still in circulation. Whether or not I am right in my view that the January bill of lading is a document of title, it was clearly wrong that two sets of what looked like original bills of lading should have been allowed to have been in circulation at the same time. … The point is even stronger if, as I have held in the earlier proceedings, the January bill of lading is a transferable document of title' (Lloyd J).

[60] Drafted, no doubt, by MSC's own legal team.

[61] Article 8:440(1) DCC stipulates: 'The shipper – or, when a bill of lading has been issued, only the lawful holder thereof in the sense of article 441 and then only against the surrender of all transferable

the ship on the quay in the port of discharge and immediately received his goods in return. Over time, however, with the increased number of ships and the increased capacity of these ships, this has simply become impossible.

In the Netherlands, this has led to the development of a custom whereby the bill of lading is first signed for discharge on its reverse and only then surrendered to the local ship's agent in exchange for a *laat volgen*.[62] The custom has been codified in article 8:481(1) of the Dutch Civil Code (DCC) which provides that the 'holder of the bill of lading, who has applied for the receipt of the goods, is held, before he has received them, to mark the bill of lading with a discharge and to surrender it to the carrier'.[63]

It is submitted, therefore, that the 'delivery order' referred to on the bill of lading is not a ship's delivery order within the framework of the Carriage of Goods by Sea Act 1992, but a delivery order in the sense of a *laat volgen*, an instruction from the carrier to the terminal to release the goods to a specific receiver.[64] Apart from the arguments above, additional evidence thereof is also found in MSC's notification that it would use the ERS and that it would 'no longer work with Delivery order (Laatvolgen)'.[65] This notification, and Steinweg's obvious understanding thereof, implies that the two documents are the same, at least in the perception of MSC and Steinweg.[66]

Since the release note with the digital PIN codes is really nothing more or less than the modern successor of the old-fashioned *laat volgen*, it qualifies as a delivery order in the sense of the attestation clause on the bill of lading.

VI. The Agreement to Deliver the Goods to the First Presenter of the PIN Codes

Apart from the qualification of the release note with the digital PIN codes, MSC also relied on estoppel. It argued that Glencore had given the impression to have

originals of this bill of lading – is entitled, in as far as the carrier can reasonably comply, to demand the delivery of the goods, or when a bill of lading has been issued, all goods mentioned thereon jointly, prior to the arrival at the destination.' The same would apply, mutatis mutandis, to a variation in the paperwork, eg the issuance of a new bill of lading or a ship's delivery order.

[62] Admittedly, it is somewhat odd to confirm good receipt before receipt, but this is not uncommon. German law, for instance, also prescribes in the first part of the first sentence of § 521(2) of the German Commercial Code (GCC) that 'The carrier shall be obliged to deliver the goods only in exchange for a bill of lading in which delivery has been confirmed'.

[63] MH Claringbould, *Parlementaire Geschiedenis van het Nieuwe Burgerlijke Wetboek* (Deventer, Kluwer, 1992) 495; H Boonk, *Zeevervoer onder cognossement* (Kluwer, Deventer, 1993) 106; M Spanjaart, 'The Surrender of the Bill of Lading "Duly Endorsed"' (2014) 20 *JIML* 327.

[64] For a recent example of such a delivery order in another jurisdiction, see for instance the wording of the delivery order discussed in *The Jag Ravi* (n 33) [26].

[65] *Glencore* (n 4) [9].

[66] Steinweg also kept on invoicing Glencore for it, see ibid [14]: 'Steinweg routinely levied €10 charges when it used the ERS and Glencore paid them, but there is no evidence that it would have reason to know that they were for electronic release notes: the charges were described as being for "delivery orders"'.

been happy enough with the ERS for the first 69 shipments, and therefore could not complain about its application this time around. That in turn implied that MSC could not have been in breach of contract because it had in fact given, and its agent Steinweg had in fact accepted, a release note with the PIN codes in exchange for an original bill of lading on the understanding that the delivery would be made to the first presenter of the PIN codes. Both Andrew Smith J and the Court of Appeal dismissed the defence. Sir Christopher Clarke held:[67]

> No representation let alone a clear one was made by Glencore or on its behalf that delivery otherwise than to it would be acceptable provided that it was made to the first presenter of the codes. The fact that cargoes had been delivered to Glencore after presentation of PIN codes on many occasions did not say anything about what the position would be if they were not.
>
> In addition, I would not accept that Steinweg had any authority to make such a representation. It had no express authority. Nor is one to be implied. Authority to make arrangements to ensure delivery to Glencore pursuant to the B/L or Delivery Order did not impliedly extend to accepting that delivery pursuant to the B/L would validly be made by delivery to the first presenter of the codes whether that was Glencore or a thief, especially when Glencore was not even aware of the ERS system.

Glencore was the party that suffered the loss, and it was also the claimant in these proceedings. It is rather likely, though, that Glencore was not exercising its own rights, but in fact the rights of its forwarding agent, Steinweg. This would not affect Glencore's rights of suit in the proceedings. Indeed, the parties settled that discussion before going to court.[68] Nevertheless, it might have an impact on the 'authority to make arrangements to ensure delivery to Glencore pursuant to the B/L or Delivery Order'.

The bill of lading in question was an order bill of lading. It is not clear from the judgments how many originals were issued to Glencore,[69] but there were clearly more than one because Glencore later sent two originals of the bill of lading to Steinweg. Steinweg then surrendered one original bill of lading to MSC and the judge noted that this bill of lading was signed and stamped by both Glencore and Steinweg.

When a bill of lading is issued 'to order' and nothing else, it is assumed to have been issued to the order of the shipper,[70] Glencore in this case. Glencore is then the lawful holder of the bill of lading, and Glencore stays the lawful holder of that bill of lading until it transfers the bill of lading to someone else. The transfer of order bill of lading requires its endorsement and delivery,[71] and Glencore basically then has two options. Glencore can endorse the bill of lading to the order of the transferee,[72] and then the bill of lading remains an order bill of lading, but

[67] *Glencore* (n 34) [67].
[68] *Glencore* (n 4) [2].
[69] Probably three, which is common, and Glencore would then have kept one original for itself.
[70] Carver (n 6) [1-011]. This rule has been codified in the Dutch Civil Code in art 8:412 DCC.
[71] Carriage of Goods by Sea Act 1992, s 5(2)(b); arts 3:93 and 8:416 DCC.
[72] Writing 'deliver to Y or order' or similar words on the reverse of the bill of lading, see SD Girvin *Carriage of Goods by Sea*, 2nd edn (Oxford, Oxford University Press, 2011) 66.

it can also endorse the bill of lading in blank. The endorsement in blank merely consists of a signature and often a company stamp without further instructions or remarks on the reverse. Such an endorsement in blank converts the order bill of lading into a bearer bill of lading,[73] and this is common in practice as it makes the process a lot easier. Whereas the transfer of an order bill of lading requires its endorsement, the transfer of a bearer bill of lading merely requires its delivery, ie the transfer of possession to the transferee.[74] The consignee of a bearer bill of lading is simply its bearer. The consignee is the party with possession of the bill of lading,[75] and ultimately the party presenting the bill of lading at the port of discharge.[76]

This would explain the presence of the Glencore stamp and signature on the bill of lading: it is an endorsement in blank. When Glencore sent that signed and stamped bill of lading to Steinweg, there were again two options. If, for instance, Glencore had sent the bill of lading to Steinweg with the instruction to keep it safe pending further instructions, there would not have been a transfer of rights, simply because they had no intention to transfer any rights. Steinweg would then only hold the bill of lading as a custodian for Glencore, and the rights of suit would have remained exactly where they had always been, with Glencore.[77]

That is not very likely, though. Steinweg did not keep the bill of lading safe pending further instructions. Steinweg presented the bill of lading to MSC in its own name, as a transferee,[78] and this is where the second stamp and signature comes in. This second stamp and signature is the discharge of the carrier, and its presence on the bill of lading identifies Steinweg as the presenter/lawful holder in the process.[79]

Section 2(1)(a) of the Carriage of Goods by Sea Act 1992 provides that 'a person who becomes … the lawful holder of a bill of lading … shall … have transferred to and vested in him all rights of suit under the contract of carriage as if he had been a party to that contract'. This implies that Steinweg was the only one with rights under the bill of lading contract at that point. It makes no difference that Steinweg acted as an agent for Glencore when it presented the bill of lading as 'there is no

[73] Carver (n 6) [1-012].

[74] *Keppel Tatlee Bank Ltd v Bandung Shipping Pte Ltd* [2002] SGCA 46, [2003] 1 Lloyd's Rep 619 [22]: 'Reverting to the instant case, it would be recalled that Shweta indorsed the B/Ls in blank and the bills eventually came into the hands of Keppel TL. The effect of such an indorsement was that each of the B/Ls had become a bearer bill, transferable with the mere passing of the bill' (Chao Hick Tin JA).

[75] Carver (n 6) [1-010].

[76] Spanjaart, 'The Surrender of the Bill' (2014).

[77] D Foxton (gen ed), *Scrutton on Charterparties and Bills of Lading*, 24th edn (London, Sweet & Maxwell, 2020) [3-013].

[78] *East West Corp v DKBS AF 1912 A/S* [2003] EWCA Civ 83, [2003] QB 1509.

[79] Obviously, a forwarding agent will not have suffered any loss or damage, but that is not a requirement under the 1992 Act. Circumventing *Albacruz (Cargo Owners) v Albazero (Owners) (The Albazero)* [1977] AC 774 (HL), s 2(4) provides that an agent 'shall be entitled to exercise those rights for the benefit of the person who sustained the loss or damage to the same extent as they could have been exercised if they had been vested in the person for whose benefit they are exercised': see *Rights of Suit* (n 56) [2.27]; DR Thomas, 'A Comparative Analysis of the Transfer of Contractual Rights under the English Carriage of Goods by Sea Act 1992 and the Rotterdam Rules' (2011) 17 *JIML* 437, 444.

exception to the extinction rule of s 2(5) in favour of a principal that transfers a bill of lading to its own agent in circumstances where s 2(1) operates in favour of an agent'.[80] In fact, the Court of Appeal in *East West Corp v DKBS AF 1912 A/S* held that[81] there was nothing 'in the statutory scheme of the 1992 Act to lend any support to the idea that, after a statutory transfer of contractual rights by a principal to its agent, the principal can still sue in contract in its own name'.

This means that Glencore cannot have been exercising any rights of its own. Glencore did not have any rights under the bill of lading contract anymore as these had already passed to Steinweg together with the bill of lading. Effectively, Glencore was exercising the rights of Steinweg, and subject to equities. All defences available to MSC against Steinweg were equally available against Glencore in these proceedings.

Again, this does not matter for the rights of suit because this was agreed upon beforehand, but it does matter for the estoppel defence. Steinweg may not have had the authority to agree on Glencore's behalf that the goods could be delivered to the first presenter of the PIN code,[82] but surely it could bind itself to that agreement. When Steinweg in full awareness of the operation of the ERS exchanged the bill of lading for the release note with the PIN codes it may just have done so.

VII. Conclusions

If the electronic release note with the PIN codes is really a modernised *laat volgen*[83] and if Glencore was really just exercising the rights of Steinweg subject to equities, including for instance a variation of the contract to the extent that the goods could be delivered to the first presenter of the PIN code, could MSC then perhaps have escaped liability?[84]

[80] *Scrutton* (n 77) [3-018]. The outcome would have been the same under Dutch law, see HR 8 November 1991, NJ 1993, 609 (ann JC Schultsz), S&S 1992, 37 (Brouwersgracht).

[81] *East West* (n 78) [18] (Mance LJ).

[82] Although that is not entirely unlikely. Glencore and Steinweg did not have a formal contract, but they had agreed that their relations would be governed by the BFF Standard Trading Conditions, art 9 of which stipulates: 'In the absence of precise instructions to the contrary or special agreements, the Freight Forwarder shall be at liberty in his choice of means to be used to organise and perform the services to the best of his abilities according to normal business practice'. Albeit not a 'formal' authority, as such, Steinweg surely had a rather free hand in the performance of its obligations towards Glencore. See also M Goldby, 'The Impact of New Commercial Practices on Liner Contracts of Carriage: New Wine in Old Skins?' in J Chuah (ed), *Research Handbook on Maritime Law and Regulation* (Cheltenham, Edward Elgar, 2019) 246 and her reference to *Sino Channel Asia Ltd v Dana Shipping & Trading Pte Singapore* [2017] EWCA Civ 1703, [2018] 1 Lloyd's Rep 17.

[83] And, as such, a delivery order in the sense of the attestation clause on the MSC bill of lading.

[84] Sir Christopher Clarke: 'If there had been a variation of the contract to the effect that delivery to the first presenter of the code was a fulfilment of the delivery obligation under the contract, Glencore would have no claim: (n 34) [67].

It is submitted that, in spite of a different analysis and dissenting opinion on these two points, the outcome of the case is correct. As to the road to that outcome, however, another perhaps more principled approach would have been preferable.

The carrier's key obligation under a bill of lading contract is the delivery of the goods against presentation of the bill of lading, namely the transfer of possession of the goods to the lawful bill of lading holder. This obligation is so fundamental that the carrier cannot be excused if he delivers against a letter of indemnity, against a forged bill of lading, or against the entry of a correct, albeit stolen, PIN code. It cannot be set aside by carrier friendly provisions in the bill of lading or release note either, whether a 'before and after' clause,[85] a clause that equals discharge to delivery, a 'variation' of the contract as argued in this particular case, and, it is submitted, not by any other 'appropriately worded clause' at all.[86]

That does not, however, mean that the carrier's period of responsibility cannot be shortened at all; it just cannot be shortened this way. The German Court of Appeal and the Dutch Supreme Court have both suggested an opening, though, namely an agreement between the terminal and the receiver.[87] Having just said that the terminal was a servant of the carrier and that the delivery required the physical handover of the goods to the receiver or its authorised agent,[88] the Court of Appeal in Hamburg then went on to remark:[89]

> A requirement for that would be that all participants agree that the terminal, upon the receipt of the goods from the carrier, no longer operates for the carrier within the framework of the terminal contract concluded with him, but only for the receiver now. From that point on, the receiver would then be liable for the payment of the terminal, which would then operate as a warehouse for him. This would then constitute a transfer of constructive possession from the carrier to the receiver.

[85] *Sze Hai Tong Bank* (n 16) 587: 'For the contract, as it seems to their Lordships, has as one of its main objects, the proper delivery of the goods by the shipping company, "unto order or his or their assigns," against production of the bill of lading. It would defeat this object entirely if the shipping company was at liberty, at its own will and pleasure, to deliver the goods to someone else, to someone not entitled at all, without being liable for the consequences' (Lord Denning).

[86] See in this respect *Motis* (n 16) [5]: 'There is no dispute that an appropriately worded clause could achieve the result for which the shipowner contends' (Mance LJ). The mere fact that such a clause has not surfaced in case law since then gives a certain support to the idea that it is in fact a fundamental obligation, and one that the courts are (as yet) reluctant to relax.

[87] Rainey, 'Pinning Down Delivery' (2019) 55 also remarks that 'there is nothing inconsistent with the terminal or sub-bailee acting as the carrier's agent during the initial stages of discharge and then the consignee's agent at the point in time at which the carrier divests itself of any control and the terminal/sub-bailee attorns to the consignee'.

[88] The Dutch Supreme Court made the same observation in *The Sriwijaya*, adding that 'it cannot be ruled out that the goods upon arrival at their destination pursuant to a different agreement with the person entitled thereto either remain in the custody of the carrier or in the custody of someone who held the goods on the basis of an agreement with the carrier, and that in these cases the contract of carriage ends at the time that this different agreement enters into force'.

[89] Hanseatisch Oberlandesgericht Hamburg 6. Zivilsenat, 4 May 2017, 6 U 133/16.

Appendix

A sample *laat volgen* (courtesy MH Claringbould)

Herfurth & Boutmy n.v.

O/REF - 705/044123	11a
DATUM	18/10/94
NR. DOC.	TLC/009288

TEL : 03/221.27.80
TLX : 72175
FAX : 03/226.35.36

Herfurth & Boutmy via Westerlund!

LAAT - VOLGEN AAN

OMSCHRIJVING - DESCRIPTION	VRACHTLIJST ART. NR.

VSL/VOY...: HEERENGRACHT/44123   ETA ANR.: 21/10/94
LAADHAVEN.: RIO DE JANEIRO, RJ   B/L NR..: RIOANR0001
LIGPLAATS.: KAAI 414   DEPOT...: WESTERLUND
ONTVANGER.: KARLSTEIN   DEM.....: 20,000000

001 CSN   204 PIECE(S)   1719279 KG
MADE IN BRASIL   TINPLATES
LAAT-VOLGEN DIENT AFGETEKEND TE WORDEN VOOR ONTVANGST TEN LAATSTE 48 UUR OF TWEE WERKDAGEN NA LOSSING DER GOEDEREN
DIT BEWIJS VAN AFLEVERING MAG NIET GEENDOSSEERD WORDEN.
EVENTUELE WAAKKOSTEN TE REGELEN OP KADE.

"Wanneer de goederen na het aftekenen van dit laat-volgen, door de ontvanger en/of zijn aangestelde niet worden weggevoerd verblijven zij op kade of waar dan ook op eigen kosten, risico en gevaar, zonder enige verantwoordelijkheid van de receptienatie, de stuwadoor, de kapitein, de rederij en/of de scheepsagent".

De Rederij aanvaardt geen verantwoordelijkheid omtrent de identiteit van de persoon die, voorzien van deze L/V, de goederen in ontvangst neemt. De Rederij beschouwt de afgetekende L/V zodra deze terug in haar bezit is als wettelijk bewijs van aflevering.

Ondergetekende erkent hiermede bovenvermelde goederen in goede staat te hebben ontvangen.

Datum: 21/10/94 as per outturn report
Coil nr. [illegible]
damaged

Behouders alle bepalingen v.h. connossement. Onder voorbehoud van goede aankomst v.h. schip en van averij-grosse.

Waakkosten op kade ~~te regelen~~.

20/10/94
Herfurth & Boutmy n.v.

MAATSCHAPPELIJKE ZETEL CASSIERSSTRAAT 19 - B-2060 ANTWERPEN 6
H.R.A. 183012   K.B. 410-0643411-33
W. 406.963.302

9

Electronic Bills of Lading, Blockchain and Distributed Ledger Technology (DLT)

STEPHEN GIRVIN* AND ELSON ONG**

I. Introduction

Transport documents[1] play a pivotal supporting role in global supply chains.[2] However, notwithstanding a rapidly changing landscape, international trade and shipping is still heavily reliant on paper. For decades, the industry has steadfastly resisted innovation.[3] One estimate for a simple trade transaction involved a multitude of actors to manage paperwork[4] with the cost of paper itself constituting eight to 10 per cent of invoice value[5] and 10 to 15 per cent of total transport costs.[6]

* MPA Professor of Maritime Law; Director, Centre for Maritime Law, Faculty of Law, National University of Singapore.

** Research Associate, Centre for Maritime Law, Faculty of Law, National University of Singapore.

[1] Including bills of lading, certificates of origin, charterparties, forwarding receipts, invoices, letters of credit, port documents, sales contracts, shipping notices and truck receipts: see UNCEFACT, 'White Paper: Technical Applications of Blockchain to UN/CEFACT Deliverables' (2019) ECE/TRADE/C/CEFACT/2019/8 5; Reed Smith, *Blockchain: Distributed Ledger Technology And Designing The Future*, 3rd edn (London, Reed Smith, 2019) 74; 'The Use Of Transport Documents In International Trade' (UNCTAD, 2003) [51].

[2] 'The Use Of Transport Documents' (ibid) [9].

[3] See, eg, MB Crutcher, 'The Ocean Bill of Lading – A Study in Fossilization' (1971) 45 *Tulane Law Review* 697.

[4] E Ganne, *Can Blockchain Revolutionise International Trade?* (Geneva, World Trade Organization, 2018) 17.

[5] HB Thomsen and B Wheble, 'Trade Facilitation and Legal Problems of Trade Data Interchange' (1985) 13 *International Business Lawyer* 313. See also P Mallon and A Tomlinson, 'Bolero: Electronic "Bills of Lading" and Electronic Contracts of Sale' (1998) 1 *International Trade Law Quarterly* 257, 258, who suggested that the cost of managing trade documentation was estimated to be '7 per cent of total value of cross-border trade'.

[6] AH Boss, 'The International Commercial Use of Electronic Data Interchange and Electronic Communications Technologies' (1991) 46 *The Business Lawyer* 1787.

A significant majority – as much as 80 per cent – of all shipping documentation continues to be in paper form.[7]

This chapter is concerned with the possible electronic or digital replacement of the core document of carriage in international trade, the bill of lading. It has been estimated that if there was a 50 per cent adoption of electronic bills of lading, the saving would be more than US $4 billion[8] per year.[9] There are, however, formidable difficulties with replicating paper bills of lading because the proprietary rights to the goods attach to the physical bill of lading and contractual rights of suit vest in the holder of the physical bill of lading.[10] This entitles a holder of a bill of lading, in the event of a misdelivery or non-delivery of the goods, to advance a claim not just for a breach of the contract of carriage but also for conversion and claiming both contractual and tortious damages. Only an electronic record which is capable of emulating the intrinsic properties of a tangible paper record is capable of replacing paper bills of lading.

This chapter explores whether emerging technologies, such as blockchain and distributed ledger technology (DLT), have features that can, if successfully employed to support digitalisation efforts, lead to productivity gains.[11]

II. Paper v Electronic Bills of Lading

A. Paper Bills of Lading

For centuries, paper has had an enduring utility as the preferred medium for transport documents. Paper is tangible and retains physical features of uniqueness,[12] transferability[13] and possessability.[14] It is trite law that bills of lading have three functions:

> (1) a receipt by the carrier acknowledging the shipment of the goods on a particular vessel for carriage to an identifiable destination; (2) a memorandum of the terms of the contract of carriage, which will usually have been concluded before the signing of the document; and (3) a document of title to the goods which enables the consignee to take

[7] Reed Smith, 'Blockchain' (2019) 75.

[8] See 'DCSA Takes on eBL Standardisation, Calls for Collaboration' (19 May 2020), available at dcsa.org/wp-content/uploads/2020/05/20200519-DCSA-taking-on-eBL.pdf.

[9] By contrast, by December 2020 electronic air waybills had an adoption rate of 74.5%. See 'e-AWB International Monthly Report (December 2020)' (IATA, 2020).

[10] See below, III(C)(i).

[11] See below, III and IV.

[12] UNCITRAL, 'Possible Future Work On Electronic Commerce: Transfer Of Rights In Tangible Goods And Other Rights' (2000) A/CN.9/WG.IV/WP.90 (Session 38) [88].

[13] ibid, [7].

[14] UNCITRAL, 'Legal Issues Relating To The Use Of Electronic Transferable Records' (2000) A/CN.9/WG.IV/WP.115 (Session 45) [6].

delivery of the goods at their destination or to dispose of them by the indorsement and delivery of the bill of lading.[15]

It is not difficult to replicate the first two of these three functions digitally, so long as there are statutory provisions that recognise electronic forms of writing and signature.[16] Since these electronic mediums are intangible, they cannot physically endow the bill of lading with those essential qualities which shape the defining characteristics of the document of title as representing title to the goods, symbolic of the cargo at sea, and the key to the door of the warehouse to the goods.[17] The negotiable[18] bill of lading, in particular, has a unique value as security under a letter of credit enabling the underlying goods to be sold during transit.[19]

Paper, however, has its limitations, being prone to inaccuracy and expensive to procure and move,[20] and logistically slow to transport. Paper can quickly pile up and overwhelm supply chain actors with clutter and may also easily be exploited for fraud.[21] The limitations of paper as a medium for transport documents have been put to the test during the COVID-19 pandemic.[22] Thus, difficulties such as endemic delay in the availability of the bills of lading at the destination port,[23] the provision of inaccurate or insufficient information, and fraud have come to the fore.[24]

In order to stand a chance of success, an electronic record must be capable of emulating the intrinsic properties of a tangible paper record. Owing to its negotiable character, a bill of lading cannot simply be converted into electronic format.

[15] *JI MacWilliam Co Inc v Mediterranean Shipping Co SA (The Rafaela S)* [2005] UKHL 11, [2005] 2 AC 423 [38] (Lord Steyn), cited with approval in *Carewins Development (China) Ltd v Bright Fortune Shipping Ltd* [2009] 3 HKLRD 409 [17]; *The Star Quest* [2016] SGHC 100, [2017] Lloyd's Rep Plus 50 [17].

[16] H Beale and L Griffiths, 'Electronic Commerce: Formal Requirements In Commercial Transactions' [2002] *LMCLQ* 467, 470–74. See, eg, Electronic Communications Act 2000, ss 7 and 7C (below, III(D)(i)). See also, Interpretation Act 1978, Sch 1 ('Writing').

[17] *Sanders Bros v Maclean & Co* (1883) 11 QBD 327, 341 (CA).

[18] See M Bridge, L Gullifer, K Low and G McMeel, *The Law of Personal Property*, 2nd edn (London, Sweet & Maxwell, 2018) [1-023]–[1-024], [5-009].

[19] UNCTAD, 'The Use Of Transport Documents In International Trade' (2003) [53]–[55].

[20] See, eg, Thomsen and Wheble, 'Trade Facilitation' (1985); AH Boss, 'The International Commercial Use of Electronic Data Interchange and Electronic Communications Technologies' (1991) 46 *The Business Lawyer* 1787.

[21] P Todd, *Maritime Fraud and Piracy*, 2nd edn (London, Informa, 2010) [5.001]; [7.065] ff.

[22] See S Chambers, 'Carriers Prepare To Bid Farewell To The Old Bill Of Lading' *Splash 247* (19 May 2020); J Baker, 'Many Hands Make Light Work In The Push To Digitalisation' *Lloyd's List* (2 July 2020); DCSA, 'DCSA Takes On eBL Standardisation, Calls For Collaboration', available at dcsa.org/wp-content/uploads/2020/05/20200519-DCSA-taking-on-eBL.pdf.

[23] See, eg, *Great Eastern Shipping Co Ltd v Far East Chartering Ltd (The Jag Ravi)* [2012] EWCA Civ 180, [2012] 1 Lloyd's Rep 637 [1]; K Grönfors, *Towards Sea Waybills and Electronic Documents* (Gothenburg, Sjörättsföreningen I Göteborg, 1991) ch 2.

[24] See G Dixon, 'Is the Time Finally Right for Electronic Bills of Lading During Pandemic?' *TradeWinds* (8 October 2020). See also 'IMB Launches Initiative to Curb Bills of Lading Fraud', available at www.icc-ccs.org/index.php?start=12.

In order to replicate the bill of lading's document of title function electronically, the electronic record, which consists of binary data, must be structured in a way which embodies each of the three intrinsic properties of a paper record. The difficulty, however, is that a paper record ceases to be tangible once it is reduced to binary data. This 'dematerialisation', as it is known, is problematic because intangible property cannot be possessed at common law.[25]

B. BOLERO and essDOCS

BOLERO was launched commercially on 27 September 1999 by BOLERO International Ltd and deploys the Core Messaging Platform (CMP), Title Registry, and BOLERO Rule Book to digitalise bills of lading.[26] essDOCS is an electronic shipping document exchange system primarily used for oil and gas transportation.[27] essDOCS, previously known as ESS-Databridge™ system, was established in 2010 and is operated by essDOCS Exchange Ltd.[28] essDOCS also offers its CargoDocs service, which covers all essential documents issued in respect of cargo shipments, including original electronic bills of lading, certificates of origin, quality and quantity, manifests and timesheets.[29]

BOLERO and essDOCS employ two contractual devices to transfer legal rights under an electronic bill of lading.[30] The first is novation, which is intended to transfer the contractual rights and duties under the contract of carriage.[31] Novation arises when two contracting parties agree to transfer the contractual rights and duties under their contract to a new contract between one of the original contracting parties and a new contracting party, terminating the old contract.[32] Here, the two original contracting parties are the carrier and the old controller[33] of the electronic record;[34] the new contracting parties are the carrier and the new controller

[25] See *Armstrong DLW GMBH v Winnington Networks Ltd* [2012] EWHC 10 (Ch) [51].

[26] R Caplehorn, 'The Bolero System' in C Reed, I Walden and L Edgar (eds), *Cross-Border Electronic Banking: Challenges and Opportunities*, 2nd edn (London, LLP, 2000) ch 4; I Kerr, 'The Electronic Bill Of Lading Leads The Digital Revolution In Global Shipping' (2016) 30 *Maritime Risk International* 13.

[27] Todd, *Maritime Fraud* (2010) [7.019].

[28] Formerly, ESS-Databridge Exchange Limited and trading as Electronic Shipping Systems (ESS). See J Tan and L Starr, 'Legal Briefing on Electronic Bills of Lading' (UK P&I Club, 2017) 3–4; 'Electronic (Paperless) Trading Systems ESS Databridge Exchange Limited (trading as Electronic Shipping Solutions ("ESS")) and Frequently Asked Questions' (Steamship Mutual, 2015). See also J Bray, 'A Long Wait but First "e-cargo" is Delivered' *TradeWinds* (10 June 2010).

[29] M Goldby, *Electronic Documents in Maritime Trade*, 2nd edn (Oxford, Oxford University Press, 2019) [11.26].

[30] See M Clarke, 'Transport Documents: Their Transferability as Documents of Title; Electronic Documents' [2002] *LMCLQ* 356, 361.

[31] Rulebook, r 3.5. Bridge, Gullifer, Low and McMeel, *Personal Property* (2018) [24-018].

[32] ibid [24-001], citing *Olsson v Dyson* (1969) 120 CLR 365, 388.

[33] BOLERO uses the phrase 'immediately preceding Holder-to-order': Rulebook, r 3.5.1.

[34] *cf* Hague and Hague-Visby Rules, art I(b).

of the electronic record.[35] Under the BOLERO system, novation brings the terms of the contract of carriage from the old controller over to the new controller,[36] ensuring that a contractual relationship is established between the carrier and the person who has agreed to take orders. For essDOCS, there is also an express novation of the contract of carriage when one electronic bill of lading is transferred from one controller to the next.[37]

The second contractual device is attornment,[38] described in *The Gudermes*[39] as 'an acknowledgement that someone other than the original bailor [of the goods] now has title … and is entitled to delivery of them'. Attornment requires an undertaking by a carrier, as bailee of the goods, to a third-party controller that it will deliver the goods to this third party,[40] in order to vest constructive possession of the goods in the third party.[41] The effect of attornment is that the bailee is estopped from denying the new bailor's rights to the goods.[42] Under the BOLERO system, a controller uses the CMP[43] to transmit a message to the Title Registry and this communicates an intention to transfer constructive possession of the goods to a new controller.[44] Upon receipt of the message, BOLERO cancels the private key, which is known only to the shipper[45] and carrier,[46] and issues a new one to the new controller.[47]

Under the BOLERO Rulebook, attornment from the carrier to the third-party controller occurs whenever BOLERO International irrevocably acts as the carrier's agent.[48] The transfer of possession occurs by designation[49] of a new holder-to-order, a new pledgee holder, a new bearer holder, or a consignee holder.[50] Where the transfer of constructive possession of the goods is concerned, BOLERO relies on the Title Registry and the provisions of the BOLERO Rulebook to achieve

[35] BOLERO uses the phrase 'new Holder-to-order': Rulebook, r 3.5.1.

[36] Rulebook, r 3.5.1.

[37] Tan and Starr, 'Legal Briefing' (2017) 5.

[38] Rulebook, r 3.4.1(2).

[39] *Mitsui & Co Ltd v Novorossiysk Shipping Co (The Gudermes)* [1993] 1 Lloyd's Rep 311, 324 (CA: Staughton LJ).

[40] Bridge, Gullifer, Low and McMeel (n 18) [12-003].

[41] ibid.

[42] See *Sonicare International Ltd v East Anglia Freight Terminal Ltd* [1997] 2 Lloyd's Rep 48, 54.

[43] Caplehorn, 'Bolero System' (2000) 94.

[44] Rulebook, r 3.4.

[45] ie a 'user which is the original contracting party with whom a Carrier enters into the contract for the carriage of goods': r 1.1(48).

[46] The Rulebook defines the carrier as 'A User which contracts with another User to carry goods by any means of transport, regardless of whether the Carrier is the owner or operator of the means of transport used. Synonym: Originator': r 1.1(17).

[47] Rulebook, r 3.4.1(2).

[48] Rulebook, r 3.4.2.

[49] The term 'designate' is 'To name or appoint a User to a role in the Title Registry': Rulebook, r 1.1(24).

[50] Rulebook, rr 3.4.1(1)(a)–(d).

the same effect that the transfer of a document of title has under English law.[51] essDOCS uses a similar process to transfer title.[52]

Both the governing law of the BOLERO Rule Book[53] and essDOCS's Databridge Services and Users Agreement (DSUA)[54] for CargoDocs is English law. However, it is submitted that, under English law, the electronic bills of lading issued under such electronic registry systems are merely de facto bills of lading and not de jure bills of lading. This point is significant because potential users prioritise the smooth running of their business operations on electronic systems over recovering losses per se.[55] If these electronic bills of lading assume a different legal character from bills of lading, the same business confidence that has been attributed to paper bills of lading will not be carried over to such electronic alternatives.

C. e-title™

e-title™ is a peer-to-peer electronic title system that employs a back-end technology which connects to the back-office systems or trade applications provided by an application service provider (ASP) of supply chain actors.[56] The service is offered by E-Title Authority Pte Ltd, a Singapore-based company founded by three previous members of BOLERO who exited BOLERO to build e-title™.[57] Its founders hope was that, unlike BOLERO, this would digitalise bills of lading without making any changes to the bill of lading or to the functionality of bills of lading.[58] Significantly, e-title™ uses the peer-to-peer network architecture and its hardware security modules (HSM) are described as being safeguarded by 'tamper-proof computers that prevent technical or physical access to stored data and software code'.[59] This technology that e-title™ uses for cybersecurity protection and the safeguarding of data resembles the workings of DLT.[60]

e-title™ is supported by a multilateral legal framework, the Electronic Title User Agreement (ETUA),[61] which requires users to agree to the incorporation of the Carriage of Goods by Sea Act 1992.[62] However, while users may agree to the incorporation of the Act, it does not mean that the Act will apply to such 'electronic

[51] M Goldby, 'Electronic Bills Of Lading And Central Registries: What Is Holding Back Progress?' (2008) 17 *Information & Communications Technology Law* 125, 130.

[52] N Gaskell, 'Bills Of Lading In An Electronic Age' [2010] *LMCLQ* 233, 261; Tan and Starr (n 28) 5.

[53] Rulebook, r 2.5(2).

[54] However, the governing law of the DSUA can be New York if the contract of carriage is governed by US Law: see Goldby, *Electronic Documents* (2019) [6.02].

[55] ibid [11.09].

[56] 'How Does e-title™ Work?', available at www.e-title.net/sol_work.php.

[57] Tan and Starr (n 28) 5.

[58] ibid.

[59] 'What is e-title™?', available at www.e-title.net/sol_what.php.

[60] Below, III(B).

[61] Tan and Starr (n 28) 5.

[62] ibid.

bills of lading' because although the Act applies to any bill of lading,[63] the references to a bill of lading do not include 'a document which is incapable of transfer either by indorsement or, as a bearer bill, by delivery without indorsement'.[64] It appears that an electronic bill of lading issued by e-title™ is 'incapable of transfer', because it uses a hybrid method to combine depositary-custodian[65] and electronic title registry[66] approaches.[67] The document is therefore 'incapable of transfer' because it is the electronic title rather than the electronic bill of lading that is transferred. Accordingly, the bill only retains the functions of an acknowledgement of receipt and contract of carriage and is transformed into an electronic sea waybill with delivery made to a unique person rather than a unique document.[68] What should have been an electronic document of title has thus been transformed into an electronic certificate of title, to be verified against a title registry.

D. Liability Insurance

The users of the electronic systems described above usually take out insurance cover to bolster business confidence in their services. essDOCS has liability cover for security breaches and associated electronic risks for up to US $20 million per electronic bill of lading.[69] However, activity has remained limited despite user growth.[70]

Since February 2010, liabilities arising from the carriage of cargo under electronic trading systems may also be covered, but only if the system is approved by the International Group of P&I Clubs (IG).[71] The recognised systems originally included BOLERO International Ltd and Electronic Shipping Solutions.[72] The recognised list was expanded in October 2015 to include E-Title Authority Pte Ltd

[63] s 1(1)(a).

[64] s 1(2).

[65] As was the case with the abortive Seadocs initiative: see K Love, 'Seadocs: The Lessons Learned' [1992] 2 *Oil & Gas Law and Taxation Law Review* 53.

[66] ie BOLERO and essDOCS.

[67] See 'Creating An Electronic Title', available at www.e-title.net/sol_work_create.php; A Mackenzie, 'Switching From Paper to Electronic Bills of Lading: Has this Led to an Increase of Documentary Fraud?' (MARSH, 2016) 1; 'Sending An Electronic Title', available at www.e-title.net/sol_work_send.php.

[68] See E Ong, 'Blockchain bills of lading and the UNCITRAL Model Law on Electronic Transferable Records' [2020] *JBL* 202, 204.

[69] Mackenzie, 'Switching From Paper to Electronic Bills of Lading' (2016) 2.

[70] C Winter and M Plaistowe, 'E-Bills of Lading on the Move' (2017) 31 *Maritime Risk International* 12; Tan and Starr (n 28) 3, 7.

[71] See, eg, Gard, Rule 63.1(j).

[72] See Gard Circular No 10/2010, available at www.gard.no/Content/8475981/Member%20Circular%20 10%202010%20Paperless%20trading%20system.pdf. This was updated in 2013: Gard Circular No 1/2013, available at www.gard.no/Content/20738185/Member%20Circular%201%202013%20 Electronic%20paper%20systems%20(paperless).pdf.

when the IG approved E-title™.[73] It was further expanded in June 2019 to include Global Share SA and its edoxOnline platform[74] and, in 2020, WAVE and CargoX.[75] Each of these systems utilises blockchain technology.

III. Blockchain, Distributed Ledger Technology (DLT) and the Law

A. Blockchain

Blockchain technology structures data as digital tokens, a digital output that has unique and transferable attributes and may be capable of emulating the intrinsic properties of a tangible paper record in an electronic form. Blockchain technology appends blocks in regular intervals over the passage of time on an electronic ledger and each block serves to clear data transfer. If a sender transfers the same electronic data to two receivers, only the first transfer will be successful. The sender no longer retains a copy,[76] the first receiver receives a copy and the second receiver will not receive a copy. Since only one copy of the electronic data survives the transfer within the electronic ledger, the electronic data before and after the transfer is one and the same.

This data transfer process is secured by a creative combination of enterprise-grade cryptographic techniques[77] that gives the electronic ledger a tamper-evident quality. If a server administrator changes a record stored in the blockchain, it will be clear from an audit of the electronic ledger. In many cases, each block will run a hash function over three sets of information: (i) the previous block's hash value; (ii) announced transfers of the digital token(s); and (iii) the timestamp.[78] This integrates identifiable information from previous blocks into future blocks with the records locked into a chain. Any alteration to a record would produce an entirely different hash value for the affected block, releasing this block from the chain. This anomaly would stand out from the rest of the chain and can serve as evidence that its record has been tampered with.

[73] See Gard Circular No 7/2015, available at www.gard.no/Content/20889007/MemberCircular_7_2015.pdf.

[74] See, eg, Gard Circular No 3/2019, available at www.gard.no/Content/27791558/MemberCircular_3_2019.pdf.

[75] IG, 'International Group Circular – Bills of Lading and Blockchain Based System' (2019); West of England P&I Club, 'No 16 2019/2020 – Electronic (Paperless) Trading – Approval of Global Share SA (CargoX)'.

[76] *cf* G Treitel and FMB Reynolds, *Carver on Bills of Lading*, 4th edn (London, Sweet & Maxwell, 2017) [8-096].

[77] N Hewett, W Lehmacher and Y Wang, 'Inclusive Deployment of Blockchain for Supply Chains: Part 1 – Introduction' (World Economic Forum, 2019) 8.

[78] See Ong, 'Blockchain bills of lading' [2020] 208.

B. Distributed Ledger Technology

Distributed Ledger Technology (DLT) is a technology that can store identical copies of an electronic ledger across a peer-to-peer network.[79] This technique involves the distribution of server rights to peers of the network. The peers operate the server through their nodes, but the process is performed by the peer's machine rather than by the human actor. The nodes ensure that human actors do not make changes to the record and if there are interferences with a node's ledger, the discrepancy will be discoverable by other nodes. These nodes override the affected ledger with the prevailing version of the ledger, replacing the tampered ledger with an untampered one. This process occurs automatically, and this makes distributed ledgers tamper-resistant. They are not, however, tamper-proof because, despite the enormous costs, sheer computing power can, theoretically, overcome the resistance.[80]

Blockchain shares a close relationship with DLT because blockchain utilises electronic ledgers and DLT is a method of storing the electronic ledger across a distributed network. The distributed network is also known as a peer-to-peer network because the data is stored with the peers as servers. It is possible to either store the blockchain ledger on one central server, some decentralised servers or across a distributed network. For the latter, this is commonly referred to 'blockchain and DLT' or 'DLT and blockchain'. The method of storage does not affect the status of the blockchain transferable record as a digital token.

A distributed storage will strengthen the integrity of digital tokens, but this cybersecurity feature has some trade-offs, like increased visibility and transparency. Supply chain players should study the pros and cons of each network architecture to identify the type of blockchain storage that best suits their needs.[81]

C. Legal Issues at Common Law

i. *Digital Tokens and Property Law*

A critical issue that arises is the relationship between digital tokens and principles of personal property law, particularly the notion of possession, which suggests a

[79] J Bacon, JD Michels, C Millard and J Singh, 'Blockchain Demystified: A Technical and Legal Introduction to Distributed and Centralised Ledgers' (2018) 25 *Richmond Journal of Law & Technology* [6].

[80] The market rate to launch a 51% attack has been estimated in 2019 to be approximately US $260,000/h: M Orcutt, 'Once Hailed As Unhackable, Blockchains are Now Getting Hacked' *MIT Technology Review* (29 February 2019).

[81] See H-C Hanebeck, N Hewett and PA McKay, 'Inclusive Deployment of Blockchain for Supply Chains: Part 3 – Public or Private Blockchains – Which One Is Right for You?' (World Economic Forum, 2019). See also below, IV.

relationship between a person and a thing.[82] When the holder is a person and the thing is a tangible object, the possessory relationship assumes a physical nature. However, when the tangible object is replaced with a digital token, it is unclear how such a possessory relationship can arise because a person would not be able to hold a digital token physically, let alone deliver it physically by the sender sending and the receiver receiving the digital token. Nevertheless, it is not impossible to draw the possessory relationship between an electronic holder and a digital token. In its traditional sense, 'holder' refers to a person, but this can be interpreted as referring to an electronic holder by way of a digital identity, akin to a pseudonym.[83] The possessory relationship between the electronic holder and the digital token will assume an electronic nature rather than a physical nature[84] and will similarly behave as 'an existence independent of a particular person'[85] and 'capable of being owned and transferred'.[86]

A proprietary relationship between an electronic holder and a digital token can also, in principle, be established.[87] The relationship between the electronic holder and the digital token is definable by the system rules[88] and this can be identified as a right or an interest by third parties to be exclusive to the holder.[89] This right or interest can be assumed by third parties through the mechanism of hashing.[90] Digital tokens can, moreover, also exist permanently on the electronic ledger[91] and while there may be some stability issues, like any other electronic system, these can be resolved technically.[92]

The follow-up question is whether a possessory relationship between an electronic holder and a digital token can meet the conditions laid down for achieving the legal status of 'property' in the Law of Property Act 1925.[93] Although there are two possibilities, one of these, an 'interest in personal property', only applies to tangible objects[94] and cannot apply to intangible objects even if it makes physical changes to the electronic system.[95] For this reason, it is unlikely that a digital token will be considered a thing in possession under English law unless a wider

[82] See Bridge (n 18) [1-002].

[83] See Ong (n 68) 214.

[84] See *Your Response Ltd v Datateam Business Media Ltd* [2014] EWCA Civ 281, [2015] QB 41 [13], [16] and [23].

[85] *OBG Ltd v Allan* [2007] UKHL 21, [2008] 1 AC 1 [309].

[86] *Dixon v R* [2015] NZSC 147, [2016] 1 NZLR 678 [38].

[87] *National Provincial Bank v Ainsworth* [1965] 1 AC 1175, 1247–48 (HL); *AA v Persons Unknown* [2019] EWHC 3556 (Comm), [2020] 4 WLR 35 [61].

[88] See L Akka, D Quest, M Lavy and S Goodman, 'Legal Statement on Cryptoassets and Smart Contracts' (UK Jurisdiction Taskforce, 2019) [49]–[57].

[89] See Bridge (n 18) [1-004]. See also *B2C2 Ltd v Quoine Pte Ltd* [2019] SGHC (I) 3, [2019] 4 SLR 17 [142] (but *cf Quoine Pte Ltd v B2C2 Ltd* [2020] SGCA(I) 2, [2020] 2 SLR 20 [144] where the appellate court reserved judgment on this point).

[90] See Akka, Quest, Lavy and Goodman, 'Legal Statement on Cryptoassets' (2019) [51].

[91] ibid [52].

[92] ibid [53]–[55].

[93] Section 205(1)(xx).

[94] Bridge (n 18) [1-016]; *Datateam* (n 84) [13].

[95] *Datateam* (n 84) [19].

interpretation is taken of the term 'possession'.[96] It is submitted that it is more appropriate for a new category of intangible things in possession to be created by statute than for the courts to enlarge the interpretation of possession. This point was addressed by Moore-Bick LJ in *Datateam*, who stated that there was

> a powerful case for recognising that the essential elements of possession can be exercised over digitised materials, of which a database is a prime example, which should therefore be amenable to the tort of conversion … [and] for reconsidering the dichotomy between choses in possession and choses in action and recognising a third category of intangible property, which may also be susceptible of possession and therefore amenable to the tort of conversion. Inevitably … this would have the beneficial effect of extending the protection of property rights in a way that would take account of recent technological developments … That course is not open to us indeed, it may now have to await the intervention of Parliament.[97]

The second possibility under the Law of Property Act 1925, a 'thing in action',[98] refers to personal rights of property that can only be claimed or enforced by legal action instead of by taking physical possession. However, a digital token is not categorised as a thing in action simply because it cannot be claimed by taking physical possession. Nevertheless they can be claimed by taking electronic possession, which may involve the use of smart contracts integrated into the blockchain system.[99] Smart contracts may provide an alternative to a claim by legal action, especially if these smart contracts do not have contractual effect. In the case of DLT it may not be feasible to enforce property rights over a digital token by legal action as the distributed network is built to resist rectification. While a court may issue an order to rectify the electronic ledger, the network may not comply with the enforcement action.[100] Notwithstanding these difficulties, provided the technical issues can be resolved, a digital token can still be categorised as a thing in action. Alternatively, it may be more appropriate to categorise a digital token as an intangible thing in possession.

ii. *Digital Tokens and Bills of Lading*

Paper bills of lading are documentary intangibles[101] and the rights of the document of title are embodied in paper form[102] and travel with the document.[103]

[96] Akka, Quest, Lavy and Goodman (n 88) [67]; M Solinas, 'Bitcoiners in Wonderland: Lessons from the Cheshire Cat' [2019] *LMCLQ* 433, 439.

[97] *Datateam* (n 84) [27].

[98] The modern wording for a 'chose in action': Bridge (n 18) [1-029]. See *Torkington v Magee* [1902] 2 KB 427, 430.

[99] P Todd, 'Electronic Bills of Lading, Blockchains and Smart Contracts' (2019) 27 *International Journal of Law and Information Technology* 339, 362 ff.

[100] Akka, Quest, Lavy and Goodman (n 88) [68].

[101] Bridge (n 18) [5-001].

[102] ibid [1-022].

[103] See E McKendrick, *Goode and McKendrick on Commercial Law*, 6th edn (London, LexisNexis, 2020) [2.58].

Since documentary intangibles in paper form, including a bill of lading, are categorised as things in action,[104] blockchain bills of lading should also be categorised as things in action. Digital tokens are unique, transferable and capable of being electronically possessed and contain the necessary features of paper required for the proper functioning of a document of title.

Digital tokens are capable of emulating the physical attributes of uniqueness and transferability that feature in tangible objects.[105] Blockchain can, by ensuring the survival of only one copy of electronic data upon a transfer, enable a digital token to behave as a representative symbol and key.[106] It is, however, a moot point whether this will effect transfer because the transfer of a digital token is different to the transfer of a tangible object. Nevertheless, merely because a digital token is transferred differently from a tangible object should not mean that it is incapable of transfer.[107] While a tangible object is transferred by moving across the distance between two places, a digital token is transferred by spending the old digital token and bringing a new digital token into existence.[108] It is submitted that a transfer by instantaneous movement can also meet the requirement of deliverability for a transfer to be possible.

Documentary intangibles are transferable either by the act of delivery or the acts of indorsement and delivery[109] and, in the case of bills of lading, these two options are available in the Carriage of Goods by Sea Act 1992.[110] Indorsement can also be performed electronically. While it is a legal requirement for the bill of lading to be sent to the receiver who must receive it into its possession for delivery to take place,[111] it does not matter how the bill of lading travels between the sender and the receiver. In order to fulfil this requirement, a platform operator should include a function for the receiver to have the option of accepting or rejecting the transfer of the blockchain bill of lading.

D. Statute and Other Forms of Regulation

i. Statute

Whatever the category of property, it must be possible to claim the legal rights attached to the digital token. Section 1(2)(a) of the Carriage of Goods by Sea Act 1992 provides that references to a bill of lading 'do not include references to a

[104] Bridge (n 18) [4-006].
[105] See above, II(A).
[106] *Sanders* (n 17).
[107] *cf* KFK Low and E Mik, 'Pause the Blockchain Legal Revolution' (2020) 69 *ICLQ* 135, 151.
[108] Akka, Quest, Lavy and Goodman (n 88) [45]–[46].
[109] Bridge (n 18) [5-008].
[110] See s 5(2)(b).
[111] *Aegean Sea Traders Corporation v Repsol Petroleo SA (The Aegean Sea)* [1998] 2 Lloyd's Rep 39, 59–60.

document which is incapable of transfer', but it does not provide an exception to contractually deem such a document which would otherwise be incapable of transfer as a document which is capable of transfer. Although section 1(2)(b) identifies a bill of lading, this is subject to section 1(2)(a). An exception should provide clear wording in order to create a statutory pathway for a document that is incapable of transfer to be contractually deemed as a document capable of transfer. An example of this wording is: 'the provisions in sub-subsection (2)(a) may be derogated from or their effect may be varied by agreement, unless that agreement would not be valid or effective under applicable law'.[112] Since this or similar wording does not exist, it is clear that BOLERO, essDOCS and e-title™ do not have a statutory option to contractually deem their electronic bills of lading as legal bills of lading. It is also for this reason that the CMI Rules for Electronic Bills of Lading would not be applicable if the applicable law is English law.[113]

The common law may or may not recognise blockchain bills of lading without any enabling legislation. Even if the common law recognises blockchain as a suitable technology to digitalise bills of lading, it may not be realistic to have all the possible permutations of implementing blockchain technology identified exhaustively. For example, Corda, developed by the R3 consortium, has abandoned the concept of blocks.[114] Would they still be considered a blockchain? Questions like these introduce uncertainty into the legal status of blockchain bills of lading and make adjudication complex because each electronic system may have to be examined on its merits.

The position is, however, clearer when bills of lading are prescribed by legislation as recorded on paper.[115] The UK Electronic Communications Act 2000 does not specifically clarify whether documents of title and bills of lading are applicable or not applicable.[116] The Singapore Electronic Transactions Act (ETA) 2010[117] provides for the security and use of electronic transactions and implements the United Nations Convention on the Use of Electronic Communications in International Contracts 2005 (ECC).[118] The ETA provides for electronic records to be used in place of writing[119] and signature,[120] when the requirements are met. Significantly, the ETA expressly states that it does not apply to documents of title

[112] This wording is adapted from art 5 of the UNCITRAL Model Law on Electronic Signatures.

[113] See also, M Goldby, 'The CMI Rules For Electronic Bills of Lading Reassessed in the Light of Current Practices' [2008] *LMCLQ* 56, 58; Chacón (ch 10) IV(C).

[114] RG Brown, J Carlyle, I Grigg and M Hearn, 'Corda: An Introduction' (2016). Note that this paper has been superseded by RG Brown, 'The Corda Platform: An Introduction' (2018), available at www.corda.net/content/corda-platform-whitepaper.pdf. See below, IV(B).

[115] See, eg, Electronic Transactions Act (ETA) 2010, First Schedule.

[116] The UK has adopted neither the MLEC nor the ECC.

[117] Revised in 2011.

[118] See ETA, s 3(a)–(g). This updates the UNCITRAL Model Law on Electronic Commerce 1996 (MLEC).

[119] ibid, s 7.

[120] ibid, s 8.

and bills of lading[121] but an amendment removing part of the First Schedule from the ETA is under consideration.[122]

In view of these difficulties, a statutory regime will help to improve certainty on the legal status of blockchain bills of lading. There are two main international frameworks that could be adopted as a statutory regime to enable digital tokens. The first is the United Nations Convention on Contracts for the International Carriage of Goods Wholly or Partly by Sea (Rotterdam Rules 2008) and the second is the UNCITRAL Model Law on Electronic Transferable Records (MLETR). This chapter will only cover them briefly.[123]

ii. Rotterdam Rules

One of the reasons for the emergence of the Rotterdam Rules was a desire to facilitate electronic commerce.[124] Chapter 3, entitled 'Electronic transport records',[125] reflects this aim and uses a catch-all term for the electronic equivalents of maritime transport documents. The reason for the wording is that the Rules focus on Electronic Data Interchange (EDI) transport documents, with 'a particular emphasis on maritime electronic bills of lading'.[126] The wording intended to encompass electronic bills of lading was 'negotiable electronic transport records',[127] but this could also include 'a new kind of document of title'.[128] One view is that Chapters 9, 10 and 11 of the Rotterdam Rules can allow for intangible electronic records to replace paper for maritime transport documents.[129]

The difficulty with the Rotterdam Rules is that they are intended to achieve a 'high degree of harmonization'[130] and, for this reason, 20 ratifications are required to bring the Rules into force.[131] As this is unlikely to happen

[121] ibid, s 4(1); First Schedule.

[122] IMDA, 'Consultation Paper issued by the Infocomm Media Development Authority on Review of the Electronic Transactions Act (ETA) (Cap 88)' (2019) paras 2.2, 2.3 and 2.5.

[123] See U-H Lee, 'Assessment of Legal Instruments and Applicability to the Use of Electronic Bills of Lading' (2020) 24 *Journal of Korea Trade* 31.

[124] MF Sturley, 'Can Commercial Law Accommodate New Technologies In International Shipping?' in B Soyer and A Tettenborn (eds), *New Technologies, Artificial Intelligence and Shipping Law in the 21st Century* (London, Informa, 2019) 29, 31; MF Sturley, T Fujita and G van der Ziel, *The Rotterdam Rules: The UN Convention on Contracts for the International Carriage of Goods Wholly or Partly by Sea*, 2nd edn (London, Sweet & Maxwell, 2020) ch 3.

[125] Rotterdam Rules, ch 3.

[126] UNCITRAL, 'Report of the Working Group on Electronic Data Interchange (EDI) on the Work of Its Twenty-Ninth Session' (1995) A/CN.9/407 (Session 28) para 113; Sturley, 'Commercial Law' (2019) 30.

[127] See Rotterdam Rules, arts 1(15), 9–10.

[128] UNCITRAL, 'Report of the Working Group on Electronic Data Interchange (EDI) on the Work of Its Twenty Seventh Session' (1994) A/CN.9/390 (Session 27) para 155; Sturley (n 124) 29.

[129] Sturley (n 124) 34.

[130] UNCITRAL, 'A Guide to UNCITRAL: Basic facts about the United Nations Commission on International Trade Law' (2013) [35]–[36].

[131] 'Status: United Nations Convention on Contracts for the International Carriage of Goods Wholly or Partly by Sea (New York, 2008) (the "Rotterdam Rules")', available at uncitral.un.org/en/texts/transportgoods/conventions/rotterdam_rules/status.

anytime soon,[132] a model law may be considered instead of a convention if a 'high degree of harmonization cannot be achieved or if a greater degree of flexibility is desired' for the subject matter under consideration.[133]

iii. UNCITRAL Model Law on Electronic Transferable Records

The UNCITRAL Model Law on Electronic Transferable Records 2017 (MLETR) is dedicated to providing a legal framework for giving functional equivalence of transferable documents or instruments, including bills of lading, to electronic transferable records (ETRs). Since the MLETR does not require a minimum number of state ratifications to be effective,[134] it can easily be adopted by states for enactment as part of national law and have statutory effect.[135] Only Bahrain has so far adopted the MLETR[136] but Singapore, Chile and New Zealand committed to adopt the MLETR when they signed the Digital Economy Partnership Agreement (DEPA) on 12 June 2020.[137] Aside from the wholesale adoption of the MLETR into legislation, states can also use the MLETR as a template for building their own enabling legislation for electronic bills of lading, especially since model laws prioritise flexibility over strict uniformity.[138] In the light of this, states are permitted to make adjustments in the MLETR to accommodate their national requirements.

IV. Blockchain Networks

The use of blockchain and DLT is projected to create an estimated USD 1 trillion in new trade volume over the next decade, resulting in a GDP growth of 1.5 per cent from 2017.[139] Recent years have seen the emergence of supply chain and trade finance consortia and independent platforms seeking to provide these services. Hyperledger Fabric, Corda, Ethereum, Open Trade Blockchain, Quorum,

[132] Just four states have ratified the Rules: Spain (2011), Togo (2012), Congo (2014) and Cameroon (2017).
[133] Sturley (n 124); UNCITRAL, 'A Guide to UNCITRAL' (2013) [35].
[134] ibid [34].
[135] ibid [37].
[136] UNCITRAL, 'Bahrain enacts the UNCITRAL Model Law on Electronic Transferable Records' (2019), available at uncitral.un.org/en/news/bahrain-enacts-uncitral-model-law-electronic-transferable-records.
[137] MTI, MCI and IMDA, 'Singapore, Chile and New Zealand sign Digital Economy Partnership Agreement electronically' (2018), available at www.mti.gov.sg/-/media/MTI/Newsroom/Press-Releases/2020/06/Joint-Press-Release--Electronic-Signing-of-Digital-Economy-Partnership-Agreement-12-June-Updated-URL.pdf. Art 2.3 of the DEPA provides that 'Each Party shall endeavour to adopt the UNCITRAL Model Law on Electronic Transferable Records (2017)'.
[138] UNCITRAL (n 130) [38].
[139] T Olsen, G Mattios and A Di Marzo, 'Trade Tech – A New Age for Trade and Supply Chain Finance' (World Economic Forum, 2018) 7.

NTT Data and Nexledger are some Blockchain-as-a-Service (BaaS) enterprise solutions that are suitable for the supply chain.[140] Others, like Wave, choose to use their own proprietary technology instead.[141] These consortia and service providers are considered in turn.

A. Hyperledger Fabric

Hyperledger Fabric is an open source collaborative effort created to advance cross-industry blockchain technologies hosted by the Linux Foundation.[142]

i. TradeLens

AP Møller Maersk A/S (Maersk) and International Business Machines Corporation (IBM) were involved in early-stage research for paperless trade. In 2014, Maersk studied a shipment containing roses and avocados from Kenya to the Netherlands and reported that the journey involved around 30 actors, more than 100 people, and more than 200 interactions.[143] The study also revealed that 10 out of 34 days of shipment were wasted from documentary processing, partly because a critical document, which was only later found amid a pile of paper, went missing.[144] These findings demonstrated that documentary clutter made paper highly inefficient as a medium for accompanying shipping activities. In another pilot shipment of avocados from Mombasa to Rotterdam, IBM assessed that the paperwork cost was US $300 out of US $2,000 and calculated that the savings that could be enjoyed from digitalisation was 15 per cent.[145] The significance of the discovery was that digitalisation could potentially save shipping carriers about US $38 billion per year.[146]

In June 2016, Maersk and IBM began collaboration to build a platform based on blockchain and cloud-based technologies.[147] This project became known as TradeLens, a trade platform intended to connect the entire supply chain ecosystem,[148] and was formally announced in January 2018.[149] The partnership

[140] See D Patel and E Ganne, 'Blockchain and DLT in Trade: A Reality Check' (World Trade Organization, 2019) 19.
[141] ibid, 7.
[142] 'About Hyperledger' (2019), available at www.hyperledger.org/about.
[143] Ganne, *Blockchain* (2018) 17.
[144] ibid.
[145] ibid 82; I Allison, 'Maersk and IBM want 10 million shipping containers on the global supply blockchain by year-end' *International Business Times* (5 March 2017), available at www.ibtimes.co.uk/maersk-ibm-aim-get-10-million-shipping-containers-onto-global-supply-blockchain-by-year-end-1609778.
[146] Ganne (n 4) 82; Allison (ibid).
[147] J Baker, 'Maersk and IBM Announce Blockchain Joint Venture' *Lloyd's List* (16 January 2018).
[148] Patel and Ganne, 'Blockchain' (2019) 31.
[149] ibid.

later grew to become an international blockchain shipping consortium. Two-thirds of all container shipping lines, over 80 terminals and ports, 17 customs authorities and corporates, banks and freight forwarders support TradeLens.[150] The wide-reaching composition of the TradeLens consortium spans the globe, comprising AP Møller-Mærsk A/S (Maersk) (Danish), CMA CGM (French), Hapag-Lloyd (German), Mediterranean Shipping Company (MSC) (Swiss–Italian), Ocean Network Express (ONE) (Japanese), Pacific International Lines (PIL) (Singaporean),[151] ZIM (Israeli),[152] APM Terminals (Dutch), DP World (Dubai), PSA International (Singaporean), Standard Chartered Bank (English), Agility (Kuwaiti) and IBM (American).[153] With the support of the participating companies, the data of nearly half of the world's ocean container cargo is available on TradeLens.[154]

ii. Global Shipping Business Network

The Global Shipping Business Network (GSBN) is a consortium that seeks to provide a trusted and secure data exchange platform – the Internet of Logistics – to facilitate collaboration with the participants of the shipping supply chain.[155] GSBN uses an open digital platform based on DLT to establish a digital baseline connecting all stakeholders, including carriers, terminal operators, customs agencies, shippers and logistics service providers, and this enables collaborative innovation and the digital transformation of the supply chain.[156] Notwithstanding the word 'Global' in its name, GSBN has a Chinese-majority composition.

GSBN was formed pursuant to a Memorandum of Understanding (MoU) signed on 6 November 2018 by five leading ocean carriers (CMA CGM, COSCO Shipping Lines, Evergreen Marine, Orient Overseas Container Line (OOCL) and Yang Ming),[157] four terminal operators (DP World, Hutchison Ports, PSA International Pte Ltd and Shanghai International Port) and a software solutions

[150] ibid, 25.

[151] See G Dixon, 'PIL Uses Blockchain eBL to Ship Oranges from China' *TradeWinds* (1 February 2019).

[152] See G Dixon, 'Zim Joins Maersk Blockchain Drive' *TradeWinds* (18 April 2019).

[153] J Baker, 'Maersk and IBM Announce Blockchain Joint Venture' *Lloyd's List* (16 January 2018); J Jiang, 'Maersk and IBM Team Up On 'Transformative' Blockchain Technology' *Splash247* (6 March 2017); J Baker, 'CMA CGM and MSC to Join TradeLens' *Lloyd's List* (28 May 2019); J Baker, 'Hapag-Lloyd and ONE Join TradeLens' *Lloyd's List* (2 July 2019); S Chambers, 'Agility In Blockchain Collaboration With Maersk and IBM' *Splash 247* (7 February 2018); S Chambers, 'Standard Chartered Becomes First Bank To Join TradeLens' *Splash 247* (11 March 2020); D Osler, 'DP World Seeks to Integrate All Terminals with TradeLens' *Lloyd's List* (28 May 2020).

[154] ibid.

[155] S Chambers, 'CMA CGM, COSCO, Hapag-Lloyd And Leading Ports Set Out To Create The Internet Of Logistics' *Splash 247* (12 July 2019).

[156] ibid.

[157] They control an estimated 31.8% TEU of the market: O Duru and M Imran Md Zin, 'Blockchain Roaming In The Maritime Industry' *Splash 247* (10 April 2019).

provider (CargoSmart).[158] A study in 2019 revealed that signatories of the GSBN Memorandum of Understanding (MoU) constituted 31.8 per cent of the global container market share.[159]

The composition of GSBN has since changed upon the signing of the GSBN shareholders' agreement. However, the GSBN is still predominantly made up of Chinese and Asian players; only two of the nine GSBN shareholders – CMA CGM and Hapag-Lloyd – are incorporated outside Asia. The nine shareholders of GSBN are CMA CGM (French), COSCO Shipping Lines (Chinese), COSCO Shipping Ports (Chinese), Hapag-Lloyd (German), Hutchison Ports (Hong Kong), OOCL (Hong Kong), Port of Qingdao (Chinese), PSA International (Singaporean) and Shanghai International Port Group (SIPG) (Chinese).[160] This shareholders' agreement was not signed by Evergreen (Taiwanese), Yang Ming (Taiwanese) and DP World (Dubai), who signed the earlier MoU.

COSCO, a Chinese state-owned enterprise,[161] owns CargoSmart[162] and plays a central role in the GSBN consortium. COSCO's ambitious plans to transform the logistic chain through GSBN[163] may be attributable to China's Digital Silk Road project.[164]

iii. We.trade

We.trade Innovation DAC, formerly Digital Trade Chain, is a joint-venture company owned by 12 European banks.[165] Its digital trade platform, we.trade.com, offers a myriad of trade finance services, such as auto-settlement, bank payment undertaking (BPU),[166] BPU financing, invoice financing, and hopes this will address the challenges of open account and documentary trading.[167]

[158] 'Container Lines and Terminal Operators Sign Blockchain MOU' *The Maritime Executive* (11 June 2018).

[159] Duru and Imran Md Zin, 'Blockchain Roaming' (2019). Seven of the top ten maritime ports in 2018 by annual throughput are Chinese: L Nightingale, *One Hundred Ports* (Maritime Intelligence, Informa, 2019) 18.

[160] I Walia, 'Progress Made In Digital Shipping Platform Network' *Lloyd's List* (27 February 2020).

[161] W Wu, 'How The Communist Party Controls China's State-Owned Industrial Titans' *SCMP* (17 June 2017).

[162] Chambers, 'The Internet Of Logistics' (2019).

[163] See, eg, C Shen, 'Cosco sets up maritime university' *Lloyd's List* (3 July 2020); C Shen, 'Cosco agrees blockchain technology deal with Alibaba' *Lloyd's List* (7 July 2020); C Shen, 'Cosco, SIPG and Tesla in blockchain test' *Lloyd's List* (7 April 2020); F Chan and C Deihl, 'GSBN Shareholders Pilot Innovative Cargo Release Application in Shanghai' (7 April 2020), available at www.cargosmart.ai/media/filer_public/d8/02/d80202fe-7fac-4871-83ff-3c2daa1c396c/20200407_cargosmart_gsbn_press_statement_en.pdf.

[164] 'The Digital Side Of The Belt And Road Initiative Is Growing' *The Economist* (6 February 2020); R Koepp, R Ward, A White and P Thaker (eds), *One Belt One Road Economic Roadmap* (The Economist | Intelligence Unit, 2016) 3; G Ouyang, '21st Century "Maritime Silk Road" and Sino–Indian Maritime Cooperation' in BR Deepak (ed), *China's Global Rebalancing and the New Silk Road* (Berlin, Springer, 2017).

[165] See Patel and Ganne (n 140) para 4.1.9.

[166] *cf* bank payment obligation (BPO): 'Frequently Asked Questions', available at we-trade.com/faq.

[167] Patel and Ganne (n 140) para 4.1.9. See also, Ganne (n 4) 24.

B. Corda

The Corda blockchain has been developed by the R3 consortium[168] and is used by Voltron and Marco Polo to deliver digital trade finance services.

i. Voltron

Voltron is a platform dedicated to letter of credit transactions.[169] Banks can use the Voltron platform to create, exchange, approve and issue letters of credit and the service accessed by customers of the participating banks, including BNP Paribas and HSBC.[170] Singapore's first fully digitalised letter of credit transaction was completed using the Voltron platform.[171] The transaction involved a bulk shipment of iron ore from Rio Tinto to Cargill and BNP Paribas issued the letter of credit on behalf of Cargill to HSBC Singapore, acting for Rio Tinto.[172] Voltron can integrate with BOLERO and essDOCS.[173] Indeed, the electronic bill of lading that was tendered by Rio Tinto to BNP Paribas was by BOLERO.[174]

ii. Marco Polo

Marco Polo is a platform that uses working capital finance solutions for open trade finance.[175] Its service offerings include receivable finance, payables finance, and payment commitment with and without financing.[176] It also provides secure, distributed data storage and book-keeping, identity management, and asset verification among other features.[177] It has received support from over 30 banks.[178]

C. Ethereum

Ethereum is a programmable blockchain that enables programmers to programme decentralised applications (Dapps).[179] CargoX, an on-chain blockchain bill of

[168] Ganne (n 4) 5, 26.
[169] ibid.
[170] Patel and Ganne (n 140) para 4.1.7.
[171] J Baker, 'Blockchain Trials Turn To Finance' *Lloyd's List* (9 November 2018).
[172] ibid.
[173] Patel and Ganne (n 140) para 4.1.7.
[174] Baker, 'Blockchain Trials' (2018). Other banks may not accept the pledge of such electronic bills of lading as security for trade finance under documentary credit because they cannot be retained in the bank's possession. See DCSA, 'DCSA Takes on eBL Standardisation' (n 8) 2; Bridge, Gullifer, Low and McMeel (n 18) para [15-011]; [15-023].
[175] Ganne (n 4) 26.
[176] Patel and Ganne (n 140) para 4.1.8.
[177] ibid.
[178] ibid.
[179] 'What is Ethereum?', available at ethereum.org/en/what-is-ethereum.

lading platform,[180] uses a blockchain document transaction system (BDTS) to tokenise, encrypt and transfer trade documents.[181]

D. Quorum

Quorum is the enterprise version of Ethereum and the blockchain unit of JP Morgan Chase & Co.[182] Komgo is a commodity trade finance platform[183] which offers digital trade finance, know your customer (KYC) and certification services.[184] Komgo completed two successful proofs-of-concept, one involving a shipment of crude cargo and another involving a transaction of soybeans.[185]

E. Open Trade Blockchain

Open Trade Blockchain (OTB) is the cross-border blockchain solution that connects trade communities developed by Global eTrade Services (GeTS) Asia Pte Ltd, a subsidiary of Singapore-based digital government services provider, Crimson Logic Pte Ltd.[186] GeTS offers a range of products, including CALISTA™,[187] a global trade facilitation and supply chain platform that it developed with PSA International Pte Ltd.[188] CALISTA™ offers a myriad of services, including CALISTA™ Finance[189] and CALISTA™ Intelligent Agent,[190] and can be divided into digital logistics, statutory compliance and financial services. Calista is featured as a value-added service on Singapore's Networked Trade Platform (NTP).[191]

The NTP is a one-stop trade and logistics ecosystem developed by Singapore Customs and the Government Technology Agency of Singapore (GovTech) to

[180] T Lyons and L Courcelas, *Blockchain in Trade Finance and Supply Chain* (The European Union Blockchain Observatory and Forum, 2019) 32.

[181] Patel and Ganne (n 140) para 4.1.8.

[182] 'What is Quorum?', available at www.jpmorgan.com/country/UK/EN/Quorum; A Irrera, 'Exclusive: JPMorgan In Talks To Merge Blockchain Unit Quorum With Startup ConsenSys – Sources' *Reuters* (11 February 2020).

[183] Lyons and Courcelas (n 180) 31.

[184] See Patel and Ganne (n 140) para 4.1.6.

[185] ibid.

[186] 'About Open Trade Blockchain', available at globaletrade.services/products/blockchain. 'Global eTrade Services (GeTS), available at globaletrade.services/sites/default/files/2019-02/GeTS%20 Brochure_2.pdf.

[187] CALISTA™ stands for CArgo Logistics, Inventory Streaming & Trade Aggregation.

[188] PSA and CrimsonLogic, 'PSA and GeTS to develop new global trade facilitation & supply chain platform "Calista™"' (24 April 2018), available at www.globalpsa.com/wp-content/uploads/nr180424.pdf. PSA International holds a majority stake in CrimsonLogic: see HH Tan, 'PSA-backed Trade Platform Takes Off On Desire To Cut Red Tape' *Lloyd's List* (3 April 2019).

[189] See HH Tan, 'Trade Compliance Speeds Up On PSA-Backed Platform' *Lloyd's List* (2 December 2019).

[190] See V Wee, 'Artificial Intelligence-Based Service To Boost Calista Supply Chain Platform' *Lloyd's List* (23 October 2019).

[191] HW Tan, 'PSA Backed Trade Platform Takes Off On Desire To Cut Red Tape' *Lloyd's List* (3 April 2019).

support digitalisation efforts and connect players across the trade value chain in Singapore and abroad.[192] The NTP collaborated with NTT Data and Bank of Tokyo-Mitsubishi UFJ in a proof of concept (PoC) to test a digital trade portal to connect the two platforms.[193]

F. NTT Data

The International Trade Data Sharing Platform using Blockchain Technology is a Japanese trade consortium involving 18 Japanese companies that seeks to streamline trade procedures.[194] This project was spearheaded by the New Energy and Industrial Technology Development Organisation (NEDO), and NTT Data Corporation was engaged as the contractor to build the system.[195]

G. Nexledger™

Nexledger™ is the blockchain developed by Samsung SDS.

i. *Export Customs Logistics Service*

An export customs logistics service consortium involving many Korean stakeholders[196] uses Nexledger™[197] to automatically track shipped cargo and record

[192] V Wee, 'Maritime Singapore Invests In A Digital Future' *Lloyd's List* (3 April 2019).

[193] Networked Trade Platform, 'Japan's BTMU and NTT Data To Test Digital Trade Portal With Singapore', available at www.ntp.gov.sg/public/news/media-releases/2017/japans-btmu-and-ntt-data-to-test-digital-trade-portal-with-singapore.

[194] NTT Data Corporation, 'International Trade Data Sharing Platform using Blockchain Technology' (2019), available at de.nttdata.com/-/media/NTTDataGermany/Files/2020-EN-Broch-International-Trade-Data-Sharing-Platform-Using-Blockchain-Technology.pdf; A Hadhi, 'MOL, NYK And K Line To Develop Trade Data Sharing Platform Using Blockchain' *Lloyd's List* (28 August 2017). The consortium's shipping lines, Mitsui OSK Lines, NYK Line, Ocean Network Express (ONE) and Kawasaki Kisen Kaisha (K Line) control an estimated 6.7% TEU of the market: Duru (n 157).

[195] NTT Data Corporation, 'Launch of the Proof of Concept (PoC) for International Trade Data Sharing System Using Blockchain Technology: Public-Private Partnership to Streamline the Trade Process in Global Supply Chain' (23 August 2018), available at www.nttdata.com/jp/ja/-/media/nttdatajapan/files/news/release/2018/082300/2018en082300-1.pdf.

[196] Samsung SDS Communication Team, 'Samsung SDS to be World's First to Apply Blockchain Tech to Export Customs Logistics Service' (17 September 2018), available at www.samsungsds.com/global/en/about/news/blockchain-tech-for-customs-logistics-service.html; T-J Kang, 'Korea's Shipping Blockchain Consortium Gets More Members' *Lloyd's List* (23 February 2018). The consortium's shipping lines, HMM and SM Line, control an estimated 1.9% TEU of the market: Duru (n 157). The Korean equivalent to BOLERO and essDOCS, KTNET, is also part of this venture: S Ji-Hye, 'Blockchain To Be Used For Logistics In Korea' (31 May 2017), available at www.koreaherald.com/view.php?ud=20170531000773. See also, UNCITRAL, 'Present and Possible Future Work on Electronic Commerce' (2010) A/CN.9/692 (Session 43) paras 26–47.

[197] Samsung SDS Communication Team, 'Samsung SDS to be World's First to Apply Blockchain Tech to Export Customs Logistics Service' (17 September 2018), available at www.samsungsds.com/global/en/about/news/blockchain-tech-for-customs-logistics-service.html.

movements, which will prevent shipment contents from being falsely advertised and shipment from being lost.[198] Indeed, SM Line tested the combination of Nexledger™ with the Internet of Things (IoT) to assess the real-time vessel monitoring system and management of reefer containers on the *SM Busan*, and installed a very-small-aperture terminal (VSAT)[199] and IoT devices[200] to monitor the condition of the ship and cargo in real-time during the voyage.[201] Two pilot voyages have also been conducted.[202]

H. Wave

Wave uses in-house blockchain and DLT to digitalise trade documents such as bills of lading, bills of exchange and promissory notes for transmission between carriers, banks, cargo owners and platforms, and has completed successful pilots since 2016.[203]

I. Observations

i. Anti-Competitive Practices

Blockchain consortiums may engage in anti-competitive or collusive practices to boost the usage of their liner services, but the economic benefits associated with a larger network effect[204] would not accrue to these smaller networks operating as data siloes independently of each other.[205] These consortiums may also call into question the relevance of the BIMCO Electronic Bills of Lading Clause 2014 for charterparties, as shipowners may not be prepared to use an electronic (paperless)

[198] See K Dotson, 'Samsung SDS Builds Blockchain Network For Korean Shipping Industry' *SiliconANGLE* (31 May 2017), available at siliconangle.com/2017/05/31/samsung-sds-builds-blockchain-network-korean-shipping-industry.

[199] The VSAT is a satellite communications system which can be used to track and check cargos.

[200] The IoT devices first transmit the cargo data to the VSAT which forwards it to SM Line's central computer server via satellite uplink.

[201] T-J Kang, 'SM Line Tests Real-Time Vessel Monitoring System Based On Internet Of Things Technology' *Lloyd's List* (28 November 2017).

[202] See T-J Kang, 'SM Line Completes First Pilot Voyage Using Blockchain Technology' *Lloyd's List* (6 November 2017); T-J Kang, 'HMM Completes Pilot Blockchain Voyage With Reefer-Laden Boxship' *Lloyd's List* (7 September 2017).

[203] See Patel and Ganne (n 140) 33; A Corbett, 'P&I Clubs Prepare for Digital Revolution' *TradeWinds* (21 January 2020).

[204] The network effect is a phenomenon where the value of a service increases with more participants in the network.

[205] S Kukman, 'How To Handle Blockchain Going Mainstream' *Splash 247* (28 August 2018).

trading system offered by a rival blockchain network. In order to foster cooperation, it is necessary to develop standardisation and interoperability regimes.

ii. Cyber-Attacks and Other Issues

Blockchain developments have raced far ahead of the underlying legal structures.[206] While attention has, perhaps inevitably, focused on blockchain issues in the banking context, it has nevertheless been warned that 'blockchain is blind and deaf to events in the real world and entirely dependent on human (or human-designed machine) input or oracles, all of which can engage in fraudulent behaviour or malfunction and hence need to properly supervised'.[207] This concern is not without foundation[208] given highly publicised cyber attacks involving Maersk[209] and MSC[210] and, more recently, CMA CGM[211] and even the IMO.[212] It has even been argued that 'in many respects quite paradoxically, shipping's greatest defence against cyber disaster lies not in technological advancement and blockchain, but in the very old-fashioned way in which its paperwork is still done'.[213]

V. Standardisation

The MLETR provides for 'any applicable industry standard'[214] to meet the general reliability standard[215] of a reliable method for functional equivalence.[216] These 'industry standards' can refer to the industry standards published by standard bodies.[217] This chapter discusses two: DCSA and ISO.

[206] See, eg, K Yeung, 'Regulation by Blockchain: the Emerging Battle for Supremacy between the Code *of* Law and Code *as* Law' (2019) 82 *MLR* 207.

[207] Low and Mik, 'Blockchain Legal Revolution' (2020) 175.

[208] See also Chacón (ch 10) III(A).

[209] I Lewis, 'Cyber Attack to Cost Maersk More Than $50m' *TradeWinds* (5 July 2017); G Dixon, 'US Charges Six Russians over NotPetya Attack that Crippled Maersk' *TradeWinds* (21 October 2020).

[210] G Dixon, 'MSC Confirms Cyber Attack But Says No Data Lost' *TradeWinds* (16 April 2020).

[211] I Lewis, 'France's CMA CGM Hit by Cyber-attack' *TradeWinds* (28 September 2020); 'CMA CGM Systems Back in Business After Dealing with Cyber-attack' *TradeWinds* (12 October 2020).

[212] A Corbett, 'IMO Hit By "Sophisticated" Hackers in Cyber-attack' *TradeWinds* (1 October 2020). See also D Ng, 'How Prepared is Shipping for the Next Cyber Attack?' *Lloyd's List* (12 October 2020).

[213] See G Gross, 'Paper Bills of Lading are Shipping's Best Defence Against Cyber Warfare' *TradeWinds* (28 July 2018).

[214] MLETR, art 12(a)(vii).

[215] ibid, art 12.

[216] ibid, art 10.1(b).

[217] See eg, L Pawczuk, JM Nielsen, PKH Sin and N Hewett, 'Inclusive Deployment of Blockchain for Supply Chains: Part 6 – A Framework for Blockchain Interoperability' (World Economic Forum, 2020) 11.

A. Digital Container Shipping Association

On 10 April 2019, four container shipping companies – MSC, Maersk, Hapag-Lloyd and ONE – established a neutral and non-profit association, the Digital Container Shipping Association (DCSA), in Amsterdam[218] to address the lack of digital standards in the container shipping industry.[219] The inspiration for the DCSA was credited to the success of the International Air Transport Association (IATA)[220] in establishing standards in the aviation industry.[221] The founding members were subsequently joined by CMA CGM, Evergreen Line, Hyundai Merchant Marine (HMM), Yang Ming and ZIM, bringing the number of major liner operators to nine, making up almost 80 per cent of the market.[222]

DCSA seeks to develop shared IT standards,[223] and has published DCSA Interface Standard for Track and Trace (version 1.2)[224] and IoT Container Standards: IoT Standard for Gateway Connectivity Interfaces (version 1).[225] The DCSA has plans to develop standards for electronic bills of lading[226] and is also working to produce an industry blueprint for container shipping.[227]

B. International Organization for Standardization

The International Organization for Standardization (ISO) is an independent, non-governmental international organisation which has been providing world-class specifications since 1947,[228] covering almost every conceivable industry, including technology.[229] ISO is building blockchain and DLT standards through its technical committee ISO/TC 307 (Blockchain and distributed ledger technologies). Three standards have been published so far: ISO 22739:2020 (Vocabulary); ISO/TR 23244:2020 (Privacy and personally identifiable information protection

[218] MSC, 'MSC to Pioneer Digital Industry Standards in New Container Line Association' (MSC, 2019).

[219] L Nightingale, 'Carriers' Digital Standardisation Lobby Means Business' *Lloyd's List* (17 May 2019). See also, MSC ibid; G van Marle, 'Digital Standards for Container Shipping on the Starting Blocks' *gCaptain* (21 June 2019), available at gcaptain.com/digital-standards-for-container-shipping-on-the-starting-blocks.

[220] J Baker, 'An INTTRA For Blockchain?' *Lloyd's List* (18 May 2018).

[221] Nightingale, 'Carriers' Digital Standardisation Lobby' (2019).

[222] ibid.

[223] The current DCSA standards and programs include Operational Vessel Schedules, IoT Connectivity, eBill of Lading, Cyber Security Guide and Track & Trace: 'Standards and programs', available at dcsa.org/initiatives#standards.

[224] DCSA, 'DCSA Interface Standard for Track and Trace 1.2' (14 May 2020).

[225] DCSA, 'IoT Container Standards: IoT Standard for Gateway Connectivity Interfaces' (29 May 2020).

[226] DCSA (n 8) 4.

[227] DCSA, 'Industry Blueprint – Container Shipping 2.0' (July 2020).

[228] ISO, 'About us', available at www.iso.org/about-us.html.

[229] ibid.

considerations); and ISO/TR 23455:2019 (Overview of and interactions between smart contracts in blockchain and distributed ledger technology systems).[230] There are eight more standards in the works.[231]

VI. Interoperability

Interoperability has been defined as the 'capacity of computer systems to exchange and make use of information; and the capacity to transfer an asset between two or more systems while keeping the state and uniqueness of the asset consistent'.[232] Its function can be described as an adapter to connect disparate systems. One interoperable framework is TradeTrust, an interoperable framework that facilitates the exchange of digital trade documentation, including bills of lading, between different digital ecosystems in Singapore and globally.[233] IMDA is working with the UN/CEFACT to build a framework on TradeTrust to comply with the reliability issues of the MLETR.[234] Accordingly, being accredited with TradeTrust may demonstrate that electronic transferable records are MLETR-compliant.

The TradeTrust initiative is jointly led by the Info-communications Media Development Authority (IMDA) and the Maritime and Port Authority (MPA), and supported by Singapore Customs, Enterprise Singapore and the Singapore Shipping Association (SSA).[235] In January 2020, the International Chamber of Commerce (ICC) and 17 global industry leaders[236] signed a Memorandum of Intent (MOI) to formalise collaboration with IMDA on TradeTrust.[237] The ICC also codeveloped the ICC TradeFlow platform, which is built on the TradeTrust framework, with IMDA, DBS Bank, Perlin (blockchain provider) and Trafigura (commodities trader).[238] In November 2019, the ICC TradeFlow platform

[230] 'Standards by ISO/TC 307 Blockchain and distributed ledger technologies', available at www.iso.org/committee/6266604/x/catalogue/p/1/u/0/w/0/d/0.

[231] ibid.

[232] Pawczuk, Nielsen, Sin and Hewett, 'Inclusive Deployment of Blockchain' (2020) 6.

[233] A Lim, 'Eliminating Paper Documents, S$300m Research Fund Top-Up Among MCI's 2019 Plans' *Channel News Asia* (Singapore). See SY Loh, 'Trade Digital: TradeTrust Trials and Partnerships' *TradeTrust Newsletter* (IMDA, April–June 2020), available at www.imda.gov.sg/-/media/Imda/Files/Programme/International-Trade-and-Logistics/FA-IMDA-TradeTrust_Newsletter.pdf.

[234] ibid.

[235] ibid. See also T Conley, 'ICC joins Singapore Government and major industry partners to launch TradeTrust' (ICC, 22 January 2020), available at iccwbo.org/media-wall/news-speeches/icc-joins-singapore-government-and-major-industry-partners-to-launch-tradetrust.

[236] See Loh, 'Trade Digital' (2020).

[237] Conley, 'ICC joins Singapore Government' (2020); O Subhani, 'World Economic Forum: Pact On Singapore-Pioneered Framework To Foster Trust In Trade Digitalisation' *The Straits Times* (23 January 2020); IMDA, 'World's Largest Business Organisation Joins Singapore Government and Major Industry Partners to Drive Global Digitalisation' (2020), available at www.imda.gov.sg/news-and-events/Media-Room/Media-Releases/2020/Worlds-Largest-Business-Organisation-Joins-Singapore-Government-and-Major-Industry-Partners-to-Drive-Global-Digitalisation.

[238] T Conley and Q Carthane, 'ICC and Blockchain Provider, Perlin, Will Pilot ICC TradeFlow, A Blockchain Platform Aimed At Simplifying The Trade Documentation Process For All'

facilitated the execution of a landmark US $20m pilot trade for the shipment of iron ore from South Africa to China.[239]

VII. Conclusions

The successful digitalisation of bills of lading depends on the economic benefits and legitimacy of electronic bills of lading and the trustworthiness of the system operators. The cost savings and productivity gains from digitalising shipping operations using technology seem attractive but have to be weighed against any potential expenses of using the service(s).[240]

There is some optimism that technological and legal developments can help spearhead the legalisation of electronic bills of lading. Although the technical problems associated with electronic bills of lading issued by BOLERO, essDOCS and e-title™ are not easily resolved by the techniques of novation, attornment and/or electronic title registry principally because these approaches do not mirror the transfer of paper bills of lading, those technical problems are becoming less of a concern. Blockchain is a suitable candidate for assuming the trinity of functions of paper bills of lading primarily because it is capable of structuring electronic records as digital tokens so as to enable the transfer the proprietary rights to the goods in the bill of lading. DLT can, optionally, be engaged to strengthen cyber-security defences, guard against fraud and protect data integrity to enhance the reliability of the electronic record.

This chapter also emphasises how a statutory regime has to be developed to give legal recognition and enforceability to electronic bills of lading, with the MLETR preferred as the regime because of its singular purpose of giving functional equivalence to transferable documents. However, for the MLETR to have any real impact it needs to be adopted and implemented by domestic regimes, a process which has only just begun.

There is also a trust problem that needs addressing if electronic bills of lading are to be workable in practice. Indeed, it has been suggested that 'the real problem in digitalisation is getting people to trust each other'.[241] The consortium and standardisation efforts are attempts at responding to this problem. This chapter has observed that there is a multiplicity of blockchain networks. The advantage of international diversity is that increasing independence between consortium

(ICC, 7 November 2019), available at iccwbo.org/media-wall/news-speeches/icc-tradeflow-blockchain-platform-launches-to-simplify-trade-processes. See also D Wainwright, 'Trafigura and DBS Start Singapore Blockchain Trade Platform' *TradeWinds* (6 November 2019).

[239] Conley (n 235).

[240] Many electronic systems usually involve the payment of a subscription and/or transaction fee: N Hewett, S Warren and M Sönmez, 'Redesigning Trust: Blockchain Deployment Toolkit' (World Economic Forum, 2020) 40.

[241] R Clayton, 'Digitalisation: Do The Numbers Stack Up?' *Lloyd's List* (9 October 2020).

members[242] and obligations to adhere to multijurisdictional data protection laws[243] enable ombudsman nodes to audit and safeguard data more effectively.[244] Conversely, the jurisdiction in which a blockchain server is located may also have laws requiring the network server to grant the authorities access to sensitive commercial data stored in the server. This may enable domestic authorities to map the web of connections between the suppliers and customers in its network, including the prices being traded.

The standardisation of the international logistics chain has frequently been described as the 'Holy Grail'.[245] The working industry standards by DCSA, ISO and other standards bodies look promising but these should also address what constitutes a 'blockchain'. Blockchain bill of lading systems should enable the receiver to choose to accept or reject the transfer of a blockchain bill of lading. TradeTrust appears to be an interoperable framework which will accredit the ETR to be compliant with MLETR and industry standards. Singapore, a trusted technological maritime hub at the crossroads of the East–West trade, is well positioned to be an interoperable node to connect the maritime and blockchain networks to facilitate blockchain roaming as a digital transshipment hub.[246]

Although these efforts are commendable and show that great strides have been made, they are by themselves no means a panacea to the problem of trust which does not have an easy solution. As one commentator pointed out, 'in a conservative, fragmented and highly competitive industry, it is not easy to build globally the key ingredient that makes all shipping projects fly: trust'.[247]

[242] Consortiums are also advised to use good blockchain governance to ensure the reliability of their system: ibid, 52.

[243] See Chacón (ch 10) V.

[244] Bacon, Michels, Millard and Singh, 'Blockchain Demystified' (2018) [57].

[245] R Meade, 'SMW: It's Time To Demand A Little More Depth From The Digital Revolution' *Lloyd's List* (24 April 2018).

[246] Duru (n 157); See 'Gateway to Asia' (2019), available at www.mpa.gov.sg/web/portal/home/maritime-singapore/introduction-to-maritime-singapore/gateway-to-asia; J Woo, 'Road Map To Boost Singapore's Edge In Maritime Industry' *Straits Times* (13 January 2018).

[247] T Mcalister, 'Trust is the Missing Link in Shipping's Bid to Harness Benefits of Blockchain' *TradeWinds* (20 May 2020).

10

Web Portals and Data Sharing by Ocean Carriers

VÍCTOR CHACÓN*

I. Introduction

The shipping industry has profited from the commercial implementation of electronic communications and digital technology. The electronic transmission of information has been common since the 1990s, when ocean carriers started transmitting data relating to freight receipts and sea waybills online.[1] Ocean carriers have substantially improved the accessibility and efficiency of their services with the introduction of web portals. Initially, these were implemented as an advertising instrument. Later, the technology evolved to web portals, which are more sophisticated, enabling the performance of commercial transactions online, now commonly known as ecommerce. Most sea carriers offer services through their own web portals or those of third parties, such as INTTRA[2] or Cargo Smart.[3] Websites display information about vessels, routes, schedules and related services. This technology makes the information more accessible, enabling customers to compare departure and arrival dates, transit times and freight rates among different carriers, and facilitating the decision-making process. The interaction provided by web portals, particularly in the liner trade, makes it possible to obtain quotations for shipments, make bookings, fill, modify and issue relevant documents, including bills of lading, give access to real-time cargo data and tracking services, and receive notification and arrival notices.[4]

Shippers or forwarding agents today enter into contracts with ocean carriers via web portals, making it possible to order remote printing of bills of lading. The information contained in the bill of lading, previously submitted through a website

* Senior Research Fellow, Centre for Maritime Law, Faculty of Law, National University of Singapore.

[1] N Gaskell, 'Bills of Lading in an Electronic Age' [2010] *LMCLQ* 233, 237.

[2] See www.inttra.com.

[3] See www.cargosmart.com/en/default.htm.

[4] See, eg, www.cma-cgm.com/products-services/ecommerce; www.maersk.com; www.msc.com/sgp; elines.coscoshipping.com/ebusiness; www.hapag-lloyd.com/en/online-business.html; www.evergreen-line.com.

or by email, can be printed at the shipper's premises or by the same carrier at the destination.[5]

Apart from the practical advantages, the digitalisation of shipping services also facilitates the contracting process and significantly reduces the cost of the associated transactions.[6] It is understandable then that the industry should migrate towards new technology[7] but industry leaders have pointed out that the maritime sector is not implementing measures fast enough to profit from digitalisation.[8] This is occurring even when the cost is affordable and 'consistently decreasing'[9] because some industry players consider digital technology as a cost rather than as an investment.[10] The slow pace is even more notorious when it comes to sharing valuable technical information among industry players.[11] This reluctance to share data is perhaps the biggest challenge for digitalisation in the shipping industry; indeed, transformation depends on this.[12] Although essential, there is a concern that such information can be used against individual companies or undermine competitiveness.[13]

Another reason for such reluctance is that technological change highlights challenges which are of concern to the international legal community, including writing and signing requirements, evidentiary value, allocation of liability for erroneous messages, the incorporation of general terms and conditions, and the safeguarding of sensitive data.[14] Data sharing and its protection has become one of the most complex aspects of this revolution. The profits that may result from the application of digitalisation depend particularly on the effective collection and sharing of data.[15] This chapter addresses the possible liabilities of ocean carriers arising from breaches of international regulations governing the exchange and protection of data collected from customers through web portals.

[5] This practice can be traced back to the early noughties when American President Lines (APL) launched a service for the remote printing of bills of lading: see M Goldby, 'The CMI Rules for Electronic Bills of Lading Reassessed in the Light of Current Practices' [2008] *LMCLQ* 56, 60.

[6] *Review of Maritime Transport 2018* (UNCTAD, 2018) 15; 'Digitalization in shipping is here to stay' *Marine & Offshore Technology* (18 December 2017).

[7] J Porter, 'Digitalisation: Overhyped or a Genuine Game-changer for Container Shipping?' *Lloyd's List* (13 April 2017).

[8] A Adamopoulos, 'Industry Still Lagging Behind on Digital Standardization and Data Sharing' *Lloyd's List* (3 June 2019); M Fuechec, 'Carrot and Stick Approach to Data-sharing' *Lloyd's List* (6 June 2019).

[9] C Roeloffs, 'Breaking the Barriers of Digital Collaboration' *Lloyd's List* (29 October 2019); OECD, 'Information Sharing for Efficient Maritime Logistics' (OECD/ITF 2018) 21, available at www.itf-oecd.org/sites/default/files/docs/information-sharing-maritime-logistics.pdf.

[10] R Clayton, 'Why is Shipping So Slow to Digitalise?' *Lloyd's List* (30 July 2019).

[11] Adamopoulos, 'Industry Still Lagging Behind' (2019).

[12] Clayton, 'Why is Shipping So Slow to Digitalise?' (2019).

[13] J Porter, 'Data Sharing is Essential in Race to Cut Shipping's Tragedies' *Lloyd's List* (30 October 2019); Clayton (n 10).

[14] J Clift, 'Electronic Commerce: The UNCITRAL Model Law and Electronic Equivalents to Traditional Bills of Lading' (1999) 27 *International Business Lawyer* 311.

[15] OECD, 'Information Sharing' (2018) 11.

II. Data Sharing Agreements and Collection and Processing of Data by Ocean Carriers

A. Background

The use of web portals supposes the availability of vast quantities of data of very high commercial value. Indeed, it has been recognised that such personal data is a key economic asset[16] and 'a new asset class'.[17] In the context of the carriage of goods by sea, digital technology depends on the submission of proper, accurate and substantial amounts of relevant, and, in some cases, sensitive data by shippers or agents through an efficient web portal. After submission, a simple click activates the supply chain and the data is processed by the ocean carrier, or a third party appointed by it, for the execution of the contract or other legitimate purposes. This information is not collected and filed on paper, but stored in codes of bytes on the carriers' servers or the cloud services of third parties contracted for that purpose.[18] It is therefore common to hear the expression that data has become the new oil.[19] Indeed, new technology, such as the Internet of Things, blockchain and artificial intelligence, all applicable in the shipping industry, have to be 'fueled' by data to be operative.

The transmission or sharing of data is essentially performed in two directions. On the one side, information is shared by customers with the ocean carrier through its web portal. On the other side, ocean carriers share data with third parties who perform the contract, and this can include affiliated companies, road carriers, subcontractors, agents at destination and also public entities, such as customs and port authorities. The practice of creating alliances among ocean carriers also means that such information is potentially shared with other ocean carriers. The largest liner companies have entered into business alliances, working together pursuant to vessel sharing agreements, and this certainly involves the exchange of customer data.[20] Sharing information with other ocean carriers under such alliances is also subject to competition law,[21] a significant area of law which falls outside the scope of this chapter.

[16] V Janeček, 'Ownership of Personal Data in the Internet of Things' (2018) 34 *Computer Law & Security Review* 1039, 1040.

[17] OECD (n 9) 15.

[18] ibid.

[19] RH Weber, 'Data Protection – An Overview' in R Schulze, D Staudenmeyer and S Lohsse (eds), *Contracts for the Supply of Digital Content: Regulatory Changes and Gaps* (Oxford, Hart, 2017) 171.

[20] For example, the various container alliances. See, eg, 'Review of Maritime Transport 2020' (UNCTAD, 2020) 56.

[21] P Marlow and R Nair, 'Liner Shipping and Information exchange – A European Perspective' (2006) 30 *Marine Policy* 681; A Pozdnakova, 'Information Exchange Agreements between Liner Shipping Companies Under EC Competition Law' in AM Antapasēs, LI Athanassiou and E Røsæg (eds), *Competition and Regulation in Shipping and Shipping Related Industries* (Leiden, Martinus Nijhoff, 2009) 26.

It is to be expected that there will be data sharing agreements, stating the type of data collected and processed, its purposes, and responsibility for its protection. The collection, processing and transmission of data involves obligations of privacy and confidentiality, depending on the provider and type of data. It also encompasses issues concerning trust, data misuse and/or abuse, and uncontrolled propagation of data.[22] For the purpose of this chapter, the focus is on the sharing and protection of data provided by the customer to the ocean carrier.

B. Data Sharing Agreements

The exchange of data between trading parties is commonly performed under a data sharing agreement (DSA). When it relates to electronic data sharing, an electronic DSA is defined as 'a human-readable, yet machine-processable contract, regulating how organisations and/or individuals share data'.[23] Such agreements regularly include user definitions, parties participating in the agreement, the data to be collected and shared, the basis on which data can be shared, and the time or duration for which data will be shared.[24] In order to access online business services, a web portal requires customer registration. Users register by submitting information to receive a password which permits access to the services provided by the web portal. Such registration is subject to the carriers' terms and conditions, its 'registered user terms', and open for acceptance through a click. In the same terms, or sometimes separately, the 'privacy and cookies policy' contains an additional set of terms and conditions regarding the collection and management of data, also requiring acceptance by a click. These two sets of terms and conditions are separate from the terms and condition for carriage, and constitute the DSA. A DSA is, therefore, presented as a pro-forma or contract of adhesion which does not enable the customer to negotiate the terms. Access and use of the services is conditional on the acceptance of those terms and if the user does not agree to these terms, it should not use the website[25] or 'must immediately stop using the website'.[26] This is essentially a 'take it or leave it' contract which may place shippers in an unfavourable position, worsened by the fact that there is no protection under consumer rights law, shippers not being considered consumers.

The user's agreement and the privacy terms and conditions explain the purpose and legal basis for the collection, management, and sharing of the data submitted by the web user. In the same agreement, the user will find provisions excluding or limiting liability and the preservation of rights concerned with the use and

[22] C Caimi, C Gambardella, M Manea, M Petrocchi and D Stella, 'Legal and Technical Perspectives in Data Sharing Agreements Definition' in B Berendt, T Engel, D Ikonomou (eds), *Privacy Technologies and Policy: Third Annual Privacy Forum, APF 2015, Luxembourg, Luxembourg, October 7–8, 2015, Revised Selected Papers* (Cham, Springer International Publishing, 2016) 178.

[23] ibid.

[24] ibid, 182.

[25] See lines.coscoshipping.com/home/item.

[26] See opensea.pro/terms.

transmission of information. But it is in the privacy policy terms where ocean carriers set out more detailed conditions regarding the collection, management, and processing of data. These terms are mostly based on the European General Data Protection Regulations (GDPR),[27] or the privacy laws of the countries where the ocean carrier has its principal place of business.

i. What Data is Collected by Ocean Carriers?

As web portals require registration by users, the submission of an individual or company name and contact details is a core requirement. As the main purpose of registration is to contract for the carriage of goods by sea, much of which is governed by the Hague (or Hague-Visby) Rules, the information requested corresponds to the information normally necessary for the bill of lading. Article III, r (3)(a) and r 3(b) of the Rules requires the carrier to issue a bill of lading describing the leading marks, the number of packages, quantity or weight of the cargo.[28] It is obvious that the shippers', consignees' and agents' names, address, contact details and contact person must be provided as well. This information is required for the carrier to perform its obligations under the contract. Some cargo liners also go beyond this and require further information that might not strictly be necessary for the execution of the carriage. Maersk Line, for example, states in its privacy policy that by using its web portal, it may collect detailed business contact information and even the business bank account of the user. Maersk also describes the categories of data it collects and processes.[29] As 'targeted data', it collects 'age, interest, any posting, comments or other content you upload or post on our websites and/or web pages'. Under 'automatically collected data', Maersk collects the IP address, browser information, operating system, and other 'Personal Data that are relevant and necessary for the service'. Biometric data, such as photographs, is also collected.[30] The use of cookies and tracking technology has become common practice and Maersk collects the unique device identifier, mobile device IP address, carrier and location information, for which another specific policy applies.[31]

The submission of certain information is expressed to be 'voluntary' and the privacy policies commonly indicate that the decision to submit all the requested information lies on the user. Some web portal functions or systems may not, however, be available if incomplete data is provided. Nevertheless, these web portals also clarify that by using the website and web pages the user is consenting to the processing of information, the use of cookies, and the potential transfer of such data to other offices. Although supposedly left to the customer, the reality is that this kind of data may be collected, stored, processed and shared. The relevant

[27] See below, V(A)(i).

[28] See, eg, G Treitel and FMB Reynolds, *Carver's Bills of Lading*, 4th edn (London, Sweet & Maxwell, 2017) [9-155].

[29] www.maersk.com/privacy-policy.

[30] See also, eg, Evergreen Line: www.evergreen-line.com/static/jsp/PrivacyPolicyStatement.jsp.

[31] www.maersk.com/cookie-policy.

privacy policies state that there is no intention to access sensitive data, but may do so if the carrier is legally allowed to do so or with the express consent of the party. A discussion may then revolve around what is considered sensitive information,[32] especially when most of the required information is open to other players in the supply chain.

ii. Purpose of Data Collection and Storage

Apart from obtaining relevant information to enable the formation of the contract, the request for additional information may have other purposes. The same privacy policies under the GDPR establish that data controllers are subject to an obligation to explain the purpose of the collection of the data. It is also clear the GDPR seeks to facilitate communication and the provision of services and products according to the particular terms agreed upon by the parties. This allows the ocean carrier to personalise the customer experience using the website, but the ocean carrier also knows who it is dealing with and this assists in the application of security precautions. The purpose of the collection of data can be categorised under three groups: (i) information for the performance of the contract; (ii) information needed to comply with regulations; (iii) information for marketing and statistical purposes.

Ocean carriers, like other companies, are subject to governmental regulation. Collecting data from clients also ensures compliance with certain regulations. Thus, in order to avoid sanctions for trading with restricted countries, such as Iran, or avoiding the carriage of illicit substances or unreported dangerous cargo, the ocean carrier must know who it is dealing with, what the cargo is, where it is from and where it is going. The collection of this data allows the carrier to comply with the regulations and avoid fines.

The collection of data is also associated with marketing strategies or analytics. It is very common for companies to send newsletters, notification of new services, or special offers to attract new business. Having access to customers' commercial behaviour and preferences simplifies targeting the right product or service for that customer. This also helps to assure the loyalty of the customer. Additionally, access to this information facilitates future planning and the customisation of future investments. The effective use of data therefore creates a competitive advantage as knowledge of customer preferences provides access to the projection of future customer behaviour and creates significant value for the business.[33]

iii. With Whom is this Data to be Shared or Disclosed?

The nature of the carriage of goods by sea obliges the exchange of information with many players in the supply chain. The international nature of the shipping industry

[32] Examples include the business bank account or the user's credit card details.

[33] SG Hoffman, *Regulation of Cloud Services Under US and EU Antitrust, Competition and Privacy Laws* (Frankfurt, Peter Lang, 2017) 23.

means that the available data may be shared globally. Ocean carriers collect and send the relevant information to and from affiliated companies around the world and this is stated as such in the terms. Thus, it is suggested that there may be 200 documentary interactions along the supply chain and that shippers and consignees may have to enter into arrangements with some 28 entities for each shipment.[34] Once a container is carried from its origin to its destination, the data concerning this movement is shared between 10 to 50 different entities, such as ports, customs offices, trucking companies, banks and industry information portals, each of them having different technological infrastructures and cybersecurity standards.[35] Privacy policies specify that such data is shared with affiliated companies and local or foreign agents. As the carriage might be performed by another company, certain data will be provided to the actual carrier, its agents and representatives. The same goes for customs and port authorities. It can be said that the data is shared in two respects. On the one hand, there is a voluntary basis, with data transmitted to the parties identified. On the other hand, there is a non-voluntary basis, when data is requested by judicial or government authorities and ocean carriers are compelled to provide the data.

III. The Risks of Hacking or Disclosure to Unauthorised Third Parties

A. Hacking and Cybersecurity

The maritime industry is not immune to the continuing trend of cyber attacks. Indeed, in the past decade, the maritime industry has witnessed some landmark examples. In August 2011, IRIS, the Iranian shipping line, was the victim of a cyber attack that damaged data relating to the core of its business. Rates, loading, cargo number, date and place were affected, leaving the company completely blind about the location of containers and making it impossible for it to know whether they were loaded or not onboard its ships.[36] Although the data was later restored, the internal communication system was seriously compromised to the point that cargo was delivered at the wrong destination, causing substantial economic loss to the company.[37] Another example was the cyber intrusion in the port of Antwerp between 2011 to 2013, a major concern in an industry that seemed to have paid little attention to this potential risk.[38] Indeed, the same port was the location for

[34] Porter, 'Digitalisation' (2017).
[35] L Jensen, 'Challenges in Maritime Cyber-Resilience' (2015) 5 *Technology Innovation Management Review* 35, 36.
[36] ibid, 37.
[37] ibid.
[38] A criminal organisation hacked the IT system and diverted the delivery of some containers loaded with illicit substances without the knowledge of the port and customs authorities: see S Cooper, 'Cyber Risk, Liabilities and Insurance in the Maritime Sector' in B Soyer and A Tettenborn (eds),

a misdelivery which led to the first court decision dealing with electronic PIN codes.[39] Other attacks have demonstrated how vulnerable electronic and digital systems are. In June 2017, Maersk was the victim of a cyber attack that reportedly caused losses amounting to US $300 million[40] and took over six months to return to normal.[41] A year later, in July 2018, COSCO Shipping Lines suffered an intrusion to its computer system.[42] There may have been other assaults that have not been reported, but these cases provide examples of how real this threat is.

It is self-evident that although ocean carriers commit to sharing information only with specific parties and for legitimate purposes, the fact that such data is stored on servers or clouds are accessible by hackers, presents an additional challenge which must be addressed. This is the threat that new technologies, such as blockchain, which preserve data, are trying to address, but they may also be vulnerable.[43] In July 2017, by way of response to this increasing threat, the International Maritime Organization (IMO) approved the Guidelines on Maritime Cyber Risk Management.[44] These guidelines are focused on, although not limited to, vulnerabilities in areas such as bridge systems, cargo handling and management, administrative and crew welfare systems, and communication systems.[45] The protection of databases with carriage and customer information, although fundamental, is not addressed. However, the Guidelines do state that the protection of information and data exchange within information and operational systems should be considered.[46] BIMCO and other maritime organisations have also produced the 'Guidelines on Cyber Security Onboard Ships'.[47] These are designed for shipowners and operators and provide recommendations for the procedures and actions to be taken to protect the company and the ships against cyber attacks.[48] The main shortcomings of the IMO and BIMCO guidelines is that they are recommendations without legal

Maritime Liabilities in a Global and Regional Context (London, Informa Law, 2019); O Daum, 'Cyber Security in The Maritime Sector' (2019) 50 *Journal of Maritime Law and Commerce* 1, 8.

[39] *Glencore International AG v MSC Mediterranean Shipping Co SA* [2017] EWCA Civ 365, [2017] 2 Lloyd's Rep 186. See Spanjaart (ch 8).

[40] 'Maersk Hit by Cyber Attack' *World Maritime News* (27 June 2017), available at worldmaritimenews.com/archives/223747/maersk-hit-by-cyber-attack; Daum, 'Cyber Security' (2019) 8.

[41] J Porter, 'Six-month Recovery Time for Maersk After Cyber-attack' *Lloyd's List* (8 November 2017).

[42] 'COSCO Shipping Lines Falls Victim to Cyber Attack', *World Maritime News* (25 July 2018), available at worldmaritimenews.com/archives/257665/cosco-shipping-lines-falls-victim-to-cyber-attack.

[43] J Baker, 'Ports Sector Failing to Take Cyber Security Seriously' *Lloyd's List* (20 February 2019).

[44] MSC-FAL.1/Circ.3 of 5 July 2017, available at www.gard.no/Content/23896593/MSC-FAL.1-Circ.3.pdf. It superseded the interim guidelines previously adopted by the circular MSC.1/Circ.1526 of 1 June 2016, available at www.gard.no/Content/21323229/MSC.1-Circ.1526.pdf.

[45] Guidelines on Maritime Cyber Risk Management, 2.1.2.

[46] ibid.

[47] These Guidelines are authored by BIMCO, CLIA, the International Chamber of Shipping, Intercargo, InterManager, Intertanko, the International Union of Marine Insurance, OCIMF and the World Shipping Council. See www.ics-shipping.org/docs/default-source/resources/safety-security-and-operations/guidelines-on-cyber-security-onboard-ships.pdf?sfvrsn=16.

[48] ibid, 1.

effect.[49] Furthermore, these instruments are focused mostly on the protection of ship navigation systems, while the majority of cyber attacks in recent years have affected IT systems on-shore.[50] BIMCO has also drafted a standard Cyber Security Clause to be used in a broad range of contracts requiring the parties to employ cybersecurity systems and processes to reduce risks.[51] This clause is, however, optional.

Carriers might exclude liability for cyber attacks. Indeed, carriers routinely exclude their liability for breaches of data from hacking or viruses in their electronic systems. If the terms and conditions of usage of the web portals contain an exclusion, shippers may not have an action for damages caused by data breaches due to hackers. Carriers may also protect themselves by buying insurance against cyber attacks, but insurers may also reject insuring a risk that is not well known, given the lack of reporting of these kinds of incidents.[52] The impossibility of making a proper assessment of the potential risk also makes it difficult to set a premium.

B. Unlawful Acts by Employees

Another possible threat is the acts of imprudent, dissatisfied or disloyal employees who have access to the carriers' data. A poll on trade secrets revealed that 17 per cent of employees might reveal company secrets for reward, and eight per cent reported having done so.[53] Although employees carry out their tasks under employment contracts which commonly contain confidentiality clauses, they might ignore such clauses if there was a reward in exchange for disclosing privileged information. It is, in reality, an old threat. The difference now, however, is that while in the past the theft of privileged information might signify the subtraction of hundreds of paper pages, digital data enables the storing of data in small USB devices or the sending of it to third parties by emails or similar technology. Employees may also, whether voluntarily or unintentionally, compromise the company's cyber systems and data.[54] Potential options for shipping companies might be implementing trade secret protection procedures (TSPP), limiting employee access to certain physical areas,

[49] Baker, 'Ports Sector' (2019).

[50] J Baker, 'Maritime Cyber-crime under the spotlight' *Lloyd's List* (18 April 2019). At the European level, the European Parliament has enacted the Directive (EU) 2016/1148 of the European Parliament and of the Council of 6 July 2016 concerning measures for a high common level of security of network and information systems across the Union, available at eur-lex.europa.eu/legal-content/EN/TXT/?uri=uriserv:OJ.L_.2016.194.01.0001.01.ENG.

[51] See www.bimco.org/news/priority-news/20190522-new-cyber-security-clause-from-bimco.

[52] Baker, 'Maritime Cyber-crime' (2019).

[53] KM Robertson, DR Hannah and BA Lautsch, 'The Secret to Protecting Trade Secrets: How to Create Positive Secrecy Climates in Organizations' (2015) 58 *Business Horizons* 669, 670.

[54] Guidelines (n 47) 10.

or the use of certain documents, computers or means of communication, or signing non-disclosure agreements which set clear rules as to what an employee can do with privileged information once having access to it.[55]

C. The Ocean Carrier's Liabilities

The alteration, modification, erasure or disclosure of data stored by ocean carriers to unauthorised parties may lead to two consequences. On the one hand, the performance of the contract of carriage might seriously be impacted. The loss or alteration of information related to delivery address, or conditions of carriage, such as temperature and humidity or particular requirements for dangerous goods, might cause serious damage.[56] If the data breach results in non-performance of the contract, misdelivery or cargo damage or loss, the carrier's liability will be assessed according to the liability rules governing the carriage of goods by sea.[57] However, the implementation and transmission of electronic transport documents and their effects fall outside the current governing international regimes, such as the Hague (and Hague-Visby) Rules and the Hamburg Rules. On the other hand, data by itself has a high value. The disclosure of commercially sensitive data to a competitor may have negative consequences for those shippers or consignees whose data is electronically stored by carriers.

The risks demand that carriers protect and secure the data. The assessment of the ocean carriers' liabilities for damages or losses resulting from data sharing activities depends on the duties and obligations assigned to them for these operations. This is where the current state of the industry causes some difficulty because, although the importance and convenience of data sharing is widely accepted, there are no specific standards.[58] The reliance of shipping companies on the sharing of information depends on how confident they are that liability, costs, authentication and access to data are securely and fairly managed.[59] Shippers, carriers, consignees and other actors in the supply chain have particular concerns about data ownership, data security, privacy, commercial sensibility and intellectual property.[60] The absence of specific standards is undermining the confidence of shipping companies in sharing information and the effectiveness of digitalisation, as it does not allow the interplay of different systems and applications.[61]

[55] DR Hannah, 'Should I Keep a Secret? The Effect of Trade Secret Protection Procedures on Employees' Obligation to Protect Trade Secrets' (2005) 16 *Organization Science* 71, 73.

[56] See above, III(A).

[57] As occurred in *Glencore* (n 39), where liability was assigned for misdelivery of the cargo. See Spanjaart (ch 8).

[58] OECD (n 9) 5.

[59] ibid, 27.

[60] ibid, 24.

[61] I Walia, 'Lack of Digital Standardisation is a Growing Issue' *Lloyd's List* (28 November 2019).

However, some standards establishing obligations to provide security of data and its sharing may be obtained from international regulations or guidelines related to these processes and activities. In that regard, the process of sharing data transmitted electronically with these various actors is subject to different, but interconnected, sets of rules. On the one hand, the action of 'sharing' involves the recognition of the legal effects of electronic data and its collection, storage and interchange, and is subject to regulations for the electronic exchange of data. On the other hand, there are regulations protecting data. 'Data' itself is subject to specific privacy and confidentiality protections. Privacy refers to the personal data of natural persons, while confidentiality relates to business information[62] or the protection of trade secrets. Therefore, the ocean carriers' liability for the possible losses or damages caused by the improper, deficient or negligent management of the data sharing process may be assessed according to the obligations stated in these different instruments.

IV. Regulation of Electronic Exchange of Data

Since the implementation of electronic communications for business, there have been various attempts to establish standardised rules to govern such communications. In the 1970s, Electronic Data Interchange (EDI) was implemented in the commercial sphere, prompting regulation. In the international arena, the United Nations Special Commissions played an initial role in the enactment of regulations. In the case of the maritime industry, and specifically electronic bills of lading, the Comité Maritime International (CMI) enacted certain rules.[63]

A. Rules for the Interchange of Electronic Data

In 1987, it became necessary to create a set of rules of conduct for users of UN/EDIFACT[64] and other systems of electronic trade data interchange. The International Chamber of Commerce (ICC) agreed to establish a Special Joint Committee with representatives of nine intergovernmental organisations, including UNCITRAL, UNCTAD, UNECE, the Custom Cooperation Council (CCC),

[62] Caimi, Gambardella, Manea, Petrocchi and Stella, 'Legal and Technical Perspectives' (2016) 185.

[63] The CMI Rules for Electronic Bills of Lading 1990. See Goldby, 'The CMI Rules' [2008].

[64] This is a series of technical rules for the interchange of electronic data adopted by the United Nations Economic Commission for Europe Working Party on Facilitation of International Trade Procedures (WP.4) in 1984: see B Wheble, 'Think Data, Not Documents' (1998) 7 *International Financial Law Review* 36, 37. The international transport industry strongly influenced the creation of these standards as the WP.4 was working on transport documents when the concerns initially arose: see GF Chandler III, 'Maritime Electronic Commerce for the Twenty-First Century' (1998) 22 *Tulane Maritime Law Journal* 463, 465.

OECD and ISO.[65] The Committee's aim was to create a code of conduct to facilitate the use of EDI between parties engaged in such transactions which applied only to the exchange of data, but not the substance of the trade message.[66] The Uniform Rules of Conduct for Interchange of Trade Data by Teletransmission 1987 (UNCID) deal with matters related to security in the exchange of messages, verification of parties' identities, confirmation of receipt of messages, protection of commercial information, and logging and storage of data by the parties.[67] The Code is a very succinct instrument of 11 articles applicable to parties using a trade data interchange protocol (TDI-AP) and was the first international cross-industry document providing general rules regulating the subject.

Among the relevant provisions, there is a duty to ensure that the transfers are correct and complete in form and secure.[68] The parties must instruct intermediaries in the transfer in order to ensure that changes without authorisation and data content should not be disclosed to any unauthorised person.[69] Articles 9 and 10 relate to the protection and storage of trade data. The former provides for the parties involved to apply special protection, through encryption or other means, to the data exchanged between them. The provision states that the parties 'may agree to apply special protection'. It does not impose a concrete duty to ensure the protection of data but merely an option to agree to protect trade data. It is subject to the condition that, if the sender for example applies encryption, the receiver must also apply it for any further transfer. This approach is insufficient in view of the relevance of data in commercial scenarios and given that the same rules provide for the storage of data. However, most electronic communications are currently encrypted, so it can be said this requirement is complied with by default. Article 10 requires minimum protection of the storage of data, providing that the parties should ensure that a trade data log[70] is maintained, completed and unchanged on computer media and, when required, must be capable of being retrieved and presented in a readable form. In order to provide assurance of the prompt availability of the data, the Code recommends that such data may be maintained in 'computer media', the current practice of storing on servers. Such storage must be retained for the period of time required by local law, or for such longer period agreed by the parties, or, failing this, for three years.[71] This provision seeks to solve problems of evidence.[72] In order to comply with this rule, the

[65] AH Boss and JB Ritter, *Electronic Data Interchange Agreements: A Guide and Sourcebook* (Paris, ICC Publishing SA, 1993) 23; AH Boss, 'The International Commercial use of Electronic Data Interchange and Electronic Communications Technologies' (1991) 46 *The Business Lawyer* 1787, 1791–92. The Committee pursued international harmonisation of ISO and other internationally accepted standards: see Wheble (ibid) 38.

[66] Boss and Ritter, *Electronic Data Interchange Agreements* (ibid) 24.

[67] UNCID, arts 5–10; Boss, 'The International Commercial use of Electronic Data' (1991) 1792.

[68] UNCID, art 5.1.

[69] ibid, art 5.2.

[70] ibid, art 2.5.

[71] ibid, art 10.3.

[72] Wheble, 'Think Data' (1998) 38.

parties will undoubtedly have to protect the relevant data logs. The suggested term for storage duration may present some problems if, for example, the stored data message contains personal or privileged information relating to trade secrets and where storage for a prolonged period may contradict local laws related to privacy or confidentiality.[73] This Code does not, however, have legal effect unless incorporated into local law or by affirmative agreement by mutual decision, expressed in writing, of the relevant parties to their transactions.[74] The Code is also recommended in rule 3.b of the CMI Rules on Electronic Bills of Lading.

B. Regulation of Ecommerce

The character of ecommerce represented by the digital services offered by ocean carriers makes it imperative to have international rules. In 1996, the UN Commission for International Trade Law (UNCITRAL) adopted a Model Law on Electronic Commerce.[75] The idea behind this was the creation of a template which would enable nations to adopt local laws on the subject.[76] The main purpose of this Model Law is to grant data messages used in electronic communications the same validity, efficacy and enforceability of information as is the case with traditional paper documents. The Model Law centres on the validity and management of 'data message',[77] which have 'functional-equivalence', meaning that electronic communications have the same legal value and effect as if written and signed as an original paper document. Under certain conditions, when the law so requires, such electronic communications have evidentiary weight[78] and this will validate transactions performed using web portals, including data sharing agreements and the contract of carriage. Pursuant to article 11, offer and acceptance of a contract can be performed by data messages and the data message generated by clicking the 'accept' button, on a web portal, constitutes a message with full effect as acceptance of an offer. The purpose of this provision gives legal effect to giving consent to an online offer by clicking on a button, a practice now widely accepted.

The Model Law foresees the need for retaining data messages.[79] Such retention is conditioned by accessibility, the preservation of the original format in which the message was generated, and the capacity to identify the origin, destination, date

[73] See below, V(B).

[74] Boss and Ritter, *Electronic Data Interchange Agreements* (1993) 23.

[75] General Assembly Resolution 51/162 of 16 December 1996, as amended in 1998, available at www.uncitral.org/pdf/english/texts/electcom/05-89450_Ebook.pdf.

[76] A Davidson, *Social Media and Electronic Commerce Law*, 2nd edn (Cambridge, Cambridge University Press, 2016) 156.

[77] Model Law, art 2(a). See also art 2(b) for a definition of EDI.

[78] Arts 5–9. See 'Guide to Enactment of the UNCITRAL Model law on Electronic Commerce' (UNCITRAL, 1996), paras 15 and 16, available at www.uncitral.org/pdf/english/texts/electcom/05-89450_Ebook.pdf; Clift, 'Electronic Commerce' (1999) 312.

[79] Art 10.

and time of the message.[80] The storage of data is obviously required for the regular operation of business. For ocean carriers, it is clear that there is a need to retain the shipment information during the period before the loading operation, during the carriage period and after carriage for delivery. After the carriage is concluded, the relevant information can be retained and used, if required, as evidence in the event of litigation.

The Model Law dedicates Part Two of its provisions to the carriage of goods by sea.[81] Electronic commerce for the carriage of goods by sea is subject to the general provisions stated in Part One, especially those regarding the guarantee of reliability and authenticity.[82] Article 16 sets out the information and actions related to this business activity which must have full validity if exchanged, ordered, or performed through data messages while article 17(3) provides that when a right or obligation is conveyed by the transfer or use of a paper document 'that requirement is met if the right or obligation is conveyed by using one or more data messages, provide that a reliable method is used to render such data message or messages unique'. This will be the case where the bills of lading are intended to grant rights of property[83] over the goods in favour of the lawful holder or named consignee or endorsee. Two of the three functions of a bill of lading,[84] namely, the receipt of the cargo, and proof of the terms of the contract[85] can be supplied by the data messages as the UN/EDIFACT but the potential function of the bill of lading as a document of title still presents considerable difficulty.[86]

The Model Law does not expressly mention an obligation to protect the information to preserve its integrity. Although it recognises the centrality and relevance of a data message, there is no specific provision expressly foreseeing the need to protect it. Such a duty may, however, be implied from the necessity to observe the reliability and integrity of the data messages to grant such messages the character of being 'original' and for the purposes of evidentiary weight.[87] In order to determine the reliability of the integrity of the message, the Model Law states that it shall have 'remained complete and unaltered', save for the normal additions or endorsements that its communication, storage and display implies. This is only possible if proper protection has been provided. Furthermore, the requirement of a 'guarantee of singularity', meaning the capacity of electronic messages to

[80] Art 10(1)(a)–(c); Chandler, 'Maritime Electronic Commerce' (1998) 493.

[81] See UNCITRAL 'Guide' (n 78), para 109.

[82] ibid.

[83] But not rights of suit at common law. In English law and Singapore law, such rights are transferred by statute: see the (UK) Carriage of Goods by Sea Act 1992 and the (Singapore) Bills of Lading Act 1993.

[84] *JI MacWilliam Co Inc v Mediterranean Shipping Co SA (The Rafaela S)* [2005] UKHL 11, [2005] 2 AC 423 [38]; *Carewins Development (China) Ltd v Bright Fortune Shipping Ltd* [2009] 3 HKLRD 409 (HKCFA), [17]; *The Star Quest* [2016] SGHC 100, [2017] 1 Lloyd's Rep Plus 50 [17].

[85] See, eg, *Sea Master Shipping Inc v Arab Bank (Switzerland) Ltd (The Sea Master)* [2018] EWHC 1902 (Comm), [2019] 1 Lloyd's Rep 101 [42].

[86] Clift (n 14) 313.

[87] Arts 8(1)(a) and 9(2).

grant title or ownership to one person,[88] certainly requires technological security systems to assure such a guarantee.[89] The Model Law does not mention terms of privacy or confidentiality of the data and does not establish a duty of controlling or restricting with whom the data may be shared. The Model Law allows the storage of data by third parties.[90] Although, as noted, the Model Law does not provide specifically for the protection of data or standards for its safe sharing, it gives legal effect to electronic data,[91] giving it great economic value.

The Model Law has been adopted by major trading nations, including China and India, and has also influenced the US Uniform Electronic Transactions Act 1999.[92] Its provisions have been also adopted in Australia, the Republic of Korea and in Singapore, among others,[93] with a total of 72 States and 151 jurisdictions passing legislation based on or influenced by the Model Law.[94] The EU has also adopted internal regulations on ecommerce.[95]

Since the Model Law, UNCITRAL has adopted a further instrument, the United Nations Convention on the Use of Electronic Communications in International Contracts (ECC).[96] This Convention relates to non-substantive issues concerning the use of electronic communications in international contracts and may be viewed as an upgrading and extension to the Model Law.[97] The ECC reaffirms the functional equivalence of data messages exchanged through electronic means used in international contracts[98] and reiterates the conditions of accessibility of the data for subsequent reference and assurance of the integrity of the information.[99] However, this Convention does not make provision for liability caused by lack of compliance with its provisions and expressly excludes bills of lading from its scope of application.[100]

C. Regulations Concerning Electronic Bills of Lading

In 1990, the CMI proposed a set of rules for electronic bills of lading, the CMI Rules for Electronic Bills of Lading, the application whereof depends on the

[88] Art 17(3).
[89] UNCITRAL (n 78) para 115.
[90] Art 10(3).
[91] Art 12.
[92] Davidson, *Social Media* (2016) 163.
[93] Clift (n 14) 312.
[94] See uncitral.un.org/en/texts/ecommerce/modellaw/electronic_commerce/status.
[95] See European e-Commerce Directive 2000/31/EC, available at eur-lex.europa.eu/legal-content/EN/ALL/?uri=CELEX%3A32000L0031.
[96] Adopted on 23 November 2005 by the United Nations General Assembly, Resolution A/RES/60/21, available at https://uncitral.un.org/sites/uncitral.un.org/files/media-documents/uncitral/en/06-57452_ebook.pdf.
[97] MF Sturley, T Fujita and G van der Ziel, *The Rotterdam Rules: the UN Convention on Contracts for the International Carriage of Goods Wholly or Partly by Sea*, 2nd edn (London, Sweet & Maxwell, 2020) [3.025].
[98] ECC, art 8.
[99] ibid, art 9.
[100] ibid, art 2.2.

agreement of the parties.[101] The Rules require the use of the UNCID to govern the conduct of the parties, subject to any conflict with the Rules.[102] That also supposes that the parties are subject to the provisions concerning the optional protection and storage of 'complete historical records of trade data interchange' on 'computer media', including the recommendation that data should be stored for a period of three years following art 10.3 of UNCID.

Rule 3.e states that, in the case of disputes concerning data actually transmitted, an electronic monitoring system may be used to verify the data received.[103] This implies a disclosure of commercial data that may affect other data not relevant to the dispute. Rule 3.e also provides that any other data not concerning the dispute must be considered as a trade secret and cannot be the subject of examination. If such disclosure is unavoidable as part of the examination, 'it must be treated as confidential and not released to any outside party or used for any other purpose'. Rule 3.f expressly states that any transfer of the right to the goods is to be considered private information and prohibits its release to other parties not connected with the carriage or clearance of goods. These two provisions underline the private and trade secret character of the information which normally appears in a paper bill of lading and imposes on ocean carriers and those subject to a contract of carriage under a bill of lading a duty to protect the data shared for the performance of the contract.

The Rules do not make provision for the carriers' liability for damage resulting from electronic transactions.[104] The Rules reflect awareness at that time about the sensitivity of data interchanged in electronic bills of lading. The Rules have, however, had almost no impact but did serve as a reference for the provision on electronic transport records in the Rotterdam Rules,[105] but these do not address issues relating to the privacy and confidentiality of the information shared by electronic communications.[106]

V. Regulations Protecting Data

The international instruments dealing with the electronic interchange of data relating to the carriage of goods by sea do not properly address issues concerning the protection of data collected and shared by ocean carriers. Although the operation of electronic systems relies on the exchange of data, there is currently no

[101] Rule 1. It was considered that a voluntary instrument would be easier to adopt than a Convention: see Chandler (n 64) 475.

[102] Rule 3.a.

[103] See the definition of Electronic Monitoring System in Rule 2.h.

[104] E Laryea, *Paperless Trades, Opportunities, Challenges and Solutions* (London, Kluwer Law International, 2002) 80, 83.

[105] Goldby (n 5) 67.

[106] Electronic bills of lading are discussed in Girvin and Ong (ch 9).

international regulation containing express provisions for the protection of data and its sharing in the ocean carriage business. What does exist is local or regional legislation enacted for the protection of personal data or regulations concerning the confidentiality of trade secrets. All businesses are affected by these regulations, and the shipping industry cannot escape its application.

A. Regulations for the Protection of Personal Data and the Right to Privacy

Regional and local regulations for the protection of the right to privacy are founded in human rights norms.[107] The right to privacy may be further divided into personal privacy and information privacy,[108] the former relating to the physical individual space of the person, the latter referring to the process and methods by which personal information is gathered, recorded, accessed, stored and transmitted.[109] Data sharing clearly falls within the second category. This part of the chapter will focus on the European and Singaporean regulations. There are good reasons for this choice: the EU regulations are the most recent and complete set of rules on the matter, and Singapore is the main maritime economy in Asia, making it an important hub for ocean carriers' services.

i. General Data Protection Regulation

There is no international convention which establishes obligations regarding the protection of data. However, the European General Data Protection Regulation (GDPR),[110] which entered into force on 25 May 2018, has extraterritorial scope and is therefore highly relevant to shipping. Four of the 10 major liner operators are European companies, while a further six are Asian companies,[111] some of which have adjusted their web portal terms and conditions and privacy policies to comply with the GDPR.[112] However, some Asian countries also have their own

[107] The right to privacy is recognised as a fundamental right in art 12 of the Universal Declaration of Human Rights, art 17 of the International Covenant on Civil and Political Rights, and art 8 of the European Convention on Human Rights (ECHR). Human rights must be observed by judicial and administrative bodies in the EU as well in the US so as to guarantee that such application will not conflict with fundamental rights and the Constitution: see A Daly, *Private Power, Online Information and EU Law: Mind the Gap* (Oxford, Hart Publishing, 2016) 31.

[108] Davidson (n 76) 102.

[109] ibid.

[110] Regulation (EU) 2016/679 of the European Parliament and of the Council of 27 April 2016, on the protection of natural persons with regards to the processing of personal data and on the free movement of such data, repealing Directive 95/46/EC.

[111] UNCTAD, 'Review' (n 20) 56.

[112] For example, Evergreen in its privacy policy states that '"Personal data" in this Policy has the same meaning as in the EU General Data Protection Regulation 2016/679/EU (GDPR)'. See www.evergreen-line.com/static/jsp/PrivacyPolicyStatement.jsp.

laws on the protection of personal data, similar to the GDPR.[113] The Asia-Pacific Economic Cooperation (APEC)[114] has also enacted a APEC Privacy Framework, which contains a set of general principles for the processing of personal data.[115] This is a basic framework, however, with no mandatory effect unless the Member Economies implement it according the methods it suggests.[116]

This chapter will focus on the GDPR and the Singapore Personal Data Protection Act (PDPA).[117] Although the GDPR and the PDPA share similar concepts and provisions, they have different approaches.[118]

a. Scope of Application

The GDPR protects personal data collected through websites and processed by automated means.[119] This is one of the most significant aspects of this regulation as companies perform data processing mostly using computers.[120] The GDPR applies primarily to EU Member States, but as noted earlier, it has extraterritorial effect. According to article 3, companies processing data in the context of activities performed within the EU are subject to the Regulation, regardless of whether the processing activity takes place within the EU or not.[121] The same also applies if the data subject is within the EU and the processing activity relates to the offering of a product or service with the collecting or processing entity not located in the EU.[122] It must be emphasised that the Regulation applies to data subject 'located' within the EU but does not necessarily require that the person is a citizen or a permanent resident of a Member State in order to be protected. Thus, most sea carriers have establishments and perform operations within the EU but, even if not physically located there, the offering of carriage services via the web to any customer located

[113] S Chesterman, 'From Privacy to Data Protection' in S Chesterman (ed), *Data Protection Law in Singapore: Privacy and Sovereignty in an Interconnected World*, 2nd edn (Singapore, Academy Publishing, 2018) para 2.22. The USA, the world's largest economy, regulates privacy and data protection variously in legislation governing different sectors, both at federal and state level: see RH Weber and D Staiger, *Transatlantic Data Protection in Practice* (Berlin, Springer, 2017) 39.

[114] APEC is a regional economic forum comprising 21 members, including most Asian economies such as China, Indonesia, The Philippines, Singapore, South Korea, but also the USA, Mexico, among others.

[115] The 2015 updated version is available at mddb.apec.org/Documents/2016/SOM/CSOM/16_csom_012app17.pdf.

[116] See APEC Privacy Framework (2015) para 37. See also ZK Yeong, 'From Compliance to Accountability' in Chesterman, *Data Protection Law in Singapore* (2018) para 11.8.

[117] No 26 of 2012 (in force 2 July 2014).

[118] While the GDPR views the protection of data as a human right to privacy, Singapore pursues a balance between the legitimate need for business and the right of individuals. The term 'privacy' is not even used in the PDPA as it is more focused in a 'management of information': see S Chesterman, 'Introduction' and 'From Privacy to Data Protection' in Chesterman (n 113) paras 1.10, 2.49.

[119] GDPR, art 1.

[120] See D Kelleher and K Murray, *EU Data Protection Law* (London, Bloomsbury Professional, 2018) para 3.01. The regulation also protects data processed in paper.

[121] GDPR, art 3.1.

[122] ibid, art 3.2(a).

in one of the Members States of the EU obliges the carrier to comply with the GDPR. This is because personal data is defined as 'any information relating to an identified or identified person'[123] and processing data includes 'disclosure by transmission, dissemination or otherwise making available'.[124]

The PDPA contains a similar provision. It applies to private 'organisations' and 'whether or not formed or recognised under the law of Singapore, or, are resident, or having an office or place of business in Singapore'.[125] It applies to companies even if they are not physically present in Singapore inasmuch as they collect, use or disclose data in Singapore.[126] However, it does not have the same extraterritorial effect as the GDPR as the processing activities must take place in Singapore.[127] The PDPA defines personal data as 'data, whether true or not about an individual that can be identified from that data, or from that data and other information to which the organisation is likely to have access'.[128] It excludes business contact information from the obligation of protection[129] as it is considered publicly available.[130] This brings into question what may happen with the consignees' business contact, essential for the delivery of the cargo, if altered or modified within the carrier's server.

b. Persons Subject to the GDPR and PDPA

The GDPR deals with the relationship between four main parties: the data subject (the party providing the information); the 'data controller' (the party who determines the means and purposes for the processing); the 'processor' (who may be the same data controller or another party who processes the data); and the 'receiver' (which could be a natural or legal person with whom the data is disclosed, including public authorities).[131] When translated into the shipping industry, the customer, usually the shipper or consignee, is the data subject. The ocean carrier will be the controller and processor if the same carrier undertakes such tasks.[132] Where this is not the case, a service provider would be a processor. The receiver will be the port and customs authorities and the carriers' affiliates or agents at the destination who receive the information to deliver the cargo to the consignee.

The PDPA simplifies this relationship, focusing on the 'organisation' that collects uses and discloses the data, and the 'individual', the equivalent of the

[123] ibid, art 4(1).
[124] ibid, art 4(2).
[125] PDPA, s 2(1), see definition of 'organization'.
[126] Chesterman (n 113) [2.68].
[127] G Greenleaf, 'The Asian Context of Singapore's Law' in Chesterman (n 113) [14.47].
[128] PDPA, s 2.
[129] H Lim, *Data Protection in the Practical Context: Strategies and Techniques* (Singapore, Singapore Academy of Law, 2017) [3.125]–[3.126].
[130] PDPA, s 4(5). See also Chesterman (n 113) [2.57].
[131] GDPR, arts 4.1, 4.8–4.10.
[132] Although some carriers establish in their web portals that the user is the controller and they are the processors, see eg www.oocl.com/eng/privacyandsecurity/Pages/default.aspx.

data subject. It contemplates the participation of a 'data intermediary', which is an organisation that processes data on behalf of another organisation, but it does not impose the same obligations as the organisation if that condition is the result of a contract evidenced or made in writing.[133] The data intermediary must comply with the obligations to protect data by making security arrangements.[134] It must also cease to retain personal data when this no longer serves the purpose of such retention and when retention is no longer necessary for legal or business purposes.[135] Under this Act, the organisation which processes personal data by itself, or intermediaries, has full obligations and liabilities.[136] The Act defines the individual whose personal data is processed as 'a natural person, whether living or deceased',[137] but does not require that the individual must be a citizen or resident or located in Singapore. This suggests that individuals abroad may be protected from the collection, use and disclosure of their data in Singapore.[138]

The GDPR, as well as the PDPA, may be of limited application between ocean carriers and their customers. In the shipping business, natural persons may contract for the carriage of personal goods or on a commercial basis, but the substantial majority of costumers are companies participating in international trade. The carrier–shipper relationship is mostly performed on a business-to-business basis. The data of companies acting as shippers, consignees or their agents are not protected by the provisions stated in the GDPR, nor by the PDPA. Article 4(1) of the GDPR expressly defines personal data as 'any information relating to an identified or identifiable natural person'. Thus, the fact that the GDPR is designed for the protection of data of natural persons excludes the possibility of protecting the data of legal entities.[139] There may, however, be an exception if the data of a legal person includes the personal data of individuals associated with the company, its function in the company or, in cases of one-man companies, where it is not possible to separate personal and company data.[140] The GDPR may also apply in cases where the name of the company acting as a shipper or as a consignee is identifiable as a

[133] PDPA, s 4(2). On the role and obligations of 'data intermediaries' see D Seng, 'Data Intermediaries and Data Breaches' in Chesterman (n 113) ch 7.

[134] ibid, s 24.

[135] ibid, s 25. A further obligation to notify potential data breaches is set out in ss 26C(3) and 26E.

[136] ibid, s 4(3).

[137] ibid, s 2(1).

[138] It has been asserted that the extraterritorial effect of data protection law in the Asian context is unusual, and, when it is so, as in Taiwan, Malaysia and the Philippines, it protects the nationals of those countries: see Greenleaf, 'Singapore's Law' (2018) 14.48.

[139] See Recital no 14 of the GDPR. See also Kelleher and Murray, *EU Data Protection Law* (2018) 4.12. The data of legal persons might be subject of a regulation which is still in proposal form: see Proposal for a Regulation of the European Parliament and of the Council on a framework for the free flow of non-personal data in the European Union COM/2017/0495 final – 2017/0228 (COD), available at eur-lex.europa.eu/legal-content/EN/TXT/?uri=COM%3A2017%3A495%3AFIN. This proposal attempts to eliminate any restrictions by Member States concerning the location of the storage and processing of non-personal data. It does not establish duties concerning the protection of that data.

[140] P Voigt and A von dem Bussche, *The EU General Data Protection Regulation (GDPR): A Practical Guide* (Cham, Springer International Publishing, 2017) 21.

natural person.[141] Large companies named after their founders may not display the personal data of that individual, but SMEs[142] might make identifiable data related to the natural living person of its owner.[143] Section 3 of the PDPA also states that the purpose of the Act is 'to govern the collection, use and disclosure of personal data by organisations' and 'personal data' is defined as 'data whether true or not, about an individual who can be identified', and an 'individual' means a natural person.[144] Hence, both instruments provide for the protection of the data of natural persons, excluding legal entities. There is no certainty that under the PDPA protection can be extended to some legal person under similar circumstances as under the GDPR. However, ocean carriers include some aspects of the GDPR in the privacy policies and terms and conditions of their web portals, with some making express reference to the GDPR and establishing certain rights grounded in the regulatory body.[145] The terms of the privacy policy may refer to 'personal data', without clarifying that this is exclusively for natural persons. Therefore, it can be said that carriers might be extending some of those rights by contract to legal entities, and binding themselves to comply with the rights established therein.

c. Consent

A key aspect of the GDPR and PDPA is that the collection and processing of data, save with some exceptions, is subject to the clear expression of consent of the individual or data subject.[146] 'Consent' under the GDPR means 'any freely given, specific, informed and unambiguous indications of the data subject's wishes by which he or she, by statement or by a clear affirmative action, signifies agreement to the processing of personal data relating to him or her'.[147] The PDPA does not define what consent means. It is clear, however, that the acceptance of the terms and conditions and the Privacy Policy of the web pages is fundamental. As noted earlier, legislation based on the Model Law on Electronic Commerce makes the mere click of the 'accept' button on a webpage amounts to consent.[148] In order to obtain valid consent, the ocean carrier must provide certain information to the customer.

[141] Kelleher and Murray (n 120) para 4.12. The European Court of Justice has stated that 'legal persons can claim the protection of Articles 7 and 8 of the Charter in relation to such identification only in so far as the official title of the legal person identifies one or more natural persons … The official title of the partnership in question directly identifies natural persons who are its partners.' See Joined Cases C-92/09 and C-93/09 *Volker und Markus Schecke GbR and Hartmut Eifert v Land Hessen* [2010] ECR 1-11063, [53]–[54].

[142] Small and medium-sized enterprises.

[143] Kelleher and Murray (n 120) para 4.12.

[144] PDPA, s 2(1). B Wong, 'Data Privacy Law in Singapore: The Personal Data Protection Act 2012' (2017) 7 *International Data Privacy Law* 287, 292.

[145] See www.hamburgsud-line.com/liner/en/liner_services/dataprotection.html; www.cma-cgm.com/legal-terms/privacy-policy.

[146] GDPR, art 7; PDPA, s 13.

[147] GDPR, art 4.11.

[148] See above IV(B).

The GDPR[149] and the PDPA[150] require the collectors or organisations to inform the customers about the purposes of that collection as a condition for obtaining valid consent. The PDPA expressly prohibits organisations requesting consent to access information beyond what is reasonable as a condition for providing the product or services.[151] Personal data can be collected, used and disclosed only for purposes that would be considered appropriate under the circumstances.[152] Hence, in the context of carriage of goods by sea, a request to obtain information, such as the details of family members, leisure activities or unclassified information of the individual, would not be required as a condition for the provision of services.[153] If that were the case, consent to access that information would be considered invalid.[154] The equivalent in the GDPR is the principle of 'data minimisation', which supposes that the personal data collected must be relevant and limited to what is necessary for the purpose that it is processed.[155] The provision on 'consent' in the GDPR does not, as the PDPA does, expressly invalidate the consent if non-necessary data is required as a condition to accessing the services. However, the GDPR states that it must be given 'utmost account' in assessing whether the consent has been freely given when unnecessary data has been required as a condition for accessing that service.[156] One main difference is that the GDPR appears to be stricter in the sense that it does not contemplate the possibility of a 'deemed consent', a concept included in the PDPA.[157] 'Deemed consent', under the PDPA, is when the individual voluntarily provides his or her personal data to the organisation for its collection, use and disclosure and it is reasonable that the individual would have provided that data voluntarily.[158] Withdrawal of consent, without affecting the processing of data submitted before the withdrawal, is also possible in both jurisdictions.[159]

Both the GDPR and PDPA establish situations in which the processing of personal data is lawful without requiring consent. In the case of the GDPR the

[149] GDPR, art 7 does not expressly mention informing about the purpose, but art 6.1(a) establishes that the collection of data is lawful if consent is given for one or more specific purposes, which implies to make known to the data subject the purpose of that collection.

[150] PDPA, s 14(1)(a) sets as condition for consent the provision to the individual of the information required in s 20 regarding the purpose of the collection. See also s 18(b); Wong, 'Data Privacy Law in Singapore' (2017) 292.

[151] ibid, s 14(2)(a).

[152] ibid, s 18(a).

[153] A clause in the privacy policy of an ocean carrier's website, such as that at www.wanhai.com/html/PrivacyPolicyEN.html, would not be considered a valid expression of consent.

[154] PDPA, s 14(3).

[155] GDPR, art 5.1(c).

[156] ibid, art 7.4.

[157] PDPA ss 14–15A.

[158] ibid, s 15. As deemed consent may present some difficulties and limitations, organisations prefer to obtain actual consent: see J Lim and YL Lee, 'Data Sharing: When Consent is not enough', in ZK Yeong, DN Alfred, S-A Chen and JB George (eds), *Personal Data Protection Digest* (Singapore, Personal Data Protection Commission, 2018) 94.

[159] GDPR, art 7.3; PDPA, s 16.

processing of data for the performance of a contract in which the data subject is a party is lawful. The same applies in respect of compliance with legal obligations to protect the vital interests of the data subject, or in performing a public interest task in the exercise of official authority vested in the controller.[160] The PDPA contains two schedules establishing the basis for the collection, use and disclosure of the personal data without consent.[161] It refers to the collection, use and disclosure necessary for any purpose in the interest of the individual whose consent cannot be obtained in a timely manner, or when the data is necessary to respond to an emergency, or when it is publicly available, or if it is necessary for the national interest.[162] These causes may not be a common occurrence in the daily operations of an ocean carrier. However, the schedules also list other causes that will be of interest to carriers. These are data to recover a debt owed to the organisation and data needed for the legal services that the organisation requires.[163] This will enable the ocean carrier to use and disclose this data for litigation, among other similar uses. Accordingly, bearing in mind the categories of data collected by the ocean carrier outlined earlier, consent might be needed only for marketing or statistical purposes.[164] The other categories may fall within those where consent is exempted. However, the lawful processing of data obtained without consent does not mean that the ocean carrier will have no obligations regarding such data.

d. Obligations

Under the PDPA, the obligations consist of nine duties: the consent obligation, purpose limitation, notification, access and correction, the accuracy of the data, protection, retention limitation, transfer limitations and openness obligation.[165] The GDPR contains a similar, but more detailed, provision holding the controller responsible for these duties and for demonstrating its compliance.[166] Both the PDPA and GDPR require the controller or processor, or the organisation, to appoint a 'data protection officer', to ensure compliance.[167] It is therefore common to see the contact details of a data protection officer in the web portal of the ocean carrier.[168] It is possible to distinguish three obligations which are relevant for the business of the ocean carrier. The first is the provision of information, which determines what must be informed in the terms and conditions or privacy policies of the websites. The second concerns the protection of the data and the third concerns limitations on the transfer of data to other countries.

[160] GDPR, art 6.1.
[161] PDPA, s 17.
[162] ibid, Parts 1 and 2 of the First Schedule.
[163] ibid, Part 3, paras 3–5 of the First Schedule.
[164] Above, II(B)(ii). However, part 5 of the First Schedule allows the processing of data without consent for business improvement purposes.
[165] L Goh and J Aw, 'Data Protection Law in Singapore' in Chesterman (n 113) [4.14].
[166] GDPR, art 5.2.
[167] GDPR, arts 37–39, PDPA, s 11(3). The title, 'data protection officer', appears in s 2 of the PDPA.
[168] GDPR, art 13.1(b); PDPA, s 11(5).

Under the GDPR, the carrier must provide information to the data subject such as its contact details, its representative and data protection officer, the purpose of the processing of data and its legal basis, the recipients of such data, and the intention to transfer such data to third countries.[169] The ocean carrier is also obliged to inform the data subject as to the period for which personal data will be stored and the right to access, rectify and delete this personal data as well as the right to lodge a complaint with a supervisory authority.[170] If the information is not collected directly from the data subject, but through a third party, as with agents or freight forwarders, the controller[171] still has an obligation to inform the data subject about these details. The data subject is also entitled to receive information about the purpose of the processing of data, the categories of data concerned, the recipients or categories of recipients of the data and recipients in third countries, and the period for which the data will be stored.[172] These are the legal foundation of the terms found in the privacy policies of ocean carriers' web portals.

The PDPA does not oblige an organisation to inform the individual of all the aspects required by the GDPR. Section 20 establishes an obligation to notify the purpose of the collection and the use and disclosure of the personal data. The organisation must notify the purpose of the collection to the individual as well as any other organisation from which personal data of an individual is collected.[173] The business contact information of the person with the capacity to answer on behalf of the organisation must be provided if the individual requests that information.[174]

Both the GDPR and the PDPA establish a clear obligation to protect personal data. The GDPR includes the obligation of 'integrity and confidentiality' of the data.[175] For this purpose, the collector and processor must process the data in a 'manner that ensures appropriate security of the personal data, including protection against unauthorised or unlawful processing and accidental loss, destruction or damage, using appropriate technical or organisational measures'.[176] Article 24 establishes the responsibility of the controller to take such measures to ensure and demonstrate that the processing is done according to the GDPR.[177] As the storage of data collected by websites is electronic, there is an obligation on the controller and the processor to implement appropriate technical and organisational measures to ensure an appropriate level of security.[178] These measures must involve the 'ability to ensure the ongoing confidentiality, integrity, availability and resilience

[169] GDPR, art 13.1.
[170] ibid, art 13.2.
[171] ibid, art 14.2. See Weber and Staiger, *Transatlantic Data Protection* (2017) 37.
[172] ibid, art 15.1.
[173] PDPA, ss 20(1) and 20(2).
[174] ibid, s 20(1)(c).
[175] GDPR, art 5.
[176] ibid, art 5.1(f).
[177] ibid, art 24.1.
[178] ibid, art 32.

of processing systems'.[179] Such storage should be for a period no longer than it is necessary for the purpose for which the data is collected, although it may be kept for longer periods for other legitimate purposes.[180]

The PDPA contains an express provision holding an organisation responsible for the personal data in its possession and under its control.[181] The organisation must make reasonable efforts to ensure that the data collected is accurate and complete. This obligation is required only if the data is used in the making of decisions that affect the individual whose data is concerned or if that data is to be disclosed to another organisation.[182] It must be noted that this obligation of ensuring the accuracy and completeness of the information is not strict, but subject to a standard of reasonableness.[183] Section 24 of the PDPA provides that 'An organisation shall protect personal data in its possession or under its control by making reasonable security arrangements to prevent unauthorised access, collection, use, disclosure, copying, modification, disposal or similar risks'. This is an essential obligation, but the Act does not suggest 'reasonable' means or measures for protection. It is reported that the majority of decisions from the Personal Data Protection Commission (PDPC) deal with infractions to this obligation.[184] The organisation is subject to this obligation for the entire period it retains the data. The retention of the data is also subject to the fulfilment of the purpose for what it was collected or until the moment the retention is no longer necessary for legal or business purposes.[185] An individual has the right to have access to its data under certain conditions[186] and the right to request the correction of errors or omissions in its data in possession of an organisation.[187] There is no right to request the deletion of its data under the PDPA as there is in the GDPR. Once the data is no longer needed for the purposes for which it was collected, the organisation must cease retaining the documents or remove the means by which it is stored. This obligation of limited retention must not, however, be confused with the right of erasure granted by the GDPR. Although the organisation is under an obligation to cease the retention of data, it does not entitle the individual to demand the ceasing of retention of his or her data.[188] However, connecting this obligation with the right to withdraw consent, once the customer withdraws its consent, there might not be a purpose for keeping the data. This may facilitate the ceasing of retention and the subsequent deletion of the data by the organisation.[189]

[179] ibid, art 32.1(b).
[180] ibid, art 5.1(e). Data might be retained for purposes of public interest, scientific or historical research purposes or statistical purposes, inasmuch as the data is subject to appropriate safeguards and the implementation of technical or organizational measures: see GDPR, art 89.1.
[181] PDPA, s 11(2).
[182] ibid, s 23.
[183] Wong (n 144) 294.
[184] ibid.
[185] PDPA, s 25.
[186] PDPA, s 21. This right is subject to some exceptions listed in the Fifth Schedule.
[187] PDPA s 22. This right is subject to some exceptions listed in the Sixth Schedule.
[188] Wong (n 144) 295.
[189] ibid.

Given the nature of the contract of carriage, the transfer of data by ocean carriers to other countries is essential. Both the GDPR and the PDPA establish conditions for such transfers.[190] The GDPR contains a set of rules which are intended to ensure that the subject whose data is transferred to a third country or international organisation holds the same rights and guarantees as under the GDPR.[191] The PDPA is complemented by the Personal Data Protection Regulations 2021 (PDPR).[192] Regulation 10 of that instrument establishes that the transferring organisation must (a) take appropriate steps to ensure the compliance of the obligations established in the Act while the data is in possession or under control of the transferring organisation; and (b) take appropriate steps to ascertain and ensure that the recipient of the personal data in that country or territory outside Singapore is bound by legally enforceable obligations comparable to those established in this Act. Therefore, the main condition for data transfer to areas outside the jurisdictions of these instruments is that the receiving country has similar standards.

e. Remedies

The GDPR and the PDPA also make provision for enforcing remedies, liabilities and penalties. For example, under the GDPR, the data subject is entitled to lodge complaints about infringement of data protection with the supervisory authority of the Member State of its residence or where the infringement has been committed.[193] Each natural or legal person is entitled to an effective judicial remedy against a decision of a supervisory authority.[194] The same is granted to the data subject if the supervisory authority does not handle a complaint or does not provide information about the progress or outcome of the case within three months.[195] Each data subject has the right to a judicial remedy where it considers its rights under the GDPR have been violated as a result of the processing of its personal data in a way which does not comply with the GDPR.[196] Thus, an ocean carrier, as controller, will be held responsible for any damage caused by processing data which infringes the GDPR, while the processor will be responsible only for the infringement of those obligations assigned to it or for acting contrary to the lawful instructions of the controller.[197] In any case, the person who has suffered material or non-material damage from any infringement of the GDPR is entitled to receive compensation from the controller or processor.[198] However, the controller or processor may be released from liability if they are able to prove they were not responsible for the

[190] GDPR, art 44, PDPA s 26.
[191] GDPR, arts 45–50.
[192] S 63/2021. See Wong (n 144) 295.
[193] GDPR art 77.
[194] ibid, art 78.1.
[195] ibid, art 78.2.
[196] ibid, art 79.1.
[197] ibid, art 82.2.
[198] ibid, art 82.1.

event that caused the damage.[199] The negligent non-compliance or intentional infringement of the provisions of the GDPR may be punished by the supervisory authority with fines up to €20 million or four per cent of the annual global turnover, whichever is higher.[200] Although this could be considered as being too severe, this shows the paramount importance granted to the right of privacy and is intended to act as a deterrence to companies to avoid infringement of the GDPR. It must, however, be emphasised that the right to judicial actions and remedies only applies if the data subject is a natural person. A company cannot found any claim for data breach under the GDPR and so a shipper company would have to seek a solution outside the GDPR. In certain limited circumstances, liabilities under the GDPR may be covered by P&I insurance and subject to the ocean carrier establishing that it has taken the necessary steps to prevent the breach.[201] Cyber insurance policies do not appear to cover such liabilities.[202]

The PDPA has also created a governmental authority called the Personal Data Protection Commission.[203] This Commission is entitled to resolve complaints from individuals for lack of compliance by an organisation of the right to access and correction of data.[204] The Commission can impose fines of up to S$1 million for lack of compliance.[205] The Act also creates some offences which can be punished by imprisonment for up to three years.[206] Apart from complaints brought before the Commission, the Act also grants a right of private action to any natural person who suffers loss or damage as a consequence of contravention of the obligations stated in the Act.[207] The claimant is entitled to seek a court order by way of injunction or damages or such other relief as the courts deems fit.[208]

The GDPR establishes that data subjects can request rectification and, more importantly, erasure of information, also known as the 'right to be forgotten'.[209] The customer has the right to request the erasure of information without undue delay, subject to specific grounds, for example, that the data is no longer necessary, or because it withdraws consent because of an absence of legal grounds for processing the data, or because it objects to the processing of data.[210] Thus, pursuant to this right, the shipper may request the erasure of its information once the contract of carriage is performed. The ocean carrier may oppose such a request if the information is necessary for exercising its defence to a claim.[211] The ocean

[199] ibid, art 82.3.
[200] ibid, art 83.5.
[201] The North of England Protecting & Indemnity Association Limited, 'FAQS: General Data Protections Regulations (GDPR) (January 2018) para 27, available at www.nepia.com/search?q=GDPR.
[202] ibid.
[203] PDPA, s 5.
[204] ibid, s 48H.
[205] ibid, s 48J(3)–(4).
[206] ibid, ss 52 and 56.
[207] ibid, s 48O. Any action is subject to a previous final decision and non appealable: see s 48O(2).
[208] ibid, s 48O(3).
[209] GDPR, art 17.
[210] ibid, art 17.1.
[211] ibid, art 17.3(e).

carrier will certainly require such information in the case of a cargo claim, where the relevant information and instructions provided by the shipper or its agents will be essential evidentiary material in support of the carriers' defence or counterclaim. In addition, as the time bar in international conventions, such as the Hague (and Hague-Visby) Rules,[212] is one year,[213] the carrier may refuse to erase the relevant information in a shorter period. As noted above, the PDPA does not grant a right to erasure.[214] Nevertheless, if the ocean carrier's privacy policy establishes the right of the user to request the modification or erasure of its data, the effect of this is that the carrier will be contractually granting such rights to that company, obliging itself to comply with it. Hence, it falls on the hands of the company to exercise this right and immediately request the erasure of its data once the carriage is concluded or after the expiration of the one-year time bar. This might be perhaps the most efficient solution in order to prevent, avoid or at least reduce the risk of its data being stolen or misused or facing any problems with its management and processing.

B. Protection of Trade Secrets

i. Background

Current international regimes do not provide clear and accurate regulation for the protection of business data shared by ocean carriers. The industry must, however, be cautious in protecting the information gathered and stored as such information may contain sensitive business data identifiable as trade secret. As stated in the CMI Rules on Electronic Bills of Lading, such data has the character of private information and trade secrets because it has a high commercial value.[215] Accordingly, when analysing the duties of ocean carriers regarding the sharing of data, the protection of trade secrets must also be assessed. The basic information that a shipper provides for the issuance of a bill of lading is displayed in the same document and will be shared with actual carriers, port and customs authorities, banks, surveyors and other actors in the supply chain. This has been the common practice of the industry for decades and even centuries. Hence, the information provided is not exactly a secret as it is shared with people, companies and authorities involved in the carriage of goods by sea. The first requirement for accessing legal actions under trade secret laws is establishing what is secret. Some companies may be reluctant to share information which they consider to be secret but, in reality, apart from customer terms and prices, most data is non-sensitive.[216]

[212] See art III, r 6.
[213] But *cf* the Hamburg Rules (art 20(1)) where the time bar is two years.
[214] See above, (A)(i)d.
[215] See above, (C).
[216] Roeloffs, 'Breaking the Barriers' (2019).

The challenge presented by new technological processes is that with web portals all business information is stored and kept electronically in order to feed intelligent machines or search engines that make the contracting process easier and faster. In addition, as already noted, such data is also kept for statistical or analytical purposes. If the shipper is a regular customer, as will often be the case, the ocean carrier will collect information about the commercial behaviour of that client over a period of time. As consignees are customarily the buyers of cargo, the ocean carrier will be collecting very valuable commercial information about that business, namely, a list of customers. On the other hand, the ocean carrier will also be collecting information about the consignee's different suppliers, along with detailed information about the type, number and weight of the merchandise it is selling and the frequency of such sales. In certain cases, the value of that cargo will also be reported to ocean carriers. In other words, the shipment of particular cargoes provides a significant part of the jigsaw puzzle that can eventually be reconstructed to provide an important part of the picture underlying the commercial operation of the company. The shipment history of a particular company may not be of much greater interest for ocean carriers other than for the purposes of analytics and business projections. But such information may be of great interest to the shipper's competitors. Using hacking technology, this valuable information could be exposed to such competitors and cause a loss of market to that shipper, among other potential damage. This brings into question whether this data constitutes a trade secret and whether it is subject to special protection under trade secrets regulations, particularly the World Trade Organization Agreements.

ii. The World Trade Organization Agreements

The protection of trade secrets has gained more attention in recent years because of the increasing threat of cyber espionage.[217] The international regulation of trade secrets is contained in the Agreement on Trade-Related Aspects of Intellectual Property Law (the TRIPS Agreement). This was adopted in 1994 as an annex to the agreement that created the World Trade Organization (WTO) and is based on the United States Uniform Trade Secrets Act (UTSA).[218] The latter Act defines a trade secret as:

> [I]nformation, including a formula, pattern, compilation, program device, method, technique, or process, that: (i) derives independent economic value, actual or potential, from not being generally known to, and not being readily ascertainable by proper means by, other persons who can obtain economic value from its disclosure or use, and (ii) is the subject of efforts that are reasonable under the circumstances to maintain its secrecy.

[217] EA Rowe and SK Sandeen, *Trade Secrecy and International Transactions: Law and Practice* (Cheltenham, Edward Elgar, 2015) [1.04], [1.36].

[218] ibid, [1.04]–[1.05].

It can be inferred from this definition that any compilation of clients and suppliers' names and particulars of the cargo, when not publicly disclosed, has an economic value which deserves special protection. The wide description provided by the UTSA permits a customer list or compilation of customer preferences, among others, to be considered a trade secret.[219] The World Intellectual Property Organization (WIPO) provides another definition that better fits the particular situation under analysis:

> The subject matter of trade secrets is usually defined in broad terms and includes sales methods, distribution methods, consumer profiles, advertising strategies, lists of suppliers and clients, and manufacturing processes. While a final determination of what information constitutes a trade secret will depend on the circumstances of each individual case, clearly unfair practices in respect of secret information include industrial or commercial espionage, breach of contract and breach of confidence.[220]

Article 39 of the TRIPS Agreement establishes an obligation on Member States to protect undisclosed information in order to prevent unfair competition. The conditions or elements for ascertaining what information is subject to protection as a trade secret are enumerated in that Article:[221]

> a) [It] is secret in the sense that it is not, as a body or in the precise configuration and assembly of its component, generally known among or readily accessible to persons within the circles that normally deal with the kind of information in question; b) [it] has commercial value because it is secret; and, c) [it] has been subject to reasonable steps under the circumstances, by the person lawfully in control of the information, to keep it secret.

Using the criteria in this provision, the information appearing in a single bill of lading does not constitute a secret in itself, as it must be disclosed to some actors in the supply chain for the execution of the contract. However, the remainder of the shipment history encompasses a list of clients and suppliers included in the definition provided by the WTO. Such lists of clients and suppliers are not known to the public and are kept secret because of their commercial value. The commercial value of confidential information is assessed according to the competitive advantage that such information may give.[222] If a competitor perceives that such information has value because it is kept secret, that may give to the holder a competitive advantage.[223] A list of customer and suppliers describing the goods, quantity and regularity of sales and, in some cases, their value, without doubt has a value as it gives a competitive advantage. However, it may be argued that such

[219] Robertson, Hannah and Lautsch, 'The Secret to Protecting Trade Secrets' (2015) 669, 670.
[220] See www.wipo.int/sme/en/ip_business/trade_secrets/trade_secrets.htm.
[221] Art 39.2.
[222] D Gervais, *The TRIPS Agreements: Drafting History and Analysis*, 4th edn (London, Sweet & Maxwell, 2012) [2.486].
[223] ibid.

information is 'readily accessible to persons within the circles that normally deal with this kind of information'. This is because the shipment history might also be reconstructed by insurers, banks, customs and port authorities with whom the information is shared as well as any individual who has access to the bills of lading of the same shipper.

The second challenge is to secure an obligation of confidentiality. The requirement entails that the 'person to whom the information is disclosed must be under an obligation to maintain the secrecy'.[224] In the terms and conditions displayed on the websites of the ocean carriers, no obligation to keep customers' information confidential is assumed. It is stated that the data will be transferred, for sales purposes, only for the performance of the contract. Such a term claims to provide the most secure treatment and management of the customer's information, but does not in itself guarantee that the data will be kept confidential. Such an expression may not constitute a duty of confidentiality, which is one of the conditions for holding someone liable for trade secret misappropriation.[225] The terms and conditions of the ocean carriers state that they are not liable for any damage that may occur from the use of their websites. In view of this, the elements for holding certain information as trade secrets under the TRIPS Agreement will not apply to the shipper's business data submitted through a website. This leaves shippers without protection for their business data.

VI. Conclusions

In the so-called Fourth Industrial Revolution, the players in international trade depend strongly on the implementation of digital technology. Web portals have demonstrated their utility and efficiency as platforms for ecommerce. Indeed, lacking an efficient website may jeopardise the competitiveness of any company. From a commercial and business perspective, this makes it mandatory to provide such technology while also creating adequate and safe policies and systems for data sharing. The shipping industry is well aware of this and has, for almost two decades, profited from this technology. The safe exchange of data among the parties to contracts for the carriage of goods by sea appears not to be regulated by existing international instruments. Apart from the fact that they do not have sufficient legal effect, international instruments on the interchange of data, ecommerce, and electronic bills of lading, barely address issues regarding the protection of data, its safe sharing or liabilities arising from a data breach. In such circumstances, local laws on these subjects have to be observed. The only set of rules which mentions confidentiality and trade secrets in the context of shipment information is the CMI Rules on Electronic Bills of Lading which has not had any legal effect.

[224] ibid.
[225] Rowe and Sandeen, *Trade Secrecy* (2015) 63.

On the other hand, the rules regarding the protection of data privacy, such as the GDPR or PDPA, have had limited effect in the shipping industry because they address the protection of the data of natural persons, not legal persons. As the shipping industry mostly involves business-to-business relationships, data protection provisions may apply only when dealing with natural persons. However, customers may have access to some rights granted in the terms and conditions of the ocean carriers' websites. From the perspective of trade secrets, international regulation does not cover such data as these do not constitute a trade secret. Thus, this data does not conform with the standards for protection of trade secrets established in the TRIPS Agreements.

The international regime does not establish a proper duty of protection for shippers' business data submitted through web portals. This situation, along with the exclusion of liability for damage resulting from the mismanagement of such data stated in the privacy policy of the web portals, leaves shippers without any effective remedy for losses caused by the disclosure of data. Damage caused by data breaches may be claimed under a general duty of care, but as this does not prohibit ocean carriers from limiting or excluding their liability for data breaches, the success of those claims is doubtful. A possible solution might be the fact that the terms and conditions established in the registered user agreement or privacy policies of the web portals state that the carriers grant certain rights to companies requesting their shipping services, such as the right to erasure of data. If so, perhaps the most efficient way to safeguard that data is for the shipper to request the immediate erasure of such data after the delivery of the cargo to the consignee. The carrier may oppose such requests because it may reasonably need the data for defence purposes in the case of a cargo claim and, in such a case, it could be mutually agreed that it will be sufficient to keep the information for up to one year. This may at least reduce the risk of the shipment history being disclosed to unauthorised parties.

Management and Organisation: Autonomous Shipping

11

Autonomous Ships and Hull and Machinery Marine Insurance

LUCI CAREY*

I. Introduction

As technology developments in autonomy increasingly drive control from ship to shore, questions arise whether the existing legal framework governing marine insurance is adequate. It is, of course, a difficult task to discuss the future and, like the algorithms that enable autonomy, the discussions can often descend to 'if this then this, if that then that'. This chapter examines some issues that may arise in relation to legal liability and insurance as autonomy in shipping becomes increasingly utilised.

Research jointly conducted by Clyde & Co and the Institute of Marine Engineering Science and Technology found that 60 per cent of the respondent marine executives think it is unclear how insurers will approach autonomous ships and this is probably because of the lack of a legal framework.[1] Nevertheless, a survey undertaken by the International Underwriting Association (IUA) found that 80 per cent of respondents believe that unmanned vessels will be in widespread use by 2028[2] and anticipate that their introduction will improve shipping safety by reducing human error.[3] However, this assumption must be accompanied by a caveat that with certain academic research into the safety of autonomous and

* Research Associate, Centre for Maritime Law, Faculty of Law, National University of Singapore. The author would like to thank Dr Ayşegül Buğra, Prof Özlem Gürses, Dr Steven Hazelwood and Prof Mikis Tsimplis for their insightful comments on earlier drafts of this chapter. The usual disclaimer applies.

[1] 'Technology in Shipping: The Impact of Technological Change on Shipping' (Clyde & Co and InMarEST, November 2017) 9, available at www.imarest.org/policy-news/thought-leadership/1010-technology-in-shipping/file.

[2] J Guy, 'Insurers Creating Unmanned Vessels Products Say IUA' *Safety at Sea* (8 October 2018), available at safetyatsea.net/news/2018/insurers-creating-unmanned-vessel-products-says-iua.

[3] 'Safety and Shipping Review 2019' (Allianz, May 2019) 7, available at www.agcs.allianz.com/news-and-insights/news/safety-shipping-review-2019.html.

unmanned vessels, the findings on the relevant safety and security risks are still on an abstract level.[4]

The principles that govern the law of marine insurance and the liability of the shipowner stem from a time when a ship was an isolated vessel with no means of communication to shore. Yet these principles remain in an era where communication is almost instantaneous. Therefore, it is likely that autonomous and unmanned ships will slot into the existing legal framework for marine insurance and shipowners' liability. However, there are specific issues that need to be resolved to ensure that shipowners comply with their legal requirements under the most commonly used Hull and Machinery clauses. The chapter examines piracy and cyber risks, Inchmaree clauses and due diligence, before briefly discussing seaworthiness warranties.

The introduction of new technology brings with it new risks and potentially exposes shipowners and managers to third-party liability. As navigation is increasingly directed by artificial intelligence, finding fault on the part of the shipowner will be difficult to establish in the event of a collision. As a result, shipowners may find that they unwittingly become strictly liable for any errors of navigation. Therefore, in order to manage and mitigate risk exposure insurers need to know whether the current maritime limitation regimes will apply equally to autonomous and unmanned ships. In particular, insurers and shipowners need to know whether the current maritime limitation regimes will apply in respect of product liability.

II. Examples of the Ships

In 1898, Nikola Tesla patented the first autonomous ship, a remote-controlled robotic boat.[5] In more recent times, autonomous ships have developed from a concept to reality and interest in the application of autonomous technology continues to build momentum. Examples of these ships are set out below.

A. Current and Planned Unmanned Ships

The current and planned ships have a variety of roles. The first registered unmanned ship is the *C-Worker 7*, a seven-metre-long subsea surveying vessel[6] which joined

[4] R Jalonen, R Tuominen and M Wahlström, 'Safety of Unmanned Ships, Safe Shipping with Autonomous and Remote Controlled Ships' Research Report, Aalto University publication series *Science and Technology* (May 2017), 4.

[5] M Novak, 'Nikola Tesla's Amazing Predictions for the 21st Century' *Smithsonian Magazine* (19 April 2013). See www.smithsonianmag.com/history/nikola-teslas-amazing-predictions-for-the-21st-century-26353702.

[6] L3 ASV Product Information. See www.asvglobal.com/product/c-worker-7.

the UK ship register in 2017.[7] It is completely unmanned and operated by remote control. There are plans for autonomous tugs in Singapore,[8] autonomous firefighting vessels,[9] autonomous ferries[10] and autonomous offshore supply vessels.[11]

The *Yara Birkeland* is probably the most well-known potential cargo carrying vessel. It is planned to be a zero-emissions autonomous container vessel that will operate within Norway's territorial waters. Autonomous testing was scheduled to begin in 2020[12] with the expectation that it will operate initially with a crew and be fully autonomous by 2022.[13]

This is an example of cargo owners driving the development of autonomous and unmanned ships. Yara is a fertiliser company and will use the *Yara Birkeland* to transport its products between its plant and the ports of Brevik and Larvik. Although owned by Yara, the *Yara Birkeland* will be managed by Massterly, a ship management company developed specifically to manage autonomous ships.[14] The *Yara Birkeland* project has led to the development of others. For instance, the grocery company ASKO plans to use autonomous ships in the Oslo fjord to replace the use of diesel trucks.[15]

Autonomous ships are not only vessels specifically constructed to be autonomous and unmanned. Autonomous technology can be attached to existing ships. At the end of November 2018, Wärtsilä tested the fully autonomous operation of a ferry on a route in Norway.

The test of Wärtsilä's autonomous shipping technology was conducted utilising the 85-metre ferry *Folgefonn* and in the presence of the Norwegian Maritime Authority. Wärtsilä has indicated that during the test, the *Folgefonn* was under full autonomous operation as it visited three different ports. The ferry was able to leave

[7] 'First Autonomous Ship Signs to the UK Registry' (Handy Shipping Guide, 15 November 2017). See www.handyshippingguide.com/shipping-news/first-autonomous-vessel-signs-to-uk-flag-registry_8601.

[8] M Hand, 'Wärtsilä in autonomous "IntelliTug" project with MPA and PSA Marine as it launches Acceleration Centre', *Seatrade Maritime News* (16 October 2018), available at www.seatrade-maritime.com/asia/w-rtsil-autonomous-intellitug-project-mpa-and-psa-marine-it-launches-acceleration-centre.

[9] 'Robert Allan Ltd and Kongsberg Maritime to Develop Remotely-operated Fireboats for Ports' (Kongsberg Press Release, 6 February 2018), available at www.kongsberg.com/maritime/about-us/news-and-media/news-archive/2018/robert-allan-ltd.-and-kongsberg-maritime-to-develop-remotely-operated-fireboats.

[10] 'Ferries showcase potential of autonomous vessel technology', available at www.rivieramm.com/opinion/opinion/ferries-showcase-potential-of-autonomous-vessel-technology-21746.

[11] Ship Technology 'Hronn Autonomous Offshore Supply Vessel', available at www.ship-technology.com/projects/hronn-autonomous-offshore-support-vessel.

[12] The hull of Yara Birkeland was launched in Romania in February 2020, however due to the Covid-19 pandemic Yara decided to pause the development of the vessel. See www.yara.com/news-and-media/press-kits/yara-birkeland-press-kit/.

[13] www.yara.com/knowledge-grows/game-changer-for-the-environment.

[14] This is a joint venture between Kongsberg and Wilhelmsen. See www.wilhelmsen.com/media-news-and-events/press-releases/2018/wilhelmsen-and-kongsberg-establish-worlds-first-autonomous-shipping-company.

[15] ØJ Rødseth, 'Improving Marine Transport in Norway with Unmanned and Autonomous Ships' (SINTEF), available at www.sintef.no/en/publications/publication/?pubid=CRIStin+1624920.

the dock, manoeuvre out of the harbour, sail to the next port of call, manoeuvre through the harbour entrance, and dock alongside the terminal without human intervention[16] although a master and crew were present on board.[17]

At the beginning of December 2018, similar technology was tested on another ferry in Finland. This time Rolls-Royce was the technology provider. The ferry sailed autonomously from Pargas to Nagu in the archipelagic waters around Turku. It did, however, experience a problem according to the master: 'the only time the system couldn't identify something in the water during a test run, it was a swimming elk'.[18]

What these examples of various autonomous and unmanned vessels demonstrate is that they are diverse in their function and purpose. Some are remote-controlled and unmanned, others are manned but operate autonomously, while others will be autonomous and unmanned but monitored from a shore control centre. The level of autonomous operation may also vary during a voyage. With this in mind, it is important to understand levels of autonomy in order to understand risk and the legal consequences in terms of liability.

B. Levels of Autonomy

A major issue affecting autonomous and unmanned ships is the lack of consistent definitions. The first challenge for the law is to define the various levels of autonomy of the vessel. This is particularly crucial when attempting to determine the liability of the shipowner and the level of control they may or may not have over software and algorithms that will govern the actions of the ship.

i. *European Defence Agency*

The European Defence Agency's Safety and Regulations for European Unmanned Systems (SARUMS), subsequently adopted by Maritime UK in its Code of Practice for Maritime Autonomous Surface Ships, provides six levels of autonomy:

AL0 The operator is onboard.
AL1 Operator has direct control via radio control or tethered.
AL2 Directed control. Authority to make decisions remains with the operator.

[16] Final tests took place in Spring 2019 with authorities expected to give the 'green light' for autonomous docking. See A Farnsworth, 'Autodocking – A Giant Leap for Merchant Shipping' (Wärtsilä), available at www.wartsila.com/twentyfour7/innovation/auto-docking-a-giant-leap-for-passenger-vessles.

[17] 'Wärtsilä Conducts Autonomous Ferry Voyage and Docking' (Maritime Executive), available at www.maritime-executive.com/article/waertsilae-conducts-autonomous-ferry-voyage-and-docking.

[18] Autonomous Vehicles 'Autonomous Ferry makes First Demonstration Voyage in Finland', available at www.autonomousvehicles-expo.co.uk/?p=293. What is unclear from the report is whether the system identified that there was an object but could not identify what it was or whether the system failed to see the obstacle and required a human to spot it.

AL3 Delegated. Decision-making shared between vessel and operator.
AL4 Monitored. Vessel makes decisions. Operator monitors events.
AL5 Vessel makes decisions. No notification to external operators.[19]

ii. Lloyd's Register

The classification society, Lloyd's Register (LR), has defined the levels in broadly the same way.[20] Autonomous does not mean unmanned, and vice versa. Within the concept of autonomous ships there are different classes of manning and it is suggested that these can be broken down into four categories:

1. Continuously manned bridge with assisted autonomy.
2. Periodically unmanned bridge.
3. Periodically unmanned ship.
4. Continuously unmanned ship.[21]

iii. The IMO

The International Maritime Organisation (IMO) is conducting a scoping exercise to determine how Maritime Autonomous Surface Ships (MASS) may be introduced in existing IMO instruments.[22] The IMO's Maritime Safety Committee divides the levels of autonomy into four layers for the purposes of the scoping exercise:

1. Ship with automated processes and decision support: seafarers are on board to operate and control shipboard systems and functions. Some operations may be automated.
2. Remotely controlled ship with seafarers on board: the ship is controlled and operated from another location, but crew remain on the ship.
3. Remotely controlled ship without seafarers on board: the ship is controlled and operated from another location. No crew remains on board.
4. Fully autonomous ship. The operating system of the ship is able to make decisions and determine actions by itself.[23]

[19] See www.maritimeuk.org/media-centre/publications/maritime-autonomous-surface-ships-industry-conduct-principles-code-practice.

[20] 'Lloyd's Register Defines Autonomy Levels for Ship Design and Operation', 8 July 2016, available at www.lr.org/en/latest=news/lr-defines-autonomy-levels-for-ship-design-and-operation.

[21] ØJ Rødseth and H Nordahl, 'Definitions for Autonomous Merchant Ships' (Norwegian Forum for Autonomous Ships), available at nfas.autonomous-ship.org/resources/autonom-defs.pdf.

[22] 'Autonomous Shipping': see www.imo.org/en/MediaCentre/HotTopics/Pages/Autonomous-shipping.aspx.

[23] Legal Committee 106th session, 'Regulatory Scoping Exercise and Gap Analysis of Conventions Emanating from the Legal Committee with Respect to Maritime Autonomous Surface Ships (MASS)', 11 January 2019.

iv. Synthesis

The various levels of autonomy and manning indicate that there is no one form of autonomous or unmanned ship. Levels of autonomy are not fixed. The level of autonomy depends upon the operation of the ship rather than the equipment.[24] On the other hand, while the definitions are different they are not completely disparate. The theme that can be extracted is that levels of autonomy are movable. As autonomy increases, human control decreases but manning levels are not necessarily impacted. At the same time, manning levels can drop to zero, but human control remains high. Therefore, legal liability for human actions will depend on the function of the vessel at any point in time and similarly the risk profile will change according to the levels of autonomy and manning.[25] Figure 11.1 illustrates the different stages.[26]

Figure 11.1 Examples of levels of autonomy and manning

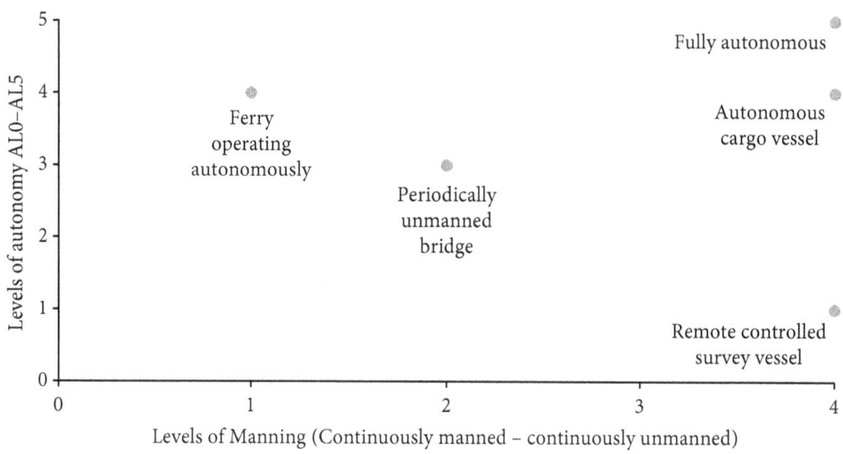

For navigation purposes, if the vessel is registered then arguably it will have the same navigational rights as a conventional ship, however, whether they will be entitled to innocent passage and transit passage through another state's territorial waters is questionable.[27] The international conventions governing shipping were

[24] H Ringbom, 'Regulating Autonomous Ships – Concepts Challenges and Precedents' (2019) 50 *Ocean Development & International Law* 141.

[25] It is worth noting that at the IMO's Maritime Safety Committee, Finland and France expressed concerns regarding the nomenclature of 'autonomous' and 'unmanned vessels', highlighting that the interpretation of certain terms may differ between stakeholders and may lead to confusion. See Maritime Safety Committee, 101st session, Agenda item 5 'Regulatory Scoping Exercise for the Use of Maritime Autonomous Surface Ships (MASS) Proposal for Terms to be Avoided, Recommended Terms and Draft of Glossary', 2 April 2019 (Finland and France).

[26] Adapted from BJ Vartdal and A Jørgensen, 'Autonomous and Remotely Operated Ships – Status and Outlook', DNV-GL webinar (2 April 2019).

[27] R Veal and M Tsimplis 'The integration of unmanned ships into the lex maritima' [2017] *LMCLQ* 303, 307.

not drafted with autonomous and unmanned ships in mind and may cause difficulties for these novel craft to comply.[28] The IMO has issued interim guidelines on the testing of MASS and these require that the trials ought to be conducted to a standard that conforms to at least the same degree of safety, security and protection of the environment as provided by the relevant instruments.[29] In addition, onboard or remote operators ought to be appropriately qualified and experienced to conduct the trials and appropriate steps should be taken to ensure cyber-risk management of the systems and infrastructure used in such trials.[30]

III. Autonomous and Unmanned Ships and Marine Insurance

The general consensus of the International Group of P&I Clubs is that autonomous ships will be covered by the normal protection and indemnity rules and deemed poolable in the mutual system.[31] However, there are concerns that the insurance industry is not ready for the introduction of autonomous ships.[32]

A. The Marine Insurance Framework

A marine insurance policy is a contract whereby an insurer undertakes to indemnify an assured against marine losses to an agreed subject matter caused by agreed perils. In many Anglo common law jurisdictions these contracts are governed by domestic legislation that in substance mirrors the UK Marine Insurance Act 1906 (MIA 1906).[33] The MIA 1906 defines certain perils that are held covered by marine insurance policies[34] and provides defences to the underwriters, such

[28] See P Dean and H Clack, 'Autonomous Shipping and Maritime Law' in B Soyer and A Tettenborn (eds), *New Technologies, Artificial Intelligence and Shipping Law in the 21st Century* (London, Informa, 2019) ch 6.

[29] IMO 'Autonomous Shipping', available at www.imo.org/en/MediaCentre/HotTopics/Pages/Autonomous-shipping.aspx.

[30] ibid. The IMO's scoping exercise of the International Conventions will identify where provisions in the international conventions preclude the operation of maritime autonomous surface vessels. It is anticipated to be completed in 2020. See www.imo.org/en/MediaCentre/MeetingSummaries/MSC/Pages/MSC-100th-session.aspx.

[31] T Howse 'Maritime Autonomous Surface Ships – Identifying and Covering the Risks', available at www.gard.no/web/updates/content/27188643/maritime-autonomous-surface-ships-identifying-and-covering-the-risks.

[32] Insurance Marine News, 'Autonomous Ships insurers not fully prepared: HFW Survey' (28 January 2019), available at iumi.com/news/blog/autonomous-ships-insurers-not-yet-fully-prepared-hfw-survey.

[33] See Marine Insurance Act 1909 (Australia); Marine Insurance Act SC 1993, c 22 (Canada); Marine Insurance Act 1908 (New Zealand); Marine Insurance Act Cap 387 (Singapore). The Marine Insurance Act 1906 applies in Malaysia by s 5(1) of the Civil Law Act 1956.

[34] MIA 1906, s 3(2) '"Maritime perils" means the perils consequent on, or incidental to, the navigation of the sea, that is to say, perils of the seas, fire, war perils, pirates, rovers, thieves, captures, seizures,

as unseaworthiness or non-disclosure of material circumstances by the assured. The purpose of the MIA 1906 was to consolidate the common law as it stood in 1900, and the principles have largely remained intact save for modifications by, inter alia, the UK Consumer Insurance (Disclosure and Representations) Act 2012 and the Insurance Act 2015. While much of the discussion that follows concerns the common law, comparisons will be made with the Nordic Plan because much of the research and development of autonomous vessels is in Scandinavia. The Nordic Plan provides that the applicable governing law and jurisdiction will be that of the claims leader where the claims leader is domiciled in a Nordic country. Otherwise, the default position is that Norwegian law is to apply but there is no provision in respect of jurisdiction.[35]

In order to recover under a marine insurance policy, both the MIA 1906 and Nordic Plan require that the assured who has paid a premium to the insurer suffers a loss, whether total or partial, of the subject matter insured and caused by one of the named perils.[36] While it is widely accepted that autonomous and unmanned ships are legally ships,[37] neither the MIA 1906 nor the Nordic Plan defines 'ship'.[38] In the absence of any changes to the legal definition of 'ship', it appears that unmanned or autonomous vessels will be deemed ships under both the MIA 1906 and Nordic Plan and legislative reform will not be required to accommodate marine insurance law and the new technology. However, the risk profile will change as autonomy increases and manning decreases.

Clause 6 of the Institute Time Clauses Hulls 1983, provides that standard and additional[39] perils insured against include:

6.1.1 perils of the seas rivers lakes or other navigable waters
6.1.2 fire, explosion
6.1.3 violent theft by persons from outside the Vessel
6.1.4 jettison
6.1.5 piracy
6.1.6 breakdown of or accident to nuclear installations or reactors
6.1.7 contact with aircraft or similar objects, or objects falling therefrom, land conveyance, dock or harbour equipment or installation

restraints, and detainment of princes and peoples, jettisons, barratry, and any other perils, either of the like kind or which may be designated by the policy.' Examples of specific perils insured against can be found in International Hull Clauses (IHC) cl 2 and Institute Time Clauses Hulls (ITCH) cl 6.

[35] The Nordic Plan 2013, version 2019, cl 1-4A.

[36] MIA 1906, ss 3, 55; Nordic Plan 2013, version 2019, cl 2-8.

[37] Veal and Tsimplis, 'lex maritima' [2017] (n 27), 308; Dean and Clack, 'Autonomous Shipping' (2019), 70–71.

[38] Although 'ship' is to include 'the hull, materials and outfit, stores and provisions for the officers and crew, and, in the case of vessels engaged in a special trade, the ordinary fittings requisite for the trade, and also, in the case of a steamship, the machinery, boilers, and coals and engine stores, if owned by the assured'. See MIA 1906, 1st schedule, Rules for Construction of Policy, r 15.

[39] Arnould highlights that in practical terms the additional perils are almost as important as the standard perils, however some of the additional perils cause greater problems with interpretation: J Gilman (gen ed), *Arnould: Law of Marine Insurance and Average*, 19th edn (London, Sweet & Maxwell, 2018) [23.02].

6.1.8 earthquake volcanic eruption or lightning.
6.2.1 accidents in loading discharging or shifting cargo or fuel
6.2.2 bursting of boilers breakage of shafts or any latent defect in the machinery or hull
6.2.3 negligence of Master Officers Crew or Pilots
6.2.4 negligence of repairers or charterers provided such repairers or charterers are not an Assured hereunder
6.2.5 barratry of Master Officers or Crew,

The perils in clause 6.2 are covered 'provided such loss or damage has not resulted from want of due diligence by the Assured, Owners or Managers'.

Certain perils will not cause a problem of interpretation with an autonomous or unmanned vessel. For example, 'perils of the seas'[40] would cover an autonomous unmanned ship in respect of loss or damage by bad weather and for damage received in a collision. A fire causing damage would similarly be covered. However, there are potential issues with the interpretation of certain perils and clauses, in the event of a claim by the owner of an autonomous ship. These will now be considered.

B. Piracy

The United Nations Convention on the Law of the Sea 1982 ('UNCLOS'), provides:

> Piracy consists of any of the following acts:
>
> (a) any illegal acts of violence or detention, or any act of depredation, committed for private ends by the crew or the passengers of a private ship or a private aircraft, and directed:
>
> (i) on the high seas, against another ship or aircraft, or against persons or property on board such ship or aircraft;
>
> (ii) against a ship, aircraft, persons or property in a place outside the jurisdiction of any State;
>
> (b) any act of voluntary participation in the operation of a ship or of an aircraft with knowledge of facts making it a pirate ship or aircraft;
>
> (c) any act of inciting or of intentionally facilitating an act described in subparagraph (a) or (b).[41]

This makes it clear that piracy must be on the high seas and by persons on another ship, which conceivably could happen by the use of craft surrounding an autonomous ship in order make the autonomous system slow the vessel down or stop so to as avoid a collision. Pirates could then board and steal cargo (inevitably it will depend on the design of the ship as to whether this will be possible). Land-based

[40] Defined as 'fortuitous accidents or casualties of the seas. It does not include the ordinary action of the winds and waves'. See MIA 1906, 1st schedule, Rules for Construction of Policy, r 7.

[41] Art 101.

criminal activities, such as hacking of the computer systems operating the ship or violent threats to the shore-based operator in order to make them redirect the ship, directed against a ship at sea will not fall within this definition although, as will be seen, this will not preclude recovery under a marine insurance policy.

For insurance purposes, the requirement that the act of piracy has to take place on the high seas is removed by the Nordic Plan. The reason was that the committee believed that placing a geographical limit was inappropriate.[42] The MIA 1906 includes 'pirates, rovers, thieves, captures, seizures' as maritime perils[43] while the International Hulls clauses provide cover for both piracy and violent theft from persons outside the vessel.[44] The requirement for the act to take place on the high seas has been unequivocally dispelled in Singapore[45] and in *The Andreas Lemos*[46] Staughton J confirmed that although an act of piracy can take place inside a state's territorial waters, the vessel must be 'at sea' within the ordinary meaning of the word.[47]

The MIA 1906 removes the requirement that 'pirates' must be external to the ship because 'pirates' is defined to 'include passengers who mutiny and rioters who attack from the shore'.[48] Rioters are defined in the Public Order Act 1986 as a group of 12 or more persons who use or threaten unlawful violence for a common purpose, in such a way to cause a person of 'reasonable firmness' to fear for their personal safety.[49]

Piracy is a 'war risk' in the Nordic Plan and a 'marine peril' in English law.[50] Therefore, if a shipowner chooses to insure for marine perils on the Nordic Plan (without a war risks policy) they are not insured for an act of piracy. If the assured takes out a 'war risks policy' on an English policy they are still not covered for an act of piracy as this is considered a 'marine peril' and not a 'war risk'. Therefore, if choosing to split insurance policies between the Nordic Plan and English policies it is important to prevent any unnecessary gaps in cover because of the differences in the definitions of perils insured against.[51] This highlights how important it is to be clear about the definition of perils insured against.

As currently defined, piracy requires the presence of a human, threatening or using violence.[52] If the shore-based operator is forced by threats of violence to renavigate the ship so that a person may steal the cargo this would be a loss caused

[42] Nordic Plan 2013, version 2019, Commentary.

[43] MIA 1906, s 3(2).

[44] For example, International Hull Clauses 01/11/03.

[45] *Bayswater Carriers Pte Ltd v QBE Insurance (International) Pte Ltd* [2005] SGHC 185, [2006] 1 SLR(R) 69.

[46] *Athens Maritime Enterprises Corp v Hellenic Mutual War Risks Association (Bermuda) Ltd (The Andreas Lemos)* [1983] QB 647.

[47] ibid 658. See also SJ Hazelwood, 'The Perils of "Pirates" – All "at sea"' [1983] *LMCLQ* 283.

[48] MIA 1906, 1st schedule, Rules for Construction of Policy, r 8.

[49] See s 1.

[50] MIA 1906, 1st schedule, Rules for Construction of Policy, r 8. However, piracy is classed as a war risk in the Institute Cargo (B) and (C) clauses. See Arnould, *Law of Marine Insurance* (2018) [2–39].

[51] Nordic Plan 2013, version 2019, Commentary.

[52] *The Andreas Lemos* (n 46); *McKeever v Northernreef Insurance* Co SA [2019] 2 Lloyd's Rep 161.

by piracy or violent theft. However, if a person hacks the system and takes control of navigation for a nefarious purpose, for example to extort money from the owner by threatening to crash the vessel if a ransom is not paid or to steal the cargo, this will not be piracy as it lacks the element of actual or threatened violence. This would, however, be a loss caused by a cyber risk.

C. Cyber Risks

It is argued that cyber risk poses the biggest challenge to the development of autonomous and unmanned ships.[53] Those who pose a cyber risk to autonomous ships include the following:

1. Disruptive activists with ideological goals, who are normally non-aggressive towards people, may attack an autonomous ship as there is no risk to human life;
2. Competitors may use cyber-attacks to access data in order to improve their market position or sabotage the ship;
3. Criminals to steal or smuggle cargo or even the ship itself;
4. Terrorists may target the ship to smuggle weapons or steal the ship to turn it into a weapon.[54]
5. Disgruntled employees
6. States and State sponsored organisations[55]

These risks are carved out from many insurance contracts by the Institute Cyber Attack Exclusion Clause (CL380),[56] which provides:

> [I]n no case shall this insurance cover loss damage liability or expense directly or indirectly caused by or contributed to, by or arising from the use or operation, as a means for inflicting harm, of any computer, computer system, computer software programme, malicious code, computer virus or process or any other electronic system.[57]

If any of the above-listed events occurred, this would be an excluded risk from the assured's policy by the use of CL380. The clause has been in operation since 2003 and has been criticised for being archaic[58] and as using a 'sledgehammer to crack a nut' because it overlooks the extent to which information technology is

[53] F Wang, 'The Warranty of Seaworthiness and Cyber Risk of Unmanned Ships' [2020] *JBL* 311, 312.

[54] K Tam and K Jones, 'Cyber Risk Assessment for Autonomous Ships' Cyber Security 2018, 4, available at pearl.plymouth.ac.uk/bitstream/handle/10026.1/11245/PID5305125.pdf?sequence=1&isAllowed=y.

[55] BIMCO, 'The Guidelines to Cyber Security onboard ships' (2018) 9.

[56] It is estimated that CL380 is used in 75–100% of hull and machinery policies: see Lloyd's Market Association 'Cyber Risks and Exposures Model Clauses – Class of Business Review' (January 2018).

[57] For a report on the use of the clause and a copy of the model clause see: IUA 'Cyber Risks and Insurance. An Introduction to Cross-class Liabilities' (Maritime London, January 2016), available at www.maritimelondon.com/wp-content/uploads/2016/01/005_Cyber_Risks_Combined_110116.pdf.

[58] Insurance Marine News, 'Clause 380 A Controversy at IUMI 2018', available at insurancemarine-news.com/insurance-marine-news/clause-380-a-controversy-at-iumi-2018.

used by assureds.[59] Shipowners can buy back the cover for the exclusions in the clause but this cover is usually subject to limitations.[60]

P&I Club cover does not expressly exclude maritime cyber risks, but some risks do not come within the scope of P&I cover because they do not arise from the operation of a ship. Examples include the risk of monetary loss where a shipping company is blackmailed to pay a ransom for the restoration of IT data or restoration of IT systems that have been compromised by cyber attack.[61] The Shipowners' Club[62] has created specific cover for autonomous vessels that covers 'third party liabilities that arise in connection with the MAV following a cyber-attack on your shoreside systems that control the MAV, or the MAV itself'.[63]

Non-malicious cyber incidents can occur on ships as a result of a failure in software updates or patching and loss of external data, such as Global Navigation Satellite Systems (GNSS).[64] In 2017, a maritime incident relating to GPS interference in the Black Sea was reported to the US Coastguard[65] after the master of a merchant vessel noticed his GPS put the vessel 32 km inland at the airport. After checking that the vessel's navigation equipment was working correctly, the master contacted nearby ships. It appeared that at least 20 ships off the port of Novorossiysk were shown by their automatic identification systems (AIS) to be at the same airport.[66] It is believed this may have been a 'spoofing' incident, where GPS is misdirected and 'lies' to the user. AIS typically relies on GNSS. When there is a GNSS deception attack, a ship may transmit misleading AIS reports.[67] In July 2019, Iranian forces seized the British registered product tanker *Stena Impero* for an alleged breach of international maritime navigation rules,[68] but it is suspected that the tanker too was the victim of a spoofing attack.[69]

[59] C Chatfield, 'Cyber Exclusion Clauses – Are they Fit for Purpose?' (Kennedys, 19 June 2018), available at www.kennedyslaw.com/thought-leadership/article/cyber-exclusion-clauses-are-they-fit-for-purpose.

[60] For example, in the energy sector, XL Caitlin offers full cover but the assured must demonstrate that the attack was targeted; QBE provides cover up to 50% of the 'All Risks' limit purchased JLT, 'Cyber Risks for Companies Operating in the Energy Sector' (28 March 2018), available at www.jltspecialty.com/our-insights/publications/energy/cyber-risks-for-companies-operating-in-the-energy-sector.

[61] UK P&I Club 'Q&A Cyber Risks and P&I Insurance' (March 2018), available at www.ukpandi.com/fileadmin/uploads/uk-pi/Documents/2018/Brochure/Cyber_Risks_and_PandI_Insurance.pdf.

[62] Thus far, the Shipowners' Club is the only P&I Club to have a separate policy for autonomous vessels but Gard is providing P&I and Hull and Machinery cover for *Yara Birkeland*. See www.gard.no/web/updates/content/27107214/maritime-autonomous-surface-ships-on-the-horizon.

[63] The policy can be viewed at www.shipownersclub.com/media/2018/07/MAV-Liability-Insurance-Brochure_160718.pdf.

[64] BIMCO (n 55) 3.

[65] United States Department of Transportation, Maritime Administration: www.maritime.dot.gov/content/2017-005a-black-sea-gps-interference.

[66] D Hambling, 'Ships Fooled in GPS Spoofing Attack Suggest Russian Cyberweapon', *The New Scientist* (10 August 2017), available at www.newscientist.com/article/2143499-ships-fooled-in-gps-spoofing-attack-suggest-russian-cyberweapon.

[67] J Bhatti and T E Humphrys, 'Hostile Control of Ships via False GPS Signals Demonstration and Detection' (2017) 64 *Journal of the Institute of Navigation* 51.

[68] For a discussion on the law of the sea and this particular incident, see A Serdy, 'Iran: What the Law of the Sea Says About Detaining Foreign Ships in Transit' (2019) 19 *Lloyd's Shipping & Trade Law* 7.

[69] MW Brockman, 'Seized UK Tanker Likely 'Spoofed' by Iran' *Lloyd's List* (16 August 2019).

CL380 is an exclusion clause and this means that cover is presupposed unless the insurer has excluded it.[70] The proximate cause maxim is removed because of the use of the words 'directly or indirectly'[71] and in order to rely on the clause the insurer will have to prove that the loss falls within the description and that the loss was caused by one of the described exclusions.[72] This will not be difficult unless proof is required of *who* intended to cause harm and that such harm was targeted at the person suffering the loss. Damage to computer systems is often via computer viruses, of which the very creation usually[73] contains the intent to cause harm. The spread of a computer virus is often innocent and caused by insufficient cyber-security or cyber-secure practices.

CL380 has not been tested in litigation but malicious intent has been defined in the context of marine insurance in *The Grecia Express*,[74] where Colman J held that:

> [P]rovided that the evidence establishes that the vessel was lost or damaged due to the conduct of someone who was intending to cause it to be lost or damaged or was reckless as to whether such loss or damage would be caused, that is enough to engage the liability of [war risks] underwriters. The words [malicious intent] therefore cover causal or random vandalism and do not require proof that the person concerned had the purpose of injuring the assured or even knew the identity of the assured.[75]

In *The B Atlantic*[76] Lord Mance explained that:

> What the context and authorities indicate is that an element of spite, ill-will or the like is required. But I would not limit the concept to conduct directed towards the insured interest. An act directed with the relevant mental element towards causing the loss of or damage or injury to other property or towards a person could lead to consequential loss of or damage to an insured interest [within clause 1.5], whether the actor was a terrorist, a person acting maliciously or a person acting from a political motive.

Most recently, in *McKeever v Northernreef Insurance Co SA*,[77] Julia Dias QC clarified that:

> It would be wholly artificial to hold that the definition of malice differs according to whether the focus is on the actor or the act – not least because acts are themselves inanimate and can only be malicious by reference to the motive of the actor.

[70] J Dunt, *Marine Cargo Insurance*, 2nd edn (London, Informa, 2015) [6.37].

[71] This is not new. See *Coxe v Employers' Liability Assurance Corp Ltd* [1916] 2 KB 629 where an insurance policy excluded death caused directly or indirectly by war. Scrutton J (at 634) said the effect of the words 'directly or indirectly' is that 'a more remote link in the chain of causation is contemplated than the proximate and immediate cause'.

[72] Dunt, *Marine Cargo Insurance* (2015) [6.38].

[73] Computer viruses can also be created for security research. See F Stevens, 'Cyber Clauses in Insurance Policies: A Legal Analysis' (2019) 25 *JIML* 134.

[74] *Strive Shipping Corporation v Hellenic Mutual War Risks Association (The Grecia Express)* [2002] EWHC 203 (Comm), [2002] 2 Lloyd's Rep 88. See also *North Star Shipping Ltd v Sphere Drake Insurance PLC* [2005] EWHC 665 (Comm), [2005] 2 Lloyd's Rep 76.

[75] ibid, 96.

[76] *Atlasnavios-Navegação lda v Navigators Insurance Co Ltd (The B Atlantic)* [2018] UKSC 26, [2019] AC 136 [28].

[77] [2019] 2 Lloyd's Rep 161 [90].

Based on this reasoning, the insurer will not need to prove that the assured was the intended target but where the identity of the culprit is unknown, it may be impossible to establish intent. In addition, the contra proferentem doctrine means that any ambiguity in the clause will be construed against the party seeking to rely upon it.[78]

If CL380 (or any cyber-risk exclusion clause) is *not* part of the hull and machinery policy and a spoofing event occurs causing a collision, this would be a peril of the seas as this is a fortuitous casualty of the seas[79] and the policy does not exclude cyber risks.[80] However, if CL380 is invoked and the insurer can show that the interference was caused with an intent to cause harm the assured will not recover.[81] If the GPS is interfered with in a manner that causes the vessel to sail into the hands of criminals, the CL380 would be effective. There is no threat of violence and no piracy as defined by the MIA 1906 or the Nordic Plan.

As almost any event causing loss to an autonomous or unmanned ship will involve some aspect of cyber risk, stakeholders in the autonomous ship would be unlikely to ever recover for loss under their policy. The joint Cefor and Core Advokatfirma project raised concerns at a potential widening of the CL380 clause to include 'non-malicious' cyber events[82] given the inextricable aspects of cyber technology and the operation of the ship.

It has been recognised that the CL380 clause is out of date and the market is reviewing its use.[83] A solution may be for insurers to define the events they are prepared to insure and events that they perceive to be higher risk and should be subject to additional cover or excluded, rather than looking at the cause of the event. An example is the theft of cargo or the vessel as an ordinary marine peril, with the vessel used as weapon by terrorists hacking the system as a war risk. So as to balance the interests of both insurer and assured, those events can be made subject to the shipowner's exercise of due diligence in the same way as the Inchmaree clause.

IV. The Inchmaree Clause

In addition to the traditional maritime perils, hull and machinery policies provide cover for loss or damage to the subject matter insured caused by the bursting of boilers, breakage of shafts, latent defects in the hull or machinery and the negligence of the master, officers, crew or pilot. Such cover is commonly referred to as

[78] See HG Beale (gen ed), *Chitty on Contracts*, 33rd edn (London, Sweet & Maxwell, 2018) [15-012].

[79] MIA 1906, 1st schedule, Rules for Construction of Policy, r 7.

[80] T Savage and H Thomas, 'Putting the Theory into Practice' (2018) 32 *Maritime Risk International* 16.

[81] ibid.

[82] Core Advokatfirma and Cefor, 'Report: Maritime Autonomous Surface Ships: Zooming in on Civil Liability and Insurance' (December 2018) 18, available at cefor.no/industry-policy/news/mass-study.

[83] Chatfield, 'Cyber Exclusion Clauses' (2018).

an 'Inchmaree' clause[84] and is found in the Institute Hull Clauses.[85] Such clauses extend coverage beyond the traditional perils insured against and provide cover for, inter alia, loss or damage to hull and or machinery caused by the negligence of 'masters, mariners, engineers or pilots, or through any latent defect in the machinery or hull' provided that such losses do not result from a failure of due diligence on the part of the shipowner.

The particular relevance to autonomous and unmanned ships is what constitutes a latent defect, what constitutes master/crew negligence and what is required of the assured to fulfil its due diligence obligations. While the clause dates back to the end of the nineteenth century, there are relatively few cases that have considered these issues.

A. Interpretation of Latent Defects at Common Law

Initially, what was considered a latent defect was strictly and narrowly construed. For instance, weakness in design was not initially considered a latent defect as there had to be some defect in material.[86] A latent defect becoming patent was also excluded from the scope of the clause[87] and the damage caused by a latent defect had to be to another part of the hull and machinery in order for the assured to recover.[88]

The first case to positively find a latent defect was *The Caribbean Sea*,[89] where Robert Goff J held that 'the mere fact that the historical reason for a defect in hull or machinery is defective design would not of itself preclude recovery under the Inchmaree clause'.[90] In this case the casualty was not attributed to wear-and-tear, but there were fatigue cracks attributed to the manner in which the ship was designed. The owners were entitled to their claim.

The decision of Robert Goff J in *The Caribbean Sea* signalled a more expansive approach to the interpretation of the Inchmaree clause. *The Nukila*[91] extended this further and is now considered the leading authority for what is considered damage by a latent defect.

Hobhouse LJ held that there are three questions that must be asked with respect to latent defect: (1) Was there damage to the subject matter insured? (2) Did that damage occur during the period covered by the policy? (3) Was that damage

[84] Arnould (n 39) [2.32].

[85] Examples include International Hull Clauses (1 November 2003), cl 2.2; Institute Voyage Clauses Hulls, cl 4.2; Institute Voyage Clauses Freight, cl 4.2; Institute Time Clauses Hulls, cl 6.2.

[86] *Jackson v Mumford* (1902) 8 Com Cas 61, 69.

[87] *Oceanic Steamship Co v Faber* (1906) 11 Com Cas 179. This can now be covered as an additional peril by the International Hull Clauses (1 November 2003), cl 41.

[88] *Scindia Steamships (London) Ltd v London Assurance* [1937] 1 KB 639.

[89] *Prudent Tankers Ltd SA v The Dominion Insurance Co Ltd (The Caribbean Sea)* [1980] 1 Lloyd's Rep 338.

[90] [1980] 1 Lloyd's Rep 338, 347.

[91] *Promet Engineering (Singapore) Pte Ltd v Sturge (The Nukila)* [1997] 2 Lloyd's Rep 146 (CA).

caused by a latent defect in the machinery or hull of the vessel? Hobhouse LJ was at pains to correct the submission that the Inchmaree clause applies only when the damage caused is to a different part of the Hull or Machinery:[92]

> The submission based upon the use of the word part is in my judgment open to the same objections. It leads to absurd results. It provides no criterion for distinguishing between what is and what is not damage. The suggested criteria – what can be physically separated, what performs a separate function – are not derived from anything contained in the clause nor from anything said by Mr Justice Walton and Mr Justice Branson. The word part is capable of being used in a whole variety of ways depending upon the context. Its use provides no answer to any relevant question. The weld is a part just as much as is a bracket or bulkhead or plate or the totality of the leg structure.

This case led underwriters to develop the anti-*Nukila* clause found in the International Hull Clauses 2003.[93]

B. Latent Defects and the Nordic Plan

The Nordic Plan is a standard contract and an All Risks policy, meaning all perils are covered unless expressly excluded.[94] The list of exceptions includes error in design:

> Clause 12-4. Error in design, etc.
>
> If the damage is a result of error in design or faulty material, the insurer is not liable for the costs of renewing or repairing the part or parts of the hull, machinery or equipment which were not in proper condition, unless the part or parts in question had been approved by the classification society.

The commentary to the Nordic Plan states that this means:

- the part has suffered damage as a consequence of faulty material or error in design, and
- the part in question has not been approved by class in the sense described below.

If the defect in design has caused damage and was approved by a classification society, then the insurer is not liable for the cost of repairing or replacing the part itself but remains liable for the cost of repairing all consequential damage to other parts of the vessel.[95] For a fault to be an error in design it must relate to how

[92] ibid, 156.

[93] Clause 2.2.2 provides cover for damage caused by latent defects but not the cost of correcting the latent defect.

[94] The Nordic Insurance Plan of 2013, Version 2019, cl 2-8. See www.nordicplan.org/The-Plan/Part-One/Chapter-2/Section-21/#-2-8-Perils-covered-by-an-insurance-against-marine-perils.

[95] T-L Wilhelmsen, 'Hull Insurance of "Latent defects" – i.e. Errors in Design, Material or Workmanship' (2004) 46 *Scandinavian Studies in Law* 257, 262.

the ship is built, rebuilt or repaired. It includes the form or functioning of the ship, the choice of material and the process of manufacture.[96] In the same way as the common law requires a latent defect to cause some form of damage over and above the discovery of the latent defect, the Nordic Plan requires 'demonstrable damage'.[97]

The expansive interpretation of 'latent defect' is beneficial to owners of autonomous and unmanned vessels. If there are no crew on board to undertake continuous maintenance, such ships are likely to spend longer in port. They will also be subject to extensive monitoring via sensors and defects are likely to be quickly discovered and repaired. A latent defect caused by a defect in design will be recoverable both in English law[98] and under the Nordic Plan provided the vessel has been passed by a class society.

What is less clear is whether a latent defect in software is included. On the current wording of the hull and machinery policies, this appears to be unlikely at common law because the policies expressly refer to 'latent defect in the machinery or hull'. Computer software is neither of these and the words 'machinery or hull' imply some form of weakness in material, rather than code.[99] A possible alternative construction is that software is part of the machinery of the autonomous ship and, provided the owner has exercised due diligence in selecting the software and ensuring that it is updated, loss or damage caused by a defect in the software will be covered. Certain Hull and Machinery policies have separate clauses that deal with loss and damage caused by 'computer equipment' which includes software.[100] This issue clearly needs to be clarified.

The Nordic Plan does not require the element of design to be attributable to faulty material in hull or machinery. All that is required is that a defect in design or faulty material must cause demonstrable damage. Taking this a step further, if there is a design fault in the navigational software that causes the vessel to ground which causes consequential damage to the hull, arguably the shipowner could recover under the Nordic Plan but not the English hull and machinery policies.[101] This is a concern for insurers who may find themselves insuring risks that are related to research and development[102] and is likely to lead to carve-outs for coverage of errors in design relating to Hull and Machinery insurance for autonomous ships.[103]

[96] ibid.
[97] ibid, 265.
[98] *Prudent Tankers Ltd SA v The Dominion Insurance Co Ltd (The Caribbean Sea)* [1980] 1 Lloyd's Rep 338.
[99] Art IV(2)(p) of the Hague (and Hague-Visby) Rules provides a defence to the carrier and the ship for latent defects not discoverable by due diligence. Although this is not a new issue, Sir Bernard Eder has highlighted that 'as automation systems become more complex, one may assume that these issues will perhaps become increasingly important': B Eder, 'Unmanned Vessels: Challenges Ahead' [2019] *LMCLQ* 47.
[100] See, eg, British Marine's Hull and Machinery policy, available at britishmarine.com/products.
[101] At the time of writing there do not appear to be any cases on this point.
[102] Core Advokatfirma and Cefor, 'Report' (2018).
[103] ibid 17.

C. Crew Negligence

The MIA 1906 provides that the insurer is liable for the negligence of the master or crew 'even though the loss would not have happened but for the misconduct or negligence of the master or crew'.[104] The Inchmaree clauses also provide that the insurance covers loss or damage to hull and machinery caused by the 'negligence of Master Officers Crew or Pilots' subject to the shipowner's due diligence.[105]

The courts have been generous in their interpretation of this section and clause. This may be illustrated by *The Lapwing*,[106] where the master negligently docked a yacht on a slipway, not once but twice. The yacht was held to have been damaged by stranding, which was interpreted *ejusdem generis* with a peril of sea. However, Hodson J held that whether or not the damage was caused by a marine peril it was also caused by the negligence of the master and within the Institute Yacht Clauses. In *Lind v Mitchell*[107] the ship was damaged by ice and took in water. This would have been a peril of the sea if the ingress of water caused the actual total loss. However, despite only being 15 miles from the destination, the master negligently did not request towage but ordered the crew to abandon the ship and set it on fire because he thought it was a danger to navigation. The Inchmaree clause was held to be effective because the master's negligence caused the loss and the assured could recover under the policy.

In order for the assured to recover for crew negligence under this clause the obvious question is who is the functional equivalent of the 'master, officers, crew or pilot' when the ship is unmanned? The starting point is the person who is remotely controlling or monitoring an unmanned ship in the shore-control centre. Such a person potentially (but not always) has the same level of control over the navigation as an on-board master or chief navigating officer, but may not be a servant of the owner and may be employed by a third-party provider of services.[108] At present, it appears that the shore-control centres will be run and manned by ship management companies.[109] If the ship is fully autonomous, the control will be with the ship itself and not a person, making it impossible to find a functional equivalent to a master or crew.

In their responses to a CMI questionnaire on this issue,[110] some jurisdictions indicated that they did not consider shore-based operators to be equivalent

[104] s 55(2)(a).

[105] For example, International Hull Clauses (1 November 2003) cl 2.2.

[106] [1940] P 112.

[107] (1928) 31 Ll L Rep 262.

[108] In particular, vessels owned by cargo interests rather than traditional shipowners.

[109] As explained above (text to n 14), Massterly (a joint venture between Wilhelmsen and Kongsberg) will run the shore control centre for the *Yara Birkeland*: www.wilhelmsen.com/media-news-and-events/press-releases/2018/wilhelmsen-and-kongsberg-establish-worlds-first-autonomous-shipping-company.

[110] Comité Maritime International, 'Summary of the Responses to CMI Questionnaire on Unmanned Ships' (13 February 2018), available at comitemaritime.org/work/unmanned-ships.

to a master.[111] All countries that responded to the questionnaire indicated that the chief pre-programmer is not the master. Eight countries reported that the shore-based operators could not be considered crew as the legal definition required them to be on-board.[112] As it can be expected that shore control centres will operate more than one vessel, this will create a further issue as to the obligations of the shore based operator. In a scenario where two or more remote controlled vessels are at risk of collision with only one operator, that operator may find that they have to make a decision where one vessel is preserved and the other damaged.[113] The operator will have been negligent in the operation of one of the vessels. An issue also arises whether a shore-based controller ought to take control if the ship is operating autonomously and something goes wrong. If the operator fails to recognise that they ought to retake control, would that be considered negligence?

If a shore-based operator does something negligently, causing the ship to be damaged, the shipowner will arguably not recover under the Inchmaree clause as such clauses presuppose the negligent act is that of a person on board the vessel. The Institute Voyage Clauses Hulls contains a clause that covers loss caused by the negligence of the 'Master Officers Crew or Pilot' provided that the loss has not resulted from a lack of due diligence by the 'Assured, Owners, Managers or Superintendents, or any of their *onshore management*'.[114] Negligence of the shore-control centre operators would not only fall outside the clause but might also constitute a failure of due diligence by onshore management.

If the software is incorrectly preprogrammed this would not be negligence by the master or crew as the programmer would not be considered master or crew. It may be classed as a defect in design under the Nordic Plan and English law, but it is unlikely to be a latent defect, as discussed above. In the event that the negligence causes loss or damage to a third party, the shipowner's P&I Club will provide cover[115] but the shipowner is unlikely to be covered for loss or damage to the hull and machinery of the ship itself.[116]

Despite the concerns raised by the CMI, the definitions will need to be clarified as to whether the insurer will consider the shore based operators as the functional equivalent of the master. If the shore-based operators are not employed directly by the shipowner but by the provider of onshore ship management services, then any negligence of the shore-based operator will not be covered by the Inchmaree

[111] The maritime law associations of Brazil, China and Croatia stated that their law defined the master as a person on board a ship.

[112] Namely Brazil, China, Croatia, France, Holland, Singapore, the UK and the US.

[113] A Buğra, 'Insuring Remotely Operated Vessels: Tempestuous Waters for Hull Insurers?' CML Working Paper Series 19/08 (October 2019), available at https://law.nus.edu.sg/cml/wp-content/uploads/sites/8/2020/04/023_2019_Aysegul-Bugra.pdf.

[114] Institute Voyage Clauses Hulls, cl 4.2–4.3. Emphasis added.

[115] For example, the Shipowners' Club provides all risks cover for autonomous ships. See www.shipownersclub.com/insurance/autonomous.

[116] It may also be unseaworthiness and void a voyage policy. See Tsimplis (ch 12).

clause. Rather, the shipowner will need to seek damages in negligence or for breach of contract from the ship management company.[117]

A shipowner is covered for loss caused by the negligence of a pilot[118] who boards the ship to assist in the conduct of navigation in pilotage areas.[119] The requirement for a pilot to board a ship also raises issues for autonomous and unmanned ships.[120] Finland has introduced laws allowing remote pilotage subject to authorisation[121] while in Singapore it is anticipated that when an autonomous vessel enters the port there will be shore-based pilotage.[122] At common law, once a pilot has control of the vessel the pilot is in charge with the master retaining overall command.[123] This means that a shore-based operator in one jurisdiction will hand over control to a shore-based pilot in another jurisdiction. If remote pilotage is lawful there is nothing to preclude recovery for damage caused by the negligence of a pilot under the policies.

D. Due Diligence

The Inchmaree clause contains a proviso that the insurer will not be liable in the event that there has been a lack of due diligence on the part of the assured.[124] However, in order to recover under the policy, it appears the assured only needs to prove they have exercised due diligence when the insurer has made a prima facie case of want of due diligence.[125] Due diligence refers to the standard of negligence, not recklessness[126] and lack thereof means a lack of reasonable care.[127] It is a non-delegable duty[128] and the shipowner will be liable for a lack of due diligence on the part of ship managers to whom they have delegated the duty.[129]

[117] The BIMCO standard ship management agreement, SHIPMAN 2009, cl 17(b), sets out the liabilities of ship managers to shipowners.

[118] A pilot means any person not belonging to a ship who has the conduct thereof: Pilotage Act 1987, s 31(1).

[119] See European Maritime Pilots' Association: empa-pilots.eu/pilotage.

[120] L Carey, 'All Hands off Deck? The Legal Barriers to Autonomous Ships' (2017) 23 *JIML* 202, 214.

[121] Ministry of Transport and Communications (Finland) 'Remote Pilotage Allowed' (17 January 2019), available at www.lvm.fi/en/-/remote-pilotage-allowed-995692.

[122] Maritime and Port Authority 'Singapore Maritime Week 2019 Focuses on Connectivity, Innovation and Talent to position Maritime Singapore for Future Growth' (2 April 2019), available at www.mpa.gov.sg/web/portal/home/media-centre/news-releases/detail/ada319e7-f54b-44d0-94a9-282f87030214.

[123] *The Tactician* [1907] P 244 (CA), 250–51.

[124] '[P]rovided that such loss or damage has not resulted from want of due diligence by the Assured, Owners or Managers.' For example, International Hull Clauses cl 2.2; Institute Time Clauses Hulls cl 6.2; Institute Voyage Clauses Hulls cl 4.2.

[125] FD Rose, *Marine Insurance Law and Practice*, 2nd edn (London, Informa, 2012) [13.13].

[126] *Sealion Shipping Ltd v Valiant Insurance Co (The Toisa Pisces)* [2012] EWHC 50 (Comm), [2012] 1 Lloyd's Rep 252.

[127] *Versloot Dredging BV v HDI-Gerling Industrie Versicherung AG (The DC Merwestone)* [2013] EWHC 1666 (Comm), [2013] 2 Lloyd's Rep 131 [70].

[128] *Riverstone Meat Co Pty Ltd v Lancashire Shipping Co Ltd (The Muncaster Castle)* [1961] AC 807 (HL), 872; *Alize 1954 v Allianz Elementar Versicherungs AG (The CMA CGM Libra)* [2020] EWCA Civ 293, [2020] 2 Lloyd's Rep 565, [75].

[129] *Papera Traders Co Ltd v Hyundai Merchant Marine Co Ltd (The Eurasian Dream)* [2002] EWHC 118 (Comm), [2002] 1 Lloyd's Rep 719 [130].

The development of technology used in autonomous and unmanned ships is likely to change what will be considered 'due diligence'. The use of sensors which monitor and report data back to shore will, in theory, alert the shipowner to problems before they cause damage. The increasing reliance on software means that maintaining, updating and backup of systems will be critical in ensuring the shipowner has performed their due diligence obligations.

The selection and training of the shore-based operators will be subject to due diligence on the part of the shipowner. Absent direction from the IMO, it is likely that the shore-based operators will, at a minimum, need to at least be held to the standards in the International Convention on Standards of Training, Certification and Watchkeeping and the International Safety Management (ISM) Code. It is anticipated that a competently trained remote operator will need to be compliant with self-regulatory industry standards and also be trained as a seafarer.[130]

V. Seaworthiness

The MIA 1906 implies a warranty of seaworthiness in a voyage policy which, if breached, provides the insurer with a defence.[131] There is no implied seaworthiness warranty for a time policy, but if the ship is sent to sea in an unseaworthy condition with the privity of the assured, the insurer will not be liable for any loss due to unseaworthiness.[132] Under section 39(4) of the MIA, a 'ship is deemed to be seaworthy when she is reasonably fit in all respects to encounter the ordinary perils of the seas of the adventure insured'.

Incompetence or inefficiency of the master and crew can render a ship unseaworthy[133] if they have a 'disabling want of skill' or 'disabling want of knowledge'.[134] Incompetence is not the same as negligence and can derive from:

(a) an inherent lack of ability.
(b) a lack of adequate training or instruction.
(c) a lack of knowledge about a particular vessel and/or its systems.
(d) a disinclination to perform the job properly.
(e) physical or mental disability or incapacity.[135]

It is crucial that the role of the shore-based operators is clarified. If such operators are considered crew and they are incompetent, an unmanned ship can be rendered unseaworthy. The test is whether 'a reasonably prudent owner, knowing the

[130] Veal and Tsimplis (n 27) 323.
[131] MIA 1906, s 39(1).
[132] ibid, s 39(5).
[133] *The Eurasian Dream* (n 129); *Hongkong Fir Shipping Co Ltd v Kawasaki Kisen Kaisha Ltd* [1962] 2 QB 26 (CA).
[134] *The Eurasian Dream*, ibid [127].
[135] ibid.

relevant facts, [would] have allowed this vessel to put to sea with this Master and crew, with their state of knowledge, training and instruction'.[136] What a reasonably prudent owner should do is assessed against the universal practice amongst competent owners and managers.[137] This may initially raise evidential issues as there will not be established universal practice. In the short term, industry-led codes of practice, such as Maritime UK's Maritime Autonomous Surface Ships (MASS) UK Conduct Principles and Code of Practice, will be crucial in providing standards of practice.[138]

VI. Liability and Limitation

A. Liability

There are concerns that if an autonomous and unmanned ship navigates independently of human decision making utilising preprogrammed algorithms it will be difficult to find room for an assessment of fault on the part of the shipowner. In turn, this will, de facto, lead to strict liability.[139] While some believe this is a problem,[140] others believe that strict liability is the solution and a more appropriate route to take for autonomous vessels.[141]

Strict liability is an ancient concept in maritime law. At common law, the owner of a ship was a common carrier and absolutely liable for the loss of goods even if they were lost or stolen without the shipowner's privity until 1734 when the UK Parliament passed the first of the Merchant Shipping Acts.[142] Today, the International Convention on Civil Liability for Oil Pollution Damage 1992 (CLC Convention) holds a shipowner liable for damage caused by oil pollution without any requirement that a plaintiff prove negligence on the part of the shipowner.[143] In return, the shipowner is entitled to limit liability provided the damage was not caused recklessly nor with the shipowner's knowledge and intent.[144]

[136] ibid, [129], quoting Salmon J in *Hongkong Fir Shipping Co Ltd v Kawasaki Kisen Kaisha Ltd* [1961] 1 Lloyd's Rep 159, 168.

[137] *Versloot Dredging BV v HDI-Gerling Industrie Versicherung AG (The DC Merwestone)* [2013] EWHC 1666 (Comm), [2013] 2 Lloyd's Rep 131 [85].

[138] Available at www.maritimeuk.org/media-centre/publications/maritime-autonomous-surface-ships-industry-conduct-principles-code-practice.

[139] Core Advokatfirma and Cefor (n 82).

[140] ibid.

[141] B Soyer, 'Autonomous Vessels and Third-party Liabilities: The Elephant in the Room' in Soyer and Tettenborn, *New Technologies* (2019) ch 8.

[142] 7 Geo II c 65. See Lord Denning MR's discussion in *Compania Maritima San Basilio SA v The Oceanus Mutual Underwriting Association (Bermuda) Ltd (The Eurysthenes)* [1976] 2 Lloyd's Rep 171, 178 (CA).

[143] CLC Convention 1992, art III.

[144] ibid, art V.

It may seem logical to impose strict liability on the owners of autonomous and unmanned vessels. However, it is submitted that this is not desirable. First, unlike oil tankers which are all of a similar nature and carry the same risks, autonomous and unmanned vessels will fulfil different roles. Some will be cargo-carrying, some will be electric, some will be harbour vessels, some will be surveying vessels, and some passenger vessels. Some will be unmanned and remote-controlled, while others will be manned but autonomous. Second, in the short-to-medium term, some conventional ships will be operating autonomously while the crew rests.[145] Applying strict liability across the board would mean that as the manning levels and autonomy levels change throughout the voyage the shipowner will find that their liability regime shifts from the existing fault-based to strict liability. This will make identifying the risk difficult for insurers and lead to an increase in premiums.[146]

Hull and machinery policies provide 3/4ths liability cover for collisions[147] and, in the event of such a collision, the International Convention for the Unification of Certain Rules of Law Relating to Collision between Vessels 1910 (the Collision Convention 1910)[148] allocates liability based upon fault. The degree of causative (not moral)[149] fault must be proved.[150] Applying strict liability to autonomous and unmanned ships will not work within the existing framework. Indeed, it will lead to undesirable outcomes because in the event of a collision between an unmanned ship and a conventional manned ship, the unmanned ship would be strictly liable and have to prove fault on the part of the manned ship. This may be contrasted with the manned ship which would be relieved of its obligation to prove fault on the part of the unmanned vessel.

Thus, it is preferable that the liability of the shipowner continues to be treated the same way for AL0–AL3 and IMO levels 1–3, where autonomy ought to be seen as a function of a ship rather than a type of ship. This will ensure that insurers can continue to underwrite the liabilities arising from a collision in the traditional manner.[151] However, for fully autonomous ships operating at AL4–5 and IMO level 4, strict liability regime analogous to that found in the UK's Automated and Electric Vehicles Act 2018 would be appropriate. The legislation provides that in the event of an accident caused by an autonomous vehicle, the insurer will be liable for the damage.[152] If the vehicle is not insured, the owner of the vehicle is liable

[145] L Swoboda, 'Steps and Stones. En Route to (More) Autonomy', paper given at BIMCO Seminar (27 March 2019).

[146] Soyer (n 141), 107.

[147] See, for example, Institute Voyage Clauses Hulls cl 6; Institute Time Clauses cl 8 and International Hull Clauses cl 6 but note that cl 38 permits parties to agree that cl 6 is amended to provide 4/4ths cover.

[148] Maritime Conventions Act 1911 (Singapore), s 1. *cf* the UK Merchant Shipping Act 1995, s 187(1).

[149] *The Dream Star* [2017] SGHC 220, [2017] 2 Lloyd's Rep 538.

[150] *The Anneliese* [1970] 1 Lloyd's Rep 355, 363 (CA).

[151] Under the traditional hull insurance clauses an owner will have collision liability cover for 3/4ths of the damage caused by a collision. When this is the case, P&I Club cover will extend to indemnify the shipowner for 1/4th of the damage to the other vessel and cargo and property on the other vessel to the extent that those liabilities are not recoverable under the hull policy: see S Hazelwood & D Semark, *P&I Clubs Law and Practice*, 4th edn (London, Informa, 2010) [10.2].

[152] Automated and Electric Vehicles Act 2018, s 2(1).

for the damage.[153] The amount of liability insurance required is capped to the Road Traffic Act 1988.[154] The intention behind the legislation is to ensure the law relating to motor insurance and autonomous vehicles continues as 'driver-centric' rather than based on product liability.[155] In the event that the damage was caused by the fault of the car manufacturer, the manufacturer (or any third party who is liable to the injured party) is liable to the insurer.[156]

B. Limitation

That a shipowner may limit liability is 'a rule of public policy which has its origin in history and justification in convenience'.[157] Limitation ensures that shipowners can obtain insurance coverage and allows a shipowner to continue to trade in the event of a claim by depositing a fund into an appropriate court for the amount it may be liable.[158] The Convention on Limitation of Liability for Maritime Claims 1976 (LLMC 1976)[159] provides that a shipowner will lose its right to limit liability if 'if it is proved that the loss resulted from his personal act or omission, committed with the intent to cause such loss, or recklessly and with knowledge that such loss would probably result'.[160]

The LLMC extends limitation to a shipowner (which includes the owner, charterer, manager and operator of a seagoing ship)[161] and any 'person for whose act, neglect or default the shipowner is responsible'.[162] A shore-based operator will be entitled to limit its liability as the shipowner or the ship manager is responsible for its actions. However, the right to limit liability under the LLMC cannot be extended to the manufacturers and programmers of autonomous ships' navigation. If the preprogrammer of the algorithms for navigating the ship is negligent, such a person is not within the scope of the LLMC. Nor are technology providers who will have a service relationship with the shipowner as there will be continuous updates and maintenance required for the software technology.

[153] ibid, s 2(2).

[154] Under the Road Traffic Act 1988, s 145(4), the amount is £1,200,000 for damage to property. There is no limit on liability for causing personal injury or death.

[155] L Butcher and T Edmonds, House of Commons Briefing Paper, Automated and Electric Vehicles Act 2018, Briefing Paper Number CBP 8118 (15 August 2018) 3.

[156] Automated and Electric Vehicles Act 2018, s 5.

[157] *The Bramley Moore* [1964] P 200, 220 (Lord Denning MR).

[158] M Tsimplis, 'The Liabilities of the Vessel' in Y Baatz (ed), *Maritime Law*, 5th edn (London, Informa, 2020) 302. For a discussion of the moral and practical arguments for and against limitation of liability for ships, see the famous polemic between Lord Mustill, 'Ships are Different – Or are They?' [1993] *LMCLQ* 490 and D Steel, 'Ships are Different: The Case for Limitation of Liability' [1995] *LMCLQ* 77.

[159] There are currently 56 contracting states representing 58.34% of world tonnage to the LLMC 1976 and 60 contracting states representing 69.44% of world tonnage to the LLMC Protocol 1996.

[160] Art 4.

[161] ibid, art 1(2).

[162] ibid, art 1(4).

Therefore it is submitted that a model similar to the liability regime found in the Automated and Electric Vehicles Act 2018 (UK) where any loss caused by the negligence of the technology provider is channelled to the shipowner (or insurer) with the technology provider in turn indemnifying the shipowner (or insurer) for such loss.[163] Therefore the limitation of liability regime remains operative unless the shipowner has failed in their due diligence with respect to the selection of the technology provider. The LLMC has been very effective in permitting insurers to make an assessment of their maximum liability because of the tonnage limits. Removal of the protection of limitation of liability for autonomous ships may have a chilling effect on their development as the cost of insurance will be too high if underwriters are unable to assess the limit of risk.

VII. Conclusions

The introduction of autonomous and unmanned ships heralds a new era in shipping. As with any new development, new risks are bound to emerge. How those risks will be assessed by insurers will involve observation, prediction and also reflection to see how new developments have been accommodated in the past. With this in mind, it is critical that shipowners, ship managers and insurers are clear on the risks covered, the standard of due diligence required and whether the limitation regimes apply to unmanned and autonomous ships in order to manage their risk exposure and liability.

The commercial relationship between insurers and shipowners is well established and, historically, the insurance market has responded to new technology with appropriate clauses and policies. The law governing these clauses and policies has supported their development without the requirement of legal reform. Reform to insurance law is driven by the notion of fairness and balance rather than by developments in technology.[164] It would therefore appear that the law of marine insurance will continue to accommodate new developments without any significant upheaval providing the risks are not significantly different.

[163] In the absence of any legislative requirement, shipowners could contractually require technology providers to take out insurance that covers them for the cost of indemnifying the shipowner.

[164] Most significantly, the reforms introduced by the Insurance Act 2015. For background to the reforms, see Law Commission and Scottish Law Commission, 'Insurance Contract Law: Business Disclosure, Warranties, Insurers' Remedies for Fraudulent Claims, and Late Payment' Law Com No 353 / Scot Law Com No 238 (July 2014).

12

On the Carriage of Goods on Autonomous, Remotely Controlled, Crewed and Uncrewed Ships

MIKIS TSIMPLIS*

I. Introduction

Autonomous marine craft have been operating for several decades, primarily in the form of autonomous underwater vehicles (AUV), used for surveying, research and military purposes. The legal status[1] of such vehicles has not been clear in all respects[2] but their use has not been problematic because their small size and underwater usage diminished the risk of substantial damage to other sea users. The development of autonomous commercial ships has been considered more recently, following the development of prototype autonomous cars and the use of aerial drones. While there is a common thread amongst autonomous cars, air drones and marine craft, the differential development of each led to the incorporation of each type of craft to the corresponding sectoral law instead of the development of a law of robotics applicable to all unmanned craft on land, air, and sea.

A. The Legality of Autonomous Ships

Accompanying advances in engineering, there have been several studies discussing the legal difficulties of operating autonomous ships.[3] A number of points can be

* Professor, School of Law, City University of Hong Kong.

[1] ED Brown and NJJ Gaskell, 'The Operation of Autonomous Underwater Vehicles', Vol 2: Report on the Law (London, Society for Underwater Technology, 2000).

[2] K Bork, J Karstensen, M Visbeck and A Zimmermann, 'The Legal Regulation of Floats and Gliders – in Quest of a New Regime?' (2008) 39 *Ocean Development and International* Law 298, 307; RB Wynn, VAI Huvenne, TP Le Bas, BJ Murton, DP Connelly, BJ Bett, HA Ruhl, KJ Morris, J Peakall, DR Parsons, EJ Sumner, SE Darby, RM Dorrell and JE Hunt, 'Autonomous Underwater Vehicles (AUVs): Their Past, Present and Future Contributions to the Advancement of Marine Geoscience' (2014) 352 *Marine Geology* 451.

[3] E van Hooydonk, 'The Law of Unmanned Merchant Shipping – An Exploration' (2014) 20 *JIML* 403; R Veal, M Tsimplis, A Serdy, S Quinn, and A Ntovas, *Liability for Operation in Unmanned Maritime Vehicles with Differing Levels of Autonomy* (Brussels, European Defence Agency, 2016) (available

derived from these studies. The first is that there is consensus that a structure that looks like a ship and is commercially used in the same way as a conventional ship should be regulated as a ship. The second is that the operation of an autonomous ship within the territorial seas of a launching state is exclusively a matter for that coastal state.[4] While coastal states are under international obligations in relation to navigational safety, the way these will be resolved with respect to autonomous and uncrewed ships is a regulatory problem under the national law of the coastal state. The third is that under international law navigational rights are granted to states and not to structures of whatever kind. It is therefore a matter for the flag state to designate an autonomous system as a ship, thus granting it the corresponding navigational rights. Fourthly, difficulties could arise when an autonomous ship, which has been granted ship status by the flag state, enters the jurisdiction and, particularly, a port of a state which does not grant ship status to such an entity or implements laws inconsistent with the autonomous or uncrewed character of the visiting ship.[5] This particular difficulty is of fundamental importance for the development of autonomous commercial ships because it makes international harmonisation a prerequisite for trading. Thus, while the current law is capable of encompassing the operation of autonomous ships, it requires detailed regulatory work and clarification in order to oversee the international use of this type of ship. The greatest challenge will arguably be to prove that autonomous ships are as safe for navigation and the environment as conventional ships. This is an operational challenge quite distinct from the question as to the ability of autonomous ships to comply with existing safety regulations.[6]

B. Commercial Challenges for Autonomous Ships

As no unsurmountable legal obstacles[7] have so far been identified for the operation of autonomous or uncrewed ships, it is arguable that the success of such ships

from Paul O'Brien, European Defence Agency, paul.obrien@eda.europea.eu); R Veal and M Tsimplis, 'The Integration of Unmanned Ships into the *Lex Maritima*' [2017] *LMCLQ* 303; HM Ringbom and R Veal, 'Unmanned Ships and the International Regulatory Framework' (2017) 23 *JIML* 100; R Veal, M Tsimplis and A Serdy (2019), 'The Legal Status and Operation of Unmanned Maritime Vehicles' (2019) 50 Ocean Development & International Law 23; P Dean and H Clack, 'Autonomous Shipping and Maritime Law' in B Soyer and A Tettenborn (eds), *New Technologies, Artificial Intelligence and Shipping law in the 21st Century* (London, Informa, 2019) 67; B Soyer, 'Autonomous Vessels and Third Party Liabilities: The Elephant in the Room' in Soyer and Tettenborn (eds), *New Technologies* (ibid) 105; S Baughen, 'Who is the Master now?: Regulatory and Contractual Challenges of Unmanned Vessels' in Soyer and Tettenborn (eds), *New Technologies* (ibid) 129; F Stevens, 'Carrier Liability for Unmanned Ships. Goodbye Crew, Hello Liability' in Soyer and Tettenborn (eds), *New Technologies* (ibid) 148.

[4] Veal and Tsimplis, 'The Integration of Unmanned Ships' (2017).

[5] See, eg, the requirement that there must be a master on board, submission of Japan to the CMI: comitemaritime.org/work/mass.

[6] This is the area where great confusion exists. Many engineering studies have focused on proving compliance of autonomous ships with the Collision Regulations (COLREGS), a fundamental misunderstanding of navigational safety of which the COLREGS form only a part.

[7] L Kretschmann, H-C Burmeister and C Jahn, 'Analyzing the Economic Benefit of Unmanned Autonomous Ships: An Exploratory Cost-comparison Between an Autonomous and a Conventional Bulk Carrier' (2017) 25 *Research in Transportation Business & Management* 76.

depends primarily on the financial model supporting them.[8] Uncrewed ships can provide sustainability benefits in economic, environmental and social terms.[9] However, assessing the financial impact of the use of autonomous and uncrewed ships is no trivial matter. The construction of technologically more advanced ships with autonomous navigation systems is much more expensive than commercial ships. Where the crew is removed a significant saving is made but, with an underlying assumption that highly trained crew will be needed at the ports of loading and discharge, it appears that the crewing costs are balanced between uncrewed and conventional ships. The main financial benefit for uncrewed ships appears to stem from the removal of crew accommodation which permits a more aerodynamic and thus more energy efficient ship design. Thus it is the change in the ship's shape rather than the reduction in crew costs that provides the financial benefit.[10]

To the extent that autonomous ships reduce the risk of accidents an additional unaccounted for financial benefit is to be expected from a corresponding reduction in collision damage and insurance costs.[11]

However, while the presumed increase in navigational safety will reduce corresponding hull, cargo and third-party risks, potential increased risks for cargo damage could arise from the reduction or complete removal of the crew on board. This necessitates a reconsideration of the distribution of the risk of cargo damage between cargo interests and the carrier.

C. The Framework of Analysis

This chapter will examine the legal framework for the carriage of goods on autonomous and uncrewed ships.[12] An important working assumption is that loading, handling, stowage and discharge of the cargo will be performed in the conventional way but that the ocean leg will be performed by an autonomous ship which may have a caretaker crew or may be completely crewless. It is also assumed that pilotage in and out of ports will be undertaken conventionally and that no compulsory pilotage during the voyage will be required.[13]

[8] See Veal and Tsimplis [2017] (n 3).

[9] Kretschmann, Burmeister and Jahn, 'Unmanned Autonomous Ships' (2017).

[10] ibid. A bulk carrier was used as the basis for calculation and several assumptions were made concerning the financial changes implied by an uncrewed ship. The savings in the operational costs were almost completely counterbalanced by increases in the port call and shipbuilding costs. When the design was optimised for fuel savings, significant savings were made.

[11] Note that given the increased amount of wiring and electronics that are required on an autonomous ship, the cost of removing the hazardous materials before recycling of an uncrewed ship is likely to be higher. The lockdown response to the COVID-19 outbreak also highlights an advantage uncrewed autonomous ships will have under similar situations as the lack of crew will minimise the possibility of transmission of the virus, the difficulty with crew changes, and the problems of caring for infected seafarers when port states refuse to permit infected ships to use their ports.

[12] See T Karilis, 'Maritime Law Issues Related to the Operation of Unmanned Autonomous Cargo Ships' (2018) 17 *WMU Journal of Maritime Affairs* 119; Stevens, 'Carrier Liability for Unmanned Ships' (2019); Van Hooydonk, 'The Law of Unmanned Merchant Shipping' (2014).

[13] Discussion of the navigational and environmental requirements during the voyage of an autonomous ship will be the subject of later study.

The applicable legal and commercial standards were devised for crewed ships navigating under the command of a master. In this chapter, autonomy means navigation which, while performed, is independent of human intervention. The most challenging scenario involves an autonomous uncrewed ship, that is, a ship where navigational decision-making is left to the ship's computers and where there is no possibility of human intervention in such decisions or in incidents occurring on board. Where a caretaker crew is available, interventions may be possible when dangerous situations arise, including the possibility of switching to a conventional mode of navigation. Remotely controlled ships provide two alternative scenarios in which the navigational control has been taken away from the ship but there is supervision from a remotely located operator. The possibility of intervention in case of system failure or other contingency will, again, depend on whether a caretaker crew is on board or not.

The principal research question is whether the legal framework for the carriage of goods by sea can, perhaps with some modification, accommodate the use of autonomous or remotely controlled ships as the performing platform and, if so, whether this is the case irrespective of the presence of caretaker crew on board. If the current legal framework proves unfavourable for the development of such ships, this will have significant consequences. It is argued that in such a case the technological development of commercial ships using autonomous technology will be inhibited until the legal framework allocating liability changes or until new business models that can accept the modified allocation of risk materialise.

II. The Normative Requirement: Taking Reasonable Care of the Goods

The entrustment of the property of one person to another for carriage gives rise to several overlapping legal obligations. Bailment,[14] liability in negligence and liability in contract are all relevant and interlinked.[15]

A contract of carriage of goods by sea is considered as a bailment for reward on terms.[16] The terms are found in the contract of carriage, such as a charterparty or, more usually, a contract evidenced by a bill of lading.[17] In the absence of specific contractual terms, bailment imposes on the bailee an obligation to take reasonable

[14] See OW Holmes Jr, 'Common Carriers and the Common Law' (1879) 13 *American Law Review* 609. The argument developed there counteracts the belief by English judges that bailment was based on Roman law. See S Baughen, 'Bailment or Conversion? Misdelivery Caims Against Non-contractual Carriers' [2006] *LMCLQ* 411.

[15] For a comparison between these three heads of claim, see S Baughen, 'Bailment's Continuing Role in Cargo Claims' [1999] *LMCLQ* 393.

[16] *Volcafe Ltd v Cia Sud Americana de Vapores (trading as CSAV)* [2018] UKSC 61, [2019] AC 358 [8].

[17] The bailment may continue where the charterparty comes to an end: see, eg, *Petroleo Brasileiro SA v ENE Kos 1 Ltd (The Kos) (No 2)* [2012] UKSC 17, [2012] 2 AC 164.

care of the goods[18] and to account to the bailor for any damage or loss to the goods.[19] The bailee can only escape liability if it has exercised reasonable care in looking after the goods or by proving that the lack of care was not causative of the damage suffered. The burden of proof of establishing either reasonable care or the non-causative character of any breach of the duty is on the bailee.[20]

Where the bailed property is under risk the bailee has an additional duty to take reasonable measures to protect the property in his possession. This proposition is supported by several judicial dicta. In *Christy v Row*,[21] a case where the cargo could not be fully delivered, Lord Mansfield CJ said that:

> The natural justice of the matter seems obvious; that a master should do that which a wise and prudent man would think most conducive to the benefit of all concerned. But it appears to be wholly voluntary; I do not know that he is bound to do it; and yet, if it were a cargo of cloth or other valuable merchandise, it would be of great hardship that he might be at liberty to cast it overboard. It is singular that such a question should at this day remain undecided.[22]

This dictum was approved and formed the basis of decision by Sir Robert Phillimore in *Cargo ex Argos*, where cargo was returned to London following unsuccessful attempts for its delivery at Le Havre.[23]

In *Notara v Henderson*,[24] a cargo of beans became wet due to a collision, an excepted peril, under the contract of carriage. The claimant shippers, the owners of the cargo, requested that the beans be discharged and dried at the port reached after the collision, but the master refused to do so. Willes J, delivering the judgment of the Exchequer Chamber, held that there was a duty imposed upon

> the master, as representing the shipowner, to take reasonable care of the goods intrusted to him, not merely in doing what is necessary to preserve them on board the ship during the ordinary incidents of the voyage, but also in taking reasonable measures to check and arrest their loss, destruction, or deterioration, by reason of accidents, for the necessary effects there is, by reason of the exception in the bill of lading, no original liability.[25]

[18] *Volcafe* (n 16) [8], held that the strict liability of the common carrier, subject only to the exceptions of Act of God and Queen's enemies is 'a no longer a useful paradigm for the common law liability of the shipowner'. This is arguably sound and is supported by various analyses: see JH Beale Jr, 'Carrier's Liability Its History' (1897–1898) 11 *Harvard Law Review* 158; GJ Thompson, 'Relation of Common Carrier of Goods and Shipper and Its Incidents of Liability' (1924–1925) 38 *Harvard Law Review* 28.

[19] *Volcafe* (n 16) [9].

[20] ibid. For discussion of the boundaries of this statement see N Palmer, 'The Case of the Vanishing Lovers: Bailment and the Burden of Proof' (2011) 16 *Art Antiquity & Law* 85.

[21] *Christy v Row* (1808) 1 Taunt 300, 127 ER 849.

[22] ibid, 315; 855.

[23] (1873) LR 5 PC 134 concerned an action *in rem* against a ship for cargo. The owner of the ship claimed against the shipper for freight (payable on discharge), freight back to London and demurrage for the delays incurred. In approving the shipowner's claim, the Privy Council stated (at 165), 'a duty is cast on the master in many cases of accident and emergency to act for the safety of the cargo, in such manner as may be best under the circumstances in which it may be placed; and that, as a correlative right, he is entitled to charge its owner with the expenses properly incurred in so doing' (Sir Montague Smith).

[24] *Notara v Henderson* (1872) LR 7 QB 225 (Ex Ch).

[25] ibid, 235.

These two cases indicate that when the cargo is in the hands of the sea carrier it has to be looked after until it is handed back and, where there is an accident, an additional duty arises to reduce damage to cargo arising from it.

Both cases that support the existence of a duty on the bailee to take all reasonable measures to protect and preserve the cargo carried by sea expressly mention them as duties of the master of the ship.[26] However, because the bailment on terms is with the master's employer and not with the master, the correct position is arguably that such obligations are imposed on the carrier. Therefore, the bailee must seek assistance in the form of salvage or towage and take other reasonable actions to preserve the goods even if a master is not present on board. This is an important obligation for cargo owners and underwriters because the proper discharge of this obligation reduces cargo losses and keeps insurance costs down.[27] The existence of such an obligation is further supported by the fact that where such measures have been taken with the knowledge of the bailor liability for compensation arises.[28]

Satisfying these requirements is easier when a caretaker crew is on board, whether the platform is remotely controlled or fully autonomous. With respect to the risk of cargo damage, the presence of a crew can be considered as providing an equivalence with conventional ships. Where the ship is remotely controlled, even if uncrewed, there will be at least some awareness of the cargo situation by the controller. If communication with the ship is lost then there will be awareness of the loss of such communication and an appreciation of some degree of risk.

Where, however, an autonomous and uncrewed ship is considered, discharge of the duty to look after the cargo by the bailee will only be possible if automated systems capable of situations where assistance needs to be sought are developed. Such systems will need to be integrated with the software system managing the ship's systems and should be linked with sensory monitors on board the ship. Where, for example, there is loss of power, or a sudden rise of temperature on any part of the ship, the software should be capable of alerting the shipowner or, in appropriate cases, call for salvage services.

In order to care for the cargo on board an autonomous uncrewed ship at standards equivalent to those on a crewed ship, the controlling systems must be linked with sensors providing information on the ship's and the cargo's condition. Sensors which monitor individual containers are already in use and, similarly, environmental characterictics of cargo spaces, for example temperature and humidity, are also easy to monitor. Linking such sensors through an automated system capable

[26] See nn 23 and 24.

[27] How the bailment relationship operates where a caretaking crew brings the autonomous ship in and out of the ports could depend on the commercial relationships in place. Where, for example, the caretaking crew are independent contractors and not employees of the shipowner they and their employer may not be the bailee.

[28] See *Cargo ex Argos* (n 23) and *China Pacific SA v Food Corp of India (The Winson)* [1982] AC 939 (HL).

of identifying abnormal readings is, also, not particularly challenging, nor is the operation of fire extinguishers when fire is detected. However synthesising all the incoming information and deciding on whether assistance is needed will be more challenging for an automated system. Furthermore, accepting assistance will require facilitating unsupervised access to an uncrewed ship, increasing the ship's vulnerability to acts of piracy or theft. If such risks are practically increased they will also be factors contributing to increased risks for cargo losses and liability.

Consider a remotely controlled ship without a crew, where there is a failure of the supervisory systems. This could be caused by a developing risk, for example, a fire which is destroying the ship's computers. At the same time, it may also be caused solely by a failure of the communication systems of the ship, a software error, or even a failure in the network of the communication provider. The interruption of communication will lead to the inference ashore that a risk is developing on board the ship. However it will be impossble to tell whether the risk is real or a false alarm. What should a reasonable shipowner and bailee of the cargo do in such a case? Arguably, the appropriate approach is to act in a way that will prevent damage by seeking assistance when communications are lost, rather than risking the loss of the ship and the cargo. If the risk is real, existing salvage law will be able to resolve the contribution of each party to the assistance. On the other hand, false alarms could lead to disputes between salvors and cargo interests in respect of cargo liability for the cost of the assistance provided.[29]

In the case of an autonomous and uncrewed ship, the duty of the bailee will arguably be to program the ship's computers so as to automatically seek salvage assistance and inform the shipowner, without delay, when problems or malfunctions occur. This is because there will be no first-hand knowledge of the ship's and the cargo's situation and no possibility for self-help on board.[30] Delay in seeking such assistance could be a breach of the reasonable care requirement because such delay will probably make it more difficult to locate the ship and land crew on board in order to confirm and resolve the problem. Such delays could lead to losses for which the bailee will become accountable. If the situation becomes dangerous and requires salvage, the cargo owners will become liable to pay their share in proportion to cargo's respective salved value.[31]

Uncrewed autonomous or remotely controlled ships are more likely to need external assistance and are more prone to the consequences of false alarms. This follows from the fact that the presence of a crew could resolve at least some problems and could provide first-hand information on the situation on board. In addition, it also flows from a preventive approach to risk and the duty of a bailee to preserve the entrusted property.

[29] See below, III.

[30] Redundancy of systems in autonomous ships is expected but this scenario assumes that this has not been successful in resolving the problem.

[31] International Salvage Convention 1989, art 13(2).

III. Cargo Liability for Salvage

Will a call for assistance issued either automatically by an autonomous uncrewed ship or by the shipowner who believes that such ship may be in danger lead to an obligation on cargo to contribute to a salvage award?

The International Salvage Convention 1989 authorises the shipowner and the master to bind the cargo owner to a salvage contract,[32] provided the property involved is in danger.[33] As a consequence, even without a master on board there is express statutory authority that the shipowner should be able to agree salvage contracts which will be binding on the cargo interests.

As there is no definition of danger in the Convention, the definition of danger under pre-existing English law is normally used. This requires the existence of real danger, reasonably apprehended.[34] The danger does not need to be present at the time salvage is sought provided that it is reasonably expected that it will arise before self-help can resolve the dangerous situation. Thus a ship immobilised by an engine failure is generally in danger even if the weather is calm or where the ship is safely anchored but there is no possibility of effective repairs being undertaken.[35] The presence of danger is to be decided objectively by the judge or arbitrator. The master's opinion is not conclusive in this respect.[36] For an uncrewed ship the option of self-help will be reduced[37] and the test for the presence of danger will be more easily satisfied than for conventional ships.

Disputes are likely to arise where there is no real danger, either because there has been a false alarm or where there has been a problem that does not affect the safety, in the ordinary sense, of the ship and the cargo directly, for example a loss of communication with an autonomous ship which otherwise continues to operate normally and can perform the voyage without assistance.[38] In each of these cases, the cargo owner could, under current legal arrangements, refuse payment of a salvage contribution because if the property is not in danger, the 1989 Salvage Convention will not operate and the shipowner will have no authority to bind the cargo to any salvage contract.[39]

[32] Art 6.

[33] Salvage operations are defined in art 1(a) as 'any act or activity undertaken to assist a vessel or any other property in danger'.

[34] *The Hamtun and the St John* [1999] 1 Lloyd's Rep 883, 889.

[35] *Troilus v Glenogle* [1951] AC 820 (HL); *Tsavliris Salvage (International) Ltd v Guangdong Shantou Overseas Chinese Materials Marketing Co (The Pa Mar)* [1999] 1 Lloyd's Rep 338.

[36] *The Hamtun and the St John* (n 34).

[37] It cannot be said that self-help will be non-existent because it is possible to think of situations where a small fire is automatically extinguished, a software error corrected by automatic rebooting, or where a hardware error is covered by increased redundancy. There would be an expectation for such self-help arrangements to be built into the new generation of ships.

[38] Another case could be where there is a problem but because the ship is close to land, self-help by landing a crew may be an option.

[39] The operation of art 6 of the Salvage Convention requires that salvage operations are taking place. Under art 1, this requires that the property is in danger.

Salvage contracts normally include an undertaking that the signing party acts as agent for the owners of property on board the ship and that they are bound to the contract.[40] Where the cargo owners successfully avoid the binding nature of the shipowner's authority under art 6 of the 1989 Salvage Convention the salvors will be looking to the shipowner for the payment of the whole of any salvage reward, including any part which will normally be payable by the cargo owners. This will be claimed as a breach of the warranty of authority under the salvage contract. Of course, if there is no danger to the ship the reward due under article 13 of the Salvage Convention 1989 will be small and may not satisfy the expectations of the salvors. Frequent false alarms may make salvors reluctant to get involved with autonomous ships without some undertaking that costs and some profits will be recovered in case there is a false alarm. Modification of standard contracts to determine the cost and allocate the financial risk of false alarms with respect to autonomous ships will likely be needed.

Prior to the enactment of the 1989 Salvage Convention, English law required the master to become an agent of necessity in order to be able to bind other property owners to a salvage agreement.[41] The agency of necessity was created when there was a situation of danger making assistance necessary, coupled with difficulties in communicating with owners of the cargo such that obtaining their instructions was impractical. In these circumstances, the master must act bona fide in the interests of cargo and must also be reasonable in entering into the contract. An autonomous ship in danger but which has its communication systems intact will normally be able to communicate with all cargo owners by the sending of an automated email. In such circumstances, no agency of necessity could be claimed. For an uncrewed remotely controlled ship the operator will also retain the capacity to communicate with the cargo owners and so no agency of necessity could arguably arise. Where the communication systems fail and the ship is fully autonomous there will then be a question as to who will be the agent of necessity. If a caretaker crew is on board, it could be argued that the person in charge of the caretaker crew will be in the position of the master where danger arises, even if it is not in control of the navigation of the ship. But where there is no crew on board, it will be difficult to argue that such agency of necessity can be granted to the autonomous system itself. Attributing legal powers to computer systems to act on behalf of the property is currently too far-fetched. It is also doubtful that an automated request for assistance given to the computer's systems and resulting in the engagement of salvors could be considered as an agreement for salvage concluded under the authority of shipowner or the master of the ship and falling under art 6 of the Salvage Convention 1989. Without an express authorisation granted by cargo interests, perhaps on shipment, such a request for salvage assistance will arguably

[40] See, eg, Lloyd's Standard Form of Salvage Agreement (LOF 2020), cl K.

[41] See *Industrie Chimiche Italia Centrale v Alexander G Tsavliris & Sons Maritime Co (The Choko Star)* [1987] 1 Lloyd's Rep 508 (CA).

not be binding on the cargo and the cargo obligations for salvage will need to be determined outside any contractual agreement.

It can therefore be concluded that the obligation to protect and preserve the cargo requires that new ships have systems that can seek assistance automatically. These could lead to an increased number of salvage situations in the case of uncrewed ships due to the reduced self-help and first-hand assessment of the situation. More disputes are likely to arise when self-help could have been provided or where there is a false alarm caused by the failure of communication systems. Contractual modifications may be able to deal with such issues, provided that compulsory legal arrangements regulating the carriage of goods by sea permit them.

IV. Contracts for the Carriage of Goods by Sea

Contractual terms modify any existing bailment obligations.[42] Where the goods in transit are not to be sold to a third party, such as where the charterer ships its own goods, the parties can make any contractual arrangements permitted by the legal system where the transaction takes place. In such a case, the parties can distribute the risks of cargo damage in accordance with their commercial interests. Normally the issues that need to be resolved concern the carrier's undertakings with respect to the seaworthiness of the ship and the liability for damage to the goods, an implied or express term on deviation, and arrangements concerning the dispatch of the voyage. This is perhaps the easiest framework to perceive the usage of autonomous or remotely controlled ships whether crewed or uncrewed. The participating legal entities have the liberty to redistribute the risks and develop relevant clauses to give effect to such agreements.

V. Regulatory Interventions and the Contract of Carriage

Where the goods are consigned to a third party (or there is an option that they may be so consigned) and the contractual rights are transferred to it,[43] the freedom of the contracting parties is statutorily constrained. The statutory constraints rectify the abuse of the unequal bargaining power between carriers and shippers which transferred risks to consignees they have never had an opportunity to negotiate.[44]

[42] They do not, under English law, replace bailment with contractual rights.

[43] By virtue of statutory provisions, eg, the Carriage of Goods by Sea Act 1992.

[44] In particular, exclusion and limitation of liability clauses, though valid under English law, were considered against public policy in the former colonies of the British Empire.

International Conventions have been developed in order to resolve this problem, the first being the Hague Rules 1924.[45] Differences in the influence of colonial powers and colonies in due course gave way to differences between developed and developing economies.[46] International intervention, initiated through UNCTAD and UNCITRAL, has attempted to renegotiate the protective framework for the third parties.[47] This process led to the adoption of the Hamburg Rules,[48] which followed an earlier attempt resulting in the Hague-Visby Rules.[49] The increased negotiating powers of global shippers has led to one further effort to permit some parties to exclude the compulsory regime altogether. This perceived need together with a wish to provide a broader, optionally multimodal and more flexible international framework, has led to the development of the United Nations Convention on Contracts for the International Carriage of Goods Wholly or Partly by Sea (the 'Rotterdam Rules').[50]

VI. Normative Requirements

The regulatory regime for the carriage of goods by sea points towards four main norms. First, an identification of who should be liable for cargo loss or damage. Second, minimum standards of performance which, when complied with, discharge the responsible person from liability. These standards cannot be derogated from[51] and trump contractually made arrangements. Third, limitation of liability rights granted to the carrier. Finally, the establishment of shipper's liability for damages arising from the unauthorised shipment of goods endangering the ship or the commercial venture.

The variation of arrangements between the four international legal regimes reflect efforts to balance the negotiating powers, based on fairness and social acceptance, between shipping and cargo interests. There has been no effort to set the legal arrangements on a financial basis, although some views have been expressed that the sharing of financial responsibility is not optimal as a matter of economics because of overlapping insurance requirements. The only economic

[45] International Convention for the Unification of Certain Rules of Law Relating to Bills of Lading (Brussels, 25 August 1924).

[46] 'General Assembly Declaration on the Establishment of a New International Economic Order' (1974) 68 *American Journal of International Law* 798.

[47] See 'Consideration of Inclusion of International Shipping Legislation Among the Priority Topics in the Work Programme', UN General Assembly, A/CN.9/23, 4 February 1969.

[48] United Nations Convention on the Carriage of Goods by Sea (Hamburg, 31 March 1978).

[49] The Hague Rules amended by the Protocol to Amend the International Convention for the Unification of Certain Rules of Law Relating to Bills of Lading (Brussels, 23 February 1968).

[50] New York, 11 December 2008. The official Signing Ceremony took place in Rotterdam on 23 September 2009 but the Rules are not yet in force.

[51] Hague and Hague-Visby Rules, art III, r 8; Hamburg Rules, art 23; Rotterdam Rules, art 79. For the latter, *cf* art 80 which permits changes with respect to volume contracts and art 81 for the carriage of live animals.

studies at national level cover the extent of the applicable limits of liability and the extent that these are high enough to operate only in a small percentage of cases of loss or damage. Instead the international legal regimes are normally benchmarked by comparion to the freedom, originally available, to the carrier, to diminish its liability through contractual agreements.

The development of autonomous and remotely controlled ships, with or without crew, challenges the benchmarking exercise and the levels of limitation of liability. At this stage of technological development the risks involved are almost completely unknown and this means that they may either be too high or too low when compared with current risks. The question as to who bears the risk during the development of this technology needs to be addressed and will depend on the allocation of liability under the compulsory liability regimes.

If it can be proved that it is, financially, optimal to allocate the risk of loss or damage to one party only, then the new technology provides an opportunity to do so. The currently unquantifiable probability of the risk involved and the negotiations that are needed to allocate them, may lead to reluctance to adopt marine autonomy. The simplification of the legal and insurance framework that can be achieved by allocating all risks to the carrier could provide both a financially optimal situation, with respect to insurance costs, and also give this new type of ship a commercial advantage over conventional competitors. Leaving to one side the possibility of such a radical reassessment of risk allocation, this chapter will now examine the four main norms as potential bases for regulating the carriage of goods on board the new generation of ships with a view to identifying the increased risks to the contracting parties.

VII. The Person Liable for the Loss of or Damage to the Goods

All the international liability regimes accept that the contractual carrier[52] is liable to a third-party holder of a bill of lading or equivalent document for the loss or damage of goods.[53] While delay in the delivery of the goods is expressly dealt with under the Hamburg Rules[54] and the Rotterdam Rules[55] this is not expressly dealt with under the Hague (or Hague-Visby) Rules.[56] Additional parties involved in the

[52] Art I(a), Hague and Hague Visby Rules; art 1.1 Hamburg Rules; art 1(5) Rotterdam Rules.

[53] Delay in the delivery is expressly dealt with in art 5(1) of the Hamburg Rules and art 4 of the Rotterdam Rules, but not expressly in the Hague or Hague-Visby Rules. The increasing significance of the 'just in time' delivery which optimises the transport chain and also the use of land transport and storage facilities would arguably make the delay provisions concerning autonomous and remotely controlled ships even more important for traders.

[54] Art 5(1).

[55] Art 4.

[56] Art I defining the carrier and arts III and IV defining the carrier's obligations. Note that the wording in the Hague and Hague-Visby Rules includes references to the liability of the ship, *in rem* liability.

performance of the contract of carriage are also liable under the Hamburg Rules[57] and the Rotterdam Rules,[58] but not under the Hague and Hague-Visby Rules.[59]

The use of autonomous or remotely controlled ships is not expected to modify the contractual character of carriage of goods by sea so this is expected to remain the applicable norm. It is, however, reasonable to expect that where the performance of the contract is entrusted to automated on-board systems, cargo interests will expect the widest cover of liability for cargo damage arising from malfunctioning of such systems. This is more likely to be achieved if both the performing and the contractual carrier are liable. Thus the more recent liability regimes are, arguably, better than the Hague and Hague-Visby Rules.

VIII. The Standards of Performance

The application of the Carriage of Goods by Sea Conventions to autonomous and remotely controlled ships becomes more complicated when one considers the conditions under which the carrier's liability is discharged. The simplest arrangement is that adopted under the Hamburg Rules, and although historically this is in reverse order, it is easier to start from this point for the purposes of this chapter.

A. The Hamburg Rules

The Hamburg Rules provide that the carrier is liable during the whole period the goods are in its charge[60] unless the carrier proves that it and its servants or agents took all reasonable measures to avoid the cause and the consequences of the damage.[61] Thus, where the carrier can prove that it and its servants and agents have not been negligent in looking after the goods and have responded properly where a risk to the goods has arisen there is no liability on the carrier. The general standard adopted is very close to the standard for bailment[62] except that there are some additional exceptions of liability not available under a pure bailment arrangement. These include special rules for damage caused by fire,[63] damage to cargoes of

[57] The actual carrier, Hamburg Rules, art 1(2).

[58] Performing party and maritime performing party, Rotterdam Rules, arts 1(6) and 1(7).

[59] At least not under the English law interpretation of these Rules.

[60] Hamburg Rules, art 4.1. See art 4.2 for when the carrier is in charge of the goods.

[61] Hamburg Rules, art 5.1 (reinforced by the 'Common understanding adopted by the United Nations Conference on the Carriage of Goods by Sea').

[62] A bailment relationship between the carrier and the third-party bill of lading holder will only exist if an attornment has been effected. See, eg, *Mitsui & Co Ltd v Novorossiysk Shipping Co (The Gudermes)* [1993] 1 Lloyd's Rep 311 (CA), 324.

[63] Art 5.4. In such a case the carrier is liable only where the claimant proves that the fire or its consequences were caused by negligence by the carrier and/or his servants and agents.

live animals,[64] damage to unauthorised deck cargo[65] and situations where efforts to saving life or property are the cause of the cargo damage.[66]

For autonomous or remotely controlled ships to be attractive to cargo interests these should support standards of reasonable care of the goods at least as good as those on board conventional ships. Under the assumptions made here, concerns about the capability of preserving the standards for cargo care on board autonomous ships may only arise for the voyage period, because it is assumed that a crew oversees or undertakes cargo operations in port.

The challenge of meeting the standards for conventional ships will depend on the cargo carried and will, in general, be higher for uncrewed ships. In cases where a caretaker crew is on board, the level of cargo care should be the same as that onboard a conventional ship, with two exceptions. First, additional risks may be present due to the autonomous or remotely performed navigation of the ship. Second, concerns will be present with respect to care of the cargo that requires diversion of the ship for the preservation of the cargo. For example, where cargo has to be restowed or for preventing cargo deterioration the ability of an autonomous or remotely controlled ship to react may be questioned. If the ship is crewed and remotely controlled, such a diversion will be possible, provided the crew is able to communicate with the ship's controller. For an uncrewed ship, however, the identification of the option to divert the ship for cargo operations or seek an appropriate port of refuge will, in addition to continuous monitoring of the cargo spaces and the cargo condition, require a broader technological capability linking navigational decision-making with the cargo needs and related developing risks. Even if it is assumed that such integrated systems will be available in the future, the absence of a crew on board will still mean that immediate intervention will not be available to the extent available on a conventional ship. The degree of difference between conventional and autonomous ships will depend on the cargo carried.

Meeting the legal standards for appropriate cargo care requires, first, adequate monitoring systems for the cargo spaces and the condition of cargo; second, linkage of the cargo monitoring system with the shore controller or the decision-making system of the autonomous ship, and third, decision-making as to whether to divert the ship from a pre-programmed route. Failing to do so or failure to replicate routine cargo management tasks, for example the airing of cargo spaces for specific cargoes, will result in the standard of care falling below that for conventional ships and lead to increased cargo damage and liability for the carrier under the Hamburg Rules.

[64] Art 5.5. Liability is excluded except where the claimant proves that the loss of damage was due to fault or neglect of the cargo by the carrier or his servants and agents.

[65] Art 9.3. The liability for loss or damage for unauthorised deck cargo is absolute.

[66] Art 5.6. Liability in general average is preserved.

B. The Hague and Hague-Visby Rules

Under the Hague and Hague-Visby Rules, the carrier has three minimum obligations to discharge, two of which can be materially affected when cargo is shipped on board an autonomous or remotely controlled ship.[67] The third, which concerns the issuance of shipping documents,[68] is not affected, because a crew will be present to oversee the cargo operations in port and issue the required documents.

i. Due Diligence to Make the Ship Seaworthy

The carriers' principal obligation is a non-delegable[69] duty to exercise due diligence[70] to provide a seaworthy ship[71] before and at the beginning of the voyage.[72] The ambit of the seaworthiness obligation extends to the actual seaworthiness of the structure, cargoworthiness and manning, and also includes statutory requirements without which the contract of cargo cannot be performed. Assuming that trading with an uncrewed ship is authorised by the relevant flag state and the relevant port state permits the entry of such a ship there should not be any unseaworthiness issue arising from the formal operation of the ship. In addition, the assumption that a caretaker crew will prepare the ship for departure and take it out of the port will ensure that, in the absence of negligence by the crew or others employed by the carrier to ensure the seaworthiness of the ship, the carrier will have discharged this particular duty.

However, despite the permissive regulatory framework, and the presence of the loading/discharging crew, whether a ship is seaworthy will be determined by asking whether a reasonable shipowner[73] will have sent the particular ship on the particular journey under the specific seasonal, environmental and, perhaps, security and political conditions. The degree of autonomy and the presence or absence of a crew during the voyage adds parameters and complicates the seaworthiness obligation.[74] Where the cargo requires a specific type of care which can only be rendered by the presence of crew a reasonable shipowner should not have sent the ship on the specific voyage. Similarly, where a call to a port of refuge could be

[67] For a recent overview, see S Girvin, 'The carrier's fundamental duties to cargo under the Hague and Hague-Visby Rules' (2019) 25 JIML 443.

[68] Art III, r 3.

[69] *Riverstone Meat Co Pty Ltd v Lancashire Shipping Co Ltd (The Muncaster Castle)* [1961] AC 807 (HL).

[70] The duty of due diligence can be considered as a personal duty of care. Lack of due diligence is negligence: *Union of India v NV Reederij Amsterdam* [1963] 2 Lloyd's Rep 223, 235 (HL).

[71] Art III, r 1.

[72] *Maxine Footwear Co Ltd v Canadian Government Merchant Marine* [1959] AC 589 (PC).

[73] *McFadden v Blue Star Line Ltd* [1905] 1 KB 697, 706.

[74] Note though that the ship does not have to be perfect, it only has to be fit to encounter the perils of the contractual voyage: ibid.

reasonably required in order to preserve the cargo, the inability to detect or react to a developing risk are factors that will lead to a conclusion that the carrier has breached its article III, rule 1 obligation.

A further point arising under article III, rule 1 is that the carrier is not liable for cargo damage arising from latent defects.[75] The exemption from such liability only becomes available, however, after the carrier has proved that neither itself nor its servants and agents have been negligent in causing the damage. The extended use of technology in navigating, controlling and monitoring the ship and the cargo implies a higher risk of latent defects occurring in the various software and hardware components leading to cargo damage. In such circumstances, the exclusion of liability for latent defect is likely to increase the situations where the cargo and its underwriters will have to pay for their own losses and also for associated salvage liability.

Thus, the Hague and Hague-Visby Rules are capable of accommodating and resolving the allocation of cargo damage involving autonomous or remotely controlled ships. However the risk allocation will need to be reassessed because cargo risks will increase with respect to latent defects while the primary beneficiary of the use of such ships is likely to be the shipowner/carrier.

ii. Care of the Cargo

The second obligation imposed on the carrier under the Hague and Hague-Visby Rules concerns the duty to look after the cargo. This is expressed as follows in article III, rule 2: 'Subject to the provisions of Article IV, the carrier shall properly and carefully load, handle, stow, carry, keep, care for, and discharge the goods carried'. As the assumption is that loading, handling, stowing and discharging of the goods will be undertaken with crew on board, it is only the carrying, keeping and caring functions that are relevant to the ships under consideration.

An integrated system linking the navigational decision-making software with the hardware monitoring the condition of the cargo will be required in order for the carrier to argue that it can properly and carefully carry, keep and care[76] for the cargo on an autonomous ship. There is no difference with the requirements under the Hamburg Rules on this point.

The article III, rule 2 obligation imposes liability on the carrier subject to article IV. Indeed, article IV provides a list of exceptions from liability most, but not all, of which concern situations where the damage is not caused by the carrier's fault or the fault of his servants or agents. Of interest here are those few exceptions where the liability of the carrier for negligence or acts of its servants

[75] *Union of India* (n 70). The same is also true under the Hamburg Rules.

[76] It is arguable that, as with bailment under English law, the proper care of the cargo under the Hague-Visby Rules will entail the ability to arrange for salvage or towage assistance in appropriate situations.

are exempted.[77] Two of the exceptions differ significantly from the others in that they exempt the carrier's vicarious liability.

The burden of proving that an exception protects the carrier falls on the carrier under article IV, rule 2(q), but it is unclear for many of the other exceptions. The decision of the Supreme Court in *Volcafe Ltd v Cia Sud Americana de Vapores SA*[78] has, however, now clarified that the burden of proving compliance with article III, rule 2 is on the carrier.

iii. Exception for Navigational Error

A notorious exception in the Rules excludes liability with respect to faults or omissions in the navigation or the management of the ship by the 'master, mariner, pilot or servants'.[79] The exception is not necessarily restricted to persons on board the ship. Because it excludes liability for the faults of the pilots who usually take the ship in and out of port or through areas of increased navigational risks, it covers persons navigating the ship in addition to the master. However, when this exception is read together with article III, rule 1 which applies before and at the beginning of the voyage, it is clear that it is meant to cover the period after the ship has sailed and thus, given the technology available at the time the Rules were agreed, it has to concern persons on board the ship.

The exception will cover liability for the actions of a caretaker crew on board an autonomous or remotely controlled ship. It could also be argued that the wording is wide enough to cover the liability of a person remotely controlling the ship, whether this person is the equivalent of the master or not. However, the wording will not cover navigational mistakes caused by the software of an autonomous ship, except perhaps where these can be attributed to a failure by the servant of the carrier who provided the specific voyage instructions to the navigational system after sailing. If such faulty instructions have been provided at the beginning of the voyage, there will arguably be a breach of the due diligence obligation under article III, rule 1.

For autonomous and uncrewed ships, the number of situations where the carrier is liable for cargo damage on board following faulty navigation or cargo care is likely to increase as the vicarious liability exception will not be as relevant as on conventional ships. For remotely controlled ships, however, the exception will remain available and is likely to cover the operator's negligence.

Complicated questions are likely to arise where there is a crew on board the autonomous ship and the navigational error arises from an error in the software or the hardware of the navigational equipment. Such errors could arise not only due to programming problems, but also due to a failure in the maintenance of or misuse by the caretaker crew or, even, a failure by the crew to intervene when

[77] See below, iii and iv.
[78] Above, n 16.
[79] Art IV, r 2(a).

it becomes evident that the onboard autonomous navigational system malfunctions. A literal interpretation of the exception suggests that the failure to maintain and the misuse of the navigational equipment is an act, neglect or default in the management of the ship while the failure to intervene will arguably also be covered as a default in the navigation of the ship.

iv. Fire Exception

The carrier's liability is also excluded with respect to fire except where the damage is caused by the fault or privity of the carrier itself.[80] Fault or privity of the carrier must be proved by the claimant and this is not likely to be affected by the character of the ship as conventional, autonomous or remotely controlled, although the absence of a crew may make it more difficult to identify the cause and the timing of the fire. Fire-fighting of small fires by the crew is one aspect that will need to be automated on uncrewed ships in order to bring the risks to a similar level to those on a conventional ship. Failure to do so will arguably mean that the fire exception under article IV, rule 2(b) will not be available to the carrier as it will clearly have knowledge of the inadequate fire extinguishing arrangements. The carrier will also be in breach of article III, rule 1, enabling the claimant to avoid the exceptions altogether.

While the other exceptions do not, in general, raise significant issues in respect of cargo shipped in an autonomous or remotely controlled ship, a problem may arise with respect to political[81] or physical risks[82] that occur after an autonomous and uncrewed ship has sailed. Assuming that the navigational constraints of an autonomous ship are set at sailing, changes in the political or environmental situation may risk the ship entering prohibited areas or a war zone, exposing the cargo to the risk of loss or damage. The possibility of updating the constraints imposed on the ship and enabling an autonomous ship to turn back or follow alternative routes following such updates will be crucial in ensuring protection by such exceptions. The owner will otherwise be liable for any cargo damage.

v. Limitation of Liability

All the international carriage by sea liability regimes provide for limited liability for cargo loss and damage, though with different limitation amounts.[83] Under the

[80] Art IV, r 2(b).

[81] Art IV, r 2(e) (act of war); art IV, r 2(f) (act of public enemies); art IV, r 2(g) (arrest or restraint of princes, rulers or people, or seizure under legal process); art IV, r 2(h) (quarantine restrictions); art IV, r 2(j) (strikes or lockouts or stoppage or restraint of labour from whatever cause, whether partial or general); art IV, r 2(k) (riots and civil commotions).

[82] Art IV, r 2(c) (perils, dangers and accidents of the sea or other navigable waters); art IV, r 2(d) (act of God).

[83] Hague Rules, art IV, r 5 (100 pounds sterling per package or unit, or the equivalent of that sum in other currency). There is no limitation for bulk cargo under the Hague Rules: *Kyokuyo Co Ltd*

Hague and Hague-Visby Rules, limitation of liability is not available to the carrier where the cargo value is declared on the bill of lading.[84] Under the Hamburg Rules, there is an exception from the limitation of liability rights for unauthorised deck cargo.[85]

The Hague Rules do not include a test whereby the carrier may lose its right to limit liability, enabling arguments that this can be achieved under national law. All other international conventions provide that the carrier may lose its limitation rights when the damage is due to an intentional or reckless act or omission of the carrier committed with knowledge that damage would probably result.[86] The person committing the reckless or intentional act and holding the relevant knowledge must, in law, be the ego or alter ego of the party entitled to limit.[87] Therefore, the presence or absence of crew on board the ship will not affect the question whether the person acting for the legal entity limiting its liability is acting intentionally or recklessly, or whether it holds the relevant knowledge.

Whether the very use of an autonomous or remotely controlled ship with or without a crew could be argued to be the very act, intentional or reckless, that leads to the loss of the right to limit liability is a more challenging issue for discussion. The original purpose of establishing limitation of liability was to protect the carrier from claims of very high value where it did not know the value of the cargo.[88] At that stage, however, there was no agreed test for removing the right to limit liability. The test that was later adopted in all maritime conventions was designed to remove the entitlement to limit liability only in exceptional circumstances where the wrongdoing by the party entitled to limit is at high level. Only then is the limitation right lost. Thus a general situation where the use of autonomous or remotely controlled ships automatically leads to unlimited liability for cargo damage will create a major obstacle to the development of such ships and will operate as a protectionist arrangement for conventional ships. An argument that the shipper shipped with knowledge of the relevant risks may be sufficient to establish that

v AP Møller-Maersk A/S, trading as 'Maersk Line' [2018] EWCA Civ 778, [2018] 2 Lloyd's Rep 59; Hague-Visby Rules, art IV, r 5(a) (limitation is 666.67 units of account per package or unit or 2 units of account per kilo of gross weight of the goods lost or damaged, whichever is the higher); Hamburg Rules, art 6(1)(a) (835 units of account per package or other shipping unit or 2.5 units of account per kilogram of gross weight of the goods lost or damaged, whichever is the higher); Rotterdam Rules, art 59(1) (875 units of account per package or other shipping unit, or three units of account per kilogram of the gross weight of the goods that are the subject of the claim or dispute).

[84] Hague Rules, art IV, r 5 and Hague-Visby Rules, art IV, r 5(1). The same applies under the Rotterdam Rules, art 59. Another possible situation arises in English law where the damage is caused by deviation and provided that deviation remains a fundamental breach: see now *Dera Commercial Estate v Derya Inc (The Sur)* [2018] EWHC 1673 (Comm), [2019] 1 Lloyd's Rep 57.

[85] Art 9(4). *cf* the Rotterdam Rules, art 25(5).

[86] Hague-Visby Rules, art IV, r 5(e) ('and with knowledge that damage would probably result'); Hamburg Rules, art 8.1 ('and with knowledge that such loss, damage or delay would probably result'); Rotterdam Rules, art 61(1) ('and with knowledge that such loss would probably result').

[87] ie generally the contractually carrier. Depending on the legal regime applicable, this could be the performing carrier or the maritime performing party.

[88] See F Berlingieri (ed), *The Travaux Préparatoires of the Hague Rules and of the Hague-Visby Rules* (Antwerp, CMI, 1997) 452, and the Hague Rules, art IV, r 5.

the inherent risks associated with shipment on board an autonomous ship have been accepted and that the autonomous or remotely controlled character of the ship is not 'an act or omission of the carrier done … recklessly and with knowledge that damage would probably result'. Of course, where the particular cargo or the navigational safety for a specific voyage demands human presence on board, the absence of a master and a crew is likely to lead to the loss of the right to limit liability.

vi. Liability for the Unauthorised Shipment of Dangerous Goods

The fourth norm considered under the international liability regimes is the shipper's obligation to inform the carrier when dangerous goods are being shipped.[89] Under English law, this obligation does not depend on the shipper's knowledge of the dangerous character of the goods[90] and this has been confirmed to be the case under the Hague-Visby Rules.[91]

Where the shipper fails to provide the required information it becomes liable for all losses and damages sustained by the carrier and the goods can be landed or destroyed without any liability for the carrier.[92] Where the required information has been provided and the cargo endangers the ship or other cargo, the carrier has the same options in dealing with the dangerous cargo.[93]

The current legal arrangement will remain relevant to the shipment of dangerous goods on board autonomous or remotely controlled ships because it is assumed that shipment will be undertaken by or under the supervision of crew members. Provided the shipper has given the required notification, any failure to transmit this information to the controller of a remotely controlled ship or failure to arrange for any special treatment required by an automated cargo care system will be at the risk of the carrier.

There are, however, two potential difficulties. The first is that, in the absence of a crew, the shipowners' entitlement to destroy or land or render innocuous of any dangerous cargo will not be of much use. In the case of the danger materialising and destroying other cargo, this will raise the question whether the damage is due to the breach of the shipper's obligation or due to the inability of the carrier to intervene and stop any additional damage from occurring. If the failure to have crew able to intervene on board in such a case is considered as a breach of the

[89] The relevant Hague and Hague-Visby provision is art IV, r 6; Hamburg Rules, art 13; Rotterdam Rules, art 32. The Rotterdam Rules provision broadens the scope of dangerous goods by including those which are environmentally dangerous. Although the common law obligation is wider than that established in the Conventions, it also includes legally dangerous goods: see, eg, *Mitchell, Cotts & Co v Steel Bros & Co Ltd* [1916] 2 KB 610.

[90] *Brass v Maitland* (1856) 6 El & Bl 470, 119 ER 940.

[91] *Effort Shipping Co Ltd v Linden Management SA (The Giannis NK)* [1998] AC 605, 619 (HL), confirms the common law position.

[92] Hague-Visby Rules, art IV, r 6.

[93] For an argument that the Rotterdam Rules provides a favourable regime for information exchange regarding safety, see M Sturley, 'The Rotterdam Rules and vessel safety' (Editorial) (2019) 25 *JIML* 429.

due diligence obligation to provide a seaworthy ship, there is authority suggesting that the carrier will be liable.[94] The same will be true under the Hamburg Rules because the carrier will be unable to disprove fault or negligence on its behalf in failing to provide a crew. In the case of container ships, it will be important to develop systems which can deal with dangers materialising, whether the cargo was declared or not.

A broader question concerns the effect that the uncrewed autonomous or remotely controlled character of the ship may have on the definition of dangerous goods and the duty imposed on the shipper. Because the shipper's obligation to notify is based on a contractual[95] matrix, the capabilities and the character of the ship are expected to make some cargoes which are not dangerous when carried on conventional ship, dangerous for autonomous or remotely controlled ships. Thus the shipper will be required to provide information on the cargo, taking into account the type of the ship on which the cargo will be shipped. The carrier will then have to decide whether or not to carry the particular cargo on the particular the voyage.

vii. Other Standards of Performance

International conventions exclude the liability of the carrier when there is a deviation to save life or property.[96] However, whether this exception will be relevant in the future depends on whether autonomous or remotely controlled ships will have a statutory duty to save life at sea.

The imposition of statutory duties is normally on the master of the ship.[97] It is submitted that an autonomous or remotely controlled ship with a crew on board will be bound by the same duty to assist as a conventional ship and will be effected in the relevant national and international laws. It will be unacceptable and unreasonable if technological advancement results into lives being lost because the legal norm of assisting in saving life at risk at sea could technically be avoided by the absence of a master on board the ship. Thus, it is submitted that both the obligation and the relevant liability exception will remain in use for crewed ships at least.

[94] *Northern Shipping Co v Deutsche Seereederei GmbH (The Kapitan Sakharov)* [2000] 2 Lloyd's Rep 255 (CA).

[95] In *The Athanasia Comninos and Georges Chr Lemos* [1990] 1 Lloyd's Rep 277, a charterparty case, Mustill J said (at 283): 'it is not correct to start with an implied warranty as to the shipment of dangerous goods and try to force the facts within it; but rather to read the contract and the facts together, and ask whether, on the true construction of the contract, the risk involved in this particular shipment were risks which the plaintiffs [owners] contracted to bear'.

[96] Art IV, r 4 of the Hague and Hague-Visby Rules; art 5.6 of the Hamburg Rules (which excludes liability for all measures taken for that purpose but does not mention deviation).

[97] An obligation is imposed on states to legislate to this effect under UNCLOS, art 98(1) and further developed under the Convention for the Safety of Life at Sea (SOLAS), ch V, reg 33, and the International Convention on Salvage, art 10. See also The International Convention on Maritime Search and Rescue (SAR Convention), art 5.3.3.5 recognising that 'in the majority of distress situations in ocean areas, other vessels in the vicinity are important elements for search and rescue operations'.

For an uncrewed autonomous ship, it could be argued that the absence of a master on board does not impose on the ship any obligation to help a casualty at sea but also makes the provision of such assistance practically impossible. For a remotely controlled uncrewed ship, the inability to render effective assistance in the absence of crew together with the increased vulnerability of an uncrewed ship to criminal activity if boarded, permits an argument that such obligation either does not exist at all or, if it exists, is avoidable on the ground of the potential risk to the ship.

Excluding uncrewed ships from life-saving operations will make the sea a more dangerous place for those humans who use it for work, pleasure, or out of necessity. An uncrewed ship can reduce loss to human life in a number of ways. First, by automatically releasing life-saving devices. These will have to be on board as crew will be going on board at loading and discharging ports. A second mechanism for providing assistance could be to have facilities on board which will enable shipwrecked people to get on board. A third way will be to indicate the location of a casualty to other rescuers. The argument that the absence of the master on board can be the basis for avoiding the obligation to assist in saving life at sea does not stand up to scrutiny because the obligation was imposed on the master as a way of compelling the assistance and not because the master was capable of providing assistance. The ship is the platform that provides safety. Thus, the current legal arrangements impose a norm on whoever launches and controls the ship. If the master ceases to be the way for the implementation of this norm, the law will have to follow suit and confirm that the safety of human life at sea it signifies is preserved. Thus, it is submitted that an autonomous ship should be in the position to assist others, should be appropriately designed for such a role, and should be entitled to the exception from cargo liability when it deviates to serve this purpose.

There are currently no statutory obligations to save property at sea and so it is unlikely that uncrewed autonomous ships will be involved in such operations. However they could provide a towage service in some circumstances.

Due dispatch is also a common standard of performance which is not included under the carriage conventions. As this is defined contractually, it should not be too complicated to redefine the obligation by taking into account the capabilities and constraints of the navigational system of an autonomous ship for optimising the ship's consumption and reducing its greenhouse gas emissions.

IX. Conclusions

The legal norms underlying the carriage of goods by sea on autonomous and remotely controlled ships, whether crewed or not, question whether such ships can be considered as fit for purpose. Economic arguments requiring a reduction of cargo damage and increased efficiency of sea transport imply that the standards for the carriage of the goods on board such ships cannot be reduced below those applicable to conventional ships, although the allocation of risk could be rearranged.

This chapter has adopted the least challenging scenario, one where the loading and discharge stage and the pilotage in and out of a port are undertaken by a crew. Nevertheless, there are still significant demands imposed by the compulsory legal arrangements which are designed to protect the third-party consignee.

The duty to properly look after cargo requires the development of monitoring and cargo management systems which can perform the tasks that a crew will normally undertake before the crew can be removed from such a ship. Such systems must be able to take the necessary actions to preserve the goods, intervene when risks develop to minimise damage, and take the ship to a port of refuge in order to restore the safety of the ship and the cargo.

Furthermore, as there is a requirement in bailment and as part as of the obligation to care for the cargo, the capability of such a ship to seek salvage assistance, when needed, is dictated by an important legal obligation that must be complied with.

Uncrewed ships are likely to pose additional risks for cargo damage. Liability for this damage could lead to an increase in the liability of the carrier who is assumed to be the shipowner. Additionally, for specific cargoes, the use of an uncrewed ship could lead to the loss of some of the exceptions available to the owner of a conventional ship and possibly also the loss of the right to limit liability. The latter effects are likely to be particularly relevant for cargoes requiring specialised care during the voyage.

Additional risks which will have to be borne by cargo interests exist. For example, the increased technological complexity is likely to increase the situations where latent defects cause cargo damage. Under current arrangements, such damage is not recoverable from the carrier. In addition, the inability of an uncrewed ship to provide self-help is likely to lead to more salvage incidents with increased costs for the participants to the maritime adventure, including cargo interests.

The increased risk for both cargo interests and shipowners demonstrates that the adoption of the new technology will require the renegotiation of the allocation of liability. Such renegotiation will need to involve other stakeholders too. For example, it will be necessary to develop additional contractual arrangements to ensure that salvage assistance is available when needed. These arrangements should ensure that false alarms from uncrewed ships will compensate salvors for their time and effort.

The current legal obligations require that autonomous ship systems must be able to act in matters of navigation and cargo care in an integrated manner and must be able to deal with risks developing on or outside the ship. Autonomous ships without a crew must be capable of diverting the ship to a port of refuge.[98] This requires coupling the navigational system with cargo maintenance and monitoring elements in a way that enables the decision-making system to properly identify the risk and act accordingly. Uncrewed autonomous ships will therefore only be capable of discharging the current care of cargo obligations if they are also

[98] Appropriate crew capable of dealing with the specific ship must, of course, be available.

'smart' in the aforementioned way. The presence of a crew can reduce the degree of risk significantly and the need for the integration of navigational, cargo monitoring and decision-making systems will also require powers of intervention to be available to the crew. Navigational decisions can then be made by those on board when risks develop and the ship is autonomous or the connection with the remote controller has been lost. This will require a standby master to take over in such circumstances.

Thus supervised navigational autonomy through the presence of a crew will most likely be required to discharge existing performance standards for the carriage of goods on autonomous or remotely controlled ships. This is, however, an unwanted conclusion because the financial benefits of autonomous ships arise because of the removal of crew accommodation. If a crew has to be on board, accommodation will have to be provided and the financial benefits will reduce or disappear completely. In view of this and the higher costs of construction and maintenance, it is difficult to see whether such ships will be able to compete financially with conventional ships.

Where autonomous or remotely controlled ships are used for commercial carriage of goods, the required reallocation of cargo liability will be more readily made in charterparties, where there are no statutory constraints or minimum standards. A system where liability is exclusively on the carrier could potentially lead to financial optimisation with respect to insurance, provided that the shipper's liability with respect to unauthorised dangerous cargo is preserved.

The view that the development of a regulatory system for autonomous and remotely controlled ships does not challenge the legal order and is a matter of adjustment, rather than re-examination,[99] is still, it is submitted, correct. However, this chapter has shown that the commercial exploitation of such ships requires significant technological development to cope with the multiple layers of information that need to be integrated in order to reach the same decision as a reasonable bailee of a conventional ship. These layers of information include: (i) the navigational risks present: (ii) the awareness of the condition of the cargo; (iii) the possibility of interrupting the voyage when the ship and the cargo conditions require it; (iv) the ability to seek and agree assistance when danger develops; and (v) the ability to assess whether to assist when human life is at risk. Provided that the decision-making systems are developed in such a way as to satisfy these requirements, the benefits of removing the crew can materialise by optimising the shape of ships. At that stage, a renegotiation of the rules allocating cargo and salvage liability will be unavoidable because risks will be redistributed not only between carrier and cargo interests but also for other parties, including salvors. It is submitted that when such renegotiation is undertaken, re-examining the legal framework against financial and wealth maximisation criteria for the transport chain will be beneficial and support the development of an autonomous commercial fleet.

[99] Veal and Tsimplis [2017] (n 3).

INDEX

www.ingramcontent.com/pod-product-compliance
Lightning Source LLC
Chambersburg PA
CBHW071352220926
51613CB00008B/127
9781509942916